Thoughts for Buffets

DECORATIONS BY WILLIAM BARSS

HOUGHTON MIFFLIN COMPANY BOSTON

Dear

Hostesses:

THIS CHANGING WORLD, gastronomically speaking, has been so affected by the additions of new methods, mixes, foods, and spices — plus the subtraction of household help — that we think a few fresh observations on "Thoughts for Food" are timely.

Our aims are twofold: (1) to retain the gracious art of fine dining with (2) a minimum of effort as befits the times. We have stressed the short cuts while observing an epicurean approach to both the palate and the eye.

The menus have been planned in the hope that they will be helpful. However, the recipes are interchangeable, and we leave to your discretion and imagination the mixing and matching of the various dishes.

We do suggest the use of the many new items which simplify the homemaker's task. Space does not permit us to list all the commercial timesavers on the market. Frozen foods, packaged mixes, prebaked delicacies will make your cooking simpler; wines, spices, and herbs will make it far more interesting. Also, for your convenience, we have outlined timetables for those foods which may be made in advance.

Our recipes have come from many places and many people. Some were our own "treasures" but whenever we heard of, or tasted, an unusual dish, we hunted the recipe down and tested it with alacrity. We found hostesses from all over the country generous in parting with their trade secrets. To them, we bow appreciatively.

Putting this book together has been a real adventure, a mountain of work, and, above all, a world of fun. To the reader we wish many seasons of happy parties.

THE AUTHORS

Contents

Introduction

BUFFET SERVICE

ALTHOUGH in many cases buffet parties are designed for large groups, we have planned the majority of recipes in this book to serve six. In this way, they may be used for any occasion, increased or decreased as suits your individual need. Wherever recipes are for larger numbers, it is so indicated.

The cooking time schedules which are offered below the menus are suggested in the hope that they may facilitate preparation of the meals. All the cooking need not be done at the last minute or even on the day of the party. Some dishes may be completely prepared ahead of time and refrigerated; others, precooked and frozen. Even when last-minute cooking is necessary, the component parts of a dish may be readied ahead of time. The preparation procedure for each recipe should be self-explanatory.

The cook will find it very helpful to plan and organize in advance. This often is what distinguishes the calm and serene hostess from the harassed housewife who does not have time even to greet her guests.

MEMOS TO HOSTESSES

The hors d'oeuvre merits special mention. It is sprinkled through the following pages in various forms, from the popular "dips" to the unlimited Ramaki combinations. It is not only a conversation piece but the handy gadget with which to fill the lulls often a bane to the hostess — an antidote to possible boredom. Though the guest of honor may be late and the roast delayed, there are always the hors d'oeuvres to interest the waiting company. Prepare a sufficient number of them and remember that the surplus may be frozen for a possible emergency. Although there is no special section in this book for cocktail parties and cocktail suppers, there are unlimited varieties of hors d'oeuvres accompanying most of the menus which can be used for this type of entertaining.

Informal entertaining is gay and not restrained by the technicalities of formal service. Your first course may be served from the buffet table or in the living room. Wheel the fish platter in on a teacart or set up a serving table for the tureen of chowder. For casual parties, pour the soup into mugs for easy handling.

If you are using your dining room table for the buffet or live in one of the modern apartments which do not have a dining room, it is pleasant to arrange individual places for your guests. For this you will find many aids. Newest of all are the snack and stack tables, available in metal, plastic or wood. They are a real convenience and add to the charm of informal entertaining and dining. Bridge tables are always comfortable for groups of four, and may accomodate six when covered with a round accessory table top. Also consider the collapsible aluminum tables which seat as many as eight.

Invaluable aids for arranging the buffet table are chafing dishes, ovenproof casseroles, and the new gayly decorated cooking utensils that double for service. Above all, do not clutter your table. Try to arrange your courses in natural sequence.

If your group is exceptionally large, have a duplicate of each of the various dishes on opposite sides of the tables; and have your guests form two queues instead of one.

DECOR IDEAS

The traditional floral centerpiece is lovely, of course; that is why it is the most popular. But a centerpiece can sometimes be as imaginative as the menu. For example, as an autumnal setting, casually pile interesting seasonal small gourds and squashes in harmonizing colors on a base of leaves. Use bright hothouse tomatoes (with stems), green and red peppers as accents (a suggestion for the Thanksgiving menu).

Make an arrangement of shining red apples, using silver paper doilies as a background for some of the especially lovely ones (Football Supper).

Line woven reed cornucopias with silver foil and fill them to overflowing with luscious grapes.

Accent a graceful piece of driftwood with perhaps five bright blossoms (Cantonese meal).

In a clear glass bowl filled with water, float three or four camellias, or use the less expensive floating candles.

Use coral carnations as a striking color balance for the Persimmon ring (page 26).

White tulips are lovely for Easter with the ham menu. Turn back some of the petals to give them an airy look, and be certain to drop a few pennies in the water as the copper gives them longer life.

Use a lei of small apples or pears around a large pineapple to accent the Hawaiian supper.

An old-fashioned bouquet of white carnations and limes is a cool note for a summer party. To form a tight bouquet, place chicken wire across the top of the bowl (a pedestal type is stunning) and slip the carnations through the mesh. The center should be solid blossoms about 3 inches above the wire, graduating to about 1½ inches at the edge of the bowl. Tuck the limes between the carnations on the periphery and border the arrangement with shiny green leaves.

Brunch
Buffets

Each recipe
serves six
unless otherwise
indicated

THE HOSTESS who plans to entertain her friends on Sundays and holidays with an eye-opening, start-the-day-right brunch, will find many new and unusual combinations here. She might even surprise her family with a welcome change from the weekly "ham, bacon and egg" saga.

As coffee cakes are so often used in the brunch menus, we add a few suggestions for freezing them and thus facilitating your chores.

To freeze coffee cakes: Cool, wrap in freezer paper; freeze. If frosting is indicated, do it just before serving.

To serve: While still wrapped, let thaw several hours at room temperature. Then frost, if recipe so directs.

To heat: Wrap in foil if cake is not already wrapped in this fashion, and heat in a 400° oven. Allow 15 minutes for individual rolls and 30 to 45 minutes for larger coffee cakes.

4

Brunch Buffet

Spiced Rice Crisps   Sliced Oranges — Sour Cream Dip
Tuna Amandine   Chicken Livers (Choice of three recipes)
Swiss Cheese Scrambled Eggs
Northern Corn Bread   Strawberry Preserves
Cheese Blintzes
Coffee

ADVANCE PREPARATION SCHEDULE

Previous Day	Early Morning	Deep Freeze
Spiced Rice Crisps	*Fill Blintzes*	*Blintz Wrappers*
Filling for Blintzes	*Fruit*	
Tuna Amandine	*Corn Bread*	

The Blintz wrappers may be made in advance, placed between sheets of wax paper and frozen.

SPICED RICE CRISPS

4 tablespoons butter or margarine
1 teaspoon mustard seed
½ teaspoon curry powder
¼ teaspoon salt
¼ teaspoon cinnamon

Dash of pepper
1 cup roasted, salted peanuts
3 cups oven-popped rice cereal (prepared)

Melt butter in heavy skillet; add mustard seed, cover and cook until seeds begin to pop. Add curry powder, salt, cinnamon, and pepper; mix with butter; add peanuts and cereal and stir until heated and coated with seasonings. Prepare in advance, as the crisps improve in flavor and remain crunchy.

SLICED ORANGES — SOUR CREAM DIP

4 oranges
1 cup commercial sour cream

2 tablespoons sugar
¼ teaspoon cinnamon

Wash and peel oranges; slice about ¼ inch thick and cut slices into thirds. Combine remaining ingredients. Serve orange slices, chilled, with sour cream dip.

TUNA AMANDINE

2 10-ounce packages of frozen
asparagus spears
2 6-ounce cans of tuna, flaked
and drained
6 tablespoons butter
½ cup blanched almonds, chopped
5 tablespoons flour

1 teaspoon salt
⅛ teaspoon pepper, freshly
ground
⅛ teaspoon nutmeg
3 cups milk
2 tablespoons sherry
Paprika

Cook asparagus according to the directions on the package. Drain. Arrange on bottom of a buttered baking dish 11 x 7 x 1½ inches; cover with the tuna flakes. Melt butter in a heavy saucepan, add almonds. Cook until slightly golden brown. Blend in the flour and seasonings; add the milk. Stir, cooking until sauce is smooth and thickened. Add sherry and correct seasonings. Pour the sauce over the tuna and asparagus. Sprinkle with paprika. Bake in 350° oven for 25 to 30 minutes or until slightly golden. For a more subtle flavor, first blanch tuna with scalding water and drain before preparation of recipe. Serves 8.

#1 CHICKEN LIVERS MADEIRA

2 pounds chicken livers
½ cup flour, seasoned with
½ teaspoon salt and
¼ teaspoon pepper
3 tablespoons butter

¼ cup Madeira (or sauterne)
4 large tomatoes, peeled and
diced
1 cup grated Cheddar cheese
12 eggs, beaten

½ pound salted almonds

Roll livers in the seasoned flour. Melt butter in a saucepan and sauté the livers. Add wine and tomatoes and simmer 3 or 4 minutes. Transfer liver and wine mixture to a 1½-quart casserole; sprinkle with cheese and broil until cheese melts. Pour eggs into a hot buttered skillet; let cook slowly until eggs become set on bottom of pan. With a fork or a spatula lift up the eggs at the edge of the pan, allowing the uncooked egg to run underneath. Continue this cooking and lifting until eggs are all set. To serve, place eggs in center of platter, border with livers, and sprinkle almonds over livers. Garnish with parsley. Serves 8.

#2 CHICKEN LIVERS VELOUTE

8 tablespoons butter
3 tablespoons flour
½ cup chicken stock or canned consommé
2 cups commercial sour cream

1 tablespoon minced parsley
2 pounds chicken livers
½ cup flour, seasoned with
½ teaspoon salt and
¼ teaspoon pepper

Melt 4 tablespoons of butter in saucepan. Add the flour and blend well. Stir in heated stock and cook for 5 minutes, stirring constantly. Combine with sour cream and parsley. Coat the livers in seasoned flour. Sauté in remaining 4 tablespoons of butter for about 5 minutes. Pour the sauce over the meat, cover the pan and let cook for an additional 5 minutes. Serve over vermicelli. (An eight-ounce package will serve six. Cook according to instructions on box.) Serves 8.

#3 CHICKEN LIVERS — SOY SAUCE

1 3-ounce bottle soy sauce
2 pounds chicken livers

Flour
Butter

Marinate chicken livers in soy sauce overnight (in refrigerator). Drain, dredge with flour; sauté in butter for about 5 minutes, shaking pan occasionally to brown livers gently. Serves 8.

SWISS CHEESE SCRAMBLED EGGS

1 dozen eggs
¾ cup light cream
Salt and pepper to taste

6 tablespoons butter
1 cup coarsely shredded Swiss cheese or processed American or Cheddar

Beat eggs and stir in cream, salt and pepper. Pour into heated butter in two 12-inch skillets. Cook slowly, gently lifting from sides with a spoon so mixture may run to the bottom of the skillet. Add cheese just before eggs are completely cooked; blend. Cook until set, but moist. Serves 8.

NORTHERN CORN BREAD

1½ cups all-purpose flour   ½ cup yellow corn meal
3 teaspoons baking powder   2 eggs, beaten
1 teaspoon salt   1 cup milk
¼ cup sugar   ¼ cup melted butter

Sift the first 4 ingredients together. Add corn meal and mix well. Combine eggs, milk and butter and add to the dry ingredients; stir only until well blended. Pour into well-greased 8″ x 8″ x 2″ baking pan, and bake in a 325° oven for 30 to 40 minutes. Cut into 2-inch squares.

STRAWBERRY PRESERVES

4 cups strawberries   1 tablespoon vinegar
3 cups sugar

Wash and hull strawberries. Underripe berries may be used. Place in saucepan; add vinegar, cover and bring to a boil. Boil for only one minute. Add sugar and continue to boil very gently for 20 minutes, uncovered. Stir occasionally. Pour into a bowl and let stand at room temperature overnight. Ladle into six 5½-ounce sterilized glasses and cover with paraffin. This is not a thick preserve, but has a pure strawberry flavor.

CHEESE BLINTZES

Filling:

½ pound cottage cheese   2 tablespoons butter, melted
½ pound cream cheese   2 tablespoons sugar
1 egg, well beaten   ¼ cup white raisins (optional)
1 teaspoon vanilla

Blend ingredients together. Allow 1 tablespoon filling per blintz.
Wrappers:

4 eggs   1½ cups flour
¼ teaspoon salt   2 tablespoons melted butter
2 cups milk

Beat eggs well and add combined salt and flour; add butter. Add milk gradually while beating to a smooth batter. Make one wrapper at a time. Grease a 7-inch skillet lightly and pour in 3 tablespoons batter, tilting the pan from side to side so that batter covers bottom. Sauté lightly on one side and remove to paper towel. Place 1 tablespoon of filling in center of browned side and fold pancake from opposite sides in envelope shape. Cool; refrigerate. To serve, brush lightly with butter, and sauté quickly in greased skillet until brown on all sides. They may be heated by placing them in a 350° oven for 20 minutes or until brown. Serve with preserves and commercial sour cream. Makes 24 blintzes.

Variation:
1 pint fresh strawberries, sliced   ⅓ cup ground Zwieback
½ cup sugar

Combine ingredients and mix well. Place 1 tablespoon on brown side of each wrapper and fold opposite sides toward center in envelope shape. Handle carefully. Then brown both sides by sautéing in hot melted butter as in cheese blintzes. The filled pancakes may be frozen well in advance. To serve, defrost and sauté.

Brunch Buffet

Cheese Straws
Puffy Omelet with Lobster Sauce   Deviled Chicken Breasts
on Toast
Caraway French Bread
Rhubarb and Strawberry Mold — Seasonal Fruits
Peach Kuchen   Blender Cheese Pie
Coffee

ADVANCE PREPARATION SCHEDULE

Previous Day	Early Morning	Deep Freeze
Lobster Sauce	*Cheese Pie*	*Peach Kuchen —*
Rhubarb and Strawberry Mold	*Fruit for garnish*	*remove for last 30 minutes of baking*
Chicken Breasts		*Cheese Straws*

CHEESE STRAWS

1 cup sharp cheese, grated   ⅛ teaspoon paprika
1 tablespoon melted butter   ⅛ teaspoon salt
4 tablespoons cold water   ¼ teaspoon baking powder
        1 cup all-purpose flour

Combine ingredients, adding the flour last. Roll into thin sheets on well-floured board. Cut into strips. Bake in a hot oven (400°) on cooky sheet.

PUFFY OMELET

8 egg yolks, well-beaten   8 egg whites
½ cup milk   ½ teaspoon salt
1 teaspoon baking powder   2 tablespoons butter

Working quickly and lightly is the secret in omelet cooking. Beat the egg yolks, milk and baking powder until they are fluffy and lemon yellow. Then combine the whites and the salt and beat until they are just stiff and fold with the yolk mixture. Melt the butter in a 10-inch skillet and pour batter onto skillet. Cover and cook over low heat about 10 to 12 minutes, slashing the omelet once or twice to let the heat come through. Uncover. Place in 275° oven until slightly brown. Loosen and turn out on a hot platter. Pour the lobster sauce over the top and serve.

LOBSTER SAUCE

2 6½-ounce cans diced lobster   1 teaspoon grated lemon rind
   meat, or 2 cups fresh   1 teaspoon grated onion
4 tablespoons butter   1 teaspoon salt
4 tablespoons flour   ⅛ teaspoon pepper
2½ cups milk   ⅛ teaspoon dry mustard

Remove spiny pieces from the lobster; set aside. Melt the butter in a saucepan and stir in the flour. Add the milk gradually, then remaining ingredients. Cook, stirring over low heat until smooth and thickened. Add lobster and heat thoroughly. Serves 8 generously.

DEVILED CHICKEN BREASTS

Dressing for Chicken:

1 cup soft bread crumbs	1 teaspoon onion juice
1 cup white wine *or* milk	1 teaspoon chopped parsley
¼ cup melted butter	½ cup chopped fresh mushrooms
1 teaspoon salt	3 tablespoons butter

To Prepare Breasts for Dressing:

8 chicken breasts	1 cup fine bread crumbs
4 tablespoons butter	1 egg, beaten
Prepared mustard	Vegetable shortening

Dressing: Soak bread crumbs in wine and squeeze dry. Combine with melted butter, salt, onion juice, parsley, and mushrooms. Mix well and place in saucepan with 3 tablespoons butter. Cook for 5 minutes. Set aside. *Chicken Breasts:* Bone and skin breasts. (Cut in half before preparing, if desired.) Pound breasts with the edge of a saucer until thin. Melt butter in saucepan and sauté breasts lightly. Drain and lay them flat on a board. Spread with the dressing and form into rolls. Fasten with toothpicks. Spread each roll with mustard and roll in bread crumbs. Dip in the beaten egg and roll in the crumbs again; refrigerate until ready to cook. Melt ½ cup vegetable shortening in a saucepan. Heat to about 350° so that breasts do not cook too fast. Place breasts in the shortening and fry to a golden brown for 20 minutes or until tender. Place in a moderate oven to keep warm until ready to serve. Serves 8. May be prepared previous day for cooking.

May be served with **Wine Sauce:**

2 tablespoons butter	1 10½-ounce can consommé
1 small onion, minced	2 teaspoons lemon juice
2 tablespoons flour	1 teaspoon sugar
1 cup white wine	Salt and pepper

Melt butter in a saucepan; add onion, sauté one minute, add flour, and cook, stirring constantly, until golden brown. Stir in wine, consommé, lemon juice, sugar and seasonings and blend well; cook 5 minutes

CARAWAY FRENCH BREAD

1 loaf French or Vienna Bread 2 teaspoons caraway seeds
  (1-pound size)   3 tablespoons mayonnaise or
1 cup shredded American cheese   salad dressing
              ¼ cup soft butter

Cut bread diagonally, almost through to bottom crust, into 12 equal-size slices. Combine cheese, caraway seeds, and mayonnaise. Spread butter and cheese mixture between slices of bread. Wrap loaf in aluminum foil. Heat in a hot oven (400°) for about 15 minutes.

RHUBARB AND STRAWBERRY MOLD

2 packages lemon-flavored gelatin 2 10-ounce packages frozen rhu-
2 cups boiling water   barb
2 tablespoons plain gelatin   2 10-ounce packages frozen
½ cup cold water   strawberries
              1 tablespoon lemon juice

Dissolve the lemon gelatin in the boiling water. Cool. Soften the plain gelatin in the cold water. Add to the first mixture. Cook the rhubarb for about 5 minutes. Defrost the strawberries. When the gelatin is cool and slightly thickened, add the fruits and lemon juice. Pour into a 2-quart mold. Chill until firm. Unmold on platter and surround with salad greens. Fill with seasonal fresh fruit. Serves 8 to 12.

PEACH KUCHEN

2 cups sifted all-purpose flour   12 peach halves, fresh, or
¼ teaspoon baking powder   2 10-ounce packages frozen
½ teaspoon salt   slices
¼ cup sugar   1 teaspoon cinnamon
½ cup butter or margarine   2 egg yolks
    1 cup commercial sour cream or ½ cup sweet cream

Preheat oven to 400°. Sift flour, baking powder, salt, and 2 tablespoons sugar in a mixing bowl. Cut shortening in with two knives or a pastry blender until mixture looks like coarse corn meal. Pat an even layer of this crumbly pastry over bottom and halfway up the sides of a buttered 8″ x 8″ x 2″ baking pan. Use your hands and press pastry firmly until it holds. Skin fresh peaches and cut in half, or thaw and drain frozen peaches. Arrange peaches over pastry and sprinkle with remaining sugar and cinnamon. Bake 15 minutes at 400°. Pour a mixture of slightly beaten egg yolks and cream over top. Bake 30 minutes longer. Serve warm or cold.

BLENDER CHEESE PIE

Graham cracker crust:

16 graham crackers, crushed finely	¼ cup melted butter

Blend cracker crumbs and butter thoroughly, and line a 9-inch pie pan very firmly.   .

Cheese filling:

1½ 8-ounce packages cream cheese (12 ounces)	¼ cup sugar
	1 tablespoon vanilla
2 eggs	1 teaspoon lemon juice
2 tablespoons milk	½ teaspoon grated lemon rind

Place all ingredients in blender, and whirl for 1 minute. Pour into pie shell, and bake in a 375° oven for 20 minutes. Cool, and cover with topping.

Topping:

1 cup commercial sour cream	¼ cup sugar
1 teaspoon vanilla	

Combine ingredients, spread over baked cheese pie and place in the oven again, this time in a 475° oven for 7 minutes. Cool and serve. Serves 8.

Recipe may be increased by one-half to serve 12.

Brunch Buffet

Melon Medley   Euphrates Wafers

Hoppel Poppel   Sliced Chicken Pompadour

Stuffed Tomatoes and Corn Relish

Cinnamon Apple Muffins   Peach Jam

Cheese Torte

Coffee

ADVANCE PREPARATION SCHEDULE

Previous Day	Early Morning	Deep Freeze
Marinate cantaloupes	*Tomatoes*	
Roast chicken	*Mix Hoppel Poppel*	
Corn Relish	*Mix Sauce Pompadour*	
	Cheese Torte	

MELON MEDLEY

6 small cantaloupes	1 small pineapple, peeled,
1 pint raspberries	cored and diced
¼ cup kirsch or grenadine	

Cut cantaloupes in half; remove flesh and balls with a French ball cutter. Scallop the cantaloupe shells. Wash raspberries and toss with pineapple cubes and melon balls. Marinate with kirsch. To serve, fill shells and place on grape leaves.

Variation: Pour ginger ale over fruit just before serving.

HOPPEL POPPEL

2½ cups salami, cooked and chopped	2 tomatoes, diced
½ cup finely chopped onions or	½ cup green pepper, diced
6 green onions, finely chopped	2 teaspoons salt
	¼ teaspoon pepper
	12 eggs, slightly beaten

Mix ingredients thoroughly. Pour into shallow buttered pan about 9 x 13 x 2 inches. Bake in a 350° oven for about 10 to 12 minutes, or until set. Cut into 12 pieces.

SLICED CHICKEN POMPADOUR

24 slices of cooked chicken or 12 slices turkey

Sauce:

2 10½-ounce cans cream of
    mushroom soup
1 cup sherry

2 tablespoons lemon juice
1 cup diced shrimp
½ cup chopped ham
¼ teaspoon oregano

Heat all ingredients together in a saucepan or chafing dish to the boiling point. Spice as desired; one-fourth teaspoon oregano gives an unusual flavor. Serve over the slices of chicken which have been covered and warmed in a 300° oven. Serves 12.

STUFFED TOMATOES AND CORN RELISH

12 medium tomatoes of even size
1 teaspoon salt
½ teaspoon pepper
2 cups corn cut from cob
3 cups shredded cabbage
1 cup chopped celery

½ cup chopped green onion
⅓ cup wine vinegar
½ cup salad oil
2 teaspoons Worcestershire
    sauce
¼ teaspoon dried dill (optional)

Hollow tomatoes, drain upside down, and sprinkle with salt and pepper. Combine remaining ingredients and chill for one hour or until flavors are well blended. Fill tomatoes with vegetable mixture. Serve on lettuce. Serves 12.

Variation: Serve corn relish in a lettuce cup.

CINNAMON APPLE MUFFINS

2 cups sifted all-purpose flour
4 teaspoons baking powder
½ teaspoon salt
¼ cup sugar
½ teaspoon cinnamon

1 cup milk
1 egg, well beaten
¼ cup shortening, melted
1 cup sliced apples mixed with
    ¼ cup sugar

Sift the dry ingredients together. Combine the milk and egg; blend this into the dry ingredients; add the shortening, mixing just enough to moisten dry ingredients. Fold in the apples combined with sugar. Pour into well-greased muffin pan, filling cups ⅔ full. Bake in a 350° oven for 35 minutes.

PEACH JAM

2 10-ounce packages frozen   1 tablespoon lemon juice
peaches, thawed   3½ cups sugar
1 medium orange
⅓ cup chopped maraschino cherries

Scald six jelly glasses. Chop peaches coarsely. Slice orange very thin. Remove seeds, and cut into small pieces. Combine peaches, orange, lemon juice, and sugar and cook until thick; about 20 minutes. Add cherries, mix well and pour into sterilized glasses. Seal with melted paraffin, cool and cover.

CHEESE TORTE

1 6-ounce package Zwieback   1 teaspoon cinnamon
½ cup sugar   ½ cup melted butter

Roll the Zwieback fine, mix with sugar, cinnamon, and melted butter. Set aside ¾ cup of the mixture for the top. Butter a 9-inch spring form well. Spread and press Zwieback mixture on the bottom and sides of the form.

Filling:

4 eggs   1 cup cream
1 cup sugar   1½ pounds cottage cheese,
⅛ teaspoon salt   creamed
1 lemon, juice and grated rind   ¾ cup all-purpose flour
1 teaspoon vanilla (optional)
½ cup pistachio nuts, chopped, *or* whole toasted almonds

Beat eggs, without separating, with sugar until light. Add salt, lemon and vanilla, if desired. Stir the cream in well, add cheese and flour; mix thoroughly. Strain through a fine sieve, then stir until smooth. Pour into Zwieback-lined form; sprinkle remaining crumb mixture over top. Sprinkle chopped nuts over all and bake one hour in 325° oven. Turn off heat, cool in the oven for one hour or longer, with oven door open last 30 minutes. This is very important as cake will fall if allowed to cool too fast. If toasted almonds are preferred, decorate the cake with them, after it has been baked and cooled. Stick them halfway through top, like porcupine quills. Remove rim of spring form and place cake, still on tin bottom, on serving plate. Serves 10 to 12.

Brunch Buffet

Baked Hash au Gratin with Mustard Sauce Supreme
Pancakes Casino
Pears Cardinal
Popovers   Plum Marmalade
Sour Cream Coffee Cake Grandmère
Coffee

ADVANCE PREPARATION SCHEDULE

Previous Day	Early Morning	Deep Freeze
Combine hash except for topping	*Put extra sauce on pancakes*	*Sour Cream Coffee Cake*
Mustard sauce		
Poach pears		
Pancakes Casino		

BAKED HASH AU GRATIN

Hash:

3 cups coarsely ground cooked beef or corned beef
2 cups coarsely chopped cooked potatoes
1 large onion, ground
1 green pepper, ground
1 teaspoon salt

¼ teaspoon pepper
1 teaspoon Worcestershire sauce
¾ cup leftover gravy *or*
¾ cup beef bouillon
¼ teaspoon thyme
1 tablespoon sherry

Topping:

2 tomatoes, sliced
½ cup grated cheese

¼ cup bread crumbs
2 tablespoons butter

Mix all ingredients for hash. Pour into a greased 2-quart casserole. Press tomato slices into top of mixture, sprinkle with cheese and crumbs and dot with butter. Bake in 375° oven, uncovered, for 35 minutes, or until browned.

MUSTARD SAUCE SUPREME

1 cup sugar (scant)	1 cup cream
3 tablespoons dry mustard	1 cup cider vinegar
4 eggs, well beaten	¼ cup butter

Mix sugar and mustard together and sift. Place in saucepan and add remaining ingredients. Cook very slowly, stirring constantly, until mixture bubbles; then continue cooking for 5 minutes. Cool. Refrigerate. Makes 1 quart of sauce. Exceptionally good with fish. Keeps well in refrigerator.

PANCAKES CASINO

Pancakes:

2 eggs	¼ teaspoon salt
1 tablespoon melted butter	⅓ cup unsifted all-purpose flour
¼ teaspoon sugar	⅔ cup milk

Beat eggs, add butter, sugar, salt, and flour. Beat until smooth. Add milk and mix well. Grease a 6-inch skillet lightly and pour 2 tablespoons of batter into the pan, tipping it quickly so that the batter covers the bottom. Cook until golden, turn and brown other side. Repeat until 12 pancakes are made, greasing the pan slightly if required. (Not too much greasing is necessary because of the butter in the batter.) Stack pancakes until filling is made.

Filling:

3 tablespoons butter	1 teaspoon curry powder *or* 1 table-
½ cup chopped mushrooms	spoon sherry
3 tablespoons flour	1 cup chicken broth or 1 bouillon
½ teaspoon salt	cube dissolved in 1 cup boiling
¼ teaspoon pepper	water
½ teaspoon celery salt	1 cup light cream
	2 egg yolks
2 cups diced chicken	

Melt butter and sauté mushrooms for 3 minutes. Add flour, seasonings, and broth. Cook 5 minutes. Stir in cream and beaten egg yolks. Add chicken, heat, but do not boil. To fill, spoon 2 tablespoons of the mixture across the center inside of the pancake. Roll and place, seam side down, in ungreased 12″ x 8″ x 2″ baking dish.

When ready to serve, cover with remaining cream sauce. There should be about a cup, but if insufficient, add cream to make a cup. Pour over the filled pancakes, dust with ½ cup grated cheese and bake in a 375° oven for 20 minutes or until hot and brown. The filled pancakes and extra sauce may be made the day before, and refrigerated separately until serving time.

PEARS CARDINAL

6 fresh pears   1½ cups sugar
2 cups water   2 teaspoons vanilla
¼ teaspoon salt

Peel pears, leaving stems on. Mix water, sugar, vanilla, and salt together in a saucepan. Bring to a boil. Add whole pears; simmer, turning pears occasionally in syrup, for 20 to 25 minutes or until tender. Cool pears in syrup. Remove pears.

CARDINAL SAUCE

1 12-ounce jar strawberry or other   1 tablespoon lemon juice
red jelly
3 tablespoons maraschino cherry juice or grenadine syrup

Combine ingredients and heat in top of double boiler over water, stirring until smooth. Remove from heat and chill. To serve, place pears upright either individually or together in flat dish. Spoon sauce over each pear.

POPOVERS

2 eggs, well beaten   1 cup all-purpose flour
1 cup milk   ½ teaspoon salt
2 tablespoons butter

Heat popover pans or glass custard cups in oven. Combine eggs, milk, flour, and salt. Beat thoroughly. Remove pans from oven. Place ½ teaspoon butter in each cup. Pour in the batter, filling ½ to ⅔ full. Bake in 475° oven for 15 minutes. Reduce heat to 350° and bake 20 to 25 minutes longer. Makes 12 medium-sized popovers.

PLUM MARMALADE

2 dozen purple plums, cut small   6 oranges, cut up, skins and all
¼ pound walnuts, chopped   1 cup seedless raisins
        ¾ cup sugar for each cup fruit

Cook all together for one hour on slow flame. Cool in jars and cover with paraffin. Makes six half-pints.

SOUR CREAM COFFEE CAKE GRANDMERE

½ cup butter   1 teaspoon baking soda
1 cup sugar   1 teaspoon baking powder
2 eggs   ½ teaspoon salt
2 cups all-purpose flour   1 cup commercial sour cream
        1 teaspoon vanilla

Cream the butter until soft, then add the sugar, and cream the mixture well until light and fluffy. Add the eggs, one at a time, beating well after each addition. Sift the dry ingredients together. Add the dry ingredients to the creamed mixture, alternating with the sour cream, beginning and ending with the flour mixture. Stir in the vanilla. Pour half of the batter into a well-buttered 9″ x 13″ pan, cover with half of the nut filling and topping (see below), pour the remaining batter over the filling and top with remainder of the nut mixture. Bake in a 325° oven for about 40 minutes.

Topping and filling:
        ⅓ cup brown sugar   1 teaspoon cinnamon
        ¼ cup sugar   ¼ cup finely chopped pecans

Combine all ingredients; add as directed.

Brunch Buffet

Crabmeat Blanche
Savory Eggs   Puffy French Toast
Sausage Links with Apple Rings   Hot Buttered Syrup
Frosted Mint Mold
Orange Streusel Cake
Coffee

ADVANCE PREPARATION SCHEDULE

Previous Day	Early Morning	Deep Freeze
Crabmeat mixture	*Egg mixture for*	*Coffee cake*
Apple Rings	*toast*	*to heat: add*
Mint Mold		*streusel and bake*
		15 minutes 350°

CRABMEAT BLANCHE

4 small English muffins, split   1 pound fresh crabmeat
2 tablespoons butter   Anchovy paste
1 pound fresh mushrooms   1 cup crumbled fresh bread

Split English muffins and toast lightly. Butter muffin halves with
large pieces of butter, melted, but not browned. Muffins should
bsorb butter. Make 2½ cups of thick cream sauce, using cream
see Index for recipe). Chop mushrooms and sauté lightly in butter
or 5 minutes. Add crabmeat and mushrooms to cream sauce.
Spread anchovy paste very lightly on muffins. Then pile crabmeat
mixture on English muffins, add crumbled fresh bread and little
dots of butter on top. Bake in preheated oven 350° for about 15
minutes. These may be prepared ahead of time and baked when
ready to serve. Serves 8.

SAVORY EGGS

2 cups grated American cheese
¼ cup butter
1 cup light cream
½ teaspoon salt

¼ teaspoon pepper, freshly ground
2 teaspoons prepared mustard
12 eggs, slightly beaten

Spread the cheese in a greased 13" x 9" x 2" baking dish. Dot with butter. Combine the cream, salt, pepper, and mustard. Pour half of this mixture over the cheese. Pour eggs into the baking dish. Add the remaining cream mixture. Bake in moderately slow oven (325°) until set, about 40 minutes.

PAN-FRIED SAUSAGE LINKS

2 pounds small pork sausages   ½ cup cold water

Place the sausages in water in a saucepan. Do not prick. Let cook 5 minutes, covered. Drain off the water. Let cook very slowly for 10 minutes. Turn often so that they may brown evenly. They should be browned well, but not dry. Serves 6.

APPLE RINGS

3 pounds of apples, cored, cut into ½" slices
1 cup sugar

½ teaspoon cinnamon
1½ cups water
Few drops of red coloring

Prepare a syrup by combining the sugar, water, cinnamon, and coloring, and boil 10 or 15 minutes. Drop the sliced apples into the syrup. Cook until tender, or about 3 minutes. Drain the apples well, arrange on a platter with the sausages.

PUFFY FRENCH TOAST

8 slices white bread   ½ cup jelly

Batter:

1 tablespoon flour
2 tablespoons sugar

4 eggs, separated
½ cup milk

Spread bread with jelly and make 4 sandwiches. Cut into triangles. Mix the flour, sugar, egg yolks, and milk together and fold stiffly-beaten egg whites into the batter. Dip bread triangles into batter and fry in deep fat. Sprinkle with powdered sugar.

Hot Buttered Syrup:

Serve the toast with a sauce made of 1 cup pure maple syrup, heated with ¼ cup butter. To this add a little freshly grated lemon peel.

FROSTED MINT MOLD

1 20-ounce can crushed pine-
    apple, drained
2 tablespoons unflavored gelatin

½ cup cold water
¾ cup mint jelly (6 ounces)
1 cup commercial sour cream
2 drops mint flavoring

Soak the gelatin in the cold water for 5 minutes. Add sufficient water to pineapple juice to make 2½ cups and heat. Dissolve the gelatin in the hot liquid. Melt the jelly and add. Cool and place in the refrigerator until slightly thickened. Beat until foamy with a rotary beater, add flavoring, a few drops of green coloring if desired, and fold in the pineapple and sour cream. Pour into a greased 6-cup mold. (A melon mold would be attractive.) Chill until firm. Garnish with mint leaves.

ORANGE STREUSEL CAKE

1 cup brown sugar, tightly-
    packed
½ cup butter
2 eggs, well beaten
2 cups all-purpose flour

Pinch of salt
3 teaspoons baking powder
½ cup orange juice
½ cup milk
2 teaspoons vanilla
1 teaspoon grated orange rind

Cream butter and brown sugar. Add eggs. Sift dry ingredients together, and add to the butter and sugar mixture. Beat well and add orange juice and milk. Blend in vanilla and orange rind. Pour into a 9-inch greased square pan and sprinkle with Streusel Topping. Bake in a 350° oven for 45 minutes.

STREUSEL TOPPING

⅓ cup sugar
⅓ cup flour
1 teaspoon grated orange rind

3 tablespoons butter
1 teaspoon sugar

Mix until crumbly in texture.

Brunch Buffet

Creole Eggs   Sour Cream Noodles
Celery Crackers
Ham Upside-Down Cake — Mushroom Sauce
Celery and Beets Julienne   Persimmon Ring
Almond Puffs
Bundt Kuchen   Blueberry Tarts au Cointreau
Coffee

ADVANCE PREPARATION SCHEDULE

Previous Day	Early Morning	Deep Freeze
Noodles	*Sauce for eggs*	*Almond Puffs*
Mushroom Sauce	*Blueberry Tarts*	*Bundt Kuchen*
Marinate celery and beets		
Persimmon Ring		

CREOLE EGGS

2 No. 2 cans tomatoes (4 cups)   1 8½-ounce can cooked peas
¼ cup chopped onions   (1 cup)
½ cup chopped green pepper   2 cups shredded cheese, Ameri-
1 bay leaf   can or Cheddar
1 cup diced celery   8 eggs
1½ cups soft bread crumbs   Salt and pepper to taste

Combine tomatoes, onion, green pepper, bay leaf, and celery.
Cook slowly until celery is tender. Remove bay leaf. Season to
taste with salt and pepper. Add bread crumbs and peas. Pour
half of the sauce into individual casseroles, and sprinkle with one
half of the shredded cheese. Repeat, using the remaining sauce
and cheese. With a tablespoon, make a depression in each casserole and break an egg into each. Sprinkle with salt. Bake in a
350° oven for 20 minutes, or until eggs are cooked. This may be
baked in a 1½-quart casserole. Serves 8.

SOUR CREAM NOODLES

1 8-ounce package cream cheese
¼ cup butter
1 cup commercial sour cream
½ small onion, grated

1 pound package medium noodles,
cooked and drained
4 eggs, well beaten
½ teaspoon salt
¼ teaspoon pepper

Combine cheese, butter, sour cream, and onion; add the noodles which have been combined with the eggs. Add seasonings. Bake in a 350° oven for 45 minutes in a buttered 2-quart casserole. Serves 8.

HAM UPSIDE–DOWN CAKE

4 tablespoons butter
½ cup brown sugar
8 slices canned pineapple
6 slices baked ham

8 maraschino cherries
1 12-ounce package corn-meal
bread mix

Melt butter in a 10-inch skillet. Sprinkle sugar over butter. Place pineapple slices on the sugar in one layer, and arrange cherries as decoration. Place layer of ham next. Prepare corn bread according to package directions and pour over ham. Bake as directed. When baked, turn upside down on a serving platter and serve with Mushroom Sauce or Quick Mushroom Sauce, if desired. Serves 8.

MUSHROOM SAUCE

½ pound mushrooms sliced
2 tablespoons butter
2 tablespoons flour
2 tablespoons sherry

½ teaspoon salt
¼ teaspoon oregano
1½ cups light cream

Sauté mushrooms in the butter for 4 minutes. Add flour, salt, oregano, and light cream, and cook, stirring until thick. Add sherry just before serving.

QUICK MUSHROOM SAUCE

1 10½-ounce can undiluted cream
of mushroom soup
2 tablespoons butter
⅓ cup milk *or* sherry

½ cup drained mushrooms
(canned)
Pinch of curry powder

Mix all ingredients, except sherry. Simmer for 5 minutes. Add sherry and serve.

CELERY AND BEETS JULIENNE

2 20-ounce cans julienne sliced beets

2 20-ounce cans celery hearts, julienne sliced

Vinegar and Oil Dressing (see Index for recipe)

3 hard-cooked eggs

Watercress

1 10-ounce jar salad olives

Drain and marinate beets, celery, and olives, separately; refrigerate overnight. Use wine vinegar in dressing. Serve in mounds on platter lined with watercress. Garnish with grated egg yolks and chopped whites of egg. Border with marinated salad olives.

PERSIMMON RING

1 tablespoon plain gelatin

¼ cup water

1 package lemon-flavored gelatin

¾ cup hot orange juice

1 cup cold orange juice

Juice of ½ lemon (1½ tablespoons)

½ teaspoon salt

5 large ripe persimmons, puréed

Soak plain gelatin in water for five minutes. Dissolve lemon gelatin in hot orange juice and add soaked gelatin. Add cold orange juice, lemon juice, and salt. Mix well. Place in refrigerator and chill until of jellylike consistency. Fold in the puréed persimmons; pour into 6-cup greased ring mold. (If sharper flavor is desired, 2 tablespoons tarragon vinegar may be added to recipe.) Center with Green Mayonnaise (see Index for recipe). Surround with slices of melon, wheel-fashion. Serves 8.

ALMOND PUFFS

⅓ cup almonds, blanched and finely chopped

¾ cup scalded milk, cooled to lukewarm

3 tablespoons sugar

1 teaspoon salt

¼ cup shortening

1 cake compressed yeast

2 eggs

2 cups sifted all-purpose flour

Topping:

⅓ cup almonds, blanched, and finely chopped, plus 3 tablespoons sugar

Mix together until shortening is soft, the milk, sugar, salt, and shortening. Crumble in the yeast; stir in the eggs. Add the flour;

mix well. Add the almonds. Beat until smooth and well blended. Scrape the dough from the sides of the bowl, cover with damp cloth, and let rise until about double in bulk. Beat well after the dough has risen, and drop by spoonfuls into greased muffin cups. filling each cup half full. Sprinkle with almond-sugar topping. Let rise until double. Bake in 375° oven for 15 to 20 minutes. Makes 24 small or 12 large puffs.

BUNDT KUCHEN

1½ cups pecan meat halves	2 cups sugar
3 cups cake flour	4 eggs, separated
2 teaspoons baking powder	1 cup milk
½ teaspoon salt	Juice and grated peel of one lemon
1 cup shortening	2 teaspoons whiskey (optional)

1 teaspoon vanilla

Grease and flour a fluted 9-inch tube pan; place pecan halves in grooves around bottom and sides of pan. Sift flour, measure, and sift again with baking powder and salt. Cream shortening and gradually add sugar, creaming thoroughly; beat in egg yolks, one at a time, and beat until smooth. Add dry ingredients to creamed mixture alternately with milk; stir in lemon juice and peel, whiskey if desired, and vanilla. Beat egg whites until stiff, but not dry, then fold in. Carefully spoon batter into nut-lined pan. Bake in 400° oven for 15 minutes. Reduce heat to 350° and continue baking 1 hour longer. Cool slightly and turn out of pan.

BLUEBERRY TARTS AU COINTREAU

12 tart shells	1 cup heavy cream
1 3¼-ounce package instant vanilla pudding	⅛ teaspoon salt
	1 tablespoon Cointreau
1 cup milk	

3 cups blueberries dusted with powdered sugar

Make the instant pudding according to the directions on the package, but use the milk and heavy cream for the liquid. Add salt, then add the Cointreau. Fill tarts. Heap with blueberries; sprinkle with powdered sugar. Serve with whipped cream.

TART SHELLS

2 cups all-purpose flour ½ cup salad oil
1½ teaspoons salt   ¼ cup cold milk

Mix flour and salt; add oil and milk. Mix well. Press into ball, flatten slightly. Roll pastry ⅛ inch thick between waxed paper. Cut into 3½-inch rounds and fit over inverted bottom of 12 muffin tins. Flute edges; prick entire surface with fork. Bake in a 425° oven about 10 minutes or until delicately brown. Cool before filling.

Brunch Buffet

Cold Poached Salmon
Cucumber Dressing
Chicken Hash Pump Room   Gambler's Eggs
Baked Canadian Bacon
Cinnamon Rolls   Apricot Conserve
Strawberry Pancakes
Coffee

ADVANCE PREPARATION SCHEDULE

Previous Day	Early Morning	Deep Freeze
Chicken Hash	*Make pancakes and*	*Pan Rolls*
Bake bacon, partially	*stack*	
Poach salmon	*Cucumber Dressing*	

COLD POACHED SALMON

4 pounds fresh salmon
1 quart water
3 tablespoons white wine or wine vinegar
1 tablespoon salt
1 bay leaf

2 sliced carrots
5 sprigs dill
1 stalk celery
¼ teaspoon thyme
¼ teaspoon allspice
2 cloves stuck into 1 onion

Place all ingredients except fish in a large kettle and simmer for

15 minutes. Wrap the fish in a piece of cheesecloth and lower it into the liquid very carefully. Let simmer just under the boiling point for 20 minutes. Remove carefully in the cloth, drain thoroughly and place on serving platter. Garnish with watercress, radish roses and sliced cucumbers. Chill and serve with Cucumber Dressing. Serves 8 to 12.

CUCUMBER DRESSING

1 cup commercial sour cream   ½ teaspoon dill seed
2 tablespoons lemon juice   ½ teaspoon salt
1 teaspoon prepared mustard   ½ teaspoon onion powder
1 cup finely chopped cucumber

Combine ingredients; blend well.

CHICKEN HASH PUMP ROOM

4 cups diced cooked chicken   2 egg yolks
½ cup diced celery   2 tablespoons cream
1 cup chicken broth   1 teaspoon salt
2 cups Supreme Sauce   ¼ teaspoon pepper
2 tablespoons Escoffier Sauce   ¼ teaspoon paprika
½ cup Madeira

Heat the diced chicken and celery in ¾ cup of the chicken broth. In a separate skillet, heat Supreme Sauce and Escoffier Sauce. Blend egg yolks and cream into sauce, stirring constantly and briskly. Add wine and seasonings. If sauce is too thick, add some of the remaining chicken broth. Blend chicken and sauce together. Serve in casserole or prepare and serve in a chafing dish. Decorate with paprika. Serves 8.

Variation: Serve in pastry shell.

SUPREME SAUCE

½ cup butter   2 cups broth
4 tablespoons flour   ¼ teaspoon salt
1 teaspoon onion juice

Melt the butter; stir in the flour. Add broth, salt, and onion juice, stirring constantly until sauce thickens.

GAMBLER'S EGGS

A base of French Toast covered with Scrambled Eggs and served with Tomato Sauce.

French Toast, Oven Style:

2 eggs, slightly beaten	¼ cup milk
½ teaspoon salt	6 slices white bread

Combine eggs, salt and milk in a shallow dish. Dip bread slices quickly on both sides into egg mixture. Place on a very well greased jelly-roll pan. Bake 5 minutes on each side in a 500° oven.

Special Scrambled Eggs:

3 tablespoons butter	½ cup milk
12 eggs	1 teaspoon salt
¼ teaspoon pepper	

Melt butter in top of double boiler or chafing dish at table. Beat the eggs, milk, and seasonings together, very lightly; pour mixture into the hot butter and stir briefly, and occasionally. Remove double boiler from flame when eggs are thick and creamy. Butter may be omitted from this method of preparation though your pan may need an extra bit of scrubbing.

Tomato Sauce:

2 tablespoons butter	¼ cup light cream
1 tablespoon minced onion	¼ teaspoon oregano
1 10½-ounce can condensed tomato soup, undiluted	1 teaspoon A-1 Sauce
	¼ teaspoon prepared mustard

Melt butter in saucepan and sauté onion for 5 minutes; add soup, cream, oregano, A-1 sauce and mustard, and cook another 5 minutes. Keep the French Toast hot in the oven while scrambling the eggs in a chafing dish at the table. The sauce may be brought in piping hot with the toast.

BAKED CANADIAN BACON

3 to 4 pounds Canadian bacon ½ cup orange juice
1 orange, cut into thin slices ¼ cup sugar
½ cup molasses   ¼ teaspoon dry mustard
¼ cup water   Whole cloves

Remove casing from bacon and place fat side up in an open pan. Bake in 325° oven for 2 hours. Remove from oven. Attach orange slices to Canadian bacon with whole cloves. Mix remaining ingredients, pour over bacon and bake, basting frequently, in 325° oven for 30 minutes. Serves 8.

The leftover bacon, if any, is very good with any kind of eggs.

CINNAMON ROLLS

½ pound of butter   3 cups all-purpose flour
3 tablespoons sugar   ½ teaspoon salt
1 cake compressed yeast   Cinnamon
3 eggs   Brown sugar
1 cup commercial sour cream Raisins

Cream together the butter and sugar. Put the yeast through a sieve; mix with creamed mixture. Add the eggs, sour cream, flour, and salt. Knead well; chill overnight. Use ⅓ of the dough at one time. Roll out flat, brush with butter and sprinkle with cinnamon, brown sugar and raisins; roll as a jelly roll. Cut into 1½-inch slices. Line or spread each muffin tin with one tablespoon butter and one teaspoon brown sugar. Place each slice cut side down in muffin tin. Let rise in warm place (85°) until double the original size, about 1½ hours. Bake in 350° oven for 12 to 15 minutes. Turn rolls out of pans immediately. Scrape any remaining butter and sugar from pans and apply to tops of rolls. Makes 24.

APRICOT CONSERVE

1 pound dried apricots   2 cups crushed pineapple, drained
                    4 cups sugar

Wash apricots; cover with water and soak overnight. Cook in same water until tender, about 30 minutes. Mash through a food mill or a coarse strainer. Add the pineapple and sugar. Cook slowly, stirring constantly, until thickened. Keep in refrigerator for immediate use or seal in sterilized jars. Serve with toasted prepared hard rolls or your recipe from freezer.

STRAWBERRY PANCAKES

3 egg yolks	¼ cup all-purpose flour
¾ cup cottage cheese	¼ cup milk
¼ teaspoon salt	3 egg whites, stiffly beaten

Beat the egg yolks and the cottage cheese until smooth. Mix in the salt, flour, and milk. Fold in the egg whites. Bake on a hot, lightly greased 7-inch griddle, using 2 tablespoons batter per pancake. Turn pancakes when they are puffed, and bubbles appear. Brown other side; roll or stack. To serve, place rolled or stacked pancakes in casserole and Strawberry Sauce in separate bowl. Keep hot in oven until ready to serve. Serves 4.

Strawberry Sauce:

1 10-ounce package of frozen strawberries	1 tablespoon cornstarch

Mix the cornstarch with ¼ cup of water. Add thawed berries and bring slowly to a boil. Cook 5 minutes or until clear.

Brunch Buffet

Iced Cherry Soup
Saltines
Eggs Florentine   Shrimp Fritters
Caesar Salad
Cheese Platter
Date and Nut Bread   Jiffy Coffee Cake
Coffee   Iced Tea

ADVANCE PREPARATION SCHEDULE

Previous Day	Early Morning	Deep Freeze
Cherry Soup	*Crisp greens*	*Date and Nut Bread*
	Cook spinach	*Jiffy Coffee Cake*
	Jiffy Coffee Cake;	
	may be frozen	

ICED CHERRY SOUP

1 No. 2 can sour pitted cherries (2 cups)
5½ cups water
½ cup sugar
½ lemon, thinly sliced
½ teaspoon cinnamon or 1 stick cinnamon

3 tablespoons cornstarch
½ teaspoon salt
½ teaspoon almond extract
½ teaspoon red food coloring
1 cup commercial sour cream

Mash cherries slightly. Combine 5 cups water with sugar, lemon slices, and cinnamon; cover and cook slowly for 30 minutes. Dissolve cornstarch with remaining ½ cup water and add to cherry mixture with salt, almond extract and coloring. Cook until soup clears and begins to thicken. Serve cold with a generous mound of sour cream on each portion.

EGGS FLORENTINE

1 10-ounce package frozen spinach or 2 cups chopped cooked spinach
6 eggs

1 10-ounce can cream of celery soup
1½ cups shredded process cheese

Line the bottom of a shallow baking dish with spinach. Make 6 indentations in spinach and break eggs into each. Heat the soup and 1 cup of cheese. Pour around the eggs. Sprinkle with ½ cup cheese. Bake in 350° oven for 30 minutes.

SHRIMP FRITTERS

½ cup water
2 tablespoons butter
½ cup flour
2 eggs

½ cup American cheese, grated
1 cup cooked shrimp, cut into small pieces

Bring the water to a boil with butter. Add flour all at once, stirring vigorously until mixture leaves the side of the pan. Remove from heat and add well-beaten eggs, beating until smooth and thick. Stir in shrimp and cheese; drop by small spoonfuls into shallow hot fat. Brown well on both sides. Makes 12 fritters.

CAESAR SALAD

1 clove garlic, minced
¼ cup salad or olive oil
2 cups small bread cubes
2 heads of romaine or greens
1 2-ounce can anchovies
⅓ cup salad or olive oil
½ teaspoon salt

¼ teaspoon black pepper
1 tablespoon Worcestershire sauce
¼ cup lemon juice
2 coddled eggs
½ cup grated Parmesan cheese
¼ teaspoon dry mustard

Blend garlic and oil in a large skillet; heat and add bread cubes. Sauté gently until golden brown. Refrigerate. (May be made hours in advance.) Tear chilled greens into medium-sized pieces and place in salad bowl. Mash anchovies and combine with ⅓ cup oil, salt, pepper, Worcestershire sauce, mustard, and lemon juice. Mix thoroughly and pour over greens. Pour eggs over greens and toss well. Sprinkle with cheese and bread cubes, toss again, and serve immediately. Serves 8.

Coddled Eggs:
Place eggs in boiling water. Turn off the heat; cover pan, let stand for 1½ minutes. Remove.

CHEESE PLATTER

Cheddar cubes
Swiss cheese squares
Nut-covered Cheddar cheese balls
Blue cheese triangles
Unhulled strawberries
Pineapple spears
Lemon leaves

Arrange on a large wooden platter: cheese cubes with colored toothpicks for handles; light yellow Swiss cheese squares, nut-covered Cheddar cheese balls, blue cheese triangles, bright red strawberries, and golden pineapple spears. Place on a bed of green lemon leaves. To make the cheese balls: Roll small pieces of prepared Cheddar cheese spread into round balls. Dip them in fruit juice and roll the balls in chopped nuts.

DATE AND NUT BREAD

1 cup pitted dates (1 box)
1 cup boiling water
1 teaspoon baking soda
1 cup sugar
½ cup shortening
1 cup nut meats
1¾ cups all-purpose flour

Soak the dates in boiling water with the soda for 15 minutes. Cream sugar and shortening. Mix nuts with the flour. Combine all mixtures alternately. Bake in a greased and floured 9-inch loaf pan in a 350° oven about 1 hour.

JIFFY COFFEE CAKE

1 egg
½ cup sugar
1 cup pancake mix
½ cup milk
3 tablespoons melted butter

Topping:

¼ cup brown sugar
1 tablespoon flour
1 teaspoon cinnamon
2 tablespoons melted butter
¼ cup chopped nuts

Cream the egg and sugar together until fluffy. Add pancake mix, milk, and melted butter. Pour into a greased 8" x 8" x 2" pan. Combine topping ingredients and spread on batter. Bake in 375° oven for 30 minutes.

Brunch Buffet

Carrot Sticks   Watermelon Rind   Stuffed Fresh Figs
Baked Smelts Bonne Femme   Tripe Creole
Crisp Noodle Mold
Tahiti Fruit Cup
Cinnamon Rolls
Continental Coffee Cake   Danish Kringle
Coffee

ADVANCE PREPARATION SCHEDULE

Previous Day	Early Morning	Deep Freeze
Clean smelts, prepare partially	*Complete tripe preparation*	*Continental Coffee Cake*
Cook tripe, prepare partially	*Sauce on smelts*	
Noodle Mold	*Relishes*	
Mornay Sauce	*Fruit*	

CARROT STICKS

Cut four small carrots in julienne strips and crisp in ice water.

WATERMELON RIND

2 pounds watermelon rind   1 pint vinegar
Salted water (¼ cup salt to 1   1 pint water
    quart water)   4 cups sugar
¼ cup mixed pickling spices

Pare rind, removing all green and pink membrane. Cut rind into
1-inch cubes. Cover with salt water and soak overnight. Drain
and cover with fresh water. Bring to a boil and simmer until tender; drain. Tie spices in a bag and combine with water, vinegar,
and sugar. Place in another saucepan and cook for about 15 minutes until thick and clear. Add rind and simmer until rind appears
translucent. Remove spice bag and pour into sterilized jars.

STUFFED FIGS

1 dozen fresh figs   1 3-ounce package cream cheese
2 tablespoons cream

Mix cream and cheese until smooth. Split a small opening in side of fig and stuff with the cream cheese mixture. Refrigerate.

BAKED SMELTS BONNE FEMME

3 dozen smelts   1 tablespoon lemon juice
1 cup stock (beef or fish)   Sauce Mornay for baking

Clean smelts and remove heads; split in half and lay flat in shallow baking dish. Pour stock and lemon juice over the fish, place in a 350° oven and bake for 25 minutes, basting frequently. Cover with Sauce Mornay and, when ready to serve, place 3 inches from broiler flame and broil for 10 minutes until nicely glazed and heated.

Sauce Mornay:

¼ cup butter   ½ cup grated Swiss or American
1 tablespoon minced onion   cheese
¼ cup flour   1 teaspoon salt
2 cups warm milk   ¼ teaspoon pepper
                                ¼ teaspoon thyme
                  Paprika

Heat butter in saucepan; add combined onion, flour, and milk. Blend well. Cook until thick. Stir in seasonings and cheese. Reheat.

TRIPE CREOLE

2 pounds tripe   1 clove garlic, minced
1 tablespoon salt   ¼ cup ham,
1 tablespoon vinegar   finely chopped (optional)
2 onions, finely sliced   ½ teaspoon thyme
2 tablespoons butter   1 bay leaf
Salt and pepper   1 No. 2 can tomatoes (2 cups)
Dash cayenne   1 green pepper, finely sliced

Wash tripe thoroughly in several changes of water; place in a saucepan and cover with fresh water, salt, and vinegar. Boil for three hours or until tender. Cut into strips 2 inches by ½ inch. Sauté onions in butter until brown. Add remaining ingredients except tripe, and cook for 10 minutes. Add tripe, cover and simmer 30 minutes longer. Serve around Crisp Noodle Mold with garnish of greens in center.

CRISP NOODLE MOLD

1 8-ounce package thin noodles	½ pound mushrooms
1 cup long-grain rice	½ teaspoon salt
¼ pound butter	½ teaspoon onion salt
2 cups consommé	Freshly ground pepper
¼ teaspoon thyme	

Brown uncooked noodles and rice in 4 tablespoons butter. Place in pan with consommé and cook, uncovered, for about 30 minutes or until liquid is absorbed. Chop mushrooms coarsely and sauté in 2 tablespoons butter. Combine with noodle-rice mixture and add seasonings and remaining butter. Arrange in a buttered 4-cup ring mold, place in a pan of hot water, and bake in 350° oven for 45 minutes. Serves 6 to 8.

TAHITI FRUIT CUP

2 cups orange sections	1 cup shredded coconut or
Sections of one grapefruit	1 6-ounce can shredded coconut
1 cup diced pineapple	1 tablespoon chopped ginger
2 teaspoons grated orange peel	¾ cup orange juice
¼ cup Cointreau (optional)	

Combine all ingredients thoroughly. Chill.

BROWN–AND–SERVE CINNAMON ROLLS

1 package brown-and-serve cinnamon rolls

Spread each roll with ½ teaspoon butter, 1 teaspoon brown sugar and 3 whole pecans. Bake as directed. Serving piping hot.

CONTINENTAL COFFEE CAKE

2½ cups sifted all-purpose flour
¼ teaspoon salt
1 cup butter
3 egg yolks, beaten
½ teaspoon vanilla
1 package dry yeast
¼ cup warm water
3 tablespoons sugar
3 egg whites
1 cup sugar
Chopped nuts
Raisins

Sift flour and salt into bowl. Cut in the butter, as for pie crust. Add the beaten egg yolks and vanilla. Dissolve yeast in warm water; stir in sugar. Add to the batter and stir well. Cover and place in refrigerator overnight. Remove from refrigerator. Beat the egg whites until stiff; gradually beat in the sugar and continue beating until mixture stands in stiff peaks. Divide dough into 2 pieces. Roll each piece to about ¼-inch thickness. Spread with meringue and sprinkle with nuts and raisins. Roll up each piece as for a jelly roll. Place on a greased baking sheet or in ring molds. Let rise for about 15 minutes. Bake in a moderate oven (350°) for 35 to 40 minutes or until lightly browned. While cake is still warm, drizzle on the icing (see below). For variety, add thinly sliced, peeled, sour apples to filling. Makes two cakes.

COFFEE CAKE ICING

2 tablespoons hot cream   ¾ cup confectioners' sugar
¼ teaspoon vanilla

Mix sugar with hot cream or milk; add vanilla. Drizzle over hot cake as it comes out of oven.

DANISH KRINGLE

1 cake compressed yeast
¼ cup lukewarm water
4 cups all-purpose flour
1½ teaspoons salt
1½ cups butter
3 egg yolks
½ cup commercial sour cream
Raisin filling
3 egg whites, lightly beaten
Sugar

Soften yeast in water. Sift flour and salt into large bowl; cut in butter with pastry blender until mixture is size of small peas; beat egg yolks slightly and combine with yeast and cream. Add to flour mixture. Mix well, using hands, if necessary, to get a smooth dough. Divide into 2 parts. Roll one portion on slightly floured surface into a long strip 18 x 6 inches. Spread center thinly with filling (see below). Fold sides partially over it, letting some of the filling show. Arrange on a greased cooky sheet in shape of pretzel. Repeat with remaining dough and filling. Brush with egg white. Sprinkle with sugar; bake at 350° for 20 minutes.

Filling:

1 3¼-ounce package instant va-   1½ cups milk
    nilla pudding   1 cup raisins

Rinse and drain raisins; prepare pudding according to the directions on the package, using 1½ cups milk. Cool slightly, stir in the raisins.

Brunch Buffet

Berries with Sour Cream and Brown Sugar

Eggs — Hunter's Style   Frogs' Legs Financier

Wild Rice Pancakes

Orange Biscuits

Butter Horns   Coffee

ADVANCE PREPARATION SCHEDULE

Previous Day	Early Morning	Deep Freeze
Tomato Sauce	*Frogs' legs*	*Orange Biscuits*
Boil rice	*Mix pancakes*	*Butter Horns*

BERRIES WITH SOUR CREAM AND BROWN SUGAR

2 pints strawberries, raspberries, or   1 pint commercial sour cream
    blueberries   1 cup brown sugar

Wash and hull berries, place in sherbet glasses or a bowl. Top with sour cream and sugar. Cream and sugar may be served separately.

EGGS — HUNTER'S STYLE

1 pound chicken livers
½ teaspoon salt
2 tablespoons butter
¼ cup sauterne

1 tablespoon chopped onion
6 tablespoons tomato purée
6 eggs
6 slices toast

Cut livers in halves; season with salt and sauté lightly in butter. Remove from pan. Pour wine and onion in pan; simmer onion until soft. Add tomato purée and cook 15 minutes. Add livers to sauce, and break eggs, one at a time, over them, spacing eggs evenly. Cover tightly and cook slowly for 3 or 4 minutes. Serve on toast.

FROGS' LEGS FINANCIER

12 pairs frozen frogs' legs
2 cups prepared bread crumbs
¼ cup butter

4 eggs, well beaten
1 tablespoon minced onion

Thaw frogs' legs; rinse in cold water and dry. Dip in bread crumbs, dust with salt and pepper, then dip in eggs and once again in bread crumbs. Let stand on wax paper at room temperature for 15 minutes. Melt butter, add onion and frogs' legs. Sauté over medium heat until golden brown. Turn and sauté on the other side for a total cooking time of 15 minutes. Serve with Tartar Sauce (see Index for recipe).

WILD RICE PANCAKES

½ pound mushrooms, coarsely chopped
2 tablespoons grated onion
4 tablespoons butter
3 whole eggs, beaten
2 cups boiled wild rice; may be purchased cooked in cans

2 teaspoons baking powder
1 teaspoon salt
1 cup all-purpose flour
¼ cup milk
4 tablespoons shortening for frying

Sauté mushrooms and onions in butter; add eggs. Now stir in the remaining ingredients. If batter is too thick, more milk may be added. Drop into hot shortening and fry to a light golden brown. Especially good fried in chicken fat.

ORANGE BISCUITS

3 cups all-purpose flour	4 tablespoons butter
3 teaspoons baking powder	1½ cups buttermilk
½ teaspoon soda	1 tablespoon grated orange peel
1 teaspoon salt	Orange marmalade

Sift together the dry ingredients; work in the butter and then add the buttermilk to make soft dough. Stir in orange peel. Roll out thin and cut in rounds. Place two together and on the top biscuit, place a small spoonful of orange marmalade. Bake in 375° oven for 15 minutes, or until light brown.

BUTTER HORNS

¼ cup warm water	3 cups all-purpose flour
1 ¼-ounce package active dry yeast	2 tablespoons sugar
	1 teaspoon salt
1 teaspoon sugar	1 cup butter
6 ounces evaporated milk (¾ cup)	2 egg yolks, slightly beaten
	Melted butter

Filling:

1 cup finely chopped nut meats	1 teaspoon cinnamon
	2 tablespoons brown sugar

Add water to yeast; dissolve and add sugar; allow to stand until it starts bubbling. Cut the dry ingredients into the cup of butter with pastry blender until dough is like corn meal; add milk and eggs; mix well. Add the yeast mixture and knead slightly. Divide dough into 8 parts. Roll each piece into a circle on floured board. Spread with melted butter and then the filling. Cut circle into 5 wedges. Roll toward the point of the wedge and shape into crescents. Let rise for 2 hours in warm place. Bake in a 350° oven for about 20 minutes.

Variation: Fill with apricot jam. Makes 40 pieces.

Brunch Buffet

Orange Cooler
Capon Liver Pâté
Poached Turbot — Caper or Hollandaise Sauce
German Apple Pancake
Mushroom Spoon Bread
Pineapple and Cucumber Ring
Posies   Coffee

ADVANCE PREPARATION SCHEDULE

Previous Day	Early Morning	Deep Freeze
Poach turbot	*Prepare chicken livers*	*Posies*
Caper Sauce	*Hollandaise Sauce*	
Liver Pâté		

ORANGE COOLER

2 10-ounce packages frozen straw-   1 cup orange juice
  berries (almost thawed)   ¼ cup lemon juice
Sugar to taste

Combine ingredients in blender. Place 2 cubes of ice in each 8-ounce glass. Pour in ½ cup of fruit mixture. Fill remainder with carbonated ginger ale or lime drink.

Variation: Add 1 ounce of gin or vodka to each serving, and a dash of grenadine.

CAPON LIVER PATE

1 pound capon or chicken livers   ½ pound raw mushrooms,
1 small onion, chopped   washed and cut into pieces
½ cup butter   1 ounce sherry
Salt and pepper to taste

Sauté chicken livers and onion in butter about 10 minutes. Place in a blender with remaining ingredients and mix until smooth.

Pour into a 2-cup mold and refrigerate at least 3 hours. Unmold on lettuce. Serve with melba toast. Serves 6 to 8.

POACHED TURBOT

Court Bouillon:

1 quart water *or* 2½ cups water
and 1½ cups white wine
1 carrot
1 onion

1 lemon, sliced
2 bay leaves
1 teaspoon salt
4 peppercorns

1 4- to 5-pound turbot, may be sliced or filleted

Combine all ingredients for Court Bouillon and simmer slowly for 30 minutes. Place a whole fish in cheesecloth and lower gently into bouillon. Leave ends of cloth outside of pan to use as handles so that fish may be removed easily without breaking. Liquid should just cover fish. Simmer under the boiling point for 30 minutes. Do not overcook. (Fillets should cook only 10 minutes.) Remove, drain, and place on heated platter, garnished with lemon slices and parsley. Serve with Caper Sauce or Hollandaise Sauce.

CAPER SAUCE

2 3-ounce packages of cream cheese
2 egg yolks, beaten

2 tablespoons lemon juice
¼ teaspoon salt

2 tablespoons capers

Mix cheese, yolks, lemon juice, and salt; blend thoroughly. Heat over water in double boiler, stirring occasionally. Add capers just before serving.

HOLLANDAISE SAUCE

½ cup soft butter
4 egg yolks, slightly beaten

Dash of cayenne
¼ teaspoon salt

1 tablespoon lemon juice

Divide butter into three parts. In the upper part of double boiler, combine egg yolks and one-third of butter. Bring water in lower part of double boiler to boil and place upper part on it. Remove from heat. Beat butter and yolks with rotary beater until butter is melted; add second piece of butter and beat; then the third piece. Continue to beat mixture about 2 or 3 minutes or until sauce thickens. Remove upper part of boiler from hot water. Add lemon juice and seasonings. Beat until well blended. May be kept over warm, but not boiling water until ready to be served. Should sauce curdle, add 1 or 2 tablespoons boiling water, beating constantly.

GERMAN APPLE PANCAKE

3 tablespoons lemon juice	6 eggs, beaten
4 tart apples, peeled, sliced very thin	1 teaspoon salt
	1 cup milk
2 tablespoons butter	1 cup all-purpose flour

Topping:
    1 tablespoon lemon juice   Sugar

Mix apples with the lemon juice. Melt butter in a 12-inch skillet, seeing that sides of skillet are greased. Sauté apples about 7 minutes until glazed. Add salt, milk, and flour to eggs while beating constantly. Pour the batter over the apples and place immediately in a preheated 450° oven. Bake 20 minutes, reduce the heat to 350° and bake 10 minutes more until crisp and brown. To serve, sprinkle with 1 tablespoon lemon juice and dust liberally with sugar.

MUSHROOM SPOON BREAD

¾ cup milk	1 tablespoon butter
1 10-ounce can mushroom soup	2 egg yolks, beaten
½ cup corn meal	¼ teaspoon salt
2 egg whites, stiffly beaten	

Combine the milk and soup, add corn meal, bring slowly to a boil. Cook 5 minutes, stirring constantly. Add butter, yolks, and salt. Stir well; fold in the stiffly beaten egg whites. Pour into buttered casserole and bake 1 hour in 350° oven. Serve immediately.

PINEAPPLE AND CUCUMBER RING

2 20-ounce cans crushed pineapple, drained
2 large cucumbers, chopped and
drained

3½ cups liquid (pineapple juice
and sufficient water)

2 packages lime-flavored gelatin

Drain pineapple and cucumbers thoroughly and combine. Heat 1 cup of liquid to boiling and dissolve gelatin. Add remaining cold liquid and stir. Place in refrigerator and set until slightly congealed. Fold in the pineapple and cucumbers. Pour into a greased 8-cup mold and chill until firm. Garnish center of mold with watercress and border with cantaloupe slices and pickled peaches. Sprinkle with blueberries. Serves 10.

POSIES

½ pound butter
1 cup sugar
1 egg yolk
½ cup chopped pecans

2 cups all-purpose flour
2 teaspoons cinnamon
1 egg white

Cream butter and sugar; add the egg yolk. Beat in the flour and cinnamon. Mix well until smooth. Pat, by hand, on cooky sheet; brush with egg white; cover with chopped pecans. Bake in a 350° oven for 30 minutes. Cut in squares while warm and remove from pan.

Luncheon Buffets

*Each recipe
serves six
unless otherwise
indicated*

LUNCHEONS are strictly "between us girls." Usually, both the food and conversation are on the light side. However, for the special occasions when you are honoring an old college friend or a visiting lecturer, you will want a menu that is delectable and distinctive. Incidentally, any of the brunch menus will fit the occasion just as well as the following.

Buffet Luncheon

Cold Artichokes
Mustard French Dressing
Sweetbreads Maréchal   Cheese Soufflé
Bacon Twists
Bing Cherries Royale   Muffins Rivoli — Pineapple Preserves
Party Crescents   Chocolate Angel Pie
Coffee

47

ADVANCE PREPARATION SCHEDULE

Previous Day	Early Morning	Freezer
Boil sweetbreads	*Bacon Twists*	*Party Crescents*
Boil artichokes	*Sweetbreads in sauce*	
Refrigerate cherries		
Chocolate Angel Pie		

COLD ARTICHOKES

6 whole artichokes
Boiling water
½ teaspoon salt per cup of water

6 tablespoons salad oil
6 thick slices of lemon
1 clove garlic (optional)

Cutting straight across the top, remove 1 inch of the artichoke; cut off stem close to the leaves and snip off thorns of the outer leaves. Stand upright closely together in 1 inch of boiling, salted water. Add the oil, lemon and garlic. Boil gently, covered, for 30 minutes, or until a leaf may be easily pulled from the stalk. Drain upside down. Remove choke and chill. Add more water, if necessary, when boiling. Serve with Mustard French Dressing.

MUSTARD FRENCH DRESSING

1 cup basic French dressing   3 tablespoons Bavarian-style mustard with Moselle wine

Blend the two ingredients together.

SWEETBREADS MARECHAL

2 pounds sweetbreads, soaked 15 minutes in cold water
2 large onions, finely chopped, sautéed in butter

2 10-ounce cans tomato soup, undiluted
1 cup commercial sour cream
Sugar to taste
Toast points

Cook sweetbreads in boiling, salted water for 20 minutes; drain and remove membrane. Roll the sweetbreads in the sautéed onions; add soup, sour cream, and sugar. Heat lightly, but thoroughly. Serve on toast points.

CHEESE SOUFFLE

4 tablespoons butter
4 tablespoons flour
1½ cups milk
½ pound processed American cheese, grated

1 teaspoon salt
Dash cayenne
6 egg yolks, beaten
6 egg whites, stiffly beaten

Melt the butter over boiling water in the top of a double boiler. Add the flour; stir until thick and smooth. Add the milk and then the cheese; stir until melted. Remove from heat and add the egg yolks and seasonings; mix well. Pour onto stiffly-beaten whites, gently folding until blended. Pour into ungreased 2-quart casserole. With a teaspoon, draw a line 1 inch in from the edge of casserole. It will form a "top hat." Place casserole in shallow pan of boiling water. Bake 1¼ hours in a 300° oven.

BACON TWISTS

6 slices frozen sandwich bread (defrost sufficiently to handle)
1 3-ounce package cream cheese

1 tablespoon mayonnaise
¼ teaspoon onion juice
½ teaspoon seasoning salt
9 slices bacon, halved

Cut crusts from bread slices. Combine cheese, mayonnaise, onion juice, and seasoning salt. Blend well. Spread each slice of bread with mixture. Place in refrigerator to harden. Cut each slice into three strips. Wrap bacon spirally around each strip and fasten with toothpick. Brown in broiler about 10 minutes, turning once, or until bacon is crisp.

BING CHERRIES ROYALE

1 No. 2½ can Bing cherries and juice (3 cups)

¼ cup port wine

Drain ¼ cup juice from the cherries; substitute with the port wine. Chill before serving.

MUFFINS RIVOLI

3 tablespoons butter
3 tablespoons sugar
2¼ teaspoons baking powder
2¼ cups sifted all-purpose flour

½ teaspoon salt
2 egg yolks, beaten
Cream
2 egg whites, stiffly beaten

Blend butter, sugar, baking powder, flour, and salt until well mixed, as for pie. Place the yolks in a cup and add sufficient cream to make 1 cup liquid. Add to first mixture. Mix well. Fold in the stiffly beaten egg whites. Pour into greased muffin tins; bake in a 325° oven for 25 minutes.

PINEAPPLE PRESERVES

2 cups crushed pineapple
1 10-ounce package frozen strawberries

2 tablespoons lemon juice
5 cups sugar
1 cup liquid pectin

Heat together the pineapple, strawberries, lemon juice, and sugar; bring to a full rolling boil and stir for 1 minute. Remove from heat; mix in liquid pectin; skim and stir for 5 minutes. Pour into 12 sterilized, 4-ounce glasses. Seal.

PARTY CRESCENTS

4 cups sifted bread flour
½ teaspoon salt
1 ounce household yeast
1¼ cups butter

3 egg yolks, beaten
1 teaspoon vanilla
1 cup commercial sour cream
Powdered sugar

Crumble yeast into flour and salt. Cut in the butter with a pastry blender until mixture resembles meal. Add the beaten yolks, vanilla and sour cream. Mix well. Divide into 7 balls. Roll each ball separately in powdered sugar and roll quite thin into a circle. Cut each circle into 8 pie-shaped wedges. Put 1 teaspoon filling on each triangle and roll tightly, starting at the broad end. Shape as a crescent and place on ungreased cooky sheet. Bake 15 to 20 minutes in 400° oven. Remove; sprinkle with powdered sugar. Makes 56. (These Crescents freeze well.)

Filling:

Stiffly beaten whites of the 3 eggs
1 cup sugar

1 cup ground pecans or walnuts
1 teaspoon vanilla

Fold sugar, nuts and vanilla into beaten egg whites.

CHOCOLATE ANGEL PIE

Meringue shell:

4 egg whites ¼ teaspoon cream of tartar
1 cup sugar

Beat 4 egg whites until stiff, but not dry, adding cream of tartar. Add sugar and beat until glossy. Spread in a 10-inch pie plate, making a deep ring around the edge; bake in a 300° oven for 1 hour.

Filling:

1 6-ounce package chocolate bits   2 egg whites, stiffly beaten
4 egg yolks   1 cup cream, whipped
1 teaspoon vanilla   Shaved bitter chocolate

Place chocolate pieces in top of double boiler. Melt, and remove from heat. Beat in the yolks; cool; fold in egg whites and vanilla. Fold half the whipped cream into the custard and pour into the cooled meringue shell. Spread remaining cream over the top. Sprinkle with shaved chocolate. Chill several hours.

Variation: Make individual meringues.

Buffet Luncheon

Cold Cucumber Soup   Mushroom Pizzas
Stuffed Celery
Lobster Old French Market   Chicken Almond Mousse
Potato Flour Muffins   Plum Jam
Carrot Cake   Bourbon Balls
Coffee

ADVANCE PREPARATION SCHEDULE

Previous Day	Early Morning	Deep Freeze
Cold Cucumber Soup	*Stuff celery*	*Carrot Cake*
Carrot Cake	*Potato Muffins*	*Bourbon Balls*
(may be frozen)		
Lobster		
Chicken Almond		
Mousse		

COLD CUCUMBER SOUP

2 green onions, chopped
1 small onion, finely chopped
2 tablespoons butter
4 chicken bouillon cubes
3 cups boiling water
½ cup chopped parsley
½ cup celery, finely chopped

3 medium potatoes, pared, quartered
½ teaspoon thyme
Dash Tabasco
2 cups commercial sour cream
1 teaspoon salt

1 large cucumber, finely grated

Sauté onions in butter for 5 minutes. Dissolve bouillon cubes in water and add parsley to the onions with celery, potatoes, and thyme. Bring to a boil. Cover and cook over low heat for 20 minutes. Remove from heat. Force through food mill or sieve. Chill. Add Tabasco, sour cream and cucumber. Mix well. Chill covered for several hours.

MUSHROOM PIZZAS

2 tablespoons butter
½ pound mushrooms, sliced thin
½ small onion, chopped
2 tablespoons sherry

¼ teaspoon marjoram
1 teaspoon salt
6 English muffins
1½ packages (8 ounces) sliced, sharp American cheese

Melt the butter; sauté the mushrooms and onion for several minutes. Stir in sherry, marjoram, and salt. Pull or fork muffins in half horizontally. Toast lightly and spoon mushroom combination over the top. Cover with a slice of cheese and broil until bubbly. Cut in half for easier eating. Serves 8.

STUFFED CELERY

Mix one-half cup well-drained crushed pineapple with two 3-ounce packages of cream cheese. Fill small stalks of celery. Chill before serving.

LOBSTER OLD FRENCH MARKET

4 tablespoons butter
1 small onion, minced *or*
1 shallot, minced
½ clove garlic, minced
¼ teaspoon thyme
¼ teaspoon freshly ground pepper
1 teaspoon salt
1 3-ounce can tomato paste

4 small fresh tomatoes, chopped coarsely
½ cup Burgundy
1½ pounds lobster, cooked and cubed
1 8-ounce can button mushrooms
1 cup broth

1 cup brown sauce

Melt butter, add onion and garlic; sauté until lightly browned. Add seasonings, tomatoes, tomato paste, and wine and blend well. Add lobster and mushrooms; simmer for 10 minutes. Add broth and brown sauce and simmer again for 5 minutes. Serve with fluffy ric

SHERRY BROWN SAUCE

1½ tablespoons butter
1½ tablespoons flour
1 tablespoon sherry

2 cups beef consommé
1 teaspoon Worcestershire sauce

Melt the butter. Blend in the flour; stir until quite brown. Add consommé gradually. Bring to a boil; cook for 3 to 5 minutes, stirring until smooth. Add Worcestershire sauce and sherry. Simmer gently for 15 minutes, stirring occasionally. Makes 2 cups.

CHICKEN ALMOND MOUSSE

1½ tablespoons plain gelatin
3 cups chicken stock or broth
1 teaspoon salt
½ teaspoon pepper
1 teaspoon onion, finely chopped
⅛ teaspoon paprika
3 egg yolks
¼ cup chopped pimento olives
  (optional)

½ cup almonds, blanched, finely
  chopped
3 cups chopped, cooked chicken
1 cup heavy cream, whipped
Crisp greens
Melon balls
Raspberries
Lemon wedges

Soften gelatin in ½ cup cold chicken stock. Combine remaining stock with salt, pepper, onion, and paprika in top of double boiler; stir a little of the hot stock into the egg yolks, mix well, and return to the liquid. Cook over hot water until smooth and thick. Strain, if necessary. Blend in gelatin and cool until partially thickened. Fold in olives, nuts, chicken, and whipped cream. Turn into greased mold. Chill until firm. To serve, unmold on serving platter, fill center with crisp greens and garnish with melon balls, fresh raspberries, and lemon wedges.

POTATO FLOUR MUFFINS

4 eggs, separated
½ teaspoon salt
1 tablespoon sugar

½ cup potato flour
1 teaspoon baking powder
2 teaspoons ice water

Beat egg whites until stiff and dry. Add salt and sugar to beaten yolks, and fold in the whites. Sift flour and baking powder twice. Beat well into the egg mixture. Add ice water. Bake in greased muffin tins at 400° for 15 to 20 minutes.

PLUM JAM

5 pounds blue plums
5 pounds sugar

3 tablespoons lemon juice
2 10-ounce packages frozen red
  raspberries

Pit plums. Put through food grinder. Pour sugar over the plum pulp and let stand overnight. In the morning, place in saucepan

and cook slowly for 5 minutes. Add raspberries and lemon juice.
Cook about 1½ hours, or until thick. Pour into sterilized jars and
seal.

CARROT CAKE

3 cups all-purpose flour	2 cups grated carrots
2 teaspoons baking powder	2 cups sugar
1 teaspoon baking soda	1 cup salad oil
1 teaspoon cinnamon	4 eggs, beaten
½ teaspoon salt	½ cup chopped nuts

Sift together the flour, baking powder, baking soda, cinnamon, and
salt. Combine the carrots, sugar, oil, beaten eggs, and nuts. Add
the sifted ingredients. Mix well. Bake in a 9-inch tube pan in a
350° oven for 1½ hours. Cool. Frost with Cream Cheese Frosting.

CREAM CHEESE FROSTING

1 tablespoon butter	1 teaspoon vanilla
1 3-ounce package cream cheese	⅛ teaspoon salt
1 cup sifted confectioners' sugar	

Cream together until soft, the butter, cream cheese, vanilla, and
salt. Add confectioners' sugar, working until well blended.

BOURBON BALLS

½ cup bourbon	1 cup vanilla wafers, finely rolled
1½ tablespoons white corn syrup	1 cup pecans, finely chopped
2 tablespoons cocoa	

Mix bourbon and syrup together. Add crumbs, nuts, and cocoa.
Dust hands with powdered sugar. Roll balls the size of a walnut.
Roll bourbon balls in powdered sugar. Store in refrigerator be-
tween layers of wax paper. Makes about 24 balls.

Buffet Luncheon

Cantaloupe Claret
Shrimp Soufflé
Tomato Aspic with Green   Chicken Salad
Beans Vinaigrette   Cranberry French Dressing
Minced Tongue Finger Sandwiches
Pears Chez Vale   Kolacky
Coffee

ADVANCE PREPARATION SCHEDULE

Previous Day	Early Morning	Deep Freeze
Chicken	*Shrimp Soufflé —*	*Kolacky*
Tomato Aspic	*except for egg whites*	
Beans Vinaigrette	*Cantaloupe*	
Tongue sandwich filling		
Poach pears		

CANTALOUPE CLARET

Peel cantaloupes whole; slice thin wedges lengthwise. Arrange on platter; marinate in domestic claret. Chill before serving.

SHRIMP SOUFFLE

2½ tablespoons butter, melted
2 tablespoons flour
2 cups milk
⅓ teaspoon paprika
1 teaspoon Worcestershire sauce
½ teaspoon salt

1 tablespoon catsup
¾ cup grated Swiss cheese
3 egg yolks
3 egg whites, stiffly beaten
1 pound shrimp, cleaned, deveined, coarsely chopped

Melt the butter; stir in the flour until smooth; then add the milk, stirring constantly until creamy. Add seasonings and catsup. Heat and add cheese; pour sauce, beating constantly, over the egg yolks. Cool entire mixture. Fold in the egg whites. Add the shrimp.

Buffet Luncheon

Peach Cocktail

uff with Seafood Sauce Scandia   Tropical Chicken

Shanghai Salad — Herb Dressing

Melt Away Rolls

Mocha Torte   Soup to Nuts Cake

Coffee

ADVANCE PREPARATION SCHEDULE

)ay	Early Morning	Deep Freeze
uts Cake	*Melt Away Rolls*	*Soup to Nuts Cake*
frozen)	*Pineapple for chicken*	*Mocha Torte*
roll dough	*Assemble salad*	
hicken	*Frost cake*	

PEACH COCKTAIL

p orange juice   1½ teaspoons crushed tarragon
aches, pitted and peeled   leaves
p sugar   ⅓ cup lemon juice
        5 ice cubes, crushed

ingredients in electric blender for 20 seconds on high
rve immediately in chilled glasses.

LE PUFF WITH SEAFOOD SAUCE SCANDIA

3 tablespoons butter   2 teaspoons sugar
4 tablespoons flour   ⅛ teaspoon salt
1 cup milk   2 eggs, separated
        1 cup commercial sour cream

butter, stir in the flour, and cook until it bubbles. Add
ook, stirring constantly, until sauce thickens. Reduce
d cook 5 minutes. Stir in the sugar and salt. Add small

Pour into greased 2-quart casserole. Place in a shallow pan of boiling water and bake in a 350° oven for 45 minutes. Serve immediately.

TOMATO ASPIC

2 packages lemon gelatin   1½ cups cream of tomato soup,
2 cups tomato juice cocktail   undiluted
        2 tablespoons lemon juice

Dissolve the gelatin in the boiling tomato juice cocktail; when slightly cooled, add the tomato soup and lemon juice. Pour into individual molds or a large ring mold that has been rinsed with ice water. Chill until firm; unmold, and fill center of mold with Green Beans Vinaigrette.

GREEN BEANS VINAIGRETTE

2 10-ounce packages frozen French-cut green beans, cooked 5 minutes, drained
1 cup cocktail onions, drained

Toss beans and onions with Vinaigrette Dressing; marinate for several hours. Drain excess dressing before filling tomato aspic. Serves 6.

VINAIGRETTE DRESSING

3 tablespoons sweet pickle relish   ½ teaspoon sugar
2 tablespoons snipped parsley   1 teaspoon salt
½ cup salad oil   5 tablespoons vinegar

Blend ingredients. Toss with beans and onions. Makes about 1 cup.

CHICKEN SALAD

4 cups diced, cooked chicken   ½ cup mayonnaise
1 cup celery, chopped   ½ cup commercial sour cream
2 cups seedless grapes   24 salted pecan halves or toasted
½ teaspoon salt   almonds
½ teaspoon pepper, freshly ground   Pimento strips

Combine the chicken, celery, grapes, salt and pepper. Toss lightly with the mayonnaise and sour cream. For each serving, place a mound of the salad on lettuce on a salad plate. Garnish with pecan halves and pimento and serve with Cranberry French Dressing. Serves 6 to 8.

CRANBERRY FRENCH DRESSING

¾ cup salad oil   ½ teaspoon paprika
¼ cup vinegar   ¼ teaspoon dry mustard
1 teaspoon salt   Dash of freshly ground pepper
1 teaspoon sugar   ½ cup jellied cranberry sauce

Combine the oil, vinegar, and the dry ingredients in a glass jar with a tight-fitting cover. Shake until thoroughly blended. Gradually blend this dressing into the cranberry sauce which has first been beaten until smooth with a rotary beater.

MINCED TONGUE FINGER SANDWICHES

2 cups firmly packed, cooked,   ¼ cup horse-radish
  ground tongue, pickled or   ½ cup commercial sour cream
  smoked
        8 slices thin white bread, crusts removed

Combine the tongue, horse-radish, and sour cream; spread on slices of bread. Cut each slice into 3 strips. Makes 24 sandwiches.

PEARS CHEZ VALE

Orange Sherry Sauce:

1½ cups water   ¼ cup lemon juice
¾ cup sugar   2 tablespoons orange rind
½ cup orange juice   ½ cup sweet sherry
    6 medium, firm Bartlett pears

Prepare orange sauce by combining water, sugar, fruit juices, and orange rind; cook for about 4 minutes. Add sherry and cook 2 minutes longer. Peel the pears, leaving them whole and simmer gently in sauce until tender, turning often as they cook. Place pears in individual serving dishes. Pour thickened sauce over them. Chill well and serve plain or with light cream.

KOL

1 cup milk
3 tablespoons sugar
1 teaspoon salt
    4⅓ cups sifted,

Scald the milk; add sugar, salt, a Crumble yeast into lukewarm m well. Add the flour and mix to ball and knead on floured pastry smooth and satiny. Place in a ligl over once to coat top lightly with in a warm place until double ir dough is light, spoon out with ta floured board. Shape into balls a a tablespoon of Cottage Cheese F With floured fingers, close dough a baking sheet. Make an indentatior fill with a teaspoonful of comm prune filling. (This can be made tender, then sweetening to taste, Sprinkle filling with crumb toppin almost double in bulk. Bake in Makes about 40.

COTTAGE CHEE

1 pound dry cottage cheese   1
½ teaspoon grated lemon rind   1

Mix all ingredients together until we

Crumb topping:
    1 teaspoon melted butter   1
                Confectioners'

Mix melted butter and flour together. sugar to make a crumbly mixture.

Soufflé P

1 cu
2 p
½ c

Combine
speed. S

SOUFF

Melt th
milk. (
heat, ar

amount of the hot mixture to slightly beaten egg yolks, stir well. Then add yolks to remaining hot sauce. Mix thoroughly. Beat egg whites until they are stiff and fold into first mixture. Line a 12" x 8" pan with wax paper. Butter wax paper and sprinkle lightly with flour. Pour batter into pan. Bake in a slow oven (325°) until firm and slightly brown, 30 to 35 minutes. Turn out on a cloth. Remove wax paper. Place on serving platter. Spread with Seafood Sauce Scandia and roll like a jelly roll. Then top with sour cream. Serve warm and cut into slices.

SEAFOOD SAUCE SCANDIA

2 tablespoons butter
1 cup crab or diced lobster, cooked, fresh, or frozen

2 cups cream sauce (see index for recipe)
¼ cup sherry (optional) *or* 1 teaspoon Worcestershire sauce

Sauté lobster or crab in butter. Add cream sauce, season with salt, pepper, and Worcestershire sauce.

TROPICAL CHICKEN

3 fresh pineapples
3 tablespoons butter
4 tablespoons flour
1 cup chicken or turkey broth
1 cup milk
½ teaspoon salt

½ teaspoon paprika
⅛ teaspoon pepper
1½ cups cooked chicken or turkey, diced
½ cup diced pineapple
½ cup slivered almonds
Parmesan or grated sharp cheese

Cut pineapples in half lengthwise. Do not remove stalks. Hollow each half, leaving about ½" of shell and fruit.

Prepare filling: Melt butter, add flour and stir over low heat until blended. Add cold broth and milk all at once. Cook, stirring constantly, until uniformly thickened. Then set over hot water in double boiler. Add the seasonings, chicken or turkey. Heat thoroughly. Add more seasonings if desired. Blend in diced pineapple. Fill pineapple halves with poultry mixture. Top with slivered almonds and sprinkle with grated cheese. Broil until top is lightly browned.

SHANGHAI SALAD

1 20-ounce can bean sprouts
1 16-ounce can water chestnuts,
  thinly sliced

½ cup toasted, slivered almonds
2 quarts salad greens, washed
  and chilled
1 green pepper, chopped (optional)

Toss bean sprouts, chestnuts, green pepper, and almonds with salad greens; toss again with dressing.

HERB DRESSING

1½ cups mayonnaise
1½ teaspoons prepared mustard
½ teaspoon Tabasco sauce
2 teaspoons chili powder

1 teaspoon onion juice
2 tablespoons vinegar
1½ teaspoons ground marjoram
¾ teaspoon ground thyme
1½ teaspoons minced garlic

Combine ingredients and shake in covered jar until well blended.

MELT AWAY ROLLS

½ pound dry cottage cheese
½ pound sweet butter
10 tablespoons all-purpose flour
  (⅔ cup plus 1 tablespoon)

8 ounces cream cheese
2 tablespoons butter
2 egg yolks

Put cottage cheese through a sieve. Mix cheese, butter, and flour with hands until well blended. Place in refrigerator overnight. Next day, roll thin on a floured board, cut dough in circles as for a pie, and then cut each circle into long, thin wedges. Mix the cream cheese with the butter and egg yolks. Spread on the dough. Roll each triangle from large end to small end and make a slightly crescent shape. Place on a buttered cooky sheet; set in refrigerator. Remove ½ hour before baking. Brush with slightly beaten egg yolk. Bake in a 400° oven for 25 minutes. Serve fresh and warm. These can be frozen and reheated.

MOCHA TORTE

6 eggs	2 tablespoons instant coffee
1 cup sugar	1 cup cake flour

Frosting:

1 pint whipping cream	1 teaspoon vanilla
3 tablespoons powdered sugar	1 teaspoon instant coffee

Separate eggs; beat whites until stiff; add sugar gradually. Beat yolks separately; fold into whites. Sift flour and coffee together and add slowly to first mixture, two tablespoons at a time. Butter and flour a tube pan and pour in the batter. Bake in a 325° oven for one hour. Invert, let stand for several hours until completely cooled. Cut into three layers. Spread with two-thirds of combined whipped cream, powdered sugar, powdered coffee, and vanilla mixture. Put layers together, spread cake with remaining flavored whipped cream. Top with shaved chocolate. Chill until ready to serve.

SOUP TO NUTS CAKE

1 tablespoon butter	1 cup raisins, preferably yellow,
1 cup sugar	scalded and dried
1½ cups all-purpose flour	1 cup chopped nuts
1 scant teaspoon baking soda	1 cup canned condensed tomato soup

Cream butter and sugar. Sift dry ingredients together; add nuts and raisins. Add this mixture alternately with the tomato soup to the butter and sugar. Grease a loaf pan (10" x 5" x 3") very well, and line bottom with wax paper. Bake 1½ hours in a 275° oven. Don't look; just let it bake. Frost with Vanilla Butter Cream Frosting.

VANILLA BUTTER CREAM FROSTING

⅓ cup soft butter	3 cups sifted confectioners' sugar
⅛ teaspoon salt	About ¼ cup milk or cream
1½ teaspoon vanilla	

Combine ingredients and cream until smooth.

Buffet Luncheon

Senate Salad   Escalloped Oysters
Woodchuck and Chinese Noodles
Pecan Whole Wheat Muffins   Peach Marmalade
Oranges Alaska   Drop Butter Cookies
Coffee

ADVANCE PREPARATION SCHEDULE

Previous Day	Early Morning	Deep Freeze
Orange Shells	*Bake muffins*	*Drop Butter Cookies*
	Prepare Escalloped	*Oranges may be pre-*
	Oysters	*pared and frozen*

SENATE SALAD

2 cups lettuce, bite-size pieces
2 cups romaine, bite-size pieces
1 cup watercress, bite-size pieces
3 cups diced, cooked chicken
2 cups diced celery
½ cup chopped green onions and stems

4 medium tomatoes, cubed
2 medium avocados, peeled and cubed
10 large, stuffed olives, sliced
Sections from 1 grapefruit
½ cup julienne-cut chicken

Combine all ingredients, reserving julienne of chicken as garnish. Toss with Senate Salad Dressing.

Variation: Use lobster instead of chicken. Serves 8.

SENATE SALAD DRESSING

6 teaspoons chopped chives
6 hard-cooked eggs, chopped
1 cup olive oil

1 cup mayonnaise
1 cup vinegar
Garlic (optional)

Combine olive oil and vinegar. Add remaining ingredients. Blend well.

ESCALLOPED OYSTERS

1 quart oysters
¼ pound butter, melted
6 cups bread, ½-inch cubes
¼ cup milk

½ cup oyster liquor
3 tablespoons sherry
2 teaspoons Worcestershire
sauce
1½ teaspoons salt

Drain oysters, carefully removing pieces of shell. Reserve one-half cup of liquor. Pour butter over bread cubes. Place one-third of bread in bottom of a buttered 3-quart casserole, then half of the oysters, a layer of bread, etc., alternating bread and oysters, ending with bread. Mix milk, oyster liquor, sherry, Worcestershire sauce, and salt. Pour over all. Bake in a 350° oven for 30 minutes, or until firm and golden brown. Serves 8.

WOODCHUCK AND CHINESE NOODLES

¼ pound butter
1 green pepper, chopped fine
1 pound mushrooms, sliced
½ cup chopped pimento
6 hard-cooked eggs, chopped

¼ pound butter
4 cups prepared cheese sauce
2 10½-ounce cans tomato soup
½ teaspoon salt
2 5-ounce cans Chinese fried noodles

Sauté green pepper, mushrooms, and pimento in butter for 5 minutes. Add eggs. Place additional butter, cheese sauce, soup, and salt in the top of double boiler; cook until thick; add first mixture. Serve over fried noodles. Serves 8.

PECAN WHOLE WHEAT MUFFINS

1 cup all-purpose flour
3 teaspoons baking powder
4 tablespoons sugar
1 teaspoon salt

1 cup whole wheat flour
1 cup pecans, chopped
4 tablespoons butter, melted
2 eggs
1 cup milk

Sift the flour, baking powder, sugar, and salt together. Stir in the whole wheat flour and the nuts. Combine the remaining ingredients, and work into the first mixture until batter is well moistened. Bake in greased muffin tins 15 to 18 minutes in a 375° oven. Makes 12 muffins.

PEACH MARMALADE

5 pounds peaches 5 oranges, cut into small pieces,
Sugar   including skins
1 cup maraschino cherries, drained, sliced

Peel, pit, and slice peaches into bowl. To one heaping bowl of peaches, measure one level bowl sugar. Cook together over low heat the peaches, sugar, and oranges for about 4 hours, stirring occasionally. During the last hour of cooking, add the cherries. Place in sterilized jars and seal immediately.

ORANGES ALASKA

8 navel oranges   Orange segments, chopped
3 egg whites   ½ cup crushed pineapple
6 tablespoons sugar   1 pint vanilla ice cream

Cut slices off navel ends of perfect oranges. Scoop out pulp. Place shells in the freezing compartment of the refrigerator for at least 6 hours. They will then remain cold during preparation. Beat the egg whites until stiff; gradually add the sugar, continuing to beat until all sugar is absorbed and the meringue stands in peaks. Fill shells with a layer of chilled segments and crushed pineapple. Pack with vanilla ice cream and seal with a large scoop of meringue. Place under broiler until lightly browned. Serve at once, on a bed of lemon leaves. Serves 8.

DROP BUTTER COOKIES

½ cup butter   1 egg
⅓ cup sugar   ¾ cup all-purpose flour
½ teaspoon vanilla

Cream the butter; add the sugar, continuing to beat. Beat in the egg. Add the flour, then the vanilla, beating constantly. Drop 2 inches apart on greased cooky sheet. Top each with raisin, cherry or nut. Bake in a 400° oven for 10 minutes.

Buffet Luncheon

Cold Clam Soup
New Orleans Broccoli Mold filled with
Chicken Salad garnished with Deviled Eggs
Crabmeat Puff
Cottage Cheese Rolls   Apricot Marmalade
Pineapple Sherbet with Crème de Menthe
Panocha Squares   Crumb Coffee Cake
Coffee   Iced Tea

ADVANCE PREPARATION SCHEDULE

Previous Day	Early Morning	Deep Freeze
Broccoli Mold	*Chicken Salad*	*Panocha Squares*
Chicken	*Crabmeat Puff*	*Crumb Coffee Cake*
Deviled Eggs		*Cottage Cheese Rolls*

COLD CLAM SOUP

4 cups tomato madrilene soup, chilled
2 cups commercial sour cream
¼ cup lemon juice
½ cup minced clams, drained
Chopped chives

Combine all the ingredients; chill. Beat and return to refrigerator and thoroughly chill again. Top each serving with additional chopped chives. Serves 8.

NEW ORLEANS BROCCOLI MOLD

2 10-ounce packages frozen, chopped broccoli
2 tablespoons plain gelatin
1 10-ounce can consommé
3 hard-cooked eggs, chopped
2 tablespoons lemon juice
1 teaspoon Tabasco
½ teaspoon salt
½ cup mayonnaise

Garnish:

Salad greens
Tomato wedges
Deviled eggs
2 tablespoons Worcestershire sauce

Soak the gelatin in ½ cup of the cold consommé for 5 minutes.

Heat the remaining consommé. Add to the gelatin mixture and dissolve. Cool. Cook the broccoli according to the directions on the package. Drain. Cool. Chop more thoroughly, if necessary. Combine with the remaining ingredients. Pour ½ cup of the consommé-gelatin mixture into the bottom of a 6-cup ring mold. Let set. Add remainder to the broccoli-egg mixture. Pour into ring mold over the congealed gelatin. Chill until firm. Unmold on a platter of salad greens. Fill center with Chicken Salad. Surround the mold with Deviled Eggs, and tomato wedges. Serves 8.

CHICKEN SALAD

To cook chicken for salad:

1 4-pound young hen or 4 breasts and 2 thighs of chicken	2 teaspoons salt
	2 bay leaves
2 carrots	¼ teaspoon ginger
2 small onions	

Salad:

½ cup French dressing	½ cup commercial sour cream
½ cup blender mayonnaise (see Index for recipe)	¼ cup slivered almonds

Wash chicken and place in kettle with the remaining ingredients and sufficient water to cover. Simmer slowly until tender about 2 hours. Remove chicken and cool. Cut into pieces about 1″ x ½″, but no smaller. Marinate in French dressing for at least 1 hour. Toss with mayonnaise which has been mixed with sour cream, and sprinkle with almond slivers. Serves 8.

CHICKEN SALAD VARIATION

3 cups diced, cooked chicken	⅔ cup mayonnaise
2 cups diced celery	½ cup commercial sour cream
¼ cup French dressing	2 tablespoons chili sauce
Juice of ½ lemon	1 tablespoon capers
1 hard-cooked egg	1 teaspoon salt

Mix chicken, celery, French dressing, and lemon juice. Chill for several hours. Force egg through a fine sieve. Mix with mayonnaise, cream, chili sauce, capers, and salt. Fold into chicken, and serve on crisp salad greens. Serves 6.

DEVILED EGGS

4 hard-cooked eggs
3 ounces cream cheese
1 tablespoon mayonnaise
1 tablespoon prepared mustard

¼ teaspoon salt
1 teaspoon vinegar
1 dash cayenne
⅛ teaspoon dry mustard

Cut eggs in half, lengthwise. Remove yolks; put through strainer and add remaining ingredients. Blend until smooth. Fill hollow of egg white and decorate with slices of pimento-stuffed olives.

CRABMEAT PUFF

12 slices bread, crusts removed
6 1-ounce slices American cheese
2 cups crabmeat, fresh or frozen

3 eggs
2 cups milk
1 teaspoon salt

½ teaspoon pepper, freshly ground

Place six slices of bread across the bottom of a buttered shallow pan. Cover each with a slice of cheese. Cover the cheese with crabmeat, allowing about ⅓ cup of crabmeat per sandwich. Top with remaining slices of bread, and cut each sandwich in half diagonally. Beat the eggs slightly with the milk, salt, and pepper and pour over the sandwiches. Chill for 2 hours. Bake in a 350° oven for 30 minutes or until puffy as a soufflé. Serve immediately.

COTTAGE CHEESE ROLLS

1 package dry yeast
¼ cup lukewarm water
2½ cups sifted all-purpose flour
¼ cup sugar

1 teaspoon salt
½ cup butter
1 12-ounce carton cottage cheese
1 egg, beaten

Dissolve the yeast in the water. Sift the flour, sugar and salt together into a mixing bowl. Cut in butter until the mixture resembles corn meal. Add cottage cheese, egg, and dissolved yeast; mix well. If necessary, add more flour to make a dough that can be handled. Turn out on a lightly floured board and roll into a 14-inch square. Spread filling on dough. Roll up jelly-roll fashion. Cut into 18 slices. Place, cut side down, on a greased baking sheet. Let rise in a warm place until double in bulk. Bake in a 375° oven 20 to 25 minutes. May be frozen.

Filling:

3 tablespoons melted butter   ½ teaspoon vanilla
¼ cup brown sugar   ½ teaspoon almond extract
                    ¾ cup chopped pecans

Combine all ingredients, mixing well.

APRICOT MARMALADE

4 dozen fresh apricots   2 cups canned grapefruit, drained

Cut the apricots into small pieces, combine with the grapefruit sections. Measure the quantity. Add the same amount of sugar as fruit. Cook until thick, about one hour. Pour into sterilized jars and seal.

PINEAPPLE SHERBET WITH CREME DE MENTHE

For each serving, pour 1 tablespoon of crème de menthe over a scoop of pineapple sherbet in chilled low-stem sherbet glasses.

PANOCHA SQUARES

¼ cup butter   1 teaspoon baking powder
1 cup brown sugar   ¼ teaspoon salt
1 egg   1 cup semisweet chocolate bits
½ teaspoon vanilla   ¾ cup walnuts, chopped
1 cup all-purpose flour   Powdered sugar

Melt the butter. Add the sugar, egg, and vanilla; beat until smooth. Sift together the dry ingredients; add to the first mixture. Add the chocolate bits and chopped walnuts. Spread into a greased 8-inch pan and bake in a 350° oven for 30 minutes. Cut into squares. Sprinkle with powdered sugar when cool. May be frozen.

CRUMB COFFEE CAKE

2 cups all-purpose flour
1½ cups sugar
¾ cup shortening
2 teaspoons baking powder
2 egg yolks

1 cup milk
1 teaspoon salt
1 teaspoon almond or vanilla extract
2 egg whites, beaten stiff

1 No. 2 can blueberries or 2 cups fresh blueberries

Blend the flour, sugar, and shortening together with pastry blender until it resembles coarse meal. Remove 1 cup for topping and set aside. Add the remaining ingredients, except egg whites and blueberries, in order given, to crumb mixture in bowl. Mix until very smooth. Fold in stiffly beaten egg whites. Pour into greased and slightly floured 9" x 13" x 1½" pan. Drain blueberries well, dust lightly with flour, and spead evenly over batter. Sprinkle reserved crumb topping over the fruit. Bake in a 350° oven for approximately 40 minutes.

Note: May be frozen. See instructions on page 4.

Buffet Luncheon

Toasted Pecans

Shrimp Salad en Gelée

Chicken Livers in Tomatoes Vin Blanc — Fluffy Rice

Crescent Rolls   Pinecot Preserves

Lemon Sherbet Mousse   Brownies Araby

Coffee

ADVANCE PREPARATION SCHEDULE

Previous Day	Early Morning	Deep Freeze
Pecans	*Scoop and drain*	*Brownies*
Shrimp Salad	*tomatoes*	
Lemon Mousse	*Prepare tomato filling*	
	Bayou Sauce	

SHRIMP SALAD EN GELEE

1 pound shrimp, chopped	3 tablespoons lemon juice
6 hard-cooked eggs, chopped	(1 lemon)
1 cup celery, cut fine	½ cup catsup
2 tablespoons chopped pimento	½ teaspoon sugar
1 cup mayonnaise	1 tablespoon Worcestershire sauce
1 cup chili sauce	¼ teaspoon paprika
1 tablespoon capers, chopped	2 tablespoons unflavored gelatin
	½ cup cold water

Mix all the ingredients, except gelatin and water. Set aside. Soak the gelatin in the cold water 5 minutes. Place over hot water until dissolved. Add to the egg mixture, mixing lightly, but thoroughly. Turn into a 6-cup ring mold; chill until firm. Unmold; fill center with bowl of Tarragon Mayonnaise. Border with spiced apples on pineapple rings and garnish with small bunches of frosted green grapes (see Index for recipe). Serves 6 to 8.

TARRAGON MAYONNAISE

1 cup mayonnaise	⅓ teaspoon Worcestershire sauce
¼ teaspoon paprika	½ teaspoon catsup
1 tablespoon tarragon vinegar	

Mix well and then add ½ cup whipped cream to make it fluffy.

CHICKEN LIVERS IN TOMATOES VIN BLANC — FLUFFY RICE

8 firm tomatoes	1 tablespoon chopped parsley
½ pound fresh mushrooms	1 teaspoon salt
4 tablespoons butter	⅛ teaspoon pepper
1 medium-sized onion, minced	1½ pounds chicken livers
½ cup bread crumbs	2 tablespoons white wine

Wash and dry tomatoes. Cut off a thin slice from stem end and scoop out pulp from each tomato. Season lightly with salt and pepper and set aside. Wipe mushrooms and reserve 8 caps. Chop remainder. Melt two tablespoons butter, add onion and chopped mushrooms and cook 3 minutes. Add bread crumbs, ½ of the tomato pulp, parsley, salt, and pepper. Cook 3 more minutes. Cut chicken livers in bite-size pieces, sauté in two tablespoons of butter and add to mixture with the wine. Blend well and fill tomato shells generously. Dot with butter and top with sautéed mushroom caps. Place on a well-buttered baking pan. (This may be prepared the previous day.) When ready to serve, place in a 350° oven, and bake for 20 minutes. Serve on a platter on a bed of Fluffy Rice (see Index for recipe). Serves 6 to 8.

CRESCENT ROLLS

½ cup sugar	¾ cup milk, scalded and cooled to lukewarm
½ cup soft butter	
1 teaspoon salt	2 cakes compressed yeast
2 eggs	4 cups sifted all-purpose flour

Mix sugar, butter, salt, and eggs together. Beat with a rotary beater. Stir in the milk. Crumble the yeast into the mixture; stir until dissolved. Beat in the flour with a spoon. Scrape dough from sides of the bowl. Cover with a damp cloth and let rise in warm place until doubled. Roll dough on floured board to ½-inch thickness. Make pie-shaped wedges. Brush with melted butter and roll from broad end to small end as Butter Horns (see Index for recipe). Let stand until doubled in bulk. Bake in a 425° oven for 12 to 15 minutes. They also may be sprinkled with sesame or celery seeds. Recipe makes 4 dozen, small size.

Variation: For clover-leaf rolls, pinch off dough instead of rolling it; form into 1-inch balls and place three together in greased muffin tin; proceed as for crescents.

PINECOT PRESERVES

½ pound dried apricots	2½ cups sugar
1 cup crushed pineapple, not drained	¼ teaspoon salt
	½ cup sliced almonds
1 tablespoon lemon juice	

Wash apricots, cover with hot water, and simmer 35 minutes. Cool and drain. Cut in pieces using scissors. Add remaining ingredi-

ents, except nuts; heat slowly, stirring constantly. Then increase
the heat so as to cook rapidly, and continue for about 20 minutes,
stirring very often. If a thicker consistency is desired, cook longer.
Add almonds, and reheat to boiling point. Remove. This preserve
may be made in large quantities, and poured into small sterilized
jars and sealed. This amount makes 1 quart.

LEMON SHERBET MOUSSE

1 package lemon gelatin   1½ tablespoons lemon juice
1 cup boiling water   1½ pints lemon sherbet
½ cup cold water   Fresh strawberries

Dissolve the gelatin in the boiling water; add the cold water and
lemon juice. Beat or blend in lemon sherbert. Pour into individual
molds. Chill until firm. Unmold. Garnish with fresh strawberries.
Serve with Bayou Sauce. Serves 6 to 8.

BAYOU SAUCE

1 cup cream, whipped   ¼ cup lemon juice
4 tablespoons sugar   Grated rind of lemon

Fold all ingredients together. Chill.

BROWNIES ARABY

1½ cups butter   3 cups sugar
½ pound unsweetened chocolate   1½ cups all-purpose flour
6 eggs   3 teaspoons vanilla
                  1 cup pecans, chopped

Melt butter and chocolate together. Beat eggs with electric mixer
and add sugar. Next add melted chocolate and butter and stir in
lightly. Add flour, vanilla, and pecans; mix only enough to moisten
all the flour. Bake in two greased 8-inch-square pans at 350° for
30 minutes. After brownies are slightly cooled, cut into 2-inch
squares and leave in pan until cool. Makes 32 brownies.

Buffet
Suppers

Each recipe
serves six
unless otherwise
indicated

PATTERNS of entertaining change with each generation, and with the informal, do-it-yourself attitude of today, the buffet supper came into its own. The following menus provide the "know-how" for such entertaining.

Buffet Supper

Avocado Yogurt Soup   Cheese Crisps
Red Snapper à la Memphis
Fresh Tongue in Wine Sauce — Spaetzle
Spinach Vinaigrette
Celery Slaw   Fruit Compote
Renversée
Swedish Heirloom Cookies
Mocha Walnut Cookies   Half-and-Half Bars
Coffee

ADVANCE PREPARATION SCHEDULE

Previous Day	Early Morning	Deep Freeze
Soup	Celery Slaw	Assorted Cookies
Red Snapper	Wine Sauce; add	
Boil tongue	tongue	
Renversée		
Fruit Compote		

AVOCADO YOGURT SOUP

⅔ cup sieved avocado	½ teaspoon onion juice
⅔ cup yogurt	1 teaspoon chili powder
½ cup beef bouillon	1 tablespoon lime juice
½ teaspoon salt	

Combine all ingredients; chill several hours before serving.

CHEESE CRISPS

¼ cup butter	½ cup sharp cheese spread
¼ teaspoon Tabasco sauce	⅔ cup all-purpose flour

Cream butter and Tabasco sauce; blend in cheese and the flour. Make into a 2-inch roll as for icebox cookies. Chill. Cut into thin slices. Place on greased cooky sheet; bake in a 400° oven for 12 to 15 minutes. Dough may be kept in freezer. Remove and bake as needed.

RED SNAPPER A LA MEMPHIS

1 quart water	2 tablespoons flour
1 stalk celery	2 tablespoons butter, melted
1 medium onion, sliced	1 cup light cream
1 teaspoon salt	1 cup condensed tomato soup
2 pounds red snapper, or haddock	1½ cups canned peas
1 pound fresh mushrooms	½ cup almonds, slivered
¼ cup butter, melted	¼ cup grated Parmesan cheese

Combine water, celery, onion, and salt; cover and simmer for 15 minutes. Add red snapper and cook under boiling point for 15 minutes. Remove, drain and break into small pieces. Sauté the mushrooms in the quarter-cup of butter. Make a rich cream sauce by adding the flour to the 2 tablespoons of butter over low heat;

then add cream, stirring constantly until thickened. Combine tomato soup, peas, and almonds with the sauce. Fold in the mushrooms and red snapper. Place in 2-quart casserole or individual shells. Sprinkle with Parmesan. Bake in a 350° oven for 30 to 40 minutes. May be baked in an 8-cup mold in a pan of hot water.

FRESH TONGUE IN WINE SAUCE

4- to 5-pound fresh tongue	1 cup dry red wine
½ cup butter	2 tablespoons lemon juice
3 tablespoons flour	2 tablespoons sugar
2 tablespoons grated onion	½ teaspoon salt
4 cups tongue stock	⅛ teaspoon pepper

Boil tongue as directed (see Index for recipe). Remove root and peel tongue while hot; cool and slice. Melt butter; stir in flour and brown. Add grated onion and cook slightly. Combine with tongue stock, wine, and seasonings. Heat. Place tongue in the sauce and cook for 10 minutes. Serve hot with Spaetzle.

SPAETZLE

3 eggs	1 cup milk
2 cups all-purpose flour	½ teaspoon salt
2 tablespoons butter	

Beat eggs well; add remaining ingredients and beat until the dough blisters. Drop from the tip of a wet teaspoon into boiling salted water. Cook until tender (about 15 minutes). Drain. Toss with melted butter.

SPINACH VINAIGRETTE

2 10-ounce packages frozen, chopped spinach or	½ teaspoon prepared mustard
	2 tablespoons lemon juice
2½ pounds fresh spinach	¾ teaspoon salt
6 tablespoons butter	⅛ teaspoon pepper
1 teaspoon minced onion	2 hard-cooked eggs, chopped

Cook spinach according to package directions and drain well (if using fresh spinach, chop fine). Cook the onion slightly in the butter; add remaining ingredients; heat and pour over the spinach. Toss lightly and serve at once.

CELERY SLAW

2 teaspoons salt
1 tablespoon sugar
½ teaspoon pepper
Dash paprika
⅔ cup salad oil
2 tablespoons wine vinegar

½ cup commercial sour cream
3 cups celery, thinly sliced on the diagonal
2 tablespoons pimento, slivered or
½ cup carrots, shredded

Combine the salt, sugar, pepper, paprika, oil and vinegar; beat well with rotary beater, then slowly beat in the sour cream. Pour this dressing over the celery. Marinate in the refrigerator about 3 hours; then toss in the pimento or carrots.

FRUIT COMPOTE

2 cups water
2 cups sugar
12 ripe peaches, halved, peeled
12 ripe blue plums, halved, pitted

2 limes, thinly sliced
2 oranges, thinly sliced
½ cup whole almonds, blanched
½ cup sherry wine

Boil sugar and water for 5 minutes. Add peaches, plums, lime slices, orange slices, and almonds. Boil for 10 minutes or bake in a 350° oven for 30 minutes. Add sherry. Place fruit, covered, in refrigerator and serve cold.

RENVERSEE

(Caramel Custard)

½ cup sugar
⅔ cup condensed milk
2 cups hot water

3 eggs, slightly beaten
½ teaspoon salt
1 teaspoon vanilla

Nutmeg

Melt sugar over low heat, stirring until brown. Pour a little into each custard cup, turning so that the sides are coated. Put aside and let set. Meanwhile, combine milk and water; stir gradually into eggs. Add salt and vanilla. Pour into caramel-lined cups. Sprinkle with nutmeg. Place in shallow pan in hot water to a depth of one inch. Bake in a 325° oven for one hour, or until knife inserted in center comes out clean. Let stand for 10 minutes. Unmold. Melted caramel will run down sides of pudding and form a sauce. Serve hot or cold.

ASSORTED COOKIES
Swedish Heirloom Cookies

1 cup butter	½ teaspoon salt
1 cup confectioners' sugar	2 cups sifted all-purpose flour
1 teaspoon vanilla	1¼ cups ground almonds

Cream butter; add sugar gradually, blending thoroughly. Beat in vanilla and salt. Add flour, then almonds. Shape into balls or crescents. Bake on ungreased cooky sheet in a slow oven (325°) for 15 to 18 minutes. (They should not be brown when done.) Cookies can be rolled, while warm, in a mixture of cinnamon and confectioners' sugar.

Mocha Walnut Cookies

1½ cups sifted all-purpose flour	2 teaspoons instant coffee
½ cup sugar	1 cup butter or margarine
¼ teaspoon salt	¾ cup walnuts, coarsely chopped

Sift together flour, sugar, salt, and instant coffee. Cut in the butter as for pie with pastry blender or two knives, until size of small peas. Press dough together. Pinch off small pieces, shape into balls, as for large marbles. Roll in chopped walnuts. Place 2 inches apart on ungreased cooky sheets; flatten with bottom of glass dipped in sugar. Place in 300° preheated oven about 20 minutes, or until edges are very lightly browned. Cool slightly. Remove to wire rack. Cool thoroughly before storing. Makes about 4 dozen.

Half-and-Half Bars

1 cup sifted all-purpose flour	¼ cup sugar
¼ teaspoon salt	¼ cup brown sugar
⅛ teaspoon soda	1 egg, separated
½ teaspoon baking powder	1½ teaspoons water
½ cup soft butter	1 teaspoon vanilla

Topping:

1 6-ounce package semisweet chocolate pieces	½ cup brown sugar

Sift flour, salt, soda, and baking powder. Mix butter with sugars until light and fluffy. Add egg yolk, water, and vanilla. Mix in dry ingredients. Place in buttered 12"x 8" x 2" pan. Top with chocolate. Beat egg white stiff, add brown sugar. Spread over the chocolate. Bake in a 350° oven for 30 minutes. Cut while warm. Serves 8.

Buffet Supper

Individual French Onion Soup   Tomato Canapés
Tenderloin Sandwiches with Béarnaise Sauce
Paella   Glazed Beef Balls
Dilled Cucumbers and Green Beans in Sour Cream
Platter of Spiced Fruits
Key Lime Pie   Ginger Lime Pie
Coffee

ADVANCE PREPARATION SCHEDULE

Previous Day	Early Morning	Deep Freeze
Beef Balls	*Béarnaise Sauce*	*Lime Pies*
Cucumbers	*Paella*	
Spiced Fruits	*Canapés*	

INDIVIDUAL FRENCH ONION SOUP

4 cups thinly sliced, large onions
¼ pound butter
3 12½-ounce cans chicken consommé
1 teaspoon salt
¼ teaspoon pepper
3 slices buttered white bread, toasted and cubed
¾ cup Parmesan cheese

Sauté onions in butter until glazed and golden. Add consommé, salt and pepper. Simmer. Bring to a boil, covered, and cook 30 minutes. Pour soup into 6 ovenproof bowls, float the toast cubes in each and sprinkle them with a heaping tablespoon of grated Parmesan cheese. Place under broiler until cheese is melted and golden brown.

TOMATO CANAPES

Cut three fresh tomatoes into 12 slices and place on buttered rounds of white bread of approximately the same size. Top each canapé with curry mayonnaise.

CURRY MAYONNAISE

Blend well ½ cup of mayonnaise with ½ teaspoon curry powder.

TENDERLOIN SANDWICHES

1 pound tenderloin steak   Pepper
Salt   2 tablespoons butter
20 miniature hamburger buns, buttered

Slice tenderloin very thin (¼" or less) and cut into silver-dollar size pieces. Season with salt and pepper. Have the prepared meat, additional seasonings, hamburger buns, and the Béarnaise Sauce at the tables and let each guest assemble his own sandwich. Brown butter in the electric skillet or chafing dish, which is also on the table, fry tenderloin slices quickly in the browned butter, about 30 seconds per side.

BEARNAISE SAUCE

3 egg yolks   ½ cup tarragon vinegar
1 teaspoon water   1 bay leaf
½ teaspoon lemon juice (to taste)   3 peppercorns
½ teaspoon salt   4 shallots, finely chopped, or
⅛ teaspoon pepper   green onion
1 cup melted warm butter   2 tablespoons chopped parsley

Place egg yolks, water, lemon juice, salt and pepper in top of double boiler and beat well. Cook over hot water, stirring constantly until thick. Have butter the same warm temperature as eggs; add and beat together. In another pan, combine vinegar, bay leaf, peppercorns, and shallots. Boil until reduced to half the original amount. Strain and add to egg mixture. Cool and add parsley.

PAELLA

2 cups precooked *or*
1½ cups regular white rice
½ teaspoon powdered saffron
1 pound cooked shrimp
1 7-ounce can rock lobster,
   or 1 10-ounce package frozen
   lobster

1 6½-ounce can minced clams
   with liquid
1 No. 2 can tomatoes (3½ cups)
1 clove garlic, minced
½ cup chopped green pepper
4 hot Italian sausages, cooked
   and sliced (optional)

Cook the rice according to package directions, adding saffron as it is removed from the stove, blending well with a fork. Combine remaining ingredients, mixing well; heat thoroughly, and serve at once.

GLAZED BEEF BALLS

1 pound lean ground beef
½ cup fine bread crumbs
1 teaspoon salt
¼ teaspoon pepper
1 tablespoon grated onion
1 teaspoon A-1 Sauce

½ teaspoon prepared horse-radish
1 tablespoon Worcestershire sauce
1 egg, beaten
½ cup tomato juice, *or* 1 tablespoon catsup and water to
   make ½ cup

2 tablespoons shortening

Combine all ingredients except beef; blend well and then add to meat. Refrigerate for at least one hour. Shape into balls about the size of a large walnut and sauté until golden brown in the melted shortening. Place in glaze and bring to a boil. Remove from heat and, when ready to serve, place meat balls, well coated with the glaze, on a sheet of foil or a pan and broil for 10 minutes, turning as they broil. If necessary, add glaze so that they have a shiny glow. May be prepared in advance. Makes about 24.

Glaze:

¼ cup brown sugar
2 tablespoons flour
1 teaspoon dry mustard
4 tablespoons chili sauce
2 tablespoons prepared barbecue
   sauce

¼ cup dark corn syrup
½ teaspoon salt
Dash Tabasco
¼ cup fruit juice, orange or
   apricot

Combine in saucepan and cook until slightly thickened.

DILLED CUCUMBERS AND GREEN BEANS
IN SOUR CREAM

2 10-ounce packages frozen
French-cut string beans
¼ cup boiling water, salted
2 cups commercial sour cream
2 tablespoons dill weed, crushed

½ teaspoon salt
¼ teaspoon pepper
1 tablespoon lemon juice
2 cucumbers, sliced paper-thin
and dried

Cook beans in water four to five minutes. Drain and chill. Combine the sour cream, dill, salt, pepper, and lemon juice; allow to stand for 2 hours. Toss with cucumber and beans. Refrigerate for at least 4 hours.

KEY LIME PIE — GINGER LIME PIE
2 pies; may be frozen

Crumb pie shell:
4 cups graham cracker crumbs
1 cup melted butter
⅔ cup sugar

Combine all the ingredients; mix well. Press mixture firmly against sides and bottoms of two 9-inch pie pans. Bake for 10 minutes in a 350° oven. Cool before filling.

Filling:
2 tablespoons unflavored gelatin
½ cup cold water
6 eggs, separated
2 cups sugar

⅔ cup lime or lemon juice
1 teaspoon salt
4 teaspoons grated lime peel
Chopped, candied ginger

Soften gelatin in cold water. Beat the egg yolks; add 1 cup sugar, lime juice and salt. Cook over hot water, stirring constantly, until thickened. Add grated peel and softened gelatin; stir until gelatin dissolves. Cool. Beat the egg whites until they form soft peaks; add remaining cup of sugar slowly, beating well after each addition; fold into the gelatin mixture. Divide in half. To one half, fold in the candied ginger and fill one shell. Fill the other shell with remaining mixture. Pies may be prepared in advance and frozen. To thaw, loosen wrappings; let stand at room temperature, on cake rack, for about 1 hour. Garnish pies just before serving, using grated lime for one, and additional chopped candied ginger for the other. Serve with whipped cream.

Buffet Supper

Mushroom Soup in Mugs
Stuffed Brazilian Whitefish — Dressing — Fruits de Mer
Cantonese Pork Chops — Almond Rice
Sautéed Zucchini   Old-Fashioned Salad
Vanilla Bisque Ice Cream   Chocolate Pecan Cookies
Caramel Sauce
Coffee

ADVANCE PREPARATION SCHEDULE

Previous Day	Early Morning	Deep Freeze
Prepare stuffing	*Stuff fish*	*Chocolate Pecan*
Pork chops	*Caramel Sauce*	*Cookies*
Soup		*Vanilla Bisque Ice*
		Cream

MUSHROOM SOUP IN MUGS

2 ounces dried black mushrooms   ½ cup dried barley (optional)
1 quart soup stock   1 teaspoon salt
1 quart boiling water   1 small onion, grated
                     2 tablespoons butter

Wash mushrooms thoroughly. Cover with fresh water and let
stand overnight; chop mushrooms and place them and the water
in which they were soaked in a kettle with stock, water, barley, and
salt. Cook for one hour. Brown onion and add. If barley is
omitted and a thicker soup is desired, add a paste of 2 tablespoons
cornstarch or arrowroot at this point. Simmer another 30 minutes.

STUFFED BRAZILIAN WHITEFISH — FRUITS DE MER

3–4 pounds whitefish	¼ teaspoon pepper
Seasoning salt and 1 tablespoon	1 tablespoon chopped parsley
Worcestershire sauce	¾ pound cooked shrimp
4 tablespoons butter	¾ cup bread crumbs
1 onion, chopped	1 cup dry white wine
1 teaspoon salt	1 pint oysters

Have fish cleaned and boned. Do not remove head or tail. Wash in cold water and dry. Season well, inside and out, with seasoning salt and Worcestershire sauce. Set aside. Melt butter in skillet. Add onion, salt, pepper, and parsley. Cook until onion is golden. Add shrimps, and sauté for a minute. Add crumbs and oyster liquid. Stuff fish loosely and close cavity by fastening with skewers, laced with string. Place in shallow baking pan, brush with additional butter and pour wine over. Bake in a 400° oven for 45 minutes, basting occasionally with wine. Add oysters last 5 minutes of baking time.

Note: Allow ten minutes per pound baking time. Fish is tender when meat flakes easily with a fork.

CANTONESE PORK CHOPS — ALMOND RICE

6 rib or loin pork chops	1 tablespoon vinegar
1½ teaspoons salt	¼ teaspoon prepared mustard
¼ cup water	2 tablespoons cornstarch
1 chicken bouillon cube	2 tablespoons cold water
1 cup hot water	1 9-ounce can cubed pineapple
½ teaspoon Worcestershire sauce	½ green pepper, sliced
1 teaspoon soy sauce	1 tomato, cubed
⅓ cup pineapple juice	½ cup celery, chopped

4 cups hot, cooked rice

Salt and brown the chops slowly for 15 to 20 minutes. Add ¼ cup water and simmer for 45 minutes. Remove the chops and pour off the fat. In a skillet, melt the bouillon cube in 1 cup of hot water. Add Worcestershire sauce, soy sauce, pineapple juice, vinegar, and mustard. Combine the cornstarch with 2 tablespoons of water. Stir into the skillet mixture; simmer until thick, stirring constantly.

Add chops and all ingredients, except the rice. Simmer 5 minutes. Serve over the steamed rice (see Index for recipe). Top with ¼ cup slivered, sautéed almonds, blanched and browned.

SAUTEED ZUCCHINI

3 pounds zucchini   2 tablespoons water
¼ cup butter   ½ teaspoon salt
Freshly ground pepper

Wash zucchini and snip off ends; slice thin. Sauté in ¼ cup butter or salad oil, with 2 tablespoons water. Cover; cook only 4 minutes; salt and sprinkle with freshly ground pepper.

OLD-FASHIONED SALAD

1 cup light cream   ½ teaspoon salt
2 teaspoons sugar   2 medium heads of lettuce, cut
½ cup vinegar   into bite-size pieces
1 cup chopped scallions

Combine the cream, sugar, vinegar, and salt. Chill. Toss with lettuce and scallions just before serving.

VANILLA BISQUE ICE CREAM

1 quart French vanilla ice cream   1 cup Grape-Nuts cereal

Soften the ice cream slightly. Mix thoroughly with the Grape-Nuts. Return to freezer until ready to serve. Scoop into balls and place in a large bowl. Serve with Caramel Sauce.

CARAMEL SAUCE

1 pound cellophane-wrapped   ¾ cup light cream
   caramels   ½ cup miniature marshmallows
1 tablespoon rum (optional)

Place the caramels in the top of a double boiler with cream. Cook until melted. Just before serving, heat and add marshmallows to the sauce. Do not let them melt completely as sauce should have a fluffy appearance. The rum, if used, should be added last. This may be stored and reheated for later use. Makes 3 cups sauce.

CHOCOLATE PECAN COOKIES

1¼ cups butter	2 cups all-purpose flour
1 cup powdered sugar	1 teaspoon vanilla
½ cup cocoa	1 cup chopped pecans
Powdered sugar	

Cream the butter and sugar. Add cocoa, flour, vanilla, and pecans. Refrigerate about an hour so that dough is easier to handle. Pinch off pieces about the size of a marble and place on ungreased cooky sheet. Bake in a 350° oven for 16 minutes. Remove from oven and, while still hot, roll in powdered sugar. To make a thick coating, roll the cookies again when cold.

Buffet Supper

Madrilène with Red Caviar   Relishes
Sliced Tenderloin Sandwiches
Glazed Sweetbreads or Sweetbreads Velouté
Alfredo's Fettucini
Artichokes Polonaise   Gourmet Prunes
Lemon Fluff
Coffee

ADVANCE PREPARATION SCHEDULE

Previous Day	Early Morning	Deep Freeze
Fillet of beef	*Sweetbreads*	
Prunes		
Lemon Fluff		

MADRILENE WITH RED CAVIAR

6 10-ounce cans consommé   Sour cream
madrilène   Lemon wedges
1 small can red caviar (4 ounces)

Before chilling consommé madrilène, remove from can and stir
in the red caviar. Chill until jelled. Serve topped with sour cream
and lemon wedges. Serves 12.

SLICED TENDERLOIN SANDWICHES

3-pound beef tenderloin   Miniature hamburger buns

Season meat with salt, pepper, paprika, and seasoning salt. Bake
in a 450° oven until medium rare, 30 to 35 minutes. Slice one-
half inch thick; cut in portions of correct size to serve on miniature
hamburger buns.

GLAZED SWEETBREADS

3 pounds sweetbreads or   2 8-ounce cans consommé, undi-
3 10-ounce packages frozen   luted
sweetbreads   1 pound medium mushrooms
2 tablespoons lemon juice or vine-   4 tablespoons butter
gar   ¼ cup cream
2 tablespoons butter   ¼ cup sherry wine

Cook frozen sweetbreads according to package directions. For
fresh sweetbreads, cook as in following recipe. Cook about 10
minutes, drain and remove membrane and skin; cool. Slice and
brown lightly in butter; pour off butter and add ¼ can of consommé. Cook, turning frequently and adding more consommé
when necessary, until sweetbreads are browned. Add remaining
lemon juice and consommé. In a separate pan, sauté the mushrooms
in the butter, turning frequently. Serve the sweetbreads and mushrooms on hot platter surrounded by toast points. Mix remaining
mushroom broth with cream and sherry and pour over all. Serves 12.

SWEETBREADS VELOUTE

3 pounds sweetbreads	1 pound mushrooms
3 tablespoons lemon juice	½ pound chipped beef
2 tablespoons butter	3 cups thin white sauce
1 small onion, grated	2 tablespoons sherry

To prepare sweetbreads: Cover with water, adding 1 teaspoon salt and 1 teaspoon vinegar for each quart of water. Simmer, covered, for 15 minutes. Drain, run cold water over sweetbreads to whiten flesh. Remove membrane and tubes. Cut in cubes and mix with lemon juice.

Melt butter; sauté onion and mushrooms for 5 minutes. Add chipped beef and heat through. Blend in white sauce. Adjust seasoning. Add sweetbreads and sherry and simmer for 5 minutes. Serve on buttered Holland rusks. Serves 8 to 12.

THIN WHITE SAUCE

3 tablespoons butter	1 teaspoon salt
3 tablespoons floor	Dash paprika
Freshly ground pepper	1 teaspoon Worcestershire sauce
3 cups milk or light cream	

Melt butter; add flour and seasonings; stir until smooth and blended. Add milk gradually, stirring constantly, to avoid lumps. Cook until thickened.

ALFREDO'S FETTUCINI

½ pound unsalted butter   ½ pound grated Parmesan cheese
1 pound noodles, cooked (see recipe below for noodles)

Melt the butter and stir in the grated cheese. Pour into a heated serving dish. Top with cooked noodles and toss with a spoon and fork until noodles are evenly coated with butter-cheese mixture. Serve at once. Serves 12.

Noodles:

2 cups sifted all-purpose flour   Dash of salt
3 whole eggs plus 1 or 2 egg yolks

Sift flour and salt into bowl; beat eggs and stir into flour. Roll out on lightly floured board and cut into ribbons about ¼ inch wide.

Separate; spread on board to dry. Cook in plenty of boiling salted water until tender. Serves 12.

ARTICHOKES POLONAISE

3 packages frozen artichoke hearts	1 tablespoon chopped parsley
¼ pound butter	¼ clove garlic, minced
1 tablespoon olive oil	4 tablespoons white wine
½ cup cracker crumbs	2 tablespoons catsup
2 hard-cooked eggs, diced finely	Salt and pepper to taste

Cook artichokes according to package directions. Melt butter in a skillet. Add all other ingredients except artichokes and cook about 5 minutes over low heat. Drain the artichokes and place in serving dish. Pour the sauce over the artichokes. Serves 12.

GOURMET PRUNES

1 pound prunes	Rind of ½ orange, cut in strips
4 cups strong black tea	⅓ inch cinnamon stick
¼ cup sugar	

Wash prunes in clear water and drain; soak overnight in tea. Add orange rind and the cinnamon stick and simmer gently for about 25 minutes. Add sugar and cook about 5 minutes longer, or until prunes are tender. Chill before serving. Serves 12.

LEMON FLUFF

Crust:

¾ pound vanilla wafers, finely crushed	½ pound butter, softened

Combine butter and vanilla wafers and line a 9-inch spring form. Set aside.

Filling:

4 lemons, juice and rind	1 tablespoon unflavored gelatin
1 cup sugar	½ cup cold water
7 egg yolks, beaten	7 egg whites, stiffly beaten
¾ cup sugar	

Place the lemon juice, rind, and 1 cup sugar in top of double boiler. Stir until dissolved. Add yolks, slowly. Cook and stir until mixture coats spoon. Soak gelatin in cold water for 5 minutes. Add to the egg yolk mixture and stir until dissolved. Remove and cool. Beat ¾ cup sugar in gradually to stiffly beaten egg whites. Fold into the gelatin mixture and pour into lined spring form. Refrigerate for several hours. To serve, decorate with whipped cream, if desired.

Buffet Supper

Caviar-Stuffed Artichoke Bottoms
Cocktail Rye   Sweet Sour Meat Balls
Chicken Portuguese   Crabmeat Tetrazzini
Southern Carrots
Gazpacho Salad   Butter Crisps
Louisiane Icebox Cake
Coffee

ADVANCE PREPARATION SCHEDULE

Previous Day	Early Morning	Deep Freeze
Meat Balls	*Gazpacho Salad*	*Chicken, partially*
Crabmeat Tetrazzini	*Carrots*	*cooked*
Louisiane Icebox		*Add oranges and*
Cake		*potatoes, cook as*
		directed and serve

CAVIAR-STUFFED ARTICHOKE BOTTOMS

1 8-ounce can small artichoke   1 2-ounce can caviar
  bottoms   1 cup commercial sour cream

Scoop bottoms with a French cutter if necessary, though as a rule there is a sufficient depression. Fill with a small amount of caviar and place on a platter around the bowl of sour cream. A bed of lettuce for the appetizers, with scattered cherry tomatoes, and a dash of paprika on the sour cream will provide color.

SWEET SOUR MEAT BALLS

1½ pounds ground beef	⅛ teaspoon pepper
1 small onion	2 tablespoons cracker meal
1 egg, beaten	1 teaspoon Worcestershire sauce
1 teaspoon salt	2 tablespoons butter

Mix together all ingredients except butter; refrigerate at least 2 hours before cooking. Form into small balls. Heat butter in saucepan and brown meat balls. Drop into Sweet Sour Sauce and cook about 30 minutes. These may be made in advance, as flavor improves with standing. Serves 8.

SWEET SOUR SAUCE

1 tablespoon shortening	½ cup brown sugar
1 tablespoon flour	1 sliced lemon
1 cup hot water	¼ cup vinegar
¼ cup raisins	6 ginger snaps, crumbled
	Salt

Melt shortening, add flour and brown slightly; stir in water gradually and blend well. Add remaining ingredients and simmer about ½ hour, stirring occasionally. *Suggestion:* Canned cocktail meat balls may be used instead. Heat and drain before placing in sauce.

CHICKEN PORTUGUESE

1 2 to 3 pound broiling or frying chicken, cut into serving pieces	½ teaspoon ginger
	1½ cups orange juice
½ cup butter	2 cups water
¼ cup flour	½ teaspoon Tabasco
½ teaspoon salt	2 whole oranges, unpeeled
Paprika	1 18-ounce can vacuum-packed
⅛ teaspoon pepper	sweet potatoes
2 tablespoons brown sugar	

Sprinkle chicken with a little salt and paprika; brown in butter on all sides. Remove chicken from skillet and stir into the butter the flour, salt, pepper, sugar, Tabasco, and ginger until smooth. Gradually add orange juice and then water, cooking and stirring until sauce is smooth and thickened. Replace chicken in sauce; cover skillet and cook about 30 minutes, or until the chicken is almost tender.

If sauce is too thick, add additional liquid. Slice the whole orange about ½ inch thick, and quarter slices; add with potatoes to chicken. Cover again and continue cooking about 15 minutes longer or until chicken is tender and potatoes thoroughly heated. Serves 8.

CRABMEAT TETRAZZINI

3 tablespoons butter
1 small onion, grated
⅓ green pepper, chopped
1 pound fresh mushrooms, sliced
1 10½-ounce can condensed tomato soup, diluted with 1 18-ounce can tomato juice

2 6½-ounce cans crabmeat, flaked or 2 10-ounce packages frozen crabmeat
1 8-ounce package spaghetti, cooked
1 8-ounce package sharp cheese spread

Salt and pepper to taste

Melt butter, sauté onion, green pepper, and mushrooms; cook 5 minutes. Stir in tomato soup, crabmeat, cooked spaghetti, and three-fourths of the cheese spread and season to taste. Pour into a greased 13" x 9" x 2" casserole and dot with remaining cheese spread. Bake in a moderate oven (350°) for 30 to 45 minutes, or until thoroughly heated and browned. Serves 8.

SOUTHERN CARROTS

2 bunches carrots (about 10)
Boiling salted water
½ cup minced green pepper

1 teaspoon dry basil
2 tablespoons salad oil

Slice carrots diagonally in very thin slices. Add to boiling salted water with basil. Cook about 10 minutes. Put salad oil in saucepan; add green pepper, sauté for 5 minutes. Toss with drained carrots. Serves 8.

GAZPACHO SALAD

2 cucumbers, sliced
4 tomatoes, peeled and sliced
2 Italian onions (red), peeled and sliced

⅔ cup dry bread crumbs
½ cup Garlic French Dressing (see Index for recipe)
Lettuce and watercress

In a glass bowl, place alternate layers of cucumber, tomato and onion slices, sprinkling bread crumbs between all layers. Refrigerate until very cold. When ready to serve, pour dressing over the vegetables. Garnish with lettuce leaves and watercress.

BUTTER CRISPS

Spread 2 packages of ready-to-bake rolls generously with butter. Heat in moderate oven until crispy.

LOUISIANE ICEBOX CAKE

½ cup sweet butter	1 teaspoon vanilla
1½ cups confectioners' sugar	½ cup slivered, blanched almonds
4 egg yolks	2 cups heavy cream, whipped
2 jiggers rum or cognac or sherry	2 dozen ladyfingers
2 heaping teaspoons instant coffee	2 dozen large almond macaroons

Cream butter and sugar until fluffy. Beat in egg yolks, rum, coffee, vanilla, and nuts. Fold in 1 cup whipped cream. Place ladyfingers in a flat, oblong pan or 9-inch spring form and cover with one-half of the cream mixture; then put in a layer of macaroons and pour over them the remaining cream mixture. Let stand at room temperature for about 30 minutes, then refrigerate for at least 24 hours before serving. Cover with whipped cream and fresh berries.

Short-notice Buffet Supper

Pirozhski   Olive Tarts
Pigs in Blankets
Boulevard Sandwich Platter
Applecot Compote
Angel Food Cake with Hot Fudge Sauce
Coffee   Tea

ADVANCE PREPARATION SCHEDULE

Previous Day	Early Morning	Deep Freeze
Chicken (may be frozen)	Hot Fudge Sauce	Olive Tarts
		Pirozhski
Applecot Compote		Pigs in Blankets
Angel Food Cake		Cooked Chicken

PIROZHSKI

Dough:

½ cup butter, melted and cooled   1 teaspoon baking powder
1 cup commercial sour cream   1 teaspoon salt
2 eggs   2 cups all-purpose flour

Combine the butter, sour cream, and one egg; mix thoroughly. Add baking powder, salt, and enough flour to make a stiff dough. Roll out thin and cut dough into circles about 2½ inches in diameter. Place 1 teaspoon of filling on each circle, fold over and pinch edges together. Brush with other egg, beaten. Bake until lightly browned, about 15 minutes, on well-greased cooky sheet in a 425° oven. Serve hot or cold.

Filling:

1 tablespoon shortening   ¼ cup bouillon
1 medium onion, chopped   1½ teaspoons salt
1 pound ground beef   ½ teaspoon pepper
2 hard-cooked eggs, chopped

Heat shortening in saucepan; add onions and sauté until brown.

Add beef and cook until slightly browned, then pour in bouillon with salt and pepper. Remove from heat and combine thoroughly with eggs.

OLIVE TARTS

2 cups grated natural sharp American cheese	½ teaspoon salt
	1 teaspoon paprika
½ cup soft butter	48 stuffed olives
1 cup sifted all-purpose flour	

Blend cheese with butter. Stir in flour, salt, paprika; mix well. Wrap one teaspoon of this mixture around each olive, covering it completely. Arrange on a baking sheet or a flat pan, and freeze firm. Then place in two or three small plastic bags, tie and return to freezer. To serve, bake 15 minutes at 400°.

PIGS IN BLANKETS

1 pound cocktail frankfurters
1 package biscuit dough, prepared according to package directions

Roll dough thin; cut into 2-inch squares. Place frankfurters in pan of boiling water. Let water return to a boil and then turn off heat. Let stand 5 minutes. Place one link in center of dough square, roll up and press edges together. Bake on greased baking sheet 15 minutes in a 375° oven. Serves 8.

BOULEVARD SANDWICH PLATTER

For each portion:

1 slice rye bread	1 slice tomato
Lettuce	2 strips bacon, crisp
1 slice Swiss cheese	Thousand Island Dressing
1 slice chicken	Sliced hard-boiled egg
Parsley	

These are open sandwiches. Place the slices of bread separately on a platter (or one on each plate for individual service). Top with first the lettuce; then the cheese, chicken, and tomato in that order, and finish with two strips of bacon, crossed. Center the platter with a large bowl of Thousand Island Dressing, or pour a generous helping over each sandwich before adding the bacon. Garnish with parsley and sliced hard-boiled egg.

APPLECOT COMPOTE

2 No. 2 cans applesauce (4½ cups)   ½ pound dried apricots

To cook apricots: Wash and place in a saucepan with water to cover; simmer 30 to 45 minutes or until tender. Sweeten to taste the last 5 minutes of cooking as they may toughen if sugar is added sooner. Combine with applesauce. Refrigerate and serve very cold. Serves 8.

ANGEL FOOD CAKE WITH HOT FUDGE SAUCE

Use favorite cake mix or see Index for recipe.

HOT FUDGE SAUCE

4 ounces bitter chocolate (4 squares)
¼ cup butter
1 cup sugar
1 teaspoon vanilla
1 cup milk
1 teaspoon baking powder
½ teaspoon instant coffee (optional)

Place all ingredients except vanilla in top of double boiler, over boiling water. Cook uncovered about one hour or until thickened. Add vanilla. This sauce keeps well under refrigeration and may be reheated to serve. Freezes well.

Variation: Omit vanilla and add 2 tablespoons cognac.

Buffet Supper

Party Cheese Ball   Calf's Liver Pâté
Thin Rye Bread Squares
Pepper Steak   Seafood Curry Amalie
Rice Marguery   Peas French Market
Dinner Rolls
Watermelon Bowl
Assorted Fruits   Frosted Grapes
Mocha Marshmallow Torte
Coffee

ADVANCE PREPARATION SCHEDULE

Previous Day	Early Morning	Deep Freeze
Calf's Liver Pâté	*Complete beef*	*Calf's Liver Pâté*
Frosted Grapes	*cooking*	*Rolls*
Mocha Torte	*Make Watermelon*	
Pepper Steak partial	*Bowl*	
Party Cheese Ball	*Fruit*	

PARTY CHEESE BALL

2 3-ounce packages cream cheese
1 1½-ounce package Roquefort
    cheese
1 5-ounce jar smoked cheese spread
1 teaspoon Worcestershire sauce

1 tablespoon minced onion
1 tablespoon chopped, stuffed
    green olives
2 tablespoons chopped parsley
½ cup chopped walnuts

Combine all ingredients except parsley and nuts. Blend thoroughly.
Chill overnight. Form into a ball and roll in parsley and nuts.
Arrange on a tray with assorted crackers and potato chips. Serves
8.

CALF'S LIVER PATE

(Must be prepared a day in advance)

1½ pounds calf's liver
2 anchovy fillets
¼ cup shortening, butter, or chicken fat
3 eggs, well beaten

2 tablespoons cream
1 cup soft bread crumbs
2 tablespoons grated onion
2 teaspoons salt
½ teaspoon freshly ground black pepper

Grind the liver and the anchovies very fine. Combine liver, anchovies, and shortening; add remaining ingredients and mix until very smooth. Pour into a greased 9-inch loaf pan; place in a pan of hot water and bake in a 350° oven for 1½ hours. Chill overnight. Unmold. Garnish with watercress and carrot curls; slice very thin and serve with thinly sliced pumpernickel bread or dark rye. Serves 8, generously. This loaf freezes well.

PEPPER STEAK

3 pounds beef tenderloin, sliced thin and cut into 2-inch squares
¼ cup butter
Salt, garlic salt and freshly ground pepper to taste
1 teaspoon oregano

1 pound fresh mushrooms
3 green peppers, cut in 1-inch squares
3 tomatoes, quartered
¼ cup tomato paste
¼ cup sherry wine

Brown meat in 2 tablespoons of butter. Add seasonings and cook until tender, about 15 minutes. Sauté mushrooms and green pepper in remaining butter 5 minutes; add to the meat mixture along with the tomatoes and tomato paste. Heat thoroughly. Add sherry and serve at once. Serves 8.

SEAFOOD CURRY AMALIE

¼ cup olive oil
1 small onion, finely chopped
2 tablespoons flour
1 teaspoon curry powder, or to taste
1 teaspoon salt

1 10½-ounce can cream of mushroom soup
3 cups combined lobster, shrimp, crabmeat
¼ cup sherry
1 cup commercial sour cream

Heat oil, add onion and brown lightly; blend in the flour, curry powder, and salt, and add to onion mixture. Stir until smooth. Add soup and cook over low heat until sauce comes to a boil. Mix in the seafood, sherry, and the sour cream. Serve hot over rice. Serves 8.

RICE MARGUERY

½ cup butter
1 medium onion, chopped
1 pound fresh mushrooms, ground

2 cups white rice, regular
2 8-ounce cans undiluted consommé
3 cups water

Melt butter in a heavy skillet. Sauté onions and mushrooms for 5 minutes. Set aside. Wash rice and drain well. Place rice in skillet in which mushrooms were sautéed. Brown and add consommé; combine with water, add mushroom and onion mixture. Bring to a boil, cover and simmer about 25 minutes until liquid is absorbed and rice is tender. Serve at once. Serves 8.

PEAS FRENCH MARKET

3 pounds fresh peas or 2 packages frozen
1 tablespoon butter
½ cup water
10 large lettuce leaves, shredded coarsely
8 peeled, small white onions, or 1 20-ounce can

1 16-ounce can water chestnuts, drained and sliced
½ teaspoon thyme
1 teaspoon salt
1 teaspoon sugar
1 sprig parsley, chopped
¼ cup liquid from vegetables
1 tablespoon flour
2 tablespoons butter

Melt 1 tablespoon butter in saucepan. Add water, lettuce leaves, onions, water chestnuts, peas, and seasonings. Mix. Cover and cook slowly for 25 minutes, or until onions are tender. Blend flour, remaining butter, and vegetable liquid and add. Cook 5 minutes more. Sprinkle with chopped parsley.

Variation: Substitute for onion and peas two No. 2 cans *petit pois* with onions, drained. Blend flour and butter with ¼ cup pea stock; add seasoning and combine with peas, onions, lettuce, and water chestnuts. Steam, covered for 15 minutes. Serves 8.

DINNER ROLLS

1 package dry granular yeast	4 teaspoons sugar
¼ cup warm water	⅛ teaspoon soda
1 cup commercial sour cream	1 teaspoon salt
3 cups sifted all-purpose flour	

Dissolve yeast in lukewarm water. Scald cream. Add sugar, soda, and salt. Stir well. Cool to lukewarm. Stir yeast solution thoroughly and add to cream mixture. Add flour gradually and mix thoroughly. When dough is stiff, turn out on lightly floured board and knead quickly for about three minutes. Shape into round biscuits and place in greased 9-inch shallow round pan. Cover and let rise in a warm place until double in bulk. Bake in a 400° oven about 20 minutes. Makes 1½ dozen rolls.

WATERMELON BOWL

Cut a watermelon in half lengthwise, using desired size of melon. (To make a basket, leave a strip of rind attached for a handle.) Scallop the cut edge of watermelon. Scoop out the edible portion into wedges or balls. Make honeydew and Persian melon balls or wedges and place with watermelon pieces in a large bowl. Pour a mixture of lime juice and grenadine over the fruit and let stand for one hour in the refrigerator. (Meanwhile, the watermelon bowl should be chilling, too.) Fill the watermelon bowl with the melon balls. Place on a platter on a bed of lemon leaves and surround with pineapple slices, orange sections, fresh strawberries and frosted grapes.

FROSTED GRAPES

Wash the grapes and dry thoroughly. Dip small clusters of grapes into slightly beaten egg white and, when nearly dry, dip into sifted confectioners' sugar. Allow to dry thoroughly and use as garnish for Watermelon Bowl.

MOCHA MARSHMALLOW TORTE

1 cup boiling water	½ cup coarsely chopped nut
2 tablespoons instant coffee	meats
1 pound marshmallows (60)	2 dozen ladyfingers
⅛ teaspoon salt	¼ cup halved pistachio nuts
1½ cups heavy cream, whipped	

Dissolve instant coffee in water in top of double boiler. Add marshmallows and salt. Place over hot water. Stir until marshmallows are melted. Cool and add ½ cup whipped cream and the nuts. Split the ladyfingers and line bottom and sides of a 9-inch greased spring form with 18 split ladyfingers. Pour in half of the marshmallow filling; make a layer of six remaining split ladyfingers, add remaining filling and refrigerate. To serve, spread with one cup of whipped cream and decorate with pistachio nuts.

Buffet Supper

Cocktail Franks — Sauce Mimosa   Bacon Crackers

Ragout Fin   Filet de Sole en Papillote d'Argent

Potato Scones

Eggplant Patrice   Orange Salad Mold

Brandy Black Bottom Pie

Coffee

ADVANCE PREPARATION SCHEDULE

Previous Day	Early Morning	Deep Freeze
Ragout Fin, partial	*Potato Scones*	*Ragout Fin may be*
Sole en Papillote, partial	*Bacon Crackers*	*frozen*
Orange Salad Mold	*Eggplant*	
Brandy Black Bottom Pie		

COCKTAIL FRANKS — SAUCE MIMOSA

1 pound cocktail frankfurters

Sauce Mimosa:
½ cup prepared mustard   ½ cup grape jam
1½ tablespoons lemon juice

For sauce, heat mustard, jam, and lemon juice together in the top of a double boiler. Pan-broil cocktail frankfurters until brown. Spear franks with toothpicks and arrange around bowl of sauce.

BACON CRACKERS

12 long salted crackers, about 4" x 1"
12 slices bacon

Wrap one slice bacon tightly in spiral fashion around each cracker. Place under the broiler. Broil until crisp. Drain on paper towels. Serve hot.

RAGOUT FIN

(Preparation is made day before serving)

1 to 1½ pounds sweetbreads   6 cups water
1 teaspoon vinegar   1 whole onion
1 teaspoon salt   1 tablespoon salt
4 chicken breasts   2 stalks celery
4 chicken legs   Small bunch of parsley

Sauce:

4 tablespoons butter   ½ pound mushrooms, sliced
4 tablespoons flour   2 tablespoons butter
1½ cups chicken stock   1 onion, grated
½ cup light cream or milk   Grated Romano cheese
Juice of 1 lemon   Bread crumbs
3 tablespoons white wine   Butter
½ teaspoon seasoning salt

Drop the sweetbreads in boiling water to cover, adding one teaspoon vinegar and one teaspoon salt. Simmer 25 minutes; then place in cold water and slip off membrane and skin. Cube. Cook chicken in 6 cups of water with whole onion, one tablespoon salt, celery, and parsley for one hour (or until tender). Drain and cut into cubes.

To make sauce: Melt the butter. Add flour and mix; add chicken stock, cream, and lemon juice, and cook, stirring constantly until thick. Then add white wine. Sauté mushrooms in butter with grated onion. Add to sauce and then stir in the chicken and sweetbreads. Let stand overnight in refrigerator. Place in indivdual casseroles or one large, shallow one. Sprinkle top with grated cheese and bread crumbs and dot with butter. Bake in a 375° oven for 20 minutes. If necessary, brown top under broiler. Serves 6 to 8.

FILET DE SOLE EN PAPILLOTE D'ARGENT

8 small fillets of flounder or sole	¼ teaspoon pepper
½ pound mushrooms	½ teaspoon paprika
½ pound shrimp	1 teaspoon lemon juice
1 teaspoon salt	¼ cup chopped parsley

Rinse and dry fish; arrange one portion in the center of a 14-inch square of foil. Chop stems of the mushrooms and sauté stems and caps. Peel raw shrimp and remove center vein. Arrange shrimp and mushrooms over fillets. Season with salt, pepper, paprika, and lemon juice. Prepare white sauce and spoon it over fish. Sprinkle with chopped parsley. Bring foil edges together and double fold to make a tight seal. Fold outer edges to form a square bag. Put bags on cooky sheet and bake in hot oven (425°) for 40 minutes. When the fish is done, place bags on serving plates and, at the table, snip through foil with scissors to form a crisscross on top. To serve: Turn back the edges decoratively. Serves 8.

Thick white sauce:

4 tablespoons butter	½ teaspoon seasoning salt
4 tablespoons flour	½ teaspoon salt
1 cup milk	1 teaspoon Worcestershire sauce
Dash paprika	

Melt butter; add flour and seasoning. Stir until blended. Slowly add milk, stirring constantly. Cook until thick and smooth.

POTATO SCONES

8 medium potatoes
6 tablespoons butter or margarine
½ teaspoon salt
Dash pepper

3 egg yolks
1 egg white
¼ cup poppy seeds (optional)
Paprika

Peel and boil potatoes in salted water for 25 minutes or until soft. Drain well. Put through ricer or sieve; add butter, salt and pepper. Add egg yolks, one at a time, beating after each addition. Potatoes should be very smooth and thick enough to handle. Turn the mixture onto a sheet of lightly floured wax paper and form into 2-inch mounds. Brush with egg white and sprinkle with poppy seeds. Dust with paprika. Place on a greased cooky sheet and bake in a 400° oven about 15 minutes or until brown. May be prepared in advance and baked at serving time.

Variation: These little puffs lend themselves to many toppings. For example, instead of the poppy seeds, a piece of pimento, some grated orange peel, or a cube of cheese may be used. Serves 8.

EGGPLANT PATRICE

1 small eggplant
4 medium tomatoes, sliced
2 medium green peppers, chopped
2 medium onions, chopped
½ pound sharp Cheddar cheese, sliced ⅛ inch thick

1 tablespoon sugar
1 teaspoon salt
¼ teaspoon pepper
½ teaspoon garlic salt
½ teaspoon monosodium glutamate

Slice unpeeled eggplant ½ inch thick; place a layer of eggplant slices in a greased 2-quart casserole; add layer of sliced tomatoes. Cover with a mixture of chopped green pepper and onions. Sprinkle lightly with seasonings. Add a layer of cheese. Repeat until casserole is heaped high, ending with cheese. There is considerable shrinkage during cooking. Cover; bake in hot oven (400°) about 30 minutes. Remove cover, reduce heat to 350° and continue cooking until the eggplant is tender and the sauce is thick and golden, about 45 minutes. Serves 8.

ORANGE SALAD MOLD

2 packages orange gelatin
2 cups boiling water
½ cup orange juice
1 pint orange sherbet

1 11-ounce can mandarin oranges, drained
Mint leaves
Pear halves
Avocado slices

Dissolve the gelatin in the boiling water. Add the orange juice or cold water. Beat in the sherbet. Let set to jellylike consistency. Grease 6-cup mold. Arrange slices of drained oranges in the bottom of the mold. Pour slightly congealed gelatin mixture over them and return to the refrigerator. Chill. This mold sets very quickly. Unmold on a bed of mint leaves. Garnish with pears and avocado slices. Serves 8.

BRANDY BLACK BOTTOM PIE

Crust:

1⅓ cups graham crackers, crushed
4 tablespoons butter

1 4-ounce bar German sweet chocolate
2 tablespoons hot water

Filling:

3 egg yolks, slightly beaten
½ cup sugar
¾ cup milk

1 envelope unflavored gelatin
¼ cup cold water
2 tablespoons brandy or rum

3 egg whites, stiffly beaten

Topping:

1 cup heavy cream, whipped

2 tablespoons sugar
2 tablespoons rum

For the crust, mix graham crackers with melted butter and press evenly over bottom and sides of a 9-inch pie pan. Melt chocolate with water; stir and pour gently over graham crackers.

For the filling, cook egg yolks, sugar, and milk in top of double boiler over boiling water until thickened (mixture will coat spoon). Remove from heat. Meanwhile, soften gelatin in cold water; heat over hot water until melted and add to custard mixture. Cool until mixture starts to set. Add rum and fold in stiffly beaten egg whites. Pour filling into chocolate crust. Chill. When ready to serve, prepare topping by folding sugar and rum into whipped cream. Spread over top of filling.

Buffet Supper

Chinese Cucumber Soup   Olives, Celery Hearts
Fish Piquante   Chicken Divan
Noodle Pudding Soufflé
Creole Salad
Jubilee Bavarian Cream
Coffee

ADVANCE PREPARATION SCHEDULE

Previous Day	Early Morning	Deep Freeze
Soup	*Complete Noodle*	*Rolls*
Chicken	*Pudding*	*Chicken, if desired*
Bavarian Cream	*Creole Salad*	
Jubilee Sauce		
Noodle Pudding,		
partial		

CHINESE CUCUMBER SOUP

2 pounds marrow soup bones   1 teaspoon salad oil
1 large cucumber, cut in chunks   1 thin slice ginger root
8 cups boiling water   1 pound flank or round steak,
¼ teaspoon sugar   sliced paper-thin
1 teaspoon sherry   Salt and pepper to taste
1 8-ounce package thin noodles, boiled (optional)

Place marrow bones, cucumber, and water in soup kettle. Simmer one hour. Combine other ingredients in a mixing bowl. After one hour add to the soup. Continue cooking for 15 minutes more. Skim off excess fat. Thin noodles, boiled and drained, may be added if desired. Serves 8.

FISH PIQUANTE

4 pounds pike or salmon fillets   1 cup hot fish stock
2 lemons, juice and rind   1 teaspoon sugar
2 egg yolks   ⅛ teaspoon salt
1 tablespoon chopped parsley

Cut fish in serving-size pieces and prepare as in Swedish Trout
(see Index for recipe). Add the grated lemon rind and juice to
well-beaten egg yolks. Then gradually add the hot fish stock, stirring constantly. Season with sugar, salt, and parsley. If sauce is
not thick enough, add 1 tablespoon of cornstarch, dissolved in a
small amount of fish stock. Cook slowly for 10 minutes. Arrange
fish on platter, pour over sauce, and garnish with lemon slices and
parsley. Serves 8.

CHICKEN DIVAN

2 10-ounce packages frozen broc-   ½ cup heavy cream, whipped
coli   3 tablespoons sherry
4 tablespoons butter   Salt and pepper
4 tablespoons flour   1 cup grated Parmesan cheese
2 cups chicken stock
16 generous slices chicken, preferably breasts

Cook broccoli according to directions on package. Place in a
large casserole or baking dish. Make sauce as follows: Melt butter
in saucepan, blend with flour; add chicken stock gradually and
cook, stirring constantly, until thick and smooth. Cook for 10 minutes. Add cream, sherry, and seasonings. Pour half the sauce
over the broccoli; to the remainder of the sauce add the grated
cheese.

Arrange the chicken slices on the broccoli in the casserole; pour
the remaining sauce over the chicken. Sprinkle with additional
cheese. Bake uncovered in a 375° oven for 30 minutes. Serves 8.
This is an excellent way to use leftover poultry.

NOODLE PUDDING SOUFFLE

3 eggs, separated
½ cup melted butter
2 tablespoons sugar
1 pound creamed cottage cheese

1 cup commercial sour cream
½ pound medium cooked noodles
½ cup cornflakes, crushed
Butter

Beat egg yolks; add melted butter and sugar. Fold in the cottage cheese, sour cream, and noodles. Fold in the stiffly beaten egg whites. Place in a 2-quart buttered casserole, and sprinkle top with crushed cornflakes. Dot generously with butter. Bake 45 minutes in a 375° oven. Serves 8.

CREOLE SALAD

8 small zucchini, sliced thin (do not peel)
4 tomatoes, chopped
1 green pepper, finely chopped
1 avocado pear, cubed

1 small onion grated *or*
3 green onions, chopped
1 teaspoon sugar
1 teaspoon salt
½ teaspoon ground pepper

Wash zucchini thoroughly and cut into thin slices. Toss with remaining ingredients and seasoning. Let set for one hour and serve at room temperature. Serves 8.

JUBILEE BAVARIAN CREAM

1 tablespoon unflavored gelatin
¼ cup cold water
5 egg yolks
½ cup powdered sugar

½ cup hot milk
1 tablespoon vanilla
1 cup cream, whipped
12 ladyfingers

Soften the gelatin in water for a few minutes. Beat egg yolks and sugar with rotary egg beater until very light. Add milk; then add softened gelatin. Cook over hot water in a double boiler until mixture coats spoon, stirring constantly. Cool. Add vanilla and fold in whipped cream. Turn into spring form or other 2-quart mold which has been greased and lined with ladyfingers. Refrigerate until firm. Garnish with chopped candied fruits. Serve with Jubilee Sauce. Serves 8.

JUBILEE SAUCE

2 cups of Bing cherries, pitted Juice of 1 lemon
and drained 1 teaspoon cinnamon
½ cup sugar 2 tablespoons brandy

Place cherries in a saucepan with sugar, lemon juice, and cinnamon. Boil slowly for 15 minutes. After the mixture is cool, pour into a chafing dish. Just before serving add brandy and heat; set aflame if desired. If you don't mind extra calories, serve with heavy whipped cream. Serves 8.

New Orleans Buffet

Delta Seafood Gumbo — Rice
Broiled Flounder   Orange Almond Sauce
Green Salad Française   French Dressing
Herb-Buttered French Bread
Platter of Assorted Cheeses   Crisp Crackers
Pêches au Vin   Mardi Gras Cake
Café Diable

ADVANCE PREPARATION SCHEDULE

Previous Day	Early Morning	Deep Freeze
Poach peaches	*Seafood Gumbo*	*French Bread*
Mardi Gras Cake	*Orange Almond*	*Mardi Gras Cake*
(may be frozen)	*Sauce*	
Hard Sauce		

DELTA SEAFOOD GUMBO

1 can condensed tomato soup (10½ ounces)
1 can condensed chicken gumbo soup (10½ ounces)
1 can clam chowder (10½ ounces)
1 can condensed chicken bouillon (10½ ounces)

3 cups seafood (frozen or canned), one or more kinds of your choice — shrimp, crabmeat, lobster
½ cup chopped onions
2 tablespoons butter
½ 10-ounce package okra (optional)
¼ cup sherry
3 cups cooked white rice

Mix together in a large kettle the tomato soup, chicken gumbo soup, clam chowder, chicken bouillon, and seafood. Heat until almost boiling. Sauté onions in butter about 5 minutes and add to seafood mixture; stir in okra, and bring to a boil. Simmer 10 minutes. Add sherry. Keep hot. When ready to serve, pack hot rice into custard cups and immediately unmold in the center of large soup plates, one for each serving. Pour hot gumbo around rice and serve immediately. Serves 8.

GREEN SALAD FRANCAISE

2 quarts salad greens, washed, drained, dried and chilled. Varieties suggested:

French endive
Boston lettuce
Bibb lettuce
Limestone lettuce
Romaine
Watercress

FRENCH DRESSING

1 cup olive oil (or salad oil)
¼ cup tarragon vinegar
1 teaspoon salt
1 teaspoon sugar
1 teaspoon fresh or ¼ teaspoon dried sweet basil

1 clove garlic, split
1 teaspoon paprika
½ teaspoon dry mustard
1 tablespoon grated onion
1 tablespoon Worcestershire sauce

Place all ingredients in a jar and shake thoroughly. Before using, remove garlic.

HERB-BUTTERED FRENCH BREAD

½ cup butter
1 tablespoon chopped parsley

1 tablespoon chopped chives
½ teaspoon dried sweet basil
(optional)

Cream all ingredients together until soft and thoroughly blended. Cut a loaf of French bread in thick slices to, but not through, bottom. Spread slices apart, leaving bottom intact. Cover both sides of each slice with herb butter. Press loaf back into shape. Wrap in brown paper and secure with twine. Heat in a 250° oven for 10 to 15 minutes.

BROILED FLOUNDER

3 pounds fillet of flounder
¼ cup melted butter

¼ teaspoon salt
¼ teaspoon pepper

Place fish, skin side down, on preheated greased broiler pan. Season with salt and pepper. Brush generously with butter. Broil 2 inches under heat for 12 minutes, or until tender. Turn skin side up and broil just until skin becomes crisp. Serve with Orange Almond Sauce.

ORANGE ALMOND SAUCE

2 tablespoons butter
2 tablespoons blanched almonds
1½ teaspoons brown sugar
2 teaspoons cornstarch

1 cup orange juice
1½ tablespoons grated orange rind
¼ teaspoon powdered cloves
½ teaspoon seasoned salt

Melt butter in skillet. Sauté almonds until golden brown. Remove almonds. In the same skillet, combine sugar, cornstarch, and orange juice. Cook over medium heat, stirring constantly until clear and thickened. Add rind, cloves, seasoned salt and almonds.

PLATTER OF ASSORTED CHEESES
(see Index)

PECHES AU VIN

8 ripe peaches ⅓ cup water
¾ cup sugar ⅓ cup white wine

Peel fruit and leave whole. Combine sugar and water. Cook 5 minutes. Add wine. Add peaches and simmer, covered, for 10 minutes or until just tender. Baste while cooking. Set in shallow dish, cover with syrup. Refrigerate. Serves 8.

MARDI GRAS CAKE

2 cups sugar
2 cups water
2 cups raisins
1 teaspoon salt
⅔ cup butter
1½ teaspoons ground cloves

½ teaspoon nutmeg
4 cups sifted all-purpose flour
2 teaspoons baking soda
2 teaspoons baking powder
1 cup coarsely chopped nuts
1 cup assorted gumdrops, cut up
2 eggs, beaten

Combine first seven ingredients. Boil for 5 minutes. Cool; sift together flour, soda, baking powder and add to first mixture. Add nuts and gumdrops, and mix. Fold in eggs. Pour into two well-greased 9″ x 5″ x 3″ pans. Bake in a 275° oven for 1½ hours. Set small pan of water in oven below cake as it bakes. Serve with whipped cream, Custard Sauce (see Index) or Brandy Hard Sauce.

BRANDY HARD SAUCE

½ cup butter 1½ cups powdered sugar
2 tablespoons brandy

Cream butter until light. Gradually beat in powdered sugar and brandy. Add more brandy, if desired. Chill.

CAFE DIABLE

Use prepared mix or see Index for recipe.

Football Buffet Supper

Shrimp Dip
Topside Cheese Sandwiches
Jambalaya   Chili Con Carne
Sour Cream Cole Slaw
Eggnog Pretzel Pie   Apple Pie Mirage
Coffee

ADVANCE PREPARATION SCHEDULE

Previous Day	Early Morning	Deep Freeze
Eggnog Pie	*Assemble sandwiches*	*Chili Con Carne*
Chili Con Carne	*Cole Slaw*	
(may be frozen)	*Apple Pie Mirage*	
Jambalaya, except for		
oysters		

SHRIMP DIP

2 10-ounce cans frozen shrimp soup   1 teaspoon Worcestershire sauce
2 3-ounce packages cream cheese   ½ teaspoon curry powder
½ cup chopped ripe olives

Combine ingredients in electric blender; whirl for one minute.
Serve with potato chips or crackers. Serves 8.

TOPSIDE CHEESE SANDWICHES

24 slices white bread   12 thin slices boiled or baked ham
12 slices processed American   8 tablespoons butter
cheese

Place a slice of cheese and slice of ham on each of 12 slices of
bread. Cover with the remaining bread and press firmly together.
Melt two tablespoons of butter in a skillet and, when hot, fry the
sandwiches until brown. Turn on other side, adding more butter
when necessary. Sauté again until golden brown. Cut sandwiches
into triangles or strips; serve hot. Serves 8 to 12.

JAMBALAYA

1 pound cooked shrimp (fresh or frozen)
1½ cups cooked ham, diced
2 tablespoons salad oil
2 tablespoons butter
½ clove garlic, minced
2 onions, finely chopped
½ teaspoon thyme

1 teaspoon salt
¼ teaspoon pepper
1 bay leaf
1 cup raw rice, brown or white
2 cups bouillon, heated
1 chopped green pepper
1 No. 2 can tomatoes (2 cups)
1 pint oysters (optional)
½ cup sherry (optional)

Devein shrimp; add to ham and sauté lightly in salad oil. Add butter, garlic, onions, seasonings, bay leaf, and uncooked rice. Sauté until rice is golden brown. Stir in the bouillon, green pepper, and tomatoes, and blend well. Bring to a boil; cover tightly and simmer very slowly for 30 to 35 minutes or until rice is tender and has absorbed most of the liquid. Add oysters and heat just until the edges curl; add sherry, heat and serve. Do not cook. Serve in a chafing dish or casserole.

CHILI CON CARNE

¼ cup butter
3 pounds ground beef
1 large onion, grated
1 stalk celery, diced
1 green pepper, diced
2 10-ounce cans tomato soup
2 10-ounce cans water

2 teaspoons chili powder
1 teaspoon paprika
1 teaspoon salt
¼ teaspoon pepper
2 No. 2 cans kidney beans (4 cups), drained

Melt butter in large saucepan. Sauté beef until lightly browned, and add onion, celery, and green pepper. Stir in soup and water. Bring to a boil. Cover and simmer one hour. Add chili powder, paprika, salt, pepper, and kidney beans. Serve hot, over spaghetti. Serves 8 to 12.

SOUR CREAM COLE SLAW

1 large head finely shredded cabbage

2 teaspoons salt

Mix and let stand in the refrigerator for several hours; drain and toss with Sour Cream Dressing.

SOUR CREAM DRESSING

1 cup commercial sour cream   1 teaspoon salt
3 tablespoons sugar   1 teaspoon dry mustard
            4 tablespoons lemon juice

Mix dry ingredients, fold in cream and add lemon juice. Chill.

EGGNOG PRETZEL PIE

Pie crust:
¾ cup pretzel sticks, coarsely   ¼ cup soft butter or margarine
crushed   3 tablespoons sugar

Combine ingredients and press to bottom and sides of well-greased
9-inch pie plate. Chill.

Filling:
            1 envelope plain gelatin   ½ teaspoon nutmeg
            2 cups prepared eggnog   1 cup heavy cream
            ⅛ teaspoon salt   2 tablespoons rum or brandy

Soften gelatin in ¼ cup cold eggnog in top of double boiler. Place
over hot water. Stir until dissolved. Add balance of eggnog, salt
and nutmeg. Blend well. Refrigerate until slightly thickened.
Whip cream until stiff. Fold with rum into the eggnog mixture.
Pour into pie shell and chill. To serve, garnish with shaved chocolate. Serves 8.

APPLE PIE MIRAGE

            2 cups water   22 Ritz crackers, whole
            1 cup sugar   ¼ teaspoon nutmeg
            3 teaspoons cream of tartar   ¼ teaspoon cinnamon

Streusel:
            1 cup all-purpose flour   ½ cup sugar
            ¼ cup butter

Boil water, sugar, and cream of tartar together for 5 minutes. Add
crackers, but DO NOT STIR. Boil 2 minutes. Add nutmeg and cinnamon, and stir. Cool; pour into a greased 9-inch pie pan. Cover with
Streusel. Bake 30 minutes in a 350° oven.

To make Streusel, combine ingredients until consistency of corn
meal. Believe it or not, this is Apple Pie — no apples, no errors!

Foreign Menus

*Each recipe
serves six
unless otherwise
indicated*

IN THIS SECTION, you will find recipes of international flavor. Some are old; some are new; all are typical of the faraway places they represent. Well-known classics, such as Hungarian Goulash and Italian Spaghetti, are naturalized Americans by usage and adaptation. Others are fresh imports recently acquired by world travelers. While the character of the recipes remains the same, substitutions have been made where the original ingredients have not been available in the local food stores.

Buffet Française

Vichyssoise   Bread Sticks
Crabmeat Quiche   Chicken Parisienne — Wild Rice
Salade Champignon
Patisseries Framboises   Macédoine of Fruit
Café Brûlot   Liqueurs

117

ADVANCE PREPARATION SCHEDULE

Previous Day	Early Morning	Deep Freeze
Vichyssoise	*Chicken*	*Patisseries Framboises*
	Crust for Quiche	*Quiche, if desired*
	(may be frozen)	
	Filling for Quiche	
	(may be frozen)	
	Salade Champignon	

VICHYSSOISE

4 leeks, thinly sliced
¼ cup sliced onions
3 tablespoons butter
5 medium-size potatoes, sliced

4 cups soup stock, preferably chicken
2 cups milk
1 cup cream
Salt, pepper, chopped chives

Brown leeks and onions in melted butter. Add potatoes and stock and bring to a boil. Simmer 35 minutes. Strain mixture through a sieve. Add milk to strained liquid and heat. Add cream, salt and pepper to taste. Chill. Garnish with whipped cream and chopped chives. Serve very cold.

EASY VICHYSSOISE

2 20-ounce cans vichyssoise
1 pint commercial sour cream

¼ teaspoon grated onion
¼ cup chopped chives

Place vichyssoise, cream, and grated onion in a blender or mixing bowl. Beat until thoroughly combined. Chill in refrigerator for about 3 hours. Pour into a pitcher, sprinkle with chopped chives, and serve in 3-ounce glasses with bread sticks.

CRABMEAT QUICHE

Pastry:

4 tablespoons butter
5 tablespoons vegetable shortening

½ teaspoon salt
1 egg, unbeaten
2 cups all-purpose flour
6 tablespoons cold water

Combine butter and the shortening. Add salt and egg. Work in the flour with a pastry blender; then add six tablespoons of cold water or enough to make a firm dough. Handle the pastry very gently, mixing it just long enough to combine the ingredients. Turn out dough on floured surface. Roll lightly, forming a circle. Line a 9-inch pie pan with the dough and chill for about 1 hour. Brush the surface with white of egg. Fill with crabmeat filling. Pie crust mix may be used for the shell.

Filling:

1½ cups fresh, frozen or canned crabmeat
2 tablespoons chopped parsley
2 tablespoons dry vermouth
½ teaspoon salt

⅛ teaspoon pepper
4 eggs
1½ cups milk
Pinch cayenne pepper
¼ teaspoon rosemary

Paprika

Fill the pie shell with crabmeat which has been combined with parsley, vermouth, salt, and pepper. Beat the eggs lightly; add milk, cayenne pepper, and rosemary. Pour over the crabmeat. Dust with paprika. Bake in a preheated 450° oven for 10 minutes; reduce the heat to 350° and bake 20 minutes longer or until a knife inserted near the center comes out clean. Serve warm. Serves 6 to 8. *Note:* The quiche makes delicious appetizers when cut in small pieces. It also may be served cold, and freezes successfully.

CHICKEN PARISIENNE

12 small chicken breasts
2 8-ounce glasses currant jelly
1 tablespoon cornstarch
1 cup water
¼ cup lemon juice

2 tablespoons Worcestershire sauce
2 teaspoons ground allspice
3 teaspoons salt
1 teaspoon pepper

Place chicken breasts in uncovered roasting pan, large enough so they do not overlap. Mix all other ingredients in a saucepan and bring to a boil. Let simmer for 5 minutes. Pour sauce over the chicken breasts and bake in a preheated 450° oven for 15 minutes. Reduce the heat to 375° and bake for 1 hour, basting frequently. If sauce becomes too thick during the baking period, add water. Serve on heated platter with wild rice. Serve sauce separately. (To cook wild rice, see Index for recipe, or use 1 No. 2 can prepared wild rice.)

SALADE CHAMPIGNON

1½ pounds fresh mushrooms	¼ teaspoon salt
1 teaspoon vinegar	¼ teaspoon freshly ground pepper
Juice of 1 lemon	Bibb lettuce
2 tablespoons mayonnaise	Tomato slices
1 clove garlic, minced	Parsley sprigs

Clean mushrooms. Wash in cold water to which 1 teaspoon vinegar has been added and dry in a cloth. Slice. To keep mushrooms from turning dark, sprinkle with lemon juice. Toss lightly but thoroughly with the mixture of mayonnaise, minced garlic, salt and pepper. The mixture may seem dry, but after one or two hours in the refrigerator, it will become more liquid from the juice of the mushrooms. Stir lightly several times during the chilling process. Serve on a bed of Bibb lettuce, tomato slices and parsley sprigs.

MACEDOINE OF FRUIT

6 cups fruit, diced in 1-inch pieces (1 cup each of peaches, apricots, bananas, grapes, strawberries and cherries)	6 tablespoons peach cordial or brandy Sugar

Wash, drain and cut fruits in pieces and sweeten with granulated or confectioners' sugar. Add liqueur and blend well. Place fruit in refrigerator for about 4 hours, stirring occasionally so that flavors blend.

Variation: Other combinations of fruits and liqueurs may be used If possible, match the fruit to the liqueur.

PATISSERIES FRAMBOISES

(Raspberry Bars)

1 cup butter	½ teaspoon baking powder
½ cup sugar	1 tablespoon lemon juice
2 egg yolks, well beaten	1 teaspoon lemon rind
2 cups all-purpose flour	1 cup raspberry jam

Cream the butter and sugar. Add well-beaten egg yolks. Sift the flour and the baking powder; add alternately with lemon juice and rind. Divide the dough into two balls. Line a jelly-roll pan with one-half the dough. Spread with the raspberry jam. Roll the other ball of dough into a thin square. Cut into strips ½-inch wide. Place them lattice-fashion over the jam-spread dough. Bake in a 400° oven for 25 minutes or until a light brown. Cut into bars 2″ x 3″ before completely cool.

CAFE BRULOT

1 slice lemon peel	1 3-inch piece of cinnamon stick
1 slice orange peel	¼ vanilla bean *or* ½ teaspoon
4 cubes sugar	vanilla
2 cloves	1½ cups brandy
2 cups strong, black coffee	

Place lemon and orange peel, sugar, cloves, cinnamon, vanilla, and brandy in top pan of chafing dish. Heat. Using a ladle, dip up the brandy mixture; place a lump of sugar in the ladle and ignite. When blazing brightly, lower into the chafing dish. Add coffee. Blend well. When blaze dies, serve in demitasses.

Cantonese Buffet

Sweet and Sour Ribs   Butterfly Shrimp
Polynesian Fried Chicken   Egg Foo Young
Zucchini Cantonese
Iced Pineapple Cubes   Preserved Kumquats
Almond Macaroons
Tea

ADVANCE PREPARATION SCHEDULE

Previous Day	Early Morning	Deep Freeze
Ribs (may be frozen)	*Chill pineapple*	*Ribs*
Almond Macaroons	*Prepare shrimp and*	
Chicken, partial	*reheat to serve*	
	Complete chicken and	
	reheat to serve	

SWEET AND SOUR RIBS

2 pounds spareribs, cut into 1-inch pieces
1 cup pineapple chunks with juice
1 green pepper, cut into 1-inch pieces
2 tablespoons brown sugar
1 tablespoon cornstarch
2 tablespoons vinegar
1 teaspoon salt
¼ cup soy sauce
1 piece fresh ginger *or* 2 or 3 pieces preserved ginger

Fry spareribs, pouring off excess fat frequently. When almost tender, add pineapple with juice and green pepper. Blend remaining ingredients and pour over ribs. Bake in a moderate oven (350°) for 30 minutes, basting frequently; or continue cooking on top of stove for 10 minutes.

BUTTERFLY SHRIMP

2 pounds large, raw shrimp
2 eggs, slightly beaten
Salt and pepper
1 cup prepared pancake mix
Vegetable oil for frying

Wash, rinse, and drain the shrimps; split along the back, removing shell, leaving on the first tail joint and tail. Remove the black line at the top. Chill for two hours. Dip the shrimp into the egg combined with the seasonings, then into the prepared pancake mix. Fry a few at a time in deep, hot fat until light brown. Serve hot with cocktail sauce.

POLYNESIAN FRIED CHICKEN

3 fryers, quartered
3 eggs
½ cup milk
2 tablespoons salt
1 cup orange juice
2 cups shredded coconut
1½ cups butter
3 oranges, peeled

Dip the chicken pieces into combined egg, milk, and salt. Dip in orange juice, then coconut, coating well. Melt the butter in a shallow baking pan in a 400° oven. Remove pan from the oven and arrange the chicken pieces, turning to coat with butter. Bake skin side down in a single layer for 30 minutes. Turn and bake 30 minutes longer or until tender. Serve hot with orange sections.

EGG FOO YOUNG

1 cup diced ham
2 cups canned bean sprouts, drained
½ cup finely chopped onion
2 green onions, bulb and top, chopped
¼ cup chopped celery
1 4-ounce can sliced mushrooms, drained

6 water chestnuts, sliced *or* 1 small can, drained
½ teaspoon salt
¼ teaspoon pepper
1 teaspoon monosodium glutamate
¼ teaspoon garlic salt
5 eggs, beaten with 1 ounce dry sherry

2 cups peanut oil

Mix together thoroughly all ingredients except peanut oil. Pour peanut oil into a heavy skillet (it should be about 1½ inches deep) and heat to 350°. Pour ¼ cup of the batter for each patty into the hot oil and fry until golden brown on both sides. Remove and drain on absorbent paper. Keep hot.

Gravy:

1 teaspoon water
2 teaspoons cornstarch
½ cup water

1 tablespoon soy sauce
1 teaspoon dry sherry
1 pinch monosodium glutamate

Mix the one teaspoon water and the cornstarch to a paste. Gradually add the ½ cup water, the soy sauce, sherry, and glutamate. Bring to a boil, stirring constantly, and simmer until thickened. Pour over Egg Foo Young.

ZUCCHINI CANTONESE

½ cup cooking oil
3 pounds unpeeled zucchini, sliced into ½-inch-thick pieces

3 thinly sliced onions
1 clove garlic
3 tablespoons soy sauce

Heat the cooking oil in a skillet until hot, add the zucchini, onions, and garlic. Cook covered until the zucchini is tender and crisp. Discard the garlic. Just before serving, pour 3 tablespoons of soy sauce over the zucchini. Toss lightly.

ICED PINEAPPLE CUBES

1 fresh pineapple
1 cup maraschino cherries, cut in halves, drained

Colored plastic toothpicks
1 cup shredded coconut, canned or fresh

Peel the pineapple, remove the eyes, quarter and remove the core. Cut into 1-inch lengths and cut each strip into 1-inch pieces. Serve in a bowl on a mound of ice. Decorate with cherries. Stick toothpicks in each pineapple cube, if desired. Serve with a bowl of fresh or canned coconut.

PRESERVED KUMQUATS

1½ cups granulated sugar 1½ cups water
1 quart kumquats

Boil sugar and water 5 minutes; cool. Meanwhile, wash kumquats; cut small cross in blossom end of each. Place in cooled syrup. Cover; bring to a boil and simmer 1 hour or until clear. Do not remove cover at end of cooking time or fruit will shrink. Remove covered saucepan from heat; cool, with cover on, to room temperature. Pack in hot, sterilized jars; cover with syrup; seal as jar manufacturer directs, or refrigerate.

ALMOND MACAROONS

1 pound almond paste, purchased at bakery
2 cups sugar
¼ teaspoon salt

4 tablespoons all-purpose flour
⅔ cup sifted confectioners' sugar
⅔ cup egg whites, unbeaten (about 6)

Soften almond paste with the fingers. Work in remaining ingredients. Place ungreased brown paper on cooky sheets and drop batter, 1 teaspoon at a time, 2 inches apart on it. Pat tops of cookies lightly with water. Bake in a 325° oven for 18 to 20 minutes until set and delicately browned. Makes 5 dozen macaroons. Do *not* freeze.

Mexican Buffet

Chili Con Carne
Mexican Rice   Enchiladas
Guacamole Salad — White Wine French Dressing   Fritos
Ginger Pineapple
Natilla (Mexican Custard)
Coffee

ADVANCE PREPARATION SCHEDULE

Previous Day	Early Morning	Deep Freeze
Chili Con Carne	*Enchiladas*	*Chili Con Carne*
(may be frozen)	*Ice pineapple*	
Natilla	*Prepare rice to heat*	
	when serving	

CHILI CON CARNE

3 pounds round steak
2 teaspoons salt
¼ teaspoon pepper
1 teaspoon monosodium glutamate
3 tablespoons all-purpose flour

3 tablespoons butter (or use half
bacon fat)
3 cloves garlic
4 medium onions, chopped
1 No. 2 can tomatoes (2¼ cups)
5 to 6 tablespoons chili powder
(see Note)

1 No. 2 can (2¼ cups) chili beans

Season meat with salt, pepper, and monosodium glutamate; cut
into small squares, about ¾ to 1 inch in size and dust with flour.
Brown in butter with garlic; remove garlic, add onions and cook
until they are transparent, about 5 minutes. Add tomatoes and
enough water to cover meat; mix the chili powder to a paste with
a little water (to prevent lumping) and add. Simmer, uncovered,
for at least 4 hours, stirring in small amounts of water when necessary. Add kidney beans and heat about 5 minutes longer. (Longer

cooking and overnight standing will improve flavor.) Serve with side dishes of shredded Cheddar cheese and finely minced green onions.

Note: The strength of chili powder varies greatly with different brands, and will weaken with age. The above recipe is for very hot chili, so you may wish to use less chili powder if you prefer your food milder.

MEXICAN RICE

1¼ cups long-grain rice
2 large onions, chopped
2 tablespoons butter
1 large green pepper, chopped
1 tablespoon chili powder

1 2-ounce can pimento, drained and chopped
1 No. 2½ can tomatoes (3½ cups), drained and cut into pieces

Wash rice and drain well. Cook according to package directions, and drain again. Keep hot while preparing remaining ingredients. Sauté onion in butter until transparent, about 5 minutes. Add green pepper, pimento and tomatoes. Mix chili powder to a paste with a little water and add. Carefully fold the mixture into the hot rice.

ENCHILADAS

Salad oil
2 6-ounce cans enchilada sauce
2 large onions, finely minced

18 tortillas (available in cans)
¾ pound Cheddar cheese, shredded

Pour salad oil into a small skillet to depth of one inch. Pour enchilada sauce into a separate pan and heat to boiling. Holding a tortilla with tongs, dip it quickly into the hot oil, drain well and then dip into the hot enchilada sauce. Across the center of the tortilla sprinkle about 1 tablespoon of shredded cheese, 1 teaspoon of onion, and 1 tablespoon of sauce. Roll up and place in an oblong (9" x 13" x 2") baking dish. Continue this procedure until all tortillas are filled and rolled, placing them close together in the dish. Sprinkle the remaining cheese and onion over the top and spoon on remaining sauce. Bake in a hot oven (400°) for about 20 minutes or until cheese is melted and sauce is bubbly.

GUACAMOLE SALAD

On a bed of lettuce, lay slices of avocado and sprinkle with diced tomato, lemon juice, and chili powder. Serve with White Wine French Dressing and garnish with minced, cooked bacon. Serve with Fritos.

WHITE WINE FRENCH DRESSING

½ cup olive oil	⅛ teaspoon freshly ground pepper
¼ cup dry white wine	⅛ teaspoon dry mustard
1 teaspoon lemon juice	¼ teaspoon sugar
1 teaspoon salt	¼ teaspoon minced onion
Dash of cayenne pepper	

Shake all ingredients together. Chill. Serve over Guacamole Salad.

GINGER PINEAPPLE

Sprinkle chopped candied ginger over slices of fresh or canned pineapple.

NATILLA

(Mexican Custard)

4 cups milk	½ teaspoon salt
6 egg yolks, slightly beaten	1 teaspoon vanilla
½ cup sugar	½ cup light brown sugar, sifted
½ cup all-purpose flour, sifted	

Scald 3 cups milk in top of double boiler. Stir carefully into yolks and return to double boiler. Mix sugar, flour, and salt with remaining cup of cold milk and add to the scalded milk mixture. Continue to cook, stirring until thickened. Remove from heat, cool slightly and add vanilla. Pour into shallow baking dish; when cold, sprinkle with brown sugar. Place under broiler flame until sugar caramelizes. Refrigerate for several hours until sugar forms a sauce.

Buffet à la Russe

Beet Borscht in Mugs   Russian Rye Bread
Chicken Kiev   Beef Stroganoff
Georgian Noodle Ring
Minted Peas   Pickled Fruit
Tossed Greens — Russian Dressing   Toasted Bagel
Strawberry Charlotte Russe
Tea with Lemon
Vodka

ADVANCE PREPARATION SCHEDULE

Previous Day	Early Morning	Deep Freeze
Borscht	*Beef Stroganoff,*	*Beef Stroganoff*
Chicken Kiev	*partial*	
Noodle Ring, partial	*Greens*	
Charlotte Russe		
Pickled Fruit		

BEET BORSCHT IN MUGS

2 quarts prepared beet borscht   3 egg yolks, beaten well
1 cup commercial sour cream

Bring the borscht to a boil. Pour into the well-beaten egg yolks, stirring constantly. Cool and refrigerate. Serve individually, topped with a tablespoon of sour cream. Pieces of quartered cucumber may also be added when served.

CHICKEN KIEV

(Must be prepared a day in advance)

8 boned chicken breasts   4 beaten eggs
1 cup butter   2 teaspoons salt
1 cup all-purpose flour   2 cups bread crumbs
2 cups cold milk   Fat for deep frying

Order breasts boned (do not split), leaving a short length of breast bone attached to give them body. Skin. Place each breast between two pieces of waxed paper and pound to ¼-inch thickness. Shape butter into bars, allowing 1½ tablespoons per breast; roll each piece of chicken around a butter bar. Coat the pieces of chicken with flour. Dip into the cold milk. Drain. Next, dip into the beaten egg to which the salt has been added; now dip into the crumbs and dip for a second time in the egg; now back again in the crumbs. Chill overnight in the refrigerator. Deep-fry the chicken gently for 10 minutes in sufficient fat to cover, until golden brown. Then place on a cooky sheet in a 400° oven for 20 minutes, or until tender. Serve hot or cold. Serves 8.

ORIGINAL BEEF STROGANOFF

2 tablespoons butter
3 pounds top sirloin cut into thin strips 2" x 1"
3 large onions
½ pound fresh mushrooms, sautéed, or 1 No. 2 can (2 cups) mushrooms

2 bay leaves
1 teaspoon salt
⅛ teaspoon pepper
1 teaspoon Worcestershire sauce
½ cup water
1 cup sherry
2 cups commercial sour cream

Melt the butter in a dutch oven; brown meat and onions until golden. Add mushrooms, bay leaves, salt, pepper, water, and Worcestershire sauce. Bring to a boil; cover, and cook slowly for one hour. Remove from heat and cool. Gradually add sherry, one-half cup at a time, using the balance if a more pungent flavor is desired. Reheat and cook for an additional half-hour or until meat is tender. Cool again. When ready to serve, add sour cream and reheat, but do not boil.

Note: It is important that wine is added when meat is cool, as it evaporates more quickly when added while food is cooking. If desired, the following Quick Beef Stroganoff may be substituted.

QUICK BEEF STROGANOFF

3 pounds beef, cubed
¼ cup shortening
1 teaspoon salt
½ teaspoon pepper

½ teaspoon ground ginger
½ teaspoon curry powder
3 cups commercial sour cream
2 packages onion soup mix

Brown the beef in the fat until all sides are evenly browned. Season with salt, pepper, ginger, and curry. Cover; simmer until meat is about half tender. Combine the sour cream with the onion soup mix; beat with rotary beater. Pour half of this mixture onto the meat and blend with the juices in the pan. Place in an oiled 2-quart casserole and cover with remaining sour cream mixture. Bake in a 325° oven for one hour, or until tender.

GEORGIAN NOODLE RING

2 8-ounce packages of noodles	2 teaspoons Worcestershire sauce
6 egg yolks, beaten	2 teaspoons salt
1 pound grated Cheddar cheese	½ teaspoon pepper
¼ teaspoon dry mustard	½ teaspoon thyme
	6 egg whites, stiffly beaten

Cook noodles according to the directions on the package; mash through ricer. Combine with yolks, cheese and seasonings. Fold in the beaten whites. Pour into well-greased 2-quart ring mold. Place in pan of water and bake in a preheated 350° oven for 45 minutes. Unmold and fill center of the ring with Minted Peas. Surround with Pickled Fruit.

MINTED PEAS

2 10-ounce packages of frozen peas, cooked according to directions on package
1 teaspoon dry mint (or fresh)   2 tablespoons butter

Add the mint to the cooked peas; toss with butter. Place in center of noodle ring.

PICKLED FRUIT

1 cup sugar	¼ cup vinegar
½ cup juice from drained fruit	1 stick cinnamon
1 teaspoon whole cloves	
	3 cups canned peaches, pears, or apricots

Simmer the sugar, juice, and spices together for 10 minutes; add fruit a little at a time. Heat through slowly, and remove to bowl. Cover fruit with juice and let stand 24 hours. Chill when cool.

TOSSED GREENS

Suggested greens: Bibb lettuce, romaine, watercress and curly endive.

RUSSIAN DRESSING

1 cup basic French Dressing (see Index for recipe)
1 tablespoon prepared mustard
2 tablespoons chopped chives or green onion tops
3 tablespoons horse-radish
3 tablespoons chili sauce

Combine all ingredients and blend well.

STRAWBERRY CHARLOTTE RUSSE

2 tablespoons gelatin
⅓ cup cold water
⅓ cup boiling water
¼ cup sugar
1 10-ounce package frozen strawberries, thawed
3 tablespoons lemon juice
3 egg whites, stiffly beaten
1 cup heavy cream, whipped
1 pint fresh strawberries
18 ladyfingers, split

Soak gelatin in cold water 5 minutes; then dissolve in boiling water. Add sugar, cool, and add defrosted berries and lemon juice. When cold, whisk until frothy, then fold in stiffly beaten egg whites and whipped cream. Pour into buttered 2-quart, spring form, which has been lined with split ladyfingers. Chill several hours. Remove rim and place on a platter which has been bordered with grape leaves. Spread whipped cream over the top and circle both top and bottom with fresh whole strawberries.

Continental Buffet

Swedish Trout — Sauce Tartare
Assorted English Tea Sandwiches
Hungarian Goulash Szekely   Chicken Espagnole
Crusty French Bread
Italian Fettucini   Fruit Platter Granada
Dutch Apple Cake   Vienna Sacher Torte
Café

ADVANCE PREPARATION SCHEDULE

Previous Day	Early Morning	Deep Freeze
Boil trout	*Frost torte*	*French bread*
Goulash (may be	*Fruit*	*Vienna Sacher Torte*
frozen)	*Sandwiches*	*Apple Cake*
Chicken		*Goulash*
Rum Sauce		
Sauce Tartare		

SWEDISH TROUT

2 quarts water, or enough to cover fish
2 medium onions
2 carrots
1 stalk of dill

½ cup vinegar
¼ teaspoon whole pepper
1 teaspoon thyme
2 tablespoons salt

1 6-pound trout, whole, wrapped in cheesecloth

Garnishes:
Pimento
Hard-cooked eggs

Olives
Lemon slices

Boil water, onions, carrots, dill, vinegar, and seasonings for 10 minutes. Place the whole trout, wrapped in cheesecloth, in this liquid. Simmer for about 45 minutes, very gently. Remove the trout, using ends of cheesecloth as handles, and unwrap, laying upright on a large platter. Cool. Cover with Sauce Tartare. Decorate with slices of ripe olives to form suggested fins, slices of stuffed olives for the eyes, and pimento for color. Garnish with watercress, slices of lemon, and quartered, hard-cooked eggs. Serve cold. Serves 8.

SAUCE TARTARE

2 cups mayonnaise	1 teaspoon minced onion
2 tablespoons pickle relish	1 tablespoon capers
1 tablespoon chopped parsley	2 tablespoons catsup
1 teaspoon prepared mustard	Freshly ground pepper

Blend the ingredients together. Chill before serving.

ASSORTED ENGLISH TEA SANDWICHES

I Watercress Sandwiches

1 loaf white bread, thinly sliced   Watercress
3 ounces cream cheese blended with 2 tablespoons cream

If used the same day, sandwiches may be made two hours in advance, but no earlier so bread will not become soggy. Remove crusts from the bread. Roll slices with rolling pin to flatten. Spread with the cream cheese. Roll the bread tightly into small log rolls. Tuck a sprig of watercress in the end of each sandwich. Chill before serving.

II Open Tomato Sandwiches

Bread rounds, 1½", thinly sliced   Pimento cheese spread
Thin slices of tomato

Spread the bread rounds with pimento cheese. Top with thin slices of tomato.

III Chutney–Cheese Sandwiches

1½-inch bread rounds, thinly   ½ cup chopped chutney
sliced, toasted on one side   1 cup grated Parmesan cheese
6 slices crumbled, crisp bacon

Spread toast rounds lightly with softened butter. Spread the chutney on the untoasted side of the bread rounds. Sprinkle with Parmesan cheese. Place under the broiler until the cheese melts. Serve hot. Crumbled bits of bacon may be sprinkled on the chutney for variety. These may be made in advance and refrigerated, except of course, for the broiling.

½ cup chopped chutney   6 slices bacon
1 cup cheese butter

Mix chutney with bacon bits. Place a mound on toasted rounds. Edge each round with a thick border of cheese butter. Place under broiler.

Cheese Butter:
½ cup Cheddar or Herkimer   2 tablespoons soft butter
cheese, grated

Mix well, using blender, if possible.

HUNGARIAN GOULASH SZEKELY

6 slices bacon, diced
3 large onions
2½ pounds lean pork tenderloin, cut into 1-inch cubes
1 large garlic clove, crushed (optional)
1 teaspoon dill seed

1 teaspoon paprika
1 teaspoon salt and pepper
1 No. 2½ can sauerkraut
2 tablespoons brown sugar
1 pound veal steak, cut into 1-inch cubes
2 cups commercial sour cream

Fry chopped bacon until crisp; then sauté onions in same pan until golden. Add cubed pork, garlic, and seasonings. Place in casserole and cover with sauerkraut. Sprinkle with brown sugar. Cover tightly and steam or bake in a 350° oven for one hour. Remove, add veal and mix. Cook for another 45 minutes, until veal is tender. Top with sour cream in last 15 minutes of cooking time. Serve in casserole. Prepare in advance. Flavor improves as it sets.

CHICKEN ESPAGNOLE

¼ cup olive oil
Salt and pepper
2 4 to 5 pound roasting chickens, disjointed
1 large onion, chopped
1 clove garlic, minced
1 green pepper, cut in 1-inch cubes

1 8-ounce jar pimento olives, sliced (1 cup)
2 8-ounce cans tomato soup
1 8-ounce jar pitted black olives, sliced (1 cup)
1 pound fresh mushrooms, sliced and sautéed

½ cup sweet red wine (optional)

Heat oil in saucepan; season chicken well and sauté lightly until golden brown. Discard shortening. Remove chicken and set aside.

Prepare sauce:
Place onion, garlic, and green pepper in same pan with 2 table-spoons additional shortening. Sauté about 5 minutes, until golden brown. Add tomato soup and olives and blend. Place chicken in sauce. Cover; bring to a boil and simmer for 1½ hours or until tender. Add sautéed mushrooms and wine the last 15 minutes of cooking time. May be made in advance, and the wine and mushrooms added just before reheating. Serve in casserole or chafing dish.

Variation: Roast chicken. Remove meat from bones. Add to sauce with wine and mushrooms. Heat in casserole in oven or in chafing dish.

Variation: Steamed rice is especially good with this sauce.

ITALIAN FETTUCINI

1 pound package noodles, medium   ¼ pound butter, melted
   width   ½ cup Parmesan cheese, grated
6 cups chicken soup or broth

Cook the noodles in the boiling soup or broth until tender. *Do not drain!* Place in serving bowl. Pour over the butter. Sprinkle with the cheese. Toss lightly, until the cheese starts to string. Serve hot.

FRUIT PLATTER GRANADA

2 ripe pineapples   1 cup heavy cream
1 quart fresh strawberries   ½ cup maple syrup
            Additional maple syrup

Cut the pineapples in half lengthwise, leaving tops attached to each half. Run a curved grapefruit knife around the inner edge of the pineapple and lift out the fruit. Discard the core. Cut the fruit into cubes. Wash and drain the strawberries, leaving the stems on, and pile in pineapple shells with the pineapple cubes. Chill. Place heavy cream and the ½ cup syrup in a chilled bowl. Beat until firm. Serve with two bowls — one with maple whipped cream, the other with additional maple syrup. To eat, pick up pineapple with a wood pick and strawberries by the stems. Dip first into the bowl of syrup and then into the bowl of whipped cream.

DUTCH APPLE CAKE

2 cups sifted all-purpose flour   1 cup whipping cream
3 tablespoons sugar   3 or 4 apples
3 teaspoons baking powder   ¼ cup sugar
1 teaspoon salt   ½ teaspoon cinnamon
2 tablespoons melted butter

Mix and sift first four ingredients. Whip the cream; blend in lightly with a fork. Spread in greased 9-inch-square cake pan. Pare, core, and quarter apples. Cut each quarter into three slices. Arrange in parallel rows on dough, pressing edges into dough. Combine remaining ¼ cup sugar and cinnamon; sprinkle evenly over apples. Pour melted butter over all. Bake in a 400° oven for 30 minutes. Remove and cut in squares. Serve hot or cold with Rum Sauce.

RUM SAUCE

2 cups milk   ½ cup sugar
4 egg yolks   6 tablespoons rum
½ cup heavy cream, whipped

Scald milk in top of double boiler. Beat egg yolks with the sugar, add to the milk very slowly, stirring briskly. Place over heat; cook until thickened and mixture coats the spoon. Strain and cool. Mix in the rum and fold the cream into the custard. Refrigerate. This sauce may be made in quantity and kept in the refrigerator for two weeks or more, whipped cream to be added when served.

VIENNA SACHER TORTE

½ cup sweet butter   4 ounces German sweet chocolate,
4 eggs, separated   melted in double boiler over hot
1 cup sugar   water
1 cup sifted cake flour
¼ cup soft jam

Icing:
4 ounces German sweet chocolate   2 tablespoons shortening

Cream the butter with an electric beater. Add egg yolks, one at a time, and beat after each addition. Add sugar and beat until light and fluffy. Add melted chocolate and sifted flour. Beat until well blended. Beat the egg whites until stiff and gently fold into mixture. Pour into greased and floured 8-inch spring form pan and bake at 350° for an hour. Let cool in the pan and take out of the pan upside down. Spread thin layer of jam over the surface. Melt remaining shortening and chocolate over hot water, blend well and spread over jam. Frost sides of the torte. Decorate the top, if you desire. Tradition says that whipped cream is heaped on each serving.

Chinese Buffet

Egg Roll   Barbecued Pork with Mustard Sauce
Chicken Almond   Veal Sub Gum
Shrimp Fried Rice   Chop Suey
Chinese Fried Noodles
Apricot Cream   Almond Cookies
Tea

ADVANCE PREPARATION SCHEDULE

Previous Day	Early Morning	Deep Freeze
Egg Roll; roll in wrappers	*Add tomatoes to Sub Gum and prepare for reheating*	*Almond Cookies Chop Suey*
Barbecued Pork		
Mustard Sauce		
Chicken, partial		
Shrimp Fried Rice		
Veal Sub Gum, partial		

EGG ROLL

Wrappers:

2 cups sifted all-purpose flour	1 teaspoon salt
2 eggs	2 cups water

Combine ingredients, forming a thin batter. Drop 2 tablespoonfuls at a time into a hot 5-inch skillet forming a paper-thin wrapper. Cook lightly on both sides but do not brown. *Note:* Noodle dough squares may be purchased at Chinese bakeries.

Filling:

2 ounces dried mushrooms, chopped	1 10-ounce can water chestnuts, finely chopped
1 16-ounce can bean sprouts, drained and chopped	2 teaspoons peanut oil
2 cups cooked, lean pork or chicken, shredded	2 teaspoons sesame seeds, browned in hot skillet
1 cup cooked shrimp, finely diced	1 teaspoon monosodium glutamate
	Peanut oil for deep fat frying

Soak mushrooms overnight, then chop. Combine ingredients. Use one tablespoon of mixture for each roll. Place a spoonful of filling on each wrapper, roll up, first folding in each end. Fry in deep fat (350°) until golden brown.

BARBECUED PORK — MUSTARD SAUCE

Mustard Sauce:

1 tablespoon dry mustard	½ cup catsup
1 tablespoon vinegar	1 tablespoon soy sauce
½ teaspoon curry powder	

Combine above ingredients. Mix well.

Barbecued Pork:

¼ cup soy sauce	2 ounces bourbon
2 tablespoons brown sugar	2 pork tenderloins

Combine together soy sauce, sugar, and bourbon. Marinate the tenderloins in the sauce for one hour. Remove meat from sauce. Barbecue over low heat or bake in oven (325°), basting every 10 minutes with sauce, for about one hour, or until fork tender. Cut diagonally into thin slices when cool. Serve with above mustard sauce.

CHICKEN ALMOND

3 cups cooked chicken, 1" x 2", and very flat
3 tablespoons oil
2 cups celery, cut diagonally in ½-inch pieces
2 cups Chinese pea pods, 3-inch diagonal slices, or snow peas
3 cups chicken stock
3 tablespoons soy sauce
4 tablespoons cornstarch
½ cup water
2 20-ounce cans Chinese mixed vegetables
½ cup whole, blanched almonds
1 teaspoon monosodium glutamate

Brown chicken in hot oil until golden brown. Add celery, pea pods, chicken stock, and soy sauce. Cook about 5 minutes. Mix together cornstarch and water. Add to the chicken mixture. Simmer gently until thickened. Add mixed vegetables, almonds, and monosodium glutamate. Simmer gently until ingredients are just heated through. Do not overcook. Serve over Chinese noodles. Serves 6 to 8.

VEAL SUB GUM
(or chicken)

2 pounds veal shoulder, cut into 1" x ½" pieces
2 tablespoons butter or margarine
2 cups shredded cabbage
1 cup green pepper, cut in ½-inch squares
3 cups diced celery, cut diagonally
3 chicken bouillon cubes
2 cups hot water
3 tablespoons cornstarch
3 tablespoons soy sauce
2 tablespoons dark molasses
1 tablespoon Chinese bead molasses
2 teaspoons salt
2 teaspoons vinegar
½ cup water
3 large tomatoes, cubed
½ cup blanched almonds

Sauté meat in shortening until golden brown, about 20 minutes. Add vegetables and bouillon cubes which have been dissolved in hot water. Simmer, uncovered, 10 minutes. Make a paste of the cornstarch with the soy sauce, molasses, salt, vinegar, and water. Add to the meat mixture. Stir gently until mixture boils and thickens. Add tomatoes. Stir carefully until thoroughly combined. Heat for one minute. To serve, sprinkle with almonds.

SHRIMP FRIED RICE

1 cup rice	1 cup shrimp, chopped
1½ cups broth	1 teaspoon salt
¼ cup butter	¼ teaspoon pepper
1 egg, slightly beaten	1½ tablespoons soy sauce
¼ cup onions, finely chopped	

Wash rice in cold water several times. Drain. Add broth to rice in a saucepan. Bring to a boil, cover and simmer very slowly for about 35 minutes. Remove from heat and let stand covered for 15 minutes. Heat butter in skillet. Add egg, scramble well, breaking it as it cooks. Add the remaining ingredients, blend well, and continue cooking 10 minutes. *This can be made in advance.* To reheat, place in top of a double boiler over rapidly boiling water, until thoroughly heated.

CHOP SUEY

2 large onions, cut in ½-inch squares	2 10-ounce cans water chestnuts
	2 20-ounce cans bean sprouts
¼ pound butter *or* peanut oil	½ cup soy sauce
4 pounds chop suey meat (veal, pork, beef, cut into ½-inch cubes)	2 tablespoons sugar
	½ cup Chinese bead molasses
	2 cups celery, diagonally sliced
4 cups Chinese fried noodles	

Brown onions in butter until transparent. Remove from pan. Place in large casserole or small roasting pan. Brown meat, which has been lightly floured by shaking meat in paper bag containing flour, until richly browned. Place meat in pan with the onions. Combine in skillet the liquids from the chestnuts and bean sprouts; add soy sauce and sugar. Bring to a boil and add the molasses. Combine meat, onions, and sauce. Bake uncovered in a 350° oven for one hour. During the last 15 minutes, add bean sprouts, chestnuts, and celery. Serve with fried noodles. This freezes well. Serves 6 to 8.

APRICOT CREAM

2 16-ounce cans apricot nectar 2 cups heavy cream, whipped
Juice of 2 lemons   2 13-ounce cans pineapple chunks
          2 4-ounce cans grated coconut

Combine apricot nectar and lemon juice. Fold into whipped cream.
Serve in bowl as sauce for the pineapple chunks coated with grated
coconut.

ALMOND COOKIES

½ pound butter   ¼ teaspoon salt
1 cup sugar   ¼ pound chopped almonds
1 egg yolk   1 egg white, beaten lightly with
¼ teaspoon cinnamon   fork
2 cups all-purpose flour

Cream together butter and sugar. Add egg yolk, cinnamon, flour,
salt, and one-half of the almonds. Divide dough into two parts.
Pat into two greased 8-inch-square cake pans. Brush unbeaten egg
white over each pan. Cover with remaining almonds. Bake in a 350°
oven for 30 minutes. Cool. Cut into squares, and remove from pan.

Italian Buffet

Antipasto Riviera
Lasagna Romana
Chicken Cacciatore   Pizza Pies
Finocchio Salad
Crusty Bread
Fresh Fruit   Cheeses
Chianti Wine

ADVANCE PREPARATION SCHEDULE

Previous Day	Early Morning	Deep Freeze
Antipasto	*Crisp Finocchio*	*Pizzas*
Lasagna	*Chill greens*	*Chicken*
Pizza shells (may be frozen)		
Chicken Cacciatore (may be frozen)		

ANTIPASTO RIVIERA

2 or 3 red Italian onions, thinly sliced
1 medium head cauliflower, separated into small flowerets

2 green peppers, cut into 1-inch squares
1 cup pitted and halved green and black olives (salad olives)

Drop vegetables into boiling sauce (see below) for 5 minutes. Chill in sauce and drain thoroughly. Serve on lettuce leaves with sardines, anchovies, Italian salami, sliced tomatoes, cucumber chunks, and carrot sticks. Serve with cruet bottles of wine vinegar and olive oil on the side.

Sauce:

½ teaspoon thyme
½ teaspoon rosemary
1 teaspoon whole cloves
1 bay leaf
½ teaspoon oregano
1 cup olive oil

⅓ cup vinegar
1 No. 2 can tomatoes, strained (2¼ cups)
1 teaspoon salt
½ teaspoon freshly ground pepper
1 dash Tabasco

Tie the thyme, rosemary, cloves, bay leaf, and oregano in a cheesecloth bag. Combine with remaining ingredients and boil 20 minutes.

LASAGNA ROMANA
(Prepare in advance)

2 tablespoons salad oil
½ cup minced onions
1 pound chuck, ground
1 clove garlic, minced
1½ teaspoons salt
¼ teaspoon black pepper
¼ teaspoon oregano
3 tablespoons snipped parsley

1 No. 2 can tomatoes (2½ cups)
1 8-ounce can tomato sauce
½ cup grated Parmesan cheese
½ pound lasagna (1½" wide noodles)
¾ pound thinly sliced Mozzarella cheese
1 pound ricotta or cottage cheese

The day before serving or early the same day, sauté onions in hot oil until light brown; add beef and cook until red color is lost. Mix garlic with salt and add pepper, oregano, parsley, tomatoes, sauce, and 2 tablespoons Parmesan cheese. Simmer, covered, 40 minutes. Refrigerate until final preparation. About 45 minutes before serving, cook lasagna according to package directions. Drain and cover with cold water. Arrange one-third of meat sauce in a 3-quart casserole or a 12" x 8" baking dish. Cover with a single layer of drained lasagna, placed lengthwise (leave remainder in water), next a layer of Mozzarella, then a layer of ricotta, and sprinkle with 2 tablespoons Parmesan cheese. Repeat, ending with sauce and Parmesan. Bake 30 minutes in a 350° oven. Serves 8. *Note:* Ricotta may be purchased in Italian food stores.

CHICKEN CACCIATORE

2 3-pound fryers, disjointed
Seasoned flour
6 tablespoons salad oil
1 cup minced onion
1 cup green pepper, coarsely chopped
1 clove garlic, minced

1 No. 2½ can tomatoes (3½ cups)
1 6-ounce can tomato sauce (¾ cup)
2 teaspoons salt
½ teaspoon pepper
1 teaspoon thyme
½ teaspoon ground allspice

½ cup Chianti wine

Dredge chicken with seasoned flour; place in saucepan in hot salad oil and brown lightly. Add onion, green pepper, and garlic, and brown. Add remaining ingredients except wine and simmer uncovered for 15 minutes. Pour in the wine, cover and simmer very slowly about 40 minutes, or until tender. To serve, place chicken on platter and cover with sauce. Serves 8.

TWO PIZZA PIES
One Mushroom Pizza, One Sausage Pizza

2 No. 2 cans tomatoes, drained (5 cups)
1 6-ounce can tomato paste
½ pound Mozzarella cheese
½ cup grated Parmesan cheese
2 teaspoons oregano

1½ teaspoons salt
¼ teaspoon pepper
2 3-ounce cans button mushrooms, drained
½ pound Italian sausage, thinly sliced

2 tablespoons olive oil

Combine tomatoes and tomato paste and spoon into two unbaked pizza shells. Cover with a layer of Mozzarella cheese. Sprinkle with Parmesan, oregano, salt and pepper. Top one pie with mushrooms and the other with sausage. Sprinkle with olive oil. Bake in a 400° oven for 20 minutes. If a thicker sauce is preferred, replace 1 cup tomatoes with tomato paste.

PIZZA PIE SHELLS
(For 2 pies)

1 cup warm water
1 package dry yeast
1 teaspoon sugar

1 teaspoon salt
2 tablespoons olive oil
3½ cups sifted all-purpose flour

Measure water into a bowl; sprinkle with yeast. Stir until dissolved. Add sugar, salt, olive oil, and 2 cups of flour. Beat until smooth. Stir in remaining flour, or enough to make a dough. Turn out on lightly floured board. Knead until smooth and elastic. Place in greased bowl; brush with olive oil. Cover. Let rise in a warm place, free from draft, until doubled in bulk. Punch down; divide in half. Form each half into a ball. Roll each into a circle to fill 12-inch pizza pans. Place in oiled pan and press around edge to form a standing rim of dough, or place each on an oiled cooky sheet and press out with palms of hands into a circle 12 inches in diameter. Press around edges with fingers to form a rim about ½ inch high. Brush with olive oil. One pie serves 8. *Note:* Ready-mix pizza dough can be purchased.

FINOCCHIO SALAD

2 cups diced finocchio	4 tomatoes, peeled and quartered
3 quarts salad greens	Oil and vinegar dressing (see Index for recipe)

Freshly ground pepper

Peel finocchio and let stand in ice water to become crisp as for celery. Dice when ready to serve. Place in a bowl with greens; toss with dressing, just enough to moisten the salad. Garnish with tomatoes; serve very cold. Serves 8.

PLATTER OF FRUIT AND CHEESE

Suggested fruits:	*Suggested cheeses:*
Small Jonathan apples	Bel Paese
Orange slices	Edam
Fresh pears	Port du Salut

Place cheese in center of wooden platter. Border with fruit.

Hot Italian Buffet

Melon Prosciutto

Veal Parmigiano   Spaghetti with Meat Sauce

Brussels Sprouts Tosca   Marinated Vegetables

Pears Zabaglione   Crisp Orange Cookies

Port du Salut Cheese

Sea Toast

ADVANCE PREPARATION SCHEDULE

Previous Day	Early Morning	Deep Freeze
Veal	*Cook spaghetti*	*Spaghetti Sauce*
Meat Sauce (may be frozen)	*Sauce Zabaglione*	*Orange Cookies*
Marinate vegetables		
Poach pears		

MELON PROSCIUTTO

Cut finger-sized pieces of peeled melon; wrap a thin slice of Italian ham around each and spear with a cocktail pick.

VEAL PARMIGIANO

12 veal cutlets, pounded thin
2 eggs, beaten
½ teaspoon pepper
½ teaspoon salt
1½ cups bread crumbs

6 tablespoons Parmesan cheese
½ cup butter
2 8-ounce cans tomato sauce (2 cups)
12 slices Mozzarella cheese

Dip the veal in the egg, to which the salt and pepper have been added. Then roll in the combined bread crumbs and grated cheese. Refrigerate for ½ hour. Sauté in butter until golden brown. Place in shallow baking dish. Pour tomato sauce over all and top with slices of Mozzarella cheese; sprinkle with additional Parmesan. Bake in a 350° oven for 30 minutes. Serves 6 to 8.

SPAGHETTI — MEAT SAUCE

3 onions, minced
3 cloves garlic, minced
¼ cup butter or olive oil
2 pounds ground beef
2 6-ounce cans tomato paste

3 cups tomato juice
2 teaspoons salt
½ teaspoon pepper
1 tablespoon allspice
1 pound sliced mushrooms

1 pound fine spaghetti, cooked and drained

Brown the onions and garlic in the butter or oil. Add beef and brown. Add the remaining ingredients. Bring to a boil. Cover and simmer very slowly for 2 hours. Serve over fine spaghetti. Serves 8.

BRUSSELS SPROUTS TOSCA

2 10-ounce packages frozen Brussels sprouts

2 tablespoons butter
½ teaspoon salt

Melt butter in saucepan; add frozen Brussels sprouts and salt. Cover pan tightly and simmer very slowly for 30 minutes or until completely defrosted and leaves of sprouts curl slightly. Serves 8.

MARINATED VEGETABLES

2¼ cups canned whole baby carrots
2¼ cups canned celery hearts
1 28-ounce can julienne beets

1 No. 2 can jumbo green asparagus spears
2 No. 2 cans artichoke hearts
Lettuce leaves

Place each vegetable in a separate container with the marinade (see recipe below) over it, allowing about ⅔ cup of dressing to each vegetable. Chill for several hours.

To serve: Arrange vegetables in individual mounds on a lettuce-lined platter. They should be fairly well drained of the marinade. Sprinkle with paprika and dry chopped parsley. Add an egg to the reserved dressing; beat for a minute or two and serve with vegetables. Serves 12.

Marinade:

3 cups olive oil
2½ cups red wine vinegar

4 tablespoons chopped red onion
Salt and pepper to taste

Mix the oil and vinegar together; whip somewhat briskly; add seasonings. Pour over vegetables. Reserve remaining dressing.

PEARS ZABAGLIONE

2 cups water
½ cup sugar
1 tablespoon lemon peel, grated
1 tablespoon orange peel, grated

1 stick cinnamon
12 fresh pear halves, peeled, brushed with lemon juice

Sauce:
8 egg yolks
1 cup confectioners' sugar

1 cup orange juice
1 teaspoon lemon peel, grated

Place water, sugar, grated peels, and cinnamon in saucepan and cook until a syrup forms. Simmer pears in the syrup until tender. Remove from syrup; chill. Make a sauce by beating the egg yolks until light and lemon-colored. Add the sugar while beating. Set over hot water and continue beating with a wire whisk until foamy. Flavor with orange juice and grated peel. Remove from heat; cool. Pour sauce over pears in low-stemmed sherbet dishes.

CRISP ORANGE COOKIES

1 cup butter	1 egg, unbeaten
1½ cups sifted confectioners' sugar	2 cups all-purpose flour
1 teaspoon vanilla	1 teaspoon baking soda
1 tablespoon grated orange rind	1 teaspoon cream of tartar
	½ teaspoon salt

Cream butter and sugar until light and fluffy. Add vanilla, orange rind, and egg; mix well. Add sifted dry ingredients and mix until blended. Drop from a teaspoon on ungreased cooky sheets. Bake in a moderate oven (375°) for about 8 minutes or until delicately browned. Sprinkle lightly with confectioners' sugar.

Far East Buffet

Pâté of Chicken Almond   Poppied Crackers   Ramaki
Bongo Bongo
Rice   Rijstafel — Curry Accompaniments
Kumquat Ring
Marron Ice Cream with Brandied Marron Sauce
Turkish Delights   Dates and Nuts
Coffee

ADVANCE PREPARATION SCHEDULE

Previous Day	Early Morning	Deep Freeze
Pâté of Chicken	*Bongo Bongo*	*Marron Ice Cream*
Ramaki	*Rijstafel*	
Kumquat Ring		
Turkish Delights		

PATE OF CHICKEN ALMOND

1 cup minced chicken   1 tablespoon sherry
¼ cup butter   ¼ cup coarsely chopped onion
¼ cup slivered, toasted almonds

Blend chicken with butter; add sherry and onion. Place mixture in a small bowl and sprinkle with nuts. Use as spread with crackers.

POPPIED CRACKERS

Triangle Thins   Melted butter   Poppy seeds

Brush crackers with melted butter. Sprinkle generously with poppy seeds. Place in a 400° oven for 10 minutes. Serve hot.

RAMAKI

9 slices bacon, cut in halves   9 water chestnuts, halved
9 chicken livers, halved

Marinade:
¼ cup soy sauce   2 tablespoons brown sugar
1 ounce bourbon (optional)

Wrap a piece of water chestnut and a half of chicken liver together in a strip of bacon. Fasten with a toothpick. Marinate in soy-sauce mixture for 6 to 8 hours. Drain and place on pan or foil; broil until bacon is crisp, about 3 to 4 minutes on each side. Makes 18.

BONGO BONGO

1½ quarts stewing oysters   1½ cups canned chicken broth
3 tablespoons butter   Onion salt
3 tablespoons flour   Paprika
1½ cups milk   ½ 10-ounce package frozen
chopped spinach, thawed

Remove oysters from liquid and chop very fine, using blender, if possible. Melt butter in a saucepan, add flour and blend well. Stir in milk; mix until smooth. Add broth, seasonings, oyster liquor, and spinach. Cook one minute and add oysters. If necessary, thin with additional milk or cream. Serves 8 to 10. (Preparation may be made in advance and the oysters added just before serving.)

RIJSTAFEL

4 tablespoons butter
1 pound cooked shrimp, whole
1 pound cooked lobster meat, cut in ½-inch pieces

3 cups Curry Sauce
½ cup cream
¼ cup sherry
½ pound crabmeat in chunks
Salt

Melt the butter. Add the shrimp and lobster and sauté for 5 minutes. Add Curry Sauce and simmer for 5 minutes. Then add the cream, sherry, and crabmeat and mix carefully. Heat 2 more minutes. Adjust salt to taste. To serve, pour over large mound of fluffy white rice. Serves 6 to 8.

CURRY SAUCE

2 tablespoons butter
1 small onion, finely chopped
1 small green apple, finely chopped
1 bay leaf
⅛ teaspoon ground cloves
1½ tablespoons curry powder

2 tablespoons flour
3 cups chicken stock
½ teaspoon salt
1 teaspoon lemon juice
½ teaspoon monosodium glutamate
½ cup cream

Melt the butter in a skillet. Add onion, apple, bay leaf, and cloves. Simmer about 10 minutes until apple and onion are done, but not brown. Add curry powder and flour, and simmer for 5 minutes. Stir in chicken stock and cook slowly, covered, for ½ hour. Add salt, lemon juice, glutamate, and cream. Remove bay leaf. Strain if a smoother sauce is desired.

SUGGESTED CURRY ACCOMPANIMENTS

Chutney
Peanuts
Raisins
Snipped Parsley
Pickles
Tomato Wedges

Almonds
Currant Jelly
Chopped Eggs
Pineapple Chunks
Sautéed Onion Rings
Sliced Avocado

Grated Orange Rind
Sliced Oranges
Mandarin Orange Slices
Crisp Bacon Bits
Grated Coconut

KUMQUAT RING

1 quart fresh kumquats	1 tablespoon unflavored gelatin
3 cups water	¼ cup cold water
2 cups sugar	

Your choice of:
   Coconut   Sliced oranges   Chutney   Raisins   Almonds

Wash, seed, and slice kumquats. Mix water and sugar and bring to a boil. Cook 5 minutes or until syrupy. Add kumquats and cook slowly, covered, for 30 minutes. Remove from heat. Meanwhile, soften gelatin in the cold water for 5 minutes. Dissolve in the hot syrup. Cool and refrigerate. When slightly thickened, stir in the kumquats, and arrange them so that they are evenly distributed. Pour into a 6-cup ring mold. Chill until firm. Unmold on platter garnished with salad greens and border with sliced oranges and bowls of suggested curry accompaniments or those above.

MARRON ICE CREAM

1 quart vanilla ice cream, softened	1 cup marrons, coarsely chopped
1 tablespoon sherry	

Combine the softened ice cream with the marrons and sherry. Return to the freezer until again frozen.

I Marron Sauce

¼ cup marron syrup, in which marrons were preserved	1 tablespoon cornstarch
½ cup water	⅛ teaspoon salt
	2 tablespoons sherry

Bring marron syrup and ¼ cup water to a boil. Mix cornstarch with the other ¼ cup water and add to the boiling syrup, stirring constantly, until clear and thickened. Add salt and sherry. Serve hot or cold over Marron Ice Cream. Serves 6 to 8.

II Brandied Marron Sauce

1 package instant vanilla pudding mix	¼ cup brandy
1 cup milk	1 cup heavy cream, whipped
	½ cup coarsely chopped marrons

Make instant pudding according to package directions, using only one cup of milk plus brandy. Just as it begins to stiffen, fold in marrons and whipped cream.

TURKISH DELIGHTS

1 package cherry-flavored gelatin   1 cup sugar
1 cup hot applesauce   ⅔ cup chopped nuts
                    Sugar for coating

Heat applesauce, add gelatin and dissolve. Stir in sugar over low heat and blend until dissolved. Add nuts. Pour into greased 9″ x 5″ x 3″ loaf pan. Refrigerate until firm and cut into squares. Roll in sugar. Let set for 24 hours and roll in sugar again. Makes 3 dozen.

Buffet Dinners

*Each recipe
serves six
unless otherwise
indicated*

THIS SECTION is all-inclusive, from the casual to the state-occasion dinner; from the foreign to the regional Americal meal. Most of the recipes are a far cry from the "roast beef — baked potato" pattern, but really not a great deal more complicated to prepare. These menus are designed to offer great variety, but deleting, substituting or modifying them may be done to suit the needs of the individual hostess. To adapt any of these menus for formal service, select only one entree and the complementary courses.

Buffet Dinner

Emerald Salad Mold — Herbed Shrimp
Sauce Louis   Caraway Crackers
Baked Steak   Potatoes Anna
Stuffed Beets   Spinach Casserole
Pecan Pie
Coffee

153

Previous Day	Early Morning	Deep Freeze
Emerald Salad Mold	*Pecan Pie*	*Dinner rolls*
Beets	*Arrange potato*	
	casserole	
	Shrimp	

EMERALD SALAD MOLD

2 packages lime gelatin	2 avocados
1½ cups boiling water	2 tablespoons lemon juice
1½ cups cold water	1 cup small cocktail onions, cut
1½ cups diced cucumber	into halves
1 teaspoon salt	1 cup stuffed green olives, halved
½ cup vinegar	Salad greens

Dissolve the gelatin in boiling water; add the cold water. Chill.
Marinate the cucumber in the salt and vinegar. Cut the avocados
into halves lengthwise. Remove seeds, peel, cut into cubes and
sprinkle with salt and lemon juice. When gelatin is slightly thickened, add drained cucumbers, onions, olives, and avocado cubes;
mix lightly. Pour into a wet ring mold and chill until firm. Unmold
on a platter of salad greens; fill center with shrimp and surround
with avocado slices. Serve with Sauce Louis (see Index for recipe).

HERBED SHRIMP

1 pound shrimp, deveined,	⅔ cup tarragon vinegar
cooked	½ teaspoon salt
1 clove garlic, minced	1 small bay leaf, broken
½ cup salad oil	1 tablespoon minced fresh parsley
2 medium avocados, sliced	

Combine garlic, oil, vinegar, salt, and bay leaf; simmer for 1
minute. Pour over shrimp; cool and marinate for 2 hours or more.
Add parsley. Serve in center of Emerald Salad Mold and border
with tomato and avocado slices.

BAKED STEAK

1 3-inch-thick sirloin steak
½ teaspoon salt
¼ teaspoon freshly ground pepper
1 garlic clove, minced
1 cup catsup

3 tablespoons Worcestershire sauce
½ cup butter
1 tablespoon lemon juice
1 large Bermuda onion, sliced

Place steak in shallow roasting pan and brown in broiler on one side. Season with salt and pepper. Turn over and season raw side with salt, pepper, and garlic. Spread with combined catsup, Worcestershire sauce, butter, and lemon juice. Top with onion slices. Bake uncovered in a 350° oven for 1½ hours.

POTATOES ANNA

6 medium potatoes
1 teaspoon salt

⅛ teaspoon pepper
4 tablespoons butter

Wash and pare potatoes; cut into slices ⅛ inch thick and soak in cold water. Drain and dry. Arrange a layer of the potatoes with edges overlapping in the bottom of an 8-inch cake pan. Combine salt and pepper and sprinkle over potatoes; dot with one tablespoon butter. Repeat with the remainder of the potatoes and seasoning until pan is filled, dotting with the rest of the butter. Bake in a 425° oven for 45 minutes. To serve, invert on a warm plate. Garnish with parsley and border with Stuffed Beets. Serves 6 to 8.

STUFFED BEETS

1 No. 2 can small whole beets (2 cups)

¼ cup white prepared horse-radish
1 cup heavy cream, whipped

Hollow the beets with a vegetable ball cutter, making the depression as large as possible. Combine the horse-radish and whipped cream and fill each beet with the mixture. Chill.

SPINACH CASSEROLE

2 10-ounce packages spinach, cooked according to the directions on the package

2 tablespoons butter	2 teaspoons salt
¼ cup all-purpose flour	¼ teaspoon pepper
¾ cup milk	½ teaspoon nutmeg
3 eggs, beaten	

Melt the butter in a heavy pan; add flour; stir in milk gradually; add seasonings and spinach. Stir in beaten eggs. Turn into greased 1½-quart casserole. Place in a pan of hot water and bake in a 350° oven for 30 minutes. Unmold and serve on heated platter, accompanied by hot cream seasoned with salt and pepper. Serves 6 to 8.

PECAN PIE

3 eggs, well beaten	¼ teaspoon salt
1 cup brown sugar	1 tablespoon vanilla
¾ cup dark Karo syrup	3 tablespoons melted butter
⅔ cup pecan halves	

To well-beaten eggs, add all other ingredients. Mix thoroughly and pour into a 9-inch unbaked pie shell. Bake in a 400° oven for 10 minutes; reduce heat to 325° and bake 35 minutes longer.

FOOLPROOF PIE CRUST

3 cups sifted all-purpose flour	1 egg
1 teaspoon salt	1 teaspoon vinegar
1 cup shortening	5 tablespoons cold water

Sift flour and salt together; cut in shortening until mixture resembles corn meal. Beat egg, vinegar, and water together; add to flour mixture. Blend thoroughly. Turn out on wax paper and press into a ball. Roll to shape on floured pastry cloth, or between sheets of wax paper. Cut in circle so that dough is 1½ inches larger than pie pan. Place lightly on pan; flute edges and prick bottom with a fork Bake in preheated 450° oven 12 to 15 minutes. For pastry shel Bake in preheated 450° oven for 12 to 15 minutes. Makes tw 9-inch shells.

Buffet Dinner

Oysters Imperial
Lobster and Capon Madeira   Baked Ham — Orange Glaze
Saffron Rice   Chutney Acorn Squash
Fresh Fruit Garni   Grape Juice Mold   Cream Cheese Dressing
Apricot Strudel   Banana Chocolate Loaf
Coffee

ADVANCE PREPARATION SCHEDULE

Previous Day	Early Morning	Deep Freeze
Capon	*Ham*	*Banana Cake*
Madeira Sauce	*Fruit*	*Apricot Strudel*
Grape Juice Mold	*Fruit Dressing*	
	Arrange squash	

OYSTERS IMPERIAL

Add ½ teaspoon black or red caviar to each oyster on the half shell. Sprinkle each with a trace of minced chives and six drops of lemon juice. Serve on cracked ice. Allow four large or six small oysters per serving.

LOBSTER AND CAPON MADEIRA

2 cups lobster meat, cooked and cut in chunks

2 cups capon, cooked and sliced

Madeira Sauce:

½ cup butter
1 tablespoon chopped onion
1 tablespoon chopped celery
½ cup flour
⅛ teaspoon thyme
⅛ teaspoon rosemary
1 small bay leaf

1 clove garlic, minced
1 tablespoon tomato purée
3 cups hot brown stock (consommé)
1 tablespoon orange juice
1 tablespoon sugar
2 ounces (¼ cup) Madeira wine

Melt the butter in a skillet to a foaming consistency; add the onion and celery; sauté for five minutes. Blend in flour until light in color. Add spices and tomato purée and cook slowly for five minutes, stirring constantly. Add the hot brown stock and cover. Bring to a boil and then simmer very slowly for one hour. Strain. Place the orange juice and sugar in another saucepan and cook to a light caramel color; add the wine and simmer until the sugar is dissolved. Combine both mixtures and cook five minutes more. Add lobster meat and capon and simmer 10 minutes. Serve from a chafing dish or casserole. The sauce may be prepared in advance. Serve with Saffron Rice.

SAFFRON RICE

4 tablespoons butter   ¼ teaspoon saffron
1 small onion, chopped very fine   1½ cups raw rice (long grained)
3 cups chicken broth (use cubes or canned soup)

Melt butter in a saucepan and add onion and saffron; sauté slowly for a few minutes. Do not brown; add rice and sauté until brown, being careful that rice does not burn. Bring the chicken broth to a boil in the top of a double boiler; add rice mixture and place over boiling water. Steam for an hour, stirring several times. Rice should have absorbed the water and be almost dry. Adjust seasonings. Add paprika if desired, and the necessary salt.

BAKED HAM WITH ORANGE GLAZE

6-pound precooked ham   1½ cups dark brown sugar
1½ cups dark orange marmalade   1 cup orange juice

When purchasing ham, have entire ham sliced into serving portions and tied to hold its original shape while baking. Place in a shallow roasting pan in a 325° oven. Combine the marmalade, sugar and orange juice in a saucepan and heat until sugar and marmalade dissolve. Baste the ham every fifteen minutes with this glaze. Allow twenty minutes per pound for baking of ham.

CHUTNEY ACORN SQUASH

3 acorn squash   Salt to taste
6 teaspoons brown sugar   6 teaspoons chopped chutney

Cut squash in half. Place cut side down in ¼ inch of water in shallow pan and bake one hour in a 400° oven. Upon removing from oven, turn cut side up and sprinkle each half with sugar, salt, and chutney. When ready to serve, dot with butter and place in a 400° oven for ten minutes; or under broiler until heated. To serve: Border baked ham.

Variation: Place three or four slices of cooked sliced apples in the baked squash half and then top with the brown sugar and chutney. Proceed as in first recipe.

GRAPE JUICE MOLD

2 tablespoons unflavored gelatin   3 tablespoons lemon juice
¼ cup cold water   8 peach halves
2 cups boiling water   3 ounces cream cheese
2 6-ounce cans grape juice   1 tablespoon commercial sour
    (frozen)   cream

Soak gelatin in cold water for 5 minutes. Dissolve in boiling water. Add frozen grape juice and stir until dissolved. Add lemon juice. Chill in refrigerator until of jellylike consistency. Pour half of mixture into a 6-cup ring mold. Place peach halves, hollow side up, in the jelly. Fill each peach half with a ball of cream cheese, which has been softened with the sour cream. Pour remaining gelatin over peaches. Place in refrigerator until set. To serve, turn out on salad greens, garnish with fresh fruit in season. Place a bowl of Cream Cheese Fruit Dressing in center of ring. Serves 6 to 8.

CREAM CHEESE FRUIT DRESSING

6 ounces cream cheese   ¼ cup lemon juice
½ cup pineapple juice   Dash of paprika
     Drop of red food coloring

Combine the juices and the cream cheese; add paprika and food coloring. Blend thoroughly.

APRICOT STRUDEL

1 cup butter	1 teaspoon salt
1 cup commercial sour cream	2 cups all-purpose flour

These ingredients make the dough. Mix them all together and chill in refrigerator overnight.

Strudel Filling:

1 pound dried apricots *or*	¼ cup sugar
1 12-ounce can prepared apricot filling	1 cup shredded coconut
	½ pound chopped nuts
½ teaspoon powdered cloves	½ cup maraschino cherries, diced
¼ teaspoon mace	Powdered sugar

Soak apricots overnight in enough water to cover; drain. Put drained fruit through a food mill; add spices. Add the remaining ingredients. Roll out the chilled dough ⅛ inch thick and spread with the filling. Roll jelly-roll fashion and place in shallow pan. Bake in a 350° oven for 45 minutes. Sprinkle with powdered sugar. When cool cut in slices.

BANANA CHOCOLATE LOAF

½ cup butter	4 tablespoons sour cream
1⅔ cups sugar	1 cup mashed banana
2 eggs, slightly beaten	2 cups cake flour, sifted
1½ teaspoon baking powder	¼ teaspoon salt
½ teaspoon baking soda	1 teaspoon vanilla
2 cups chocolate bits	

Cream butter and sugar; add beaten eggs and salt; mix well. Dissolve the baking powder and the baking soda in the sour cream; add to the first mixture. Stir in the banana pulp. Add the flour gradually. Now add the vanilla and the chocolate bits. Pour into a loaf pan, 9½" x 5½" x 2½", bake in a 350° oven for 90 minutes. Freezes well.

Buffet Dinner

Crabmeat in a Skillet   Cheese Puffs
Squab Savannah   Blackberry Tongue
String Bean Casserole   Potato Pudding
Horse-radish Ring
Grapefruit and Orange Slices or Brandied Fruits
Buttermilk Rolls
Fresh Orange Cake Roll   Dutch Chocolate Cake
Coffee

ADVANCE PREPARATION SCHEDULE

Previous Day	Early Morning	Deep Freeze
Boil tongue	*Orange Roll*	*Rolls*
Horse-radish Ring	*Fruit*	*Dutch Chocolate*
Brandied Fruits	*Crabmeat*	*Cake*
Ready squabs	*Stuff squabs*	
	Arrange string beans	

CRABMEAT IN A SKILLET

2 pounds fresh lump crabmeat

Sauce:

1 cup tarragon vinegar   1 tablespoon chopped chives
¾ cup melted butter   1 tablespoon Worcestershire sauce

Blend vinegar, butter, chives, and Worcestershire sauce. Heat.
Add crabmeat. Serve hot in a chafing dish. Serves 12.

CHEESE PUFFS

¼ pound soft butter   8 ounces sharp Cheddar cheese
spread, softened
1½ cups sifted all-purpose flour

Cream the butter and cheese together. Blend in the flour. Roll
dough into small balls and place on an ungreased cooky sheet.

Refrigerate until firm. Bake in a hot oven (400°) for about 20 minutes or until crisp. Serves 12.

SQUAB SAVANNAH

12 plump squabs	Softened butter
½ teaspoon salt, per squab	¾ cup hot bouillon
⅛ teaspoon pepper, per squab	1 cup vermouth
½ cup butter, melted	

Season squabs, inside and out, with salt and pepper; fill with mushroom stuffing. Truss and rub well with softened butter. Place in a shallow pan and roast for 15 minutes in a 400° oven. Reduce the heat to 300°. Combine hot bouillon, vermouth and butter. Baste every 20 minutes with this mixture. Roast one hour or until tender. Garnish with parsley and carrot curls. Serves 12.

MUSHROOM STUFFING

1 medium onion, chopped	1 cup chopped celery
½ cup butter	2 tablespoons parsley
½ pound mushrooms, ground	½ teaspoon poultry seasoning
10 slices toasted bread, cubed	1 teaspoon salt
¼ teaspoon pepper	

Sauté onion until just golden in the butter; add mushrooms and cook 5 minutes. Toss remaining ingredients with the onions and mushrooms. Use as stuffing; do not pack this dressing tightly as it swells. Serves 12.

BLACKBERRY TONGUE

5 pounds whole boiled tongue, fresh, smoked or pickled	1 cup water
½ cup raisins	3 tablespoons lemon juice
	1 cup blackberry jelly

Remove root end and skin of tongue; place in a greased baking pan. Simmer raisins in water for ten minutes; drain, blend with lemon juice and jelly and pour over tongue. Bake uncovered in a 325° oven for 45 minutes. Delicious hot or cold.

To boil tongue: Fresh

1 4- or 5-pound tongue	1 tablespoon mixed spices
2 bay leaves	1½ teaspoons salt

Boil the tongue in salted seasoned water to cover, about 3½ hours or until very tender. Simmer slowly.

Smoked

Cover tongue with cold water. If very salty, pour off the boiling water and re-cover with fresh. Boil about 3½ hours or until tender.

Pickled

Pickled tongue is usually well seasoned. Do not pour off any water. If desired, a clove of garlic and 1 tablespoon mixed spices may be added. Boil about 3½ hours or until very tender.

STRING BEAN CASSEROLE

2 packages frozen French-cut string beans, cooked with seasoning
1 16-ounce can water chestnuts, sliced
1 20-ounce can bean sprouts, washed and crisped in ice, then drained
1 20-ounce can sliced, broiled and buttered (prepared) mushrooms or
1 pound fresh mushrooms, sautéed
1 10-ounce can cream of mushroom soup, not diluted
Herkimer cheese, grated
1 3½-ounce can French-fried onions, slightly broken

Drain canned vegetables well. Place in casserole in 2 layers in order given, using Herkimer cheese topping. Bake 20 minutes at 400° in oven. Sprinkle French-fried onions on top and bake 10 minutes more. Serves 12.

POTATO PUDDING

¼ cup chicken fat or butter	½ teaspoon baking powder
½ cup matzo meal (cracker meal)	4 cups grated, raw potatoes
1 teaspoon salt	2 small onions, grated
4 eggs, beaten	

Mix dry ingredients together. Put potatoes in a tea towel; squeeze to remove excess moisture. Combine all ingredients. Blend well. Drop batter into greased muffin tins and bake at 350° for one hour. This may also be baked in a well-greased casserole for 1½ hours. Serves 6 to 8. Makes 12 muffins.

HORSE-RADISH RING

2 packages lime gelatin	¼ teaspoon paprika
1½ cups boiling water	½ cup horse-radish
2 cups cold water	3 cups sieved cottage cheese
2 teaspoons salt	2 tablespoons mayonnaise

2 teaspoons minced onion

Dissolve gelatin in boiling water. Add cold water. Cool. Add remaining ingredients and beat well with a rotary beater until smooth. Place in refrigerator and when it begins to congeal, pour into moistened 6-cup mold. When firm, unmold on large chilled platter and garnish with sections of orange and grapefruit, sprinkled with pomegranate seeds, or brandied fruits.

HOME-BRANDIED FRUITS

Allow ¼ cup brandy to 1 cup of fruit juice. Pour juice from any canned fruits you may wish to serve. Place in saucepan; add brandy. Bring to a boil. Pour over canned fruit. Let stand overnight before serving.

BUTTERMILK ROLLS

Use prepared rolls, or see Index for Buttermilk Biscuits.

FRESH ORANGE CAKE ROLL

Filling:

1 cup sugar	1 cup orange juice
¼ cup cornstarch	2 tablespoons grated orange rind
½ teaspoon salt	1½ tablespoons lemon juice

2 tablespoons butter

Cake:

1 cup sifted cake flour	3 eggs
1 teaspoon baking powder	1 cup sugar
¼ teaspoon salt	5 tablespoons orange juice

1 teaspoon grated orange rind

To make the filling, mix the ingredients together in a saucepan. Bring to a boil, stirring constantly, and boil hard for a minute. Remove from the heat, cool, then chill.

For the cake, sift flour once and measure; add baking powder and salt and sift again. Beat eggs until thick and light, then gradually beat in the sugar, continuing to beat until all has been added and the mixture is light and lemon-colored. Add orange juice and rind and beat well. Fold in the flour mixture, lightly but thoroughly, and pour into a shallow baking pan, 15½" x 10½" in size. Pan should be greased, lined with wax paper and greased again. Bake in a 375° oven 12 to 15 minutes or until the cake tests done. Loosen the edges immediately and turn upside down on a tea towel sprinkled with confectioners' sugar. Pull off the paper quickly and carefully; roll at once and cool. When cool, unroll and spread with the chilled filling, then reroll. Slice and serve with a topping of slightly sweetened whipped cream.

DUTCH CHOCOLATE CAKE

1 cup shortening	3 cups cake flour
2 cups sugar	½ teaspoon baking soda
3 eggs	1 cup milk
1 cake compressed yeast	1 teaspoon vanilla
¼ cup lukewarm water	2 ounces chocolate, melted

Cream shortening and sugar together with electric mixer until light and fluffy. Add eggs, one at a time, beating well after each addition. Add yeast which has been dissolved in water. Add combined and sifted dry ingredients alternately with milk and vanilla, one third at a time. Beat until smooth after each addition. Add chocolate; beat for 5 minutes. Cover and let rise in warm place for about 2 hours. Spread in three greased and wax paper-lined 9-inch cake pans. Bake in a moderate oven (350°) for 35 minutes. Frost with Chocolate Frosting (see Index).

Buffet Dinner

Golden Gate Ramaki   Stuffed Olives
Seafood Curry Malayan   Fillet of Beef l'Orly
Mushrooms Florentine   Avocado Ring Mold
Dill Bread Sticks
Fresh Pear Pie   Danish Pastry Pinwheels
Coffee

ADVANCE PREPARATION SCHEDULE

Previous Day	Early Morning	Deep Freeze
Avocado Mold	*Ramaki*	*Danish Pastry*
Seafood Curry	*Warm Pear Pie*	*Pinwheels*
	Fruit for garnish	
	Bread Sticks	
	Fillet of Beef	
	Mushrooms	
	Olives	

GOLDEN GATE RAMAKI

½ cup soy sauce   12 water chestnuts, halved
12 chicken livers, halved   1 cup brown sugar
12 bacon slices, halved

Soak livers in soy sauce for 4 hours. Drain, and slit each piece of liver. Insert half chestnut and dip in brown sugar. Wrap a half slice of bacon around each and fasten with a toothpick. Dip again in brown sugar. Place on a jelly-roll pan in a 400° oven and bake 20 to 30 minutes, turning occasionally until evenly brown and crisp.

STUFFED OLIVES

Large ripe, pitted olives   Swiss cheese strips, 1-inch long
Carrot strips, 1-inch long   Pecan halves

Stuff each olive with either carrot, cheese strips or pecans. Arrange on platter with Golden Gate Ramaki.

SEAFOOD CURRY MALAYAN

2 tablespoons butter	3 tablespoons curry powder
1 onion, sliced	(amount may be reduced, if you
4 tablespoons flour	prefer)
2 cups chicken bouillon	Salt to taste
(use cubes or canned)	Freshly ground pepper to taste
3 tablespoons lemon juice	2 cups crabmeat, fresh or frozen
¼ teaspoon ginger	1 cucumber, sliced

2 cups shrimp

Melt butter in a skillet. Add onion and cook over low heat 5
minutes. Blend in flour; add bouillon slowly, stirring constantly,
and cook until smooth and thickened. Stir in lemon juice, ginger,
curry powder, seasonings, crabmeat, cucumber, and shrimp. Heat.
Serve with Rice for Curry.

RICE FOR CURRY

¼ cup butter	1½ cups uncooked rice
2 tablespoons fresh green onion	2 cups hot stock (cubes, canned
1 small clove garlic	consommé or bouillon may be
½ cup cut green pepper (optional)	used)
2 tablespoons finely cut mush-rooms	

Melt butter in saucepan and sauté onions, garlic, green pepper,
and mushrooms 5 minutes. Add uncooked rice which has been
washed in cold water several times, and the stock. Cover and cook
gently for 30 to 45 minutes until the rice is tender and the liquid
is absorbed. See Index for Curry Accompaniments.

FILLET OF BEEF L'ORLY

8-pound fillet of beef	2 tablespoons Worcestershire
½ cup butter	sauce
Salt, pepper, to taste	½ bottle catsup
Garlic salt	½ cup water

Have the fillet at room temperature; do not lard it. Rub well with
butter; season with salt, pepper, garlic salt, and Worcestershire
sauce. Place in a shallow pan and broil under the hottest flame,
about three inches from broiler, for 15 minutes on each side. Set

aside until one hour before serving. Then, roast the beef in a 375° oven for 30 to 45 minutes. Fifteen minutes before fillet is done, remove all the drippings from the roasting pan to a saucepan. Add one-half bottle catsup and one-half cup water. Simmer 5 minutes. Pour this mixture over the fillet and roast for 10 more minutes. Serves 6 to 8.

MUSHROOMS FLORENTINE

1 pound fresh mushrooms
2 packages frozen spinach
1 teaspoon salt
¼ cup chopped onion

¼ cup melted butter
1 cup freshly grated Herkimer or Cheddar cheese
Garlic salt

Wash and dry mushrooms. Slice off stems. Sauté stems and caps until brown, browning cap side of mushroom first. Line a shallow 10-inch casserole (about 1½ inches deep) with the spinach which has been seasoned with the salt, chopped onion, and melted butter. Sprinkle with ½ cup grated cheese. Arrange the sautéed mushrooms, caps and stems, over the spinach. Season with garlic salt. Cover with remaining cheese. Bake for 20 minutes at 350°, or until cheese is melted and browned. This casserole may be prepared in advance and refrigerated until ready for baking. Serves 6 to 8.

AVOCADO RING MOLD

1 package lime-flavored gelatin
1 cup boiling water
1 cup cold water
1 cup mayonnaise
1 teaspoon salt

3 tablespoons lemon juice (1 lemon)
1 cup mashed avocado
1 cup heavy cream, whipped, *or* commercial sour cream

Grapefruit wedges, orange sections, strawberries with stems

Dissolve gelatin in boiling water; add cold water. Refrigerate. When of jellylike consistency, add mayonnaise, salt, lemon juice, and avocado. Fold in whipped or sour cream. Pour into a greased or wet 6-cup ring mold. Refrigerate until firm. Unmold onto a platter of greens, surround with orange and grapefruit sections, and garnish with the strawberries. Center with a bowl of Fruit or Tarragon Mayonnaise (see Index for recipes). Serves 6 to 8.

DILL BREAD STICKS

1 cup oven-toasted rice cereal	2 teaspoons salt
2 tablespoons dill seed	1 package refrigerated biscuits
	2 tablespoons milk

Crush cereal lightly and mix with seeds and salt. Cut biscuits in half and roll each piece into a pencil-thin stick about 4 inches long. Brush with milk and roll in cereal mixture. Place on a greased baking sheet and bake in a 450° oven about 10 minutes or until lightly browned. Makes 20 sticks.

FRESH PEAR PIE

Pastry:

¾ cup homogenized shortening	¼ cup boiling water
1 tablespoon milk	2 cups sifted all-purpose flour
	1 teaspoon salt

Put shortening, milk, and water in mixing bowl; break up with a fork and whip until mixture is smooth and holds soft peaks. Sift flour and salt together into this mixture and stir quickly until dough holds together and leaves side of the bowl. Work gently with hands and shape into a ball. Divide in half; roll one half of the dough between two pieces of wax paper, rolling from center to edges of paper; roll to ⅛-inch thickness. Pull off top wax paper. Center the dough in the pie pan, paper side up; pull off the other piece of paper, and prick the crust with a fork. Prepare the other half of dough for top crust. Sufficient for one 9-inch pie.

Filling:

⅔ cup sugar	⅛ teaspoon salt
3 tablespoons flour	6 cups sliced, fresh pears, pared
½ teaspoon nutmeg	1 teaspoon lemon juice
½ teaspoon cinnamon	1 tablespoon butter

Combine the sugar, flour, nutmeg, cinnamon, and salt; mix with the pears. Add lemon juice and place mixture in pastry-lined pie pan. Dot with butter. Lay top crust over filling; seal edges and flute. Cut slits in top of pie to allow steam to escape during baking. Place in a 425° oven and bake 45 minutes. Serve slightly warm.

DANISH PASTRY PINWHEELS

¼ pound butter or margarine
1 teaspoon active or dry yeast
2 tablespoons warm (not hot) water
¼ cup milk, scalded
3 tablespoons sugar
¼ teaspoon salt
1 egg, beaten

1½ cups sifted all-purpose flour
4 teaspoons shortening
½ teaspoon grated lemon rind
1 cup jam (apricot, raspberry or cherry)
Dash of cinnamon
1 egg white
1 tablespoon cold water

Cut butter into small bits and refrigerate. Sprinkle yeast on warm water and dissolve. Combine scalded milk, sugar, and salt; cool to lukewarm. Add to the yeast, stirring until well blended, and then add egg; mix well. Beat in one-half the flour until smooth. Melt shortening, cool and add to the flour mixture with the lemon rind. Add remaining flour, beating until smooth. Turn onto a lightly floured surface, cover and let rest 15 minutes.

Roll dough into a 15″ x 12″ rectangle. Cover ⅔ of the dough with chilled bits of the butter. Fold uncovered portion over half the buttered portion and fold again making three layers. Roll dough into a 12″ x 8″ rectangle. Fold as before. Repeat rolling and folding twice more. Refrigerate at least one hour. Remove half the dough from refrigerator. Roll into a 12″ x 8″ rectangle. Spread with jam, dust lightly with cinnamon and roll from 8-inch side as for jelly roll. Cut into 1-inch slices. Place on greased cooky sheet and brush with egg white, mixed with water. Repeat with other half of dough. Let rise, covered, in a warm place until doubled in bulk. Bake in a 400° oven for 20 minutes or until done. Yields 20.

Buffet Dinner

Shad Roe Ring — Cucumber Sauce   Cheese Crisps
Chicken Nancie   Harvey Roast — Yorkshire Pudding
Cranberry Molds
French-Fried Cauliflower
Mocha Torte   Strawberry Pie Glacé
Coffee

ADVANCE PREPARATION SCHEDULE

Previous Day	Early Morning	Deep Freeze
Shad Roe Ring	*Cucumber Sauce,*	*Cheese Crisps*
Cranberry Mold	*partial*	*Rolls*
Mocha Torte	*Chicken Nancie*	
	Parboil cauliflower	

SHAD ROE RING

3 pairs shad roe, or 3 cans shad roe
4 egg yolks, beaten
Salt and pepper
Paprika
1 tablespoon butter, melted
½ cup cream
4 egg whites, stiffly beaten

Cucumber Sauce:

1 onion, grated
1 tablespoon chopped parsley
1 tablespoon capers
1 teaspoon salt
¼ teaspoon pepper, freshly ground
2 tablespoons prepared mustard
4 tablespoons mayonnaise
1 tablespoon lemon juice
2 cucumbers, thinly sliced

Skin the shad roe and flake; add beaten egg yolks, seasonings to taste, melted butter, and cream; mix until blended. Fold in the beaten egg whites. Pour into a greased 1½-quart ring mold. Bake in a pan of hot water in a moderate oven (350°) for about 45 minutes, or until a silver knife inserted in the center comes out clean. Serve hot.

To prepare sauce: Blend together all the ingredients, except cucumbers. Add cucumbers just before serving.

CHICKEN NANCIE

Marinade:

1 cup olive oil	1 tablespoon crushed peppercorns
½ cup dry red wine	1 teaspoon crushed tarragon leaves
1 tablespoon cider vinegar	or ginger
1 clove garlic, sliced	

Combine ingredients and blend well.

12 chicken breasts	Half-and-half cream
½ cup butter	Sliced oranges

Allow two chicken breasts apiece. Bone or flatten chicken breasts. Season with salt and pepper. Lay chicken in marinade, skin side down, in shallow casserole or baking dish. Turn once, allowing to marinate ½ hour on each side. Drain on paper. Reserve marinade in dish. Brown chicken on both sides in butter in heavy skillet, very slowly. If more shortening is needed, add 1 tablespoon of oil used in marinade. When brown, return chicken to casserole. Add ½ cup of marinade to skillet and cook it with drippings. Reserve for basting. Add water if too thick. Bake in a 300° to 325° oven for 45 minutes, uncovered. Baste frequently and brush occasionally with marinade. Make gravy of drippings and marinade. Add enough half-and-half cream, stirring constantly, to bind. Serve on sliced oranges.

Note: The preparation may be made in advance and the roasting done in time to serve.

HARVEY ROAST

1 5-pound eye of rib roast	1 large onion, grated
4 teaspoons salt	1 tablespoon Worcestershire
½ teaspoon pepper	sauce
⅛ pound butter	1 tablespoon A-1 Sauce
½ cup chili sauce	

Rub roast well with salt, pepper and butter. Brown quickly on all sides under broiler. Place in roaster, cover with onion. Mix

Worcestershire sauce, A-1 Sauce, and chili sauce. Pour over meat. Dot with butter. Place in a 325° oven. Baste frequently with drippings. Bake 20 minutes to the pound for rare. (Meat should be room temperature before placing in oven.)

Gravy:

½ pound mushrooms	2 tablespoons butter
¼ teaspoon salt	Drippings from pan
2 tablespoons flour	

Wash mushrooms. Place in top of double boiler with salt and butter. Steam for 20 minutes. Mix drippings with flour. Add mushrooms and mushroom liquor, bring to a boil and simmer slowly for three minutes. Pour over meat.

I YORKSHIRE PUDDING

½ cup eggs (about 3)	½ teaspoon salt
1 cup sifted all-purpose flour	1 cup cool milk

Beat eggs one-half minute with electric beater. Combine all ingredients and beat another minute. Meanwhile, place 2 tablespoons butter in a shallow 10" x 6" pan. Set pan in the oven and heat thoroughly. Pour batter into heated pan and replace in a preheated 400° oven. Bake for 30 minutes; lower the heat to 250° and bake 30 minutes more. To serve, tear the pudding in portions (do not cut it) and surround Harvey Roast.

II YORKSHIRE PUDDING

1 cup all-purpose flour, sifted	2 eggs, well beaten
1 teaspoon salt	¼ cup melted shortening or roast
1 tablespoon shortening	drippings
1 cup milk	

Sift flour and salt into bowl of electric mixer; cut in 1 tablespoon shortening and cream well. Add milk and eggs and beat on high speed for 10 minutes. Chill thoroughly in refrigerator. When ready to prepare for serving, place empty popover or muffin tins in oven until very hot. Pour about a teaspoon of shortening in each and fill only half full with batter. Bake in a 425° preheated oven for 30 minutes. Serve at once. Makes 12 puddings.

CRANBERRY MOLDS

2 packages cherry gelatin   1 cup ice and water
1 cup boiling water   1 16-ounce can cranberry sauce
           1 cup commercial sour cream

Dissolve the gelatin in the boiling water; add the ice and water. Refrigerate. When slightly thickened, add the cranberry sauce and sour cream and blend in the blender or beat thoroughly. Pour into individual greased molds. Chill until firm. Unmold. Serve on bed of romaine. Makes 6 individual molds.

FRENCH-FRIED CAULIFLOWER

1 head cauliflower   1 egg, beaten with 1 tablespoon
½ cup bread crumbs   water
           Shortening for frying

Parboil cauliflower for 10 minutes; cool, separate into flowerets. Dip each piece into bread crumbs, then into beaten egg, and then again in bread crumbs. Fry in fat until golden brown. Sprinkle with salt and pepper. Arrange peas in the center of a heated platter and surround with fried cauliflowerets.

REFRIGERATOR MOCHA TORTE

1 4-ounce bar sweet German   ¾ cup butter
   chocolate   ¾ cup powdered sugar
½ cup strong coffee   2 egg whites, stiffly beaten
6 egg yolks   2 cups heavy cream, whipped
           1½ dozen ladyfingers, split

Melt the chocolate in the coffee. Beat the egg yolks, butter, and sugar together; add the chocolate mixture. Fold in the egg whites and whipped cream. Line a greased 9-inch spring form pan with ladyfingers. Pour in mixture. Chill for several hours before serving.

STRAWBERRY PIE GLACE

1 baked pie shell

Bavarian Cream Filling:

2 3-ounce packages cream cheese
4 tablespoons commercial sour
cream
1 quart fresh strawberries

¾ cup water
1 cup sugar
3 tablespoons cornstarch
1 teaspoon lemon juice

Cream the cheese and sour cream together and spread over baked pie shell. Wash strawberries and hull. Measure 1 cup of strawberries, place in saucepan with water, and simmer 5 minutes. Combine sugar and cornstarch; add to cooked fruit. Stir constantly while cooking, until syrup is clear and thick, for about 10 minutes. Add lemon juice and cool. Place remaining uncooked berries in pie shell over cheese. Pour cooked strawberry syrup over fresh berries. Chill.

WATER WHIP PIE CRUST

(For two 9-inch pie crusts or 9 tart shells)

¾ cup vegetable shortening
¼ cup boiling water
1 teaspoon salt

1 tablespoon milk
2 cups sifted all-purpose flour

Place vegetable shortening in mixing bowl and add boiling water and milk. Whip with a fork until smooth. The mixture should resemble whipped cream and stand in soft peaks when lifted with the fork. Sift flour and salt into the shortening and stir quickly into a dough that "cleans" the sides of the bowl. Knead gently until well blended. Divide in two and place one half between two 12-inch sheets of wax paper. (Place paper on a damp surface to keep it from slipping.) Roll dough from center to edge of paper. Pull off paper; center dough on pie plate with the second piece of paper on top. Remove this piece of wax paper and shape dough on pie plate. Make a rim and prick bottom. Similarly prepare second half of dough. Bake 12 to 15 minutes in preheated 450° oven.

Buffet Dinner

Marine Turkey   Crown Roast of Pork with Chestnut Dressing
Potatoes Soufflé
Sauerkraut with Caraway
Apple Compote
Apricot Mousse   Chocolate Chip Kisses
Coffee

ADVANCE PREPARATION SCHEDULE

Previous Day	Early Morning	Deep Freeze
Chestnut Dressing	*Ready roast*	
Sauerkraut	*Prepare potatoes*	
Apricot Mousse	*except for egg*	
Chocolate Chip	*whites*	
cookies		
Apple Compote		

MARINE TURKEY

Sliced breast of turkey

Marine Sauce:

1 quart oysters and their liquor   Juice of ½ lemon
¾ cup claret   ¾ teaspoon salt
¼ teaspoon marjoram   ¼ teaspoon pepper
1 small onion, grated   4 tablespoons butter
⅓ cup bread crumbs

Drain the oysters well. Heat the liquor in a double boiler. Stir
in the claret, marjoram, and onion. Cook until the onion is tender.
Add the lemon juice, salt, pepper, and butter. Mix; add oysters
and crumbs. Cook and stir until the oysters are plump and the
edges curled, 3 to 5 minutes. Do not boil. Keep hot in chafing
dish and serve over hot or cold turkey slices. Serves 8.

CROWN ROAST OF PORK

Crown roast of pork   Chestnut Dressing
Salt and pepper

Have a crown of 10 to 12 ribs made at your market. Season with salt and pepper. Place in a roasting pan, ribs end down. Roast about 2 hours (350°). Turn, ribs end up, on a rack in an open roasting pan and fill crown with dressing. Continue roasting, allowing 40 minutes per pound for over-all roasting time.

Allow roast to set 20 minutes before serving. To serve, place spiced crabapples or frills over the bone ends. Garnish the serving platter with a few sprigs of parsley. For variety, serve the crown roast filled with vegetables. Additional dressing may be baked in a separate greased casserole. Serves 8.

CHESTNUT DRESSING

½ cup chestnuts   Salt and pepper
3 cups soft bread crumbs   2 tablespoons onion, minced
            ½ cup butter, melted

Place chestnuts in cold water and cover. Bring to a boil and cook gently for 5 minutes. Drain, peel, and skin. If meats are not tender enough, drop in hot, salted water and simmer until tender. Chop coarsely. Combine with bread crumbs, seasoning, finely minced onion, and melted butter.

POTATOES SOUFFLE

3 pounds potatoes   6 tablespoons butter
1 teaspoon salt   ¾ cup hot milk
¼ teaspoon pepper   2 egg whites, stiffly beaten
2 egg yolks, beaten   1 teaspoon chopped watercress

Cook potatoes in jackets about 35 minutes, or until done. Drain and peel. Mash thoroughly with masher or in a mixer to remove all lumps; blend in seasonings. Add egg yolks, butter, and enough milk to make potatoes creamy, beating well. Fold in egg whites and watercress. Press lightly into a greased 2-quart casserole; pour melted butter over top. Bake in a 375° oven 30 minutes or until brown. Serves 8.

SAUERKRAUT WITH CARAWAY

¼ cup shortening
¼ cup flour
1 cup sauerkraut juice
2 28-ounce cans sauerkraut, drained
1 20-ounce can tomatoes
4 cups liquid (sauerkraut juice and water)

1 tablespoon caraway
2 tablespoons barley
1 onion, quartered
2 tablespoons brown sugar
½ teaspoon monosodium glutamate

Melt shortening, add flour, and brown slightly. Stir in sauerkraut juice until smooth. Cook 5 minutes. Add remaining ingredients. Cover and simmer 1½ hours. Serves 8.

APPLE COMPOTE

8 tart apples
⅔ cup sugar
1 cup water
Juice of 1 lemon

Peel, core, and cut apples into eighths. Combine sugar, water, and lemon juice and boil for about 5 minutes. Add apples to syrup and poach slowly until clear, but not mushy. Remove apples to serving bowl. Boil remaining syrup until thickened and pour over apples. Cool and refrigerate.

Variation: Add ½ cup currant or apricot jelly to syrup before pouring it over the cooked apples.

APRICOT MOUSSE

1 28-ounce can apricots
Water
1 package lemon-flavored gelatin
½ cup vanilla wafers, crumbled
1 tablespoon apricot brandy or Cointreau
1 cup cream, whipped

Drain apricots, purée them in food mill or through a strainer. Add sufficient water to juice to make 1¾ cups of liquid and heat to boiling. Add gelatin and stir until dissolved. Cool, add puréed apricots and brandy and place in refrigerator until of jellylike consistency. Remove, beat slightly with a rotary beater. Fold in whipped cream. Pour one-half of mixture into an 8″ x 8″ x 2″ square pan. Sprinkle crumbs over mousse and then pour in the remainder. Refrigerate until firm. Cut in squares to serve. Decorate with additional whipped cream and nuts or shredded coconut. Serves 8.

CHOCOLATE CHIP KISSES

2 egg whites, room temperature
⅛ teaspoon salt
¼ teaspoon cream of tartar
¾ cup sugar

1 8-ounce package semisweet
  chocolate pieces
1 teaspoon vanilla
½ cup chopped nut meats

Beat egg whites with salt until frothy; add cream of tartar and beat until stiff. Add sugar about one tablespoon at a time, beating after each addition, and continue beating until mixture stands in stiff peaks. Fold in remaining ingredients. Drop by teaspoons onto brown-paper-lined, well-buttered cooky sheet. Bake in slow oven (300°) for 25 minutes.

Buffet Dinner

Mushroom-Liver Casserole — Toast Points   Relishes
Oven-Fried Chicken   Shrimp or Lobster Louisville
Noodles Romanoff   White Rice
Baked Broccoli   Broiled Tomatoes
Parker House Rolls
Cherry Mold   Stuffed Prunes or Bing Cherries
Blender Mayonnaise
Vanilla Ice Cream   Baba au Rhum — Pineapple Rum Sauce
Coffee

ADVANCE PREPARATION SCHEDULE

Previous Day	Early Morning	Deep Freeze
Mushroom Liver Casserole	*Coat and refrigerate chickens*	*Baba au Rhum Parker House Rolls*
Shrimp Louisville	*Pineapple Cream*	
Cherry Mold	*Pears*	
Baba au Rhum (may be frozen)		

MUSHROOM-LIVER CASSEROLE

1 pound chicken gizzards diced
½ cup butter
14-ounce bottle of catsup
2 pounds chicken livers

2 large onions, finely chopped
1 pound mushrooms, sliced
2 teaspoons Worcestershire sauce
Salt and pepper

Brown gizzards in 2 tablespoons butter; add catsup and cook until tender, about ½ hour. Sauté chicken livers and chopped onion in 2 tablespoons butter and cook about 10 minutes, tossing until tender. Sauté mushrooms in 4 tablespoons butter for about 5 minutes. Mix all three together, add Worcestershire sauce and season to taste. Serve in a chafing dish. Serves 8.

OVEN-FRIED CHICKEN

3 fryers, disjointed
1½ teaspoons salt
½ teaspoon pepper

½ teaspoon seasoning salt
¾ cup melted butter
3 cups crushed corn flakes

Season chicken pieces with salt, pepper, and seasoning salt. Dip in melted butter and then into cornflakes. Place on greased shallow baking pan, skin side up. Bake for 30 minutes in a 350° oven, then baste with additional butter. Reduce the heat to 250° and bake for 1 hour longer. Cook the necks and giblets in seasoned water to cover until tender. Remove the meat from bones and chop fine. Combine with pan drippings and serve separately. If too thick, add stock from the giblets. Serves 8.

SHRIMP OR LOBSTER LOUISVILLE

¼ cup butter
1 clove garlic, quartered (optional)
4 teaspoons chopped parsley
1 No. 2½ can tomatoes (3½ cups)
¼ cup flour
½ cup cream

2 tablespoons Worcestershire sauce
½ cup sherry
Dash of Angostura Bitters (optional)
4 cups shrimp or lobster, cooked
1 pound mushrooms, sautéed
Salt and pepper

Melt two tablespoons butter, add garlic and cook slowly until garlic is golden brown. Remove garlic. Add parsley and 3 cups tomatoes to garlic butter and cook for 5 minutes. Mix flour with remaining tomatoes, forming a smooth paste, add and cook 2 minutes longer. Add cream, mixing well, then Worcestershire sauce, sherry, and bitters. Blend; cook 5 minutes and add to mixture with shrimp or lobster and mushrooms; add salt and pepper to taste. Pour into 2-quart casserole and sprinkle with bread crumbs; dot with butter. Bake 20 minutes in a 375° oven. Serve with Fluffy Rice (see page 225). Serves 8.

NOODLES ROMANOFF

2 8-ounce packages fine noodles
2 8-ounce packages cream cheese
2 cups commercial sour cream
¼ cup minced onion

1 teaspoon Worcestershire sauce
½ teaspoon garlic salt
Dash of Tabasco
1 teaspoon salt

½ cup buttered bread crumbs

Cook noodles according to package directions; drain. Combine cream cheese, sour cream, onion, and seasonings, and stir into cooked noodles. Turn into greased 2-quart casserole. Top with bread crumbs. Bake in a moderate oven (350°) for about 25 minutes. Serve hot or cold. Serves 8 to 10.

BAKED BROCCOLI

½ pound mushrooms, sliced (optional)
¼ cup butter
¼ cup flour
1 teaspoon salt

3 10-ounce packages frozen broccoli spears
1 8-ounce can tomato paste
1 chicken bouillon cube

2 tablespoons grated Cheddar cheese

Sauté mushrooms in butter about 5 minutes. Blend in flour and salt. Cook broccoli until about half done; drain and save liquids. Mix tomato paste with 2 cans of the broccoli liquid and gradually blend into the butter and flour mixture, stirring constantly and cooking until smooth and thickened. Add bouillon cube and stir until dissolved. Stir in cheese. Place broccoli spears in large, greased baking dish; cover with the sauce. Bake in a moderate oven (350°) for about 30 minutes. Serves 8.

BROILED TOMATOES

4 medium-sized tomatoes
1 teaspoon prepared mustard
¼ cup bread crumbs
1 tablespoon minced onion

¼ teaspoon salt
¼ teaspoon curry powder (optional)

Wash, but do not peel tomatoes. Cut crosswise into halves. Place cut side up in shallow baking pan. Spread first with mustard and then with combined crumbs, onion, and seasoning. Broil 15 minutes or until nicely browned. Border chicken platter.

CHERRY MOLD

2 packages black-cherry-flavored gelatin
2 cups boiling water

Juice of drained cherries
½ cup port wine
½ cup chopped walnuts

1 28-ounce can pitted Bing cherries, drained

Dissolve gelatin in boiling water. Add sufficient water to cherry juice to make one cup. Combine with wine and add to dissolved gelatin. Refrigerate until consistency of jelly; add cherries and nuts and pour into a wet 1½-quart mold. Chill until set; turn out onto serving plate and garnish with lemon leaves. Serve with Blender Mayonnaise, border with pears. Serves 8.
Variation: Cut honeydew melon in slices with a French cutter. Form six sections of fruit around mold, making one of honeydew slices, one of grapefruit sections, one of French endive, thin orange slices, strawberries, and stuffed prunes. Garnish with watercress.

BLENDER MAYONNAISE

1 egg
½ teaspoon dry mustard
1 teaspoon salt

2 tablespoons lemon juice
¼ cup salad oil
¾ cup commercial sour cream

Combine first five ingredients and beat thoroughly in blender. Fold in sour cream.

STUFFED PRUNES OR BING CHERRIES

1 pound large prunes, pitted, or
1½ cups Bing cherries, pitted

1 3-ounce package cream cheese
1 tablespoon cream

Wash prunes. Cover with cold water and let stand overnight.

Drain. Remove pits. Soften the cream cheese with the cream. Fill the cavity in the prune with ½ teaspoon cream cheese mixture. Chopped nuts may be added to the cream cheese. Cherries are filled the same way, but with about ¼ teaspoon cheese. Serves 6 to 8.

BABA AU RHUM

½ cup scalded milk	1 whole egg
1 cake compressed yeast	¼ cup sweet butter, melted
2 egg yolks, well beaten	1 teaspoon vanilla
¼ cup sugar	2 cups sifted all-purpose flour
¼ cup white raisins	

Cool milk to lukewarm, add yeast and dissolve; mix until spongy. Beat sugar gradually into thick egg yolks and then beat in whole egg vigorously. Add butter and vanilla and stir in the yeast mixture. Beat in the flour, enough to make a medium batter, and add raisins. Place in a warm spot away from drafts and let rise until doubled in bulk, about 3 to 3½ hours. Butter a 6-cup ring mold and fill one-half full. Let rise again until doubled in bulk. Bake in a 400° oven for 20 minutes; reduce the heat to 350° and bake 10 minutes more. Remove from pan and place on platter. Pour Rum Syrup over Baba and replace in mold to soak. Pour all of syrup over and refrigerate several hours. To serve, unmold and fill center with ice cream and fruit, or Fruit Cream Sauce. Serves 8.

Rum Syrup:
Boil ½ cup sugar and ¾ cup pineapple juice together for 10 minutes. Add 1 tablespoon lemon juice and ¼ cup rum and pour over Baba while still hot.

Fruit Cream Sauce:

1 3¼-ounce package instant vanilla pudding mix	1 cup heavy cream, whipped
1 cup milk	2¼ cups crushed pineapple, drained (1 No. 2 can)
2 tablespoons rum	

Add milk to pudding mix and stir in rum. As it begins to set, fold in cream and then pineapple. Refrigerate until ready to serve. Place in center of Baba.
Variation: Prepare the Baba with your favorite pound-cake mix, or split a large cake in half, using two layers with the fruit cream in between.

Buffet Dinner

Carrot Sticks, Celery and Olives in Bowl of Cracked Ice
Shrimp Louisiane   Chicken Livers in Foil
Sirloin Tip Roast   Chicken Beaucaire
Noodle Spinach Ring
Steamed Fresh Mushrooms
Salad Bohême   Spiced French Dressing
Profiterolles au Chocolat   Loganberry Torte
Coffee

ADVANCE PREPARATION SCHEDULE

Previous Day	Early Morning	Deep Freeze
Shrimp Louisiane	*Noodle Ring*	*Profiterolles*
Chicken Beaucaire	*Carrot Sticks, etc.*	*Dinner Rolls*
Loganberry Torte	*Chicken livers ready*	
Profiterolle puffs	*to cook*	
(may be frozen)	*Fill Profiterolles*	

SHRIMP LOUISIANE

2 pounds shrimp   2 onions, thinly sliced

Marinade:

1 cup salad oil	3 bay leaves
1 cup vinegar	2 tablespoons Worcestershire
¼ cup sugar	sauce
¼ cup water	1 lemon sliced
½ teaspoon whole pepper	1½ tablespoons lemon juice
1 teaspoon salt	¼ teaspoon garlic salt (optional)
¼ teaspoon mustard	

Mix all marinade ingredients together. Place shrimp (cooked) and onions in alternate layers in covered container. Pour marinade over all. Refrigerate and allow it to stand at least 24 hours. Will keep several days. Serves 8.

CHICKEN LIVERS IN FOIL

1½ pounds large chicken livers,   ¼ cup melted butter
cut in half   1 teaspoon salt
           ½ cup butter-cracker crumbs

Dip livers in butter, then roll in crumbs mixed with salt. Separate pieces and place in jelly-roll pan. Cover tightly with foil. Bake in a 350° oven for 15 minutes. Then uncover and bake 10 minutes more. Serve immediately. Serves 8.

SIRLOIN TIP ROAST

8-pound sirloin tip roast   2 tablespoons A-1 Sauce
2 teaspoons seasoning salt   ⅛ pound butter

Have roast at room temperature. Season roast with salt, A-1 Sauce, and dot with butter. Place in a 325° oven and roast uncovered 20 minutes to the pound for rare, 22 minutes for medium, and 27 minutes for well-done meat.

Gravy:
Remove the meat to a warm platter. To the drippings in the pan, add 1½ tablespoons flour mixed with ¾ cup consommé. Season with 1 tablespoon Worcestershire sauce, 1 teaspoon prepared gravy flavoring, and 1 small grated onion. Cook gently for 5 minutes.

CHICKEN BEAUCAIRE

1 large roasting chicken, plus 4
   breasts
Juice of 1 lime
Seasoned flour
½ cup butter or shortening
1 clove garlic, minced
¼ cup chopped parsley
½ teaspoon rosemary seasoning
   powder

1 stalk celery, coarsely chopped
4 medium-sized carrots
6 small, white onions
½ cup dry, white wine
2 10-ounce cans cream of mushroom soup, undiluted
¼ teaspoon freshly ground pepper
   (optional)
Paprika

Disjoint chicken. Have legs separated from thighs, and breasts halved. Brush the pieces with lime juice, and shake in a bag of seasoned flour. Sauté in a heavy skillet in the butter until they are a golden brown (about 20 minutes). Next, place a layer of chicken pieces in a casserole, sprinkle with salt, garlic, parsley, and rosemary powder. Add a second layer of chicken pieces and repeat the seasoning. Then sprinkle over the chicken the stalk of celery, chopped; cover with the carrots, sliced in half, lengthwise, and the little white onions. In the skillet in which the chicken was sautéed, pour the dry white wine (increase wine to ¾ cup if desired) and blend it well with the butter remaining in the pan. Add the cream of mushroom soup and blend again. Pour this mixture over the contents of the casserole, sprinkle the top lightly with freshly ground pepper and paprika; put into a moderate oven (300°) and bake until tender, 1½ to 2 hours. Serve from casserole. May be prepared in advance and reheated. Serves 8.

Seasoned flour:

½ cup flour	½ teaspoon salt
1 teaspoon paprika	¼ teaspoon pepper

NOODLE SPINACH RING

1 8-ounce package broad noodles	½ cup butter
2 10-ounce packages chopped, de-	1 onion
frosted spinach, drained	3 eggs, slightly beaten
1 cup commercial sour cream	

Cook noodles in salted water until barely tender and drain; mix noodles and spinach. Sauté onion in butter until slightly browned. Fold in eggs; add sour cream and blend well. Pour into a greased 6-cup ring mold. Place mold in pan of hot water in a 350° oven for 45 minutes. Unmold. Serve on heated platter with steamed mushrooms in the center. Serves 8.

STEAMED FRESH MUSHROOMS

1 pound fresh mushrooms	2 tablespoons butter
¼ teaspoon salt	

Wash, brush, and drain mushrooms. Cut thin slices from stem. Place whole in double boiler, dot with butter and season. Steam 20 minutes. With this method, the mushrooms will be plump and the remaining butter and juice from the mushrooms improves the sauce or gravy to which the mushrooms are added.

SALAD BOHEME

1 large bunch watercress
1 celery cabbage, thinly sliced
1 cucumber, sliced
4 hard-cooked eggs
4 small sliced beets, cooked fresh
  or canned

1 tablespoon chives
½ teaspoon marjoram
6 chopped anchovy fillets
Spiced French Dressing

Line a bowl with watercress. Place in layers, first, the celery cabbage, then slices of cucumber; next, slices of eggs and beets; sprinkle with herbs and top with anchovies. To serve, pour dressing over all.

SPICED FRENCH DRESSING

1 cup basic French Dressing
½ cup chili sauce
½ green pepper, sliced

1 slice of onion
½ teaspoon oregano
½ teaspoon garlic powder

Place all ingredients into a blender. Whirl one minute. May be prepared in advance.

PROFITEROLLES AU CHOCOLAT

½ cup sifted all-purpose flour
¼ cup butter
½ cup boiling water

2 eggs
Cocoa Whipped Cream
Fudge Sauce

Sift flour, measure. Add butter to water in saucepan and bring to a boil. Reduce heat; add flour all at once, stirring rapidly. Cook and stir about 2 minutes until mixture thickens and leaves sides of pan. Remove from heat. Add eggs, one at a time, beating well after each addition. Then beat until mixture is satiny and breaks off when a spoon is raised. Use a pastry bag with ⅜-inch opening or drop mixture from a teaspoon onto an ungreased cooky sheet, shaping into 1-inch mounds. Bake 20 minutes in a 425° oven until golden brown. When cool, cut off tops, fill with Cocoa Whipped Cream and replace tops. Use 4 or 5 puffs for each serving and serve with hot Fudge Sauce.

Cocoa Whipped Cream:

1 cup whipping cream	4 tablespoons confectioners' sugar
2 tablespoons cocoa	⅛ teaspoon salt
1 teaspoon vanilla	

Combine in small bowl. Chill one hour, then beat until cream holds its shape. Do not overbeat.

Fudge Sauce:

Melt 3 squares unsweetened chocolate and 5 tablespoons butter in a saucepan. Remove from heat. Add 3 cups sifted confectioners' sugar alternately with 1 cup undiluted evaporated milk; blend well after each addition. Bring to a boil over medium heat, stirring constantly. Cook and stir until mixture becomes thick and creamy, about 8 minutes. Stir in 1 teaspoon vanilla. Serve warm. Serves 8.

LOGANBERRY TORTE

3 cups loganberries or boysenberries	1 cup heavy cream, whipped
1 package cherry gelatin	1 package 12-egg angel food cake mix
1 cup heavy cream, whipped, for frosting	

Make cake according to the directions on the package. Let cool. Drain loganberries. Add sufficient water to juice to make 1¾ cups liquid. Bring one half to a boil. Dissolve gelatin and add remaining cold liquid. Set in refrigerator until it begins to congeal and is of a syrupy consistency. Set in ice-cold beater bowl with cold beaters, and whip to texture of whipped cream, preferably in electric mixer. Fold in drained loganberries and then whipped cream. In the meantime, cut off the top of the cake to a depth of one inch. Hollow the cake, removing inside, leaving a cake shell about one inch thick. Place a piece of cake over hole at bottom, left by tube of pan. Fill with loganberry mixture. Replace top of cake. Cut a four-inch strip of foil or waxed paper, and fasten it firmly around the cake to keep it from bulging. Place in the refrigerator for several hours. Frost with whipped cream and decorate with fresh berries, or flowers cut from maraschino cherries. Serves 8 generously.

Buffet Dinner

Rock Lobster Gourmet
Asparagus Sandwiches
Spiced Chicken   Brisket Arcadia
Cauliflower Polonaise   Glazed Beets
Applesauce Noodle Pudding
Fritzel Salad
Orange Sherbet — Mandarin Orange Sauce
Lace Cookies   Pecan Slices
Coffee

ADVANCE PREPARATION SCHEDULE

Previous Day	Early Morning	Deep Freeze
Lobster Gourmet	*Refrigerate sandwiches*	*Sherbet*
Gourmet Sauce	*Refrigerate salad*	*Dinner Rolls*
Marinate chicken	*Crisp cauliflower*	*Lace Cookies*
Brisket Arcadia	*Cook chicken*	*Pecan Slices*
Glazed Beets		
Prepare noodles for		
baking		
Orange Sauce		

ROCK LOBSTER GOURMET

4 rock lobster tails

Dressing:

6 ounces cream cheese	1 cup pimento-stuffed olives,
1 cup commercial sour cream	chopped
½ teaspoon garlic salt	1 tablespoon vinegar
2 teaspoons Worcestershire sauce	Dash of Tabasco

Drop frozen lobster tails into boiling, salted water. When water reboils, cook tails 3 minutes more than the weight of the largest tail in ounces. For example, if largest tail weighs 5 ounces, cook eight minutes. Thawed tails need only one minute more than the count by ounces. Drench with cold water and cut down both sides of the undershell with kitchen scissors. Remove meat from shell.

It may be removed in one piece by inserting thumb between meat and shell and gently pulling meat away from shell. Chill. Cut into thin round slices.

Dressing: Cream the cheese and beat in the sour cream. Add salt, Worcestershire sauce, Tabasco, olives, and vinegar. Add more vinegar, if needed. Arrange lobster slices in overlapping circles on greens, on a chilled plate around a bowl of dressing. Serves 8.

ASPARAGUS SANDWICHES

Drain a can of white asparagus. Trim slices of thin white bread and flatten with rolling pin. Spread with mayonnaise or Mock Hollandaise (see Index for recipe). Roll each stalk of asparagus in bread. Place sandwiches close together on cooky sheet. Refrigerate. Remove to serve.

SPICED CHICKEN

3 frying chickens, cut into serving
  pieces
½ cup sherry
2 teaspoons cinnamon

⅓ cup honey
2 tablespoons lemon juice
½ teaspoon curry powder
1 garlic bud, minced *or*
1 teaspoon garlic salt

Place chicken pieces in a bowl. Blend remaining ingredients together and pour over the chicken pieces, turning pieces so that they are well coated. Refrigerate several hours or overnight. Drain and reserve marinade. Place in a 350° oven; bake one hour or until tender, basting every 15 minutes with remaining sauce. If sauce thickens, it may be thinned with a little additional wine. Add sufficient liquid so that enough remains to serve with chicken. Serves 8.

BRISKET ARCADIA

6 pounds brisket of beef	5 white potatoes, halved
2 teaspoons salt	2 pounds prunes, extra large
1 teaspoon pepper	1 cup dark corn syrup
4 sweet potatoes, halved	

Season meat as for roasting; place in a large stewing kettle so that meat lies flat. Cover with water about 3 inches above the meat. Bring to a boil and cover; simmer for ½ hour. Add syrup, prunes, and white potatoes. Again, bring to a boil and cover; simmer for three hours. Skim fat, if desired. Add sweet potatoes; cover and again simmer for three more hours until meat is tender. Be certain that meat is always covered with liquid, and if necessary, add more water. Do NOT STIR. Only shake the pot from side to side to be certain that meat is not sticking. The meat and potatoes should all be a luscious red-brown when prepared. To serve, surround brisket with the prunes and potatoes. This dish may be prepared the day before and reheated when ready to serve. Serves 8.

CAULIFLOWER POLONAISE

1 large head cauliflower, cooked whole	½ teaspoon lemon juice
4 tablespoons butter	2 tablespoons minced parsley
2 tablespoons fine bread crumbs	¼ teaspoon salt
	⅛ teaspoon pepper
2 chopped, hard-cooked eggs	

Heat butter gently until brown; add crumbs and stir until brown. Add combined juice, parsley, salt and pepper; heat and pour over freshly cooked and drained cauliflower. Sprinkle with chopped egg.

GLAZED BEETS

2 No. 2 cans tiny whole beets (4 cups)	½ cup brown sugar
	¼ cup lemon juice
4 tablespoons butter	

Melt butter, add sugar and lemon juice, and simmer until sugar is dissolved. Add beets and stir until coated. Cook until sauce becomes syrupy and beets become glazed. May be prepared in advance. To serve: Reheat and pour sauce over beets. Serves 8 to 10.

APPLESAUCE NOODLE PUDDING

1 8-ounce package noodles	1 cup or 1 No. 1 can applesauce
½ pound cottage cheese	3 eggs, well beaten
1 cup commercial sour cream	1 teaspoon salt
¼ cup butter	

Cook the noodles according to the directions on the package; drain and rinse in cold water. Combine with remaining ingredients. Bake in a 350° oven for one hour in a greased casserole. Raise the heat to 400° the last 15 minutes so that pudding is crisp and brown.

Variation: Use drained, crushed pineapple instead of applesauce. Serves 6 to 8.

FRITZEL SALAD

12 heads Kentucky Limestone lettuce	2 avocados, sliced
1 16-ounce can artichokes (split into 4 parts)	1 20-ounce can hearts of palm, quartered
	4 hard-cooked eggs, sliced

Arrange in salad bowl.

Dressing:

Rub bowl with garlic	¼ teaspoon freshly ground pepper
¾ cup olive oil	½ cup wine vinegar
1 teaspoon salt	½ teaspoon prepared mustard

Mix ingredients thoroughly. Pour over salad; toss lightly.

ORANGE SHERBET — MANDARIN ORANGE SAUCE

3 11-ounce cans mandarin oranges	½ cup Curaçao
Same amount sugar as juice	2 quarts orange sherbet

Drain oranges. Measure juice and pour into a saucepan; add an equal amount of sugar to juice. Add Curaçao and simmer for 5 minutes. Pour over the oranges and let stand overnight in the refrigerator. Scoop sherbet into 12 balls; place in freezer. When

ready to serve, pour sauce over sherbet and serve either individually in dessert dishes or from a large bowl at the table.
Serves 8 to 12.

LACE COOKIES

⅔ cup almonds   ½ cup sugar
½ cup butter   1 tablespoon all-purpose flour
Dash of salt   2 tablespoons milk

Grind almonds. Melt butter in a skillet. Add remaining ingredients except milk, and stir over flame until sugar melts. Add
milk and blend. Drop from a teaspoon on greased and floured
cooky sheet. Bake in a 350° oven for about 10 minutes.

PECAN SLICES

4 eggs   1½ cups all-purpose flour, sifted
1 pound brown sugar   ¼ pound butter
1 cup pecan nuts, coarsely chopped

Beat together until very light the eggs, brown sugar, and flour.
Butter a large jelly-roll pan very heavily; cover with chopped
pecans. Spread the egg mixture over the nuts. Bake in a 350°
oven for 20 minutes. Frost while still warm. Cut into strips
when cool.

Frosting:

½ cup powdered sugar   ½ teaspoon softened butter
2 teaspoons lemon juice

Combine ingredients.

Buffet Dinner

Seafood Ravigote in Shells   Blue Cheese Puffs
Caneton Cerise   Chinese Beef Tenderloin
Wild Rice Ring
Carrots Vichy   Sautéed Mushrooms
Frozen Mint Soufflé
Seasonal Fruits   Norwegian Torte
Coffee

ADVANCE PREPARATION SCHEDULE

Previous Day	Early Morning	Deep Freeze
Shrimp	*Assemble beef*	*Cheese Puffs*
Sauce for shrimp	*tenderloin*	
Ready ducks	*ingredients*	
Rice Ring		

SEAFOOD RAVIGOTE IN SHELLS

2 pounds shrimp   1 cup dry sherry

Boil and clean shrimp. Marinate shrimp in sherry for 1 hour. Refrigerate.

Sauce:

2 eggs, hard-cooked	2 teaspoons lemon juice
½ cup catsup	1 teaspoon Worcestershire sauce
1 tablespoon pickle relish	½ cup mayonnaise (prepared)
1 tablespoon chopped parsley	½ cup commercial sour cream
	Salt and pepper

Rice egg yolks and white separately; reserve for decoration. Combine remaining ingredients. Drain shrimp and add. Serve in individual shells or in a lettuce-lined bowl. Sprinkle riced egg yolks over all, border with riced whites. Garnish with rolled anchovies and serve with additional mayonnaise.

BLUE CHEESE PUFFS

½ cup butter
1 cup cake flour
2 ounces blue cheese
2 ounces Herkimer cheese, grated

2 egg whites
Paprika
Caraway seeds *or*
   sesame seeds

Mix all ingredients thoroughly; roll into cylinder 1½ inches in diameter. Wrap in wax paper. Chill. Cut into thin slices; brush with egg white mixed with paprika, caraway or sesame seeds. Bake in a 450° oven for 10 minutes.

CANETON CERISE

2 5½-pound ducks
½ cup salad oil
Orange sauce

Brown sauce, equal in volume to
   orange sauce
1 28-ounce can pitted Bing cherries

Orange sauce:
1 navel orange (a) grated rind
           (b) peeling
           (c) juice and pulp

2 cups water
1 cup sugar
4 ounces currant jelly

Wipe ducks with damp cloth. Brush well with salad oil. Truss. Bake in a 325° oven for one hour. Pour off fat, raise temperature to 400° and bake an additional hour or until tender. Meanwhile, prepare sauce. Combine orange peel, rind, water, and sugar. Bring to a boil and add juice and pulp; bring to a boil again and add currant jelly. Cook until mixture coats the spoon. Strain and measure. Combine it with the same quantity of brown sauce. Bring to a boil and simmer until of syruplike consistency. Add cherries and reheat. Quarter the ducks and arrange them in a shallow casserole. Cover with the sauce and place in a 250° oven to marinate and to remain hot until served. Extra sauce may be prepared to serve separately, if desired. Serves 6 to 8.

Note: For Brown sauce, see Index for Sherry Brown Sauce.

CHINESE BEEF TENDERLOIN

5 tablespoons salad oil
3 pounds beef tenderloin, sliced thin
1 cup coarsely chopped onion
1 cup green pepper, coarsely chopped
2 6-ounce cans whole mushrooms, or 1½ pounds sautéed fresh
4 tablespoons cornstarch

½ cup water
2 garlic cloves, minced (optional)
1½ cups water chestnuts, thinly sliced
2 cups Chinese pea pods
1 quart beef broth
½ cup soy sauce
2 tablespoons bead molasses

1 tablespoon monosodium glutamate

Heat the oil over a high flame in a Dutch oven until it sizzles. Add the tenderloin. Cook 2 minutes, turning frequently. Add the onion, green pepper, and mushrooms. Cook for 3 minutes more. Blend the cornstarch and water. Add this and the remaining ingredients to the meat. Lower flame and simmer for 10 minutes. Do not overcook.

WILD RICE RING

1 cup raw wild rice or 1 No. 2 can prepared
1 teaspoon salt

4 cups water
1 pound mushrooms
¼ cup butter

Wash the raw rice very thoroughly; boil in salted water about 45 minutes, or until tender; drain. Grind or chop mushrooms and sauté in butter for 5 minutes. Blend with the rice. Pour into a buttered 4-cup mold. Set in a pan of hot water and bake 30 minutes in a 350° oven. Turn out on a platter and center with Sautéed Mushrooms and border with Carrots Vichy.

Note: Use stems from Sautéed Mushrooms with stems from Rice Ring recipe and save all the caps for center of ring.

Variation: Center the rice ring with almost any small vegetable such as peas, small beets or corn off the cob.

CARROTS VICHY

2 20-ounce cans tiny cooked carrots
¼ cup butter

White pepper
¼ cup parsley

Drain carrots and place them in saucepan with melted butter. Simmer until carrots are completely coated; sprinkle with white pepper and then the parsley. Serve hot. Border Rice Ring.

SAUTEED MUSHROOMS

1 pound mushrooms	1 teaspoon lemon juice
¼ cup butter	½ teaspoon salt
2 tablespoons minced onion	Freshly ground pepper

Scrub mushrooms and remove ends of stems. Melt butter in saucepan, add minced onion and sauté lightly. Add mushrooms, cover and sauté 12 minutes. Shake the pan occasionally to stir. Turn off heat let stand in pan about 5 minutes to absorb juices, salt and pepper. Stir. Serve in center of Rice Ring.

FROZEN MINT SOUFFLE

2 packages lime-flavored gelatin	1 cup cold water
2 cups hot water	3 or 4 drops oil of peppermint
Unhulled strawberries, watermelon balls in season	

Dissolve gelatin in hot water. Add cold water and the peppermint to taste. Set in refrigerator until it becomes of jellylike consistency. Beat with chilled beaters in ice-cold bowl until frothy and thick. Pour into a melon mold or other 6-cup greased mold and chill firm. Garnish with sprigs of fresh mint, strawberries, and melon balls.

NORWEGIAN TORTE

2 cups double strength coffee	2 eggs, unbeaten
1 cup sugar	2 cups sifted all-purpose flour
2 tablespoons cocoa	½ teaspoon soda
1 cup seedless raisins, chopped coarsely	2 teaspoons baking powder
½ cup shortening	½ teaspoon salt
1 cup sugar	1 teaspoon cinnamon
½ teaspoon vanilla	1 teaspoon nutmeg
	½ teaspoon ground cloves

Combine coffee, one cup sugar, cocoa, and raisins in a saucepan. Bring to a boil and simmer for 15 minutes. Cool. Cream shortening and add sugar gradually, creaming until light and fluffy. Add vanilla, then eggs, one at a time, beating well after each one. Mix and sift remaining ingredients and add alternately with the coffee mixture. Bake in a greased, 10″ x 10″ x 2″ pan in a 350° oven for 1 hour. When cool, place paper doily on top, dust with confectioners' sugar and then lift doily carefully from cake so as to leave pattern. Cut in squares to serve.

May be made in two 9-inch layers with a layer of whipped cream between them; or, if you need only one layer, freeze the other.

Buffet Dinner

Coquilles St. Jacques   Blinis and Caviar
Glazed Corned Beef
Cornish Hens à la Bourbon — Wild Rice Dressing
Squash Ring
Peas and Chestnuts   Green Beans Epicure
Apricot Horns   Blitz Torte
Coffee

ADVANCE PREPARATION SCHEDULE

Previous Day	Early Morning	Deep Freeze
Coquilles St. Jacques	*Prepare and stack*	
Cook Corned Beef	*Blinis*	
Blitz Torte	*Stuff Cornish hens*	
Squash Ring	*Green Beans Epicure*	

COQUILLES ST. JACQUES

2 pounds scallops	4 tablespoons butter
1 sprig parsley	1 tablespoon minced onion
3 carrots	½ pound fresh mushrooms
2 cups white wine	4 tablespoons flour
¼ teaspoon paprika	4 tablespoons cream
1 teaspoon salt	Additional salt and pepper

Wash and drain scallops; place in a saucepan with parsley, carrots, wine, and seasonings. Simmer for 10 minutes. Remove scallops, drain and dice; reserve the broth. Melt the 4 tablespoons butter in a saucepan; add mushrooms and onion, and sauté for 5 minutes. Add reserved broth. Make a paste of the flour and cream, and add to the mushroom mixture. Cook 10 minutes until thick and smooth. Add scallops and additional seasoning to taste.

Place into eight scallop shells. Sprinkle with cheese; broil until a delicate brown. May be prepared in advance. Serves 8.

BLINIS AND CAVIAR

1 cup all-purpose flour	1½ cups milk
½ teaspoon salt	3 eggs, well beaten
1 tablespoon butter, melted	

Sift the flour and salt together; add milk and eggs, and continue beating. Heat griddle; add 1 teaspoon butter. Add additional butter when needed to grease griddle. Drop one teaspoonful batter for each pancake (each one should be about 2 inches in diameter). Place between paper towels; keep hot in a 250° oven until served. Serve hot on a large platter with separate bowls of caviar, chopped onion, grated hard-cooked egg yolks and whites, and sour cream. About 36 pancakes. Serves 8.

GLAZED CORNED BEEF

4 to 5 pounds corned beef, pickled	1 clove garlic
3 onion slices	½ teaspoon rosemary
1 bay leaf	1 stalk celery

Cover meat with water; add remaining ingredients. Bring to a boil, then simmer slowly about 4½ hours, or until tender. While the corn beef is simmering, make this sauce:

2 tablespoons butter	1 tablespoon prepared mustard
5 tablespoons catsup	3 tablespoons vinegar
⅓ cup brown sugar	

Bring all ingredients to a boil. Place roast, drained, in a roasting pan; dot with cloves as for ham. Pour sauce over corned beef; roast in a 350° oven basting occasionally for 30 to 45 minutes, or until brown.

CORNISH HENS A LA BOURBON

8 Cornish hens	1½ cups melted butter
1½ teaspoons salt	½ cup bourbon
¼ teaspoon pepper	8 tablespoons currant jelly

Wash hens thoroughly. Fill breast with Wild Rice Dressing and fasten neck skin on underside with toothpick or skewer. Stuff cavity and lace with string and skewers. Bend wings into triangles and tie legs together at end joints. Place hens on a shallow baking sheet, breast side up. Mix salt and pepper with ½ cup butter and pour over them. Place in a 425° oven. Roast for 20 minutes, basting 3 times with bourbon mixed with the remaining cup of melted butter. Reduce heat to 350° and roast for 30 minutes more, continuing to baste every 15 minutes with bourbon and butter mixture. Turn breast side down and roast for 15 more minutes. If drippings evaporate, add a bouillon cube dissolved in one cup water; be certain to baste with regularity so that the fowl is juicy. Pour melted currant jelly over the hens the last half hour of roasting for a higher glaze. Serves 8.

CORNISH HEN GIBLET GRAVY

Giblets	1 carrot
1 teaspoon salt	1 onion
2 cups water	2 stalks celery
	2 tablespoons flour

Simmer giblets with combined ingredients except flour; strain and chop coarsely. Mix flour with ½ cup stock and then mix with remaining stock, pan drippings, and chopped giblets. Heat.

WILD RICE DRESSING

1 cup wild rice or 1 No. 2 can prepared	¼ cup butter
	1 medium onion, chopped
1 cup white rice, regular	2 4-ounce cans mushrooms,
6 to 8 cups water	drained, or ½ pound sliced,
1 teaspoon salt	fresh
	⅓ cup slivered almonds

Wash wild rice thoroughly. Pour into boiling, salted water. Cover. Cook 15 minutes and add the white rice; cook 30 minutes longer. Melt butter, sauté onion and mushrooms for about 5 minutes; stir in slivered almonds and then the cooked, drained rice. Stir until evenly mixed. Use as dressing for Cornish hens.

SQUASH RING

2 10-ounce packages frozen squash
1 tablespoon minced onion
1 teaspoon salt
¼ teaspoon pepper
2 tablespoons butter, melted
3 eggs, well beaten

Cook squash according to the directions on the package, but with half the amount of water. Add the onion, seasonings, butter and eggs. Pour into a greased 6-cup ring mold; place in a pan of water. Bake in a 350° oven for one hour. Unmold and serve on a large platter, filling center with Peas and Chestnuts. Serves 8.

PEAS AND CHESTNUTS

1 No. 2½ can (or 2 cups) French peas, drained
1 bouillon cube
1 cup boiling water
1 10-ounce can water chestnuts, thinly sliced
2 tablespoons butter

Dissolve the bouillon cube in the water; add thinly sliced chestnuts. Simmer for 5 minutes; drain. Add peas. Toss with butter. Place in center of Squash Ring.

GREEN BEANS EPICURE

Dressing:

½ cup prepared French dressing
1 cup chili sauce
½ cup catsup
2 tablespoons black walnut sauce
1 tablespoon Worcestershire sauce
2 tablespoons Escoffier Sauce
2 tablespoons lemon juice

Shake all ingredients together in a covered bottle or jar.

1½ pounds fresh green beans, crisply cooked
2 red Italian onions, sliced in rings (optional)

Toss beans with dressing. Serve in a large bowl lined with curly endive and topped with onions. Serves 8.

APRICOT HORNS

½ cup cream, scalded and cooled
1 cake compressed yeast
1 tablespoon sugar
1 cup butter
3 cups all-purpose flour
3 egg yolks, well beaten
1 teaspoon vanilla
1 cup apricot jam

Mix cream, yeast, and sugar together until the yeast is dissolved.

Cut the butter into the flour until the mixture resembles corn
meal. Add the egg yolks, then the yeast mixture and vanilla.
Knead for 2 minutes. Divide the dough into two parts. Roll each
piece into a circle about 12 inches in diameter. Cut into 16 pie-
shaped wedges. Spread with the jam. Roll each piece from the
outside in. Form into small crescents. Place on greased cooky
sheets. Let stand in warm place for one hour. Bake in a 350°
oven for 30 minutes.

BLITZ TORTE

Cake:

¼ cup butter	1 cup cake flour
½ cup sugar	¼ teaspoon salt
4 egg yolks, well beaten	2½ teaspoons baking powder
⅓ cup milk	

Thoroughly cream the butter and sugar; add egg yolks, beating
well. Add sifted dry ingredients alternately with the milk. Pour
into 2 wax paper-lined 8-inch square cake pans. Bake in a 350°
oven for 15 minutes. Remove layers and place on wire racks. Cool.
Spread top of each with meringue.

Meringue:

4 egg whites	1 teaspoon vanilla
¾ cup sugar	¾ cup chopped walnuts

Beat egg white to stiff foam; add one tablespoon sugar at a time,
beating constantly. Add vanilla. Spread top of each cake layer with
meringue and sprinkle with nuts. Return layers to oven. Bake 15
minutes longer. Cool and remove from pans. Place one layer,
meringue side down, on cake platter. Spread with pineapple filling.
Cover with second layer, placing it meringue side up.

Filling:

1½ tablespoons powdered sugar	¼ teaspoon vanilla
1 cup crushed pineapple, drained	1 cup heavy cream, whipped

Fold sugar, drained pineapple, and vanilla into whipped cream.

Buffet Dinner

Lobster Normandie   Chicken Livers en Aspic
Rye Bread
Beef Béchamel   Chicken Sesame
Brown Rice   Peas Orientale
Apricot Mold Garni   Fruit Dressing
Crusty Bread
Rye Bread Torte with Mocha Chocolate Icing
Blueberry Cottage Cheese Cake
Tea, Coffee, Sanka

ADVANCE PREPARATION SCHEDULE

Previous Day	Early Morning	Deep Freeze
Liver en Aspic	*Chicken Sesame*	*Beef Béchamel*
Lobster Normandie	*Prepare casserole of*	*Rye Bread Torte*
Beef Béchamel (may	*peas*	
be frozen)	*Frost Rye Bread*	
Apricot Mold	*Torte*	
Blueberry Cheese		
Cake		

LOBSTER NORMANDIE

3 cups cooked lobster, cut in medium-sized pieces
3 tablespoons butter
3 tablespoons flour
1 clove garlic, minced
2 cups cream

½ cup catsup
1½ teaspoons salt
2 tablespoons Worcestershire
sauce
2 tablespoons dry sherry
(optional)

Buttered bread crumbs

Melt butter, and flour and garlic. Cook until golden. Scald cream
and add slowly; add remaining ingredients. Cook slowly for 5
minutes. Butter a 12" x 8" x 2" casserole. Place lobster meat in
casserole, pour sauce over, and sprinkle the buttered crumbs over
all. Bake 20 minutes in a 375° oven until hot and brown. Serves 6.
Double if necessary. May be heated and served in individual
shells.

CHICKEN LIVERS EN ASPIC

Liver mixture:

1 pound chicken livers	1 tablespoon onion juice
4 eggs, separated	1 tablespoon Worcestershire sauce
2 cups coffee cream	1 tablespoon parsley, chopped fine

Aspic:

1 tablespoon unflavored gelatin (soften in ½ cup cold water)	½ teaspoon Worcestershire sauce
1 10-ounce can consommé, undiluted and heated	¼ teaspoon Tabasco

Put liver through meat grinder or food mill. Beat 2 whole eggs plus 2 yolks, add cream, seasonings, and liver. Fold in two stiffly beaten egg whites. Pour into a 10-inch bread pan which has been greased with salad oil. Place in pan of water and bake in a 350° oven for one hour; remove and cool.

Soften gelatin in cold water. Dissolve in boiling consommé. Cool and add seasonings to taste. Pour ½ inch of aspic mixture into bottom of 10-inch pan. Place in refrigerator until set. Remove and cover with liver mixture. Pour remaining aspic over liver. Chill until firm and serve cold as an appetizer. Serves 12.

BEEF BECHAMEL

2 cups onions, thinly sliced	½ teaspoon paprika
¼ cup butter	1 tablespoon salt
3 pounds round steak, bite-size pieces	¼ teaspoon marjoram
	¼ teaspoon thyme
½ cup flour	2 cups commercial sour cream
1 to 1½ cups water	1 cup sautéed mushrooms

Sauté onions in butter until transparent; remove from pan. Dust beef with flour and brown in butter in same pan on all sides. Add onions, water, and seasonings. Cover and simmer slowly for 1½ hours, or until tender, adding more water if necessary. Cool. Just before serving, add sour cream, reheat; add mushrooms. Continue cooking 5 minutes more.

BROWN RICE

4 tablespoons butter	1 cup water
1 cup brown rice	1½ teaspoons salt
1 10-ounce can consommé	Chopped parsley

Melt butter in large frying pan. Brown raw rice in butter, stirring constantly. Add consommé, water, and salt. Cover and simmer over low heat for about 30 minutes until rice is tender, and liquid is absorbed. Garnish with chopped parsley.

CHICKEN SESAME

6 small fryers, halved	2 teaspoons salt
3 eggs, beaten	3 teaspoons paprika
1½ cups milk	½ teaspoon pepper
2 cups flour	½ cup chopped nuts
2 teaspoons baking powder	½ cup sesame seeds
	1 cup butter

Rinse chicken in cold water; drain. Dip it into slightly beaten egg combined with the milk. Then shake the chicken in a paper sack which contains the flour, baking powder, salt, paprika, pepper, nuts, and sesame seeds. Coat thoroughly. Melt butter in a shallow baking pan in a 400° oven. Remove pan from oven and place pieces of coated chicken in the pan, turning each so that both sides are buttered. Then bake, skin side down, in a single layer at 400° for 20 minutes. Turn chicken and bake another 20 minutes or until tender. If chicken cannot be served at once, reduce heat and brush once more with melted butter. Serves 12.

PEAS ORIENTALE

3 10-ounce packages frozen peas, cooked	1 pound mushrooms, sautéed in butter
2 16-ounce cans water chestnuts, drained and thinly sliced	2 10½ ounce cans cream of mushroom soup, beaten with a fork
2 20-ounce cans bean sprouts, drained	2 3½-ounce cans French-fried onion rings

Mix the vegetables with the soup; place in a buttered casserole. Bake in a 350° oven for ½ hour; then top with the French-fried onion rings, and continue baking for another 15 minutes. Serves 12.

APRICOT MOLD GARNI

2 No. 2 cans apricots, drained (5 cups)
2 packages orange-flavored gelatin
1 cup boiling water
2 cups liquid (apricot juice and water)

1 cup commercial sour cream
Cranberry jelly slices
Avocado slices
Orange wedges

Dissolve gelatin in boiling water. Drain juice from apricots and add sufficient water to make two cups liquid. Add to dissolved gelatin, stir, and cool. Refrigerate. When of jellylike consistency, beat with rotary beater until stiff. Purée the apricots and fold in with sour cream. Pour into 8-cup greased mold. Chill until firm. Unmold and garnish with cranberry jelly slices, melon balls, orange wedges, and avocado slices. Serve with Fruit Dressing. Serves 12.

FRUIT DRESSING

1 pint commercial sour cream   4 cups miniature marshmallows
1 10-ounce package of frozen strawberries, thawed

Combine all ingredients, stirring until smooth. Chill.

RYE BREAD TORTE

9 eggs, separated
1½ cups confectioners' sugar
3 tablespoons whiskey
2 cups grated stale rye bread (not too fine)
1 square unsweetened chocolate, grated

1 teaspoon baking powder
1 teaspoon cinnamon
1 teaspoon ground cloves
2 tablespoons slivered citron
½ cup ground blanched almonds

Beat the egg yolks until thick and lemon-colored; gradually stir in the sugar. Pour the whiskey over the bread crumbs and mix. Combine the baking powder, cinnamon, cloves, citron, almonds, and grated chocolate. Add to egg yolk mixture, with the moistened bread crumbs. Beat the egg whites until stiff and fold into the batter. Pour into a 9-inch greased spring form pan and bake in a moderate oven (350°) for 45 minutes. Cool and frost with chocolate or coffee icing. Trim the top with additional slivered almonds.

MOCHA CHOCOLATE ICING

2 cups confectioners' sugar sifted with ½ cup of cocoa
2 tablespoons butter ⅓ cup strong, hot coffee

Put sugar and cocoa in bowl. Make hollow in center. Place butter in hollow. Using 1 tablespoon of boiling coffee at a time, pour coffee over butter and beat mixture until just thin enough to spread. If icing hardens while being used, thin with a little more coffee. One teaspoon of vanilla may be used in the icing if desired.

BLUEBERRY COTTAGE CHEESE CAKE

2 tablespoons unflavored gelatin	1 teaspoon grated lemon rind
1 cup sugar	3 cups creamed cottage cheese
¼ teaspoon salt	1 tablespoon lemon juice
2 eggs, separated	1 teaspoon vanilla
1 cup milk	1 cup heavy cream, whipped
1 cup fresh blueberries	18 ladyfingers, split

Mix gelatin, sugar, and salt together in the top of a double boiler. Beat egg yolks and milk; add to gelatin mixture. Stir in blueberries and cook over boiling water until gelatin is dissolved. Remove from heat; add lemon rind; cool. Sieve cottage cheese and add to gelatin mixture. Add lemon juice and vanilla. Chill until mixture is slightly thickened. Beat egg whites until stiff and fold in; then fold in whipped cream. Line a 9-inch spring form pan with split ladyfingers. Fill with gelatin mixture and chill until firm. To serve, remove rim of spring form and cover cheese cake with blueberry topping. Serves 12.

Topping:

2 tablespoons cornstarch ½ cup water
½ cup sugar 1 cup fresh blueberries
½ teaspoon grated lemon rind

Combine cornstarch and sugar. Add water and mix until smooth. Add blueberries and lemon rind and cook until thickened and clear. Cool. Spread on top of cheese cake.

Buffet Dinner

Bacon Tidbits   Crabmeat Monterey
Stuffed Eggs — Thousand Island Dressing
Canneloni   Chicken Tabasco
Carrot Ring
Brussels Sprouts and Water Chestnuts
Hearts of Palm Salad Bowl
Frozen Lemon Custard   Chocolate Cake
Cinnamon Leaves
Coffee

ADVANCE PREPARATION SCHEDULE

Previous Day	Early Morning	Deep Freeze
Crabmeat Monterey	*Hot Biscuits*	*Chocolate Cake*
Thousand Island	*Bacon Tidbits*	
Dressing	*Bake chicken to*	
Canneloni dough	*reheat*	
Fill Canneloni	*Carrot Ring, except*	
Lemon Custard	*egg whites*	
Cinnamon Leaves	*Frost cake*	
	Refrigerate greens	
	(washed)	

BACON TIDBITS

Split and butter tiny hot biscuits (use biscuit mix or Lightning Hot Biscuits). Generously spread bottom half of each with bottled mustard sauce; sprinkle with onion salt; then top with a 1-inch square of crisp bacon. Cover with top half of biscuit, and place in a 200° oven until ready to serve. May be made in advance and reheated.

LIGHTNING HOT BISCUITS

2 cups sifted all-purpose flour   1 teaspoon salt
3 teaspoons baking powder   ⅓ cup salad oil
⅔ cup milk

Sift dry ingredients together. Measure oil into measuring cup; add milk to make 1 cup of liquid. Do not stir. Add to dry ingredi-ents. Mix with a fork to make a soft dough which cleans sides of bowl. Form into a ball with hands. Place a sheet of wax paper on damp table surface. Place dough on paper. Knead lightly until smooth.

Pat dough ¼ inch thick, or spread a second sheet of wax paper on top of dough and roll to desired thickness. Remove top sheet. Cut into 1-inch rounds for Bacon Tidbits, using an unfloured cut-ter. Bake on ungreased cooky sheet in a 475° oven for 10 minutes or until brown. Makes 30 small biscuits for appetizers, 18 tea-sized biscuits, or 12 large biscuits.

CRABMEAT MONTEREY

1½ cups cooked shredded crab-meat   ½ cup finely diced celery
1 tablespoon finely chopped green pepper   ½ cup sliced, stuffed green olives

Aspic:

2 tablespoons plain gelatin   1 large onion, sliced
1 cup cold water   2 tablespoons sugar
2 cups tomato juice   3 tablespoons lemon juice
2 whole cloves   4 drops Tabasco
1 bay leaf   ¼ teaspoon onion juice

Soften gelatin in cold water. Simmer the tomato juice with the cloves, bay leaf, and onion for about 5 minutes; strain. Add softened gelatin, mix until dissolved. Add the remainder of the aspic ingredients; cool until jellylike. Add the crabmeat, green pepper, celery, and olives. Pour into mold. Chill until firm. Unmold on bed of greens. Serve with Thousand Island Dressing, crackers, and Deviled Eggs (see page 69). Serves 8.

THOUSAND ISLAND DRESSING

1 pint mayonnaise
¼ cup chili sauce
½ cup catsup
1 teaspoon Worcestershire sauce

1 teaspoon paprika
¼ cup sweet pickle relish
½ cup finely chopped green pepper
1 teaspoon grated onion

Mix all ingredients together; blend well. Makes 3½ cups dressing.

CANNELONI

Dough:

1 egg
1 egg yolk

1⅓ cups all-purpose flour
½ teaspoon salt

Beat the egg and yolk slightly; add the flour and salt to make a stiff dough. Roll as thin as possible. Cut into 4-inch squares. Drop in boiling water. Cook for 8 minutes. Drain.

I Filling:

6 chicken livers
2 tablespoons butter
1½ cups cooked chicken
1 onion, grated
¼ teaspoon thyme
⅛ teaspoon pepper

1 clove garlic, minced
½ teaspoon Beau Monde *or* A-1 Sauce
½ teaspoon salt
2 eggs

Topping:

2 6-ounce cans tomato paste   ½ cup Parmesan cheese, shredded

Sauté the chicken livers in the butter; combine liver mixture and chicken; grind very fine. Add the onion and garlic, cooking until golden brown. Blend in the eggs and seasonings. Put one tablespoon filling on each square; roll as a tube. Arrange in one layer in a shallow baking dish. Cover with tomato paste; sprinkle with cheese. Brown in a 400° oven for 15 minutes. Serves 12.

II Sausage and Ricotta Filling:

4 sweet Italian pork sausages
2 cups ricotta or cottage cheese

5 tablespoons grated Parmesan cheese
1 egg, beaten

Salt and pepper to taste

Prick sausages with fork, place in a small skillet, add enough water to cover, and simmer for 30 minutes or until all water has evaporated. Brown sausages in their own fat. Drain. Remove skin and mince. Add the remainder of the ingredients, mix well, and fill canneloni. Proceed as for Filling I, using same topping. Makes 24 canneloni.

CHICKEN TABASCO

12 small chicken breasts
Tabasco
¼ cup peanut oil
1 onion, finely chopped
¾ cup chopped celery
1½ tablespoons chopped parsley
1½ tablespoons scallion tops, chopped

1 clove garlic, minced
1 green pepper, finely chopped
1 teaspoon salt
½ teaspoon pepper
½ pound mushrooms
1 6-ounce can tomato paste
1½ cups water
½ teaspoon Tabasco

4 cups cooked rice (1¼ cup raw)

Rub each piece of chicken with Tabasco, using at least a drop on each side. Use additional Tabasco, if desired. Brown in oil in heavy skillet. Remove. Add to oil, onion, celery, parsley, scallion tops, garlic, green pepper, salt and pepper. Mix well; cook 5 minutes; add mushrooms; cook an additional 5 minutes; add tomato paste, water, and ½ teaspoon Tabasco. Mix well. Add the browned chicken to the sauce in the skillet. Cover and cook until tender, about 40 minutes. Place chicken on a platter, bordered with mounds of rice. To serve, spoon gravy over rice and chicken. Serves 8.

CARROT RING

1 cup shortening
¾ cup brown sugar
1½ cups grated carrots
2 beaten egg yolks
2 tablespoons lemon juice
1 tablespoon lemon rind

1½ cups cake flour
½ teaspoon baking soda
1 teaspoon cinnamon
½ teaspoon nutmeg
1 teaspoon baking powder
2 egg whites, stiffly beaten

Cream the shortening and brown sugar; add the carrots, egg yolks, lemon juice and rind. Mix well. Add the dry ingredients which

have been sifted twice; mix well. Fold in the egg whites. Bake
in a greased 6-cup ring mold for 45 minutes in a 350° oven. Unmold and fill center with Brussels sprouts.

BRUSSELS SPROUTS WITH WATER CHESTNUTS

1 quart Brussels sprouts or 2 packages frozen Brussels sprouts
1 cup water

1 teaspoon salt
1 6-ounce can water chestnuts,
thinly sliced, or ½ pound
roasted chestnuts

Boil sprouts in the boiling salted water for about 15 minutes, or
until tender. Drain. Cook the water chestnuts, sliced, in water
drained from sprouts. Cook, covered, for 5 minutes; drain. Toss
together with two tablespoons butter.

To use roasted chestnuts: Peel and cook in boiling, salted water
to cover for 20 minutes. Slice before using as above. Serves 8.

HEARTS OF PALM SALAD BOWL

3 large heads iceberg lettuce, bite-
size pieces
2 avocados
2 grapefruit, sectioned
1 cup Vinegar and Oil Dressing (see Index for recipe)

1 teaspoon lemon juice
1 14-ounce can hearts of palm,
drained, cut into ½-inch slices

Have all ingredients chilled; peel and dice avocado and moisten
with lemon or grapefruit juice. When ready to serve, pour dressing over all and toss lightly. The salad greens may be prepared in
advance and chilled until time to serve. Serves 8.

FROZEN LEMON CUSTARD

2 tablespoons butter
3 cups crushed vanilla wafers
3 egg yolks

½ cup sugar
3 tablespoons lemon juice
1 cup heavy cream, whipped

3 egg whites, stiffly beaten

Butter a 10-inch-square cake pan very well. Line pan with vanilla
wafer crumbs, reserving ¼ cup for the top. Beat the egg yolks with

the sugar and lemon juice. Add to the whipped cream. Fold in the egg whites. Pour into the lined pan. Sprinkle remaining vanilla crumbs over the top. Place in deep freeze for several hours or overnight. Makes 9 portions.

CINNAMON LEAVES

1 cup all-purpose flour	1 teaspoon grated lemon rind
½ teaspoon salt	⅓ cup sugar
1 teaspoon cinnamon	1 egg
⅓ cup butter	⅔ cup ground walnuts

Sift dry ingredients together. Cream butter and lemon rind; add sugar gradually, creaming well. Add egg and walnuts; beat well. Blend in dry ingredients gradually; mix well. Chill one hour for easy handling. Shape into a roll about 1½ inches in diameter and 8 inches long. Chill for at least two hours. Cut chilled dough into slices about ¼ inch thick. Mold each into a pear shape, tapering on end. Place on ungreased baking sheet and flatten with palm of hand to resemble leaves. Veins can be marked with a 3" x 5" card folded in half to make a V. Press down center vein with edge of card. Bake in a 375° oven for 10 minutes. Cool. Sprinkle with sugar, brushing off excess, or frost half of each leaf with chocolate.

CHOCOLATE CAKE

½ cup butter	1½ cups sifted cake flour
1½ cups sugar	1 teaspoon baking soda
2 whole eggs	1 cup buttermilk
2 squares of bitter chocolate, melted	1 teaspoon vanilla
1 pinch salt (if shortening is used instead of butter)	

Cream butter and sugar. Add unbeaten eggs, one at a time. Mix well. Add melted chocolate. Dissolve baking soda in milk. Add flour alternately with buttermilk mixture, gradually in small amounts. Add vanilla. Bake in long pan (9" x 13") at 350° for 30 minutes.

CHOCOLATE FROSTING

3 squares Baker's unsweetened chocolate
3 tablespoons butter
3 cups sifted confectioners' sugar
⅛ teaspoon salt
7 tablespoons milk
1 teaspoon vanilla

Melt chocolate and butter over hot water. Combine confectioners' sugar, salt, milk, and vanilla; blend. Add hot chocolate mixture and mix well. Let stand, stirring occasionally, until right consistency to spread on cake.

Buffet Dinner

Cream Cheese and Caviar   Sportsman's Appetizer
Melba Toast
Beef Bourguignon   Fillet of Sole Amandine
Liver and Egg-Barley Casserole
Limestone Lettuce — Vinegar and Oil Dressing
Garlic Bread
Crème de Cacao Angel Food Cake
Ice Cream Balls with Fruit en Coquille
Café Diable or Coffee

ADVANCE PREPARATION SCHEDULE

Previous Day	Early Morning	Deep Freeze
Spread for Appetizer	*Flavor cake*	*Ice Cream Balls*
Beef Bourguignon	*Crisp greens*	
Fillet of Sole		
Barley Casserole		
Angel Food Cake		
Meringue shell		

CREAM CHEESE AND CAVIAR

8 ounces cream cheese   1 tablespoon onion juice
½ cup commercial sour cream   4 ounces red caviar
Melba toast

Soften the cream cheese; add sour cream, onion juice, and finally the red caviar. Reserve one spoonful of the caviar as a garnish for the top. Chill. Serve in a bowl with melba toast.

SPORTSMAN'S APPETIZER

2 large tomatoes   6 tablespoons butter
2 6-ounce cans tuna fish   ½ cup mayonnaise
2 hard-cooked eggs   4 slices white bread, crusts re-
½ cup green pepper   moved
¼ cup Worcestershire sauce

Combine tomatoes, tuna, eggs, and green pepper. Chop coarsely. Add Worcestershire sauce. Melt 2 tablespoons butter and sauté mixture until green peppers are tender. Add mayonnaise and blend. Melt 4 tablespoons butter and sauté bread on both sides until brown. Sprinkle with Worcestershire sauce and spread with mixture. Place on cooky sheet. Heat in a 350° oven. Cut in half, then into triangles. May be prepared in advance. Serve hot.

BEEF BOURGUIGNON

¼ pound butter   ¼ teaspoon pepper
6 medium onions, sliced   ½ teaspoon thyme
3 pounds chuck, cut into cubes   ½ teaspoon marjoram
1 tablespoon flour   2 cups beef broth
1 teaspoon salt   1½ cups Burgundy wine
1 pound fresh mushrooms or 1 No. 2 can mushrooms

Sauté onions in butter in a heavy saucepan; add meat, brown on all sides; add flour, salt, and spices, stirring until smooth. Now add ½ cup broth and one cup wine. Simmer for three hours. Add mushrooms; continue cooking for another hour. Add more broth or wine as it becomes necessary during cooking. May be prepared in advance.

FILLET OF SOLE AMANDINE

6 medium fish fillets   ½ cup sherry *or* bouillon
4 green onions, chopped   1 tablespoon butter
¼ teaspoon rosemary   ½ cup cream
½ cup chopped mushrooms   ½ cup chopped almonds

Put fish in skillet with onions, rosemary, mushrooms, and enough wine to cover. Bring to a boil. Reduce the heat and simmer slowly for 8 minutes. Remove fish to a shallow baking pan. Reduce stock to one-half the amount. Add butter and cream, heat to boiling point and pour over fish, seeing that the mushrooms and onions are on top. Sprinkle almonds over all. Broil 10 minutes under medium flame (400°).

LIVER AND EGG–BARLEY CASSEROLE

1 8-ounce package toasted egg barley   6 tablespoons chicken fat *or* butter
½ pound chicken livers   1 onion, grated (optional)
½ pound mushrooms

Boil toasted barley approximately five minutes. If not toasted, cook 30 minutes. Sauté chicken livers in 2 tablespoons butter for 5 minutes. Cut into small pieces, add one more tablespoon butter, onion, and mushrooms, and sauté 5 more minutes. Mix chicken livers and mushrooms with cooked drained barley; place in a baking pan. Dot with 2 tablespoons butter to moisten mixture, and bake at 300° for about one hour. Stir occasionally to prevent burning or sticking at edges and add butter whenever mixture becomes too dry. Serve from casserole. May be prepared in advance.

LIMESTONE LETTUCE WITH VINEGAR AND OIL DRESSING

12 heads of limestone lettuce, washed, drained and chilled
Vinegar and Oil Dressing:

1 teaspoon salt   ½ teaspoon paprika
½ teaspoon sugar   ½ teaspoon dry mustard
¼ teaspoon black pepper   ¾ cup oil
½ cup vinegar

Combine seasonings, oil, and vinegar. Shake or stir thoroughly.

May be stored in refrigerator, but is best when used at room temperature.

GARLIC BREAD

¼ pound butter (½ cup)   1 clove garlic, minced
1 loaf French bread

Blend butter and garlic. Slice bread in ¾-inch slices to, but not through, bottom crust. Spread each slice with garlic butter. Press loaf into original shape. If desired, brush top with melted butter and sprinkle with grated Parmesan cheese. Place in a 400° oven for 10 minutes or until bread is brown on top.

CREME DE CACAO ANGEL FOOD CAKE

1 package angel food cake mix   2 tablespoons light cream
½ cup Crème de Cacao

Bake angel cake; cool. Remove from pan. Replace cake in pan and using a meat skewer, make many holes of various depths in the cake. Pour one-half of the combined cream and Crème de Cacao into these holes. Let stand for 2 hours. Just before serving, invert cake onto a platter. In the top of the cake, make more holes. Fill with remaining cocoa mixture. Slice and serve.

ICE CREAM BALLS WITH FRUIT
EN COQUILLE

Meringue Shell (see Index for recipe)
12 ice cream balls of various flavors (coffee, pistachio, chocolate, strawberry), about 3 pints
2 cups fruit in season, cut in pieces (Summer: peaches, pears, berries, plums, melon. Winter: oranges, strawberries, pears, canned fruit)

Make ice cream balls in advance and roll in shredded coconut. Wrap individually in wax paper and set on a platter in freezer. To serve, warm slightly with hands, remove paper and arrange ice cream balls in meringue shell; cover with fruit.

CAFE DIABLE

Peel of ½ orange, cut into 3 pieces
1 3-inch stick of cinnamon
3 whole cloves
8 lumps sugar, rubbed with orange pulp
½ cup cognac
3 cups freshly made, hot coffee

Place orange peel, spice and sugar in a skillet or chafing dish; pour cognac over. Set it aflame with lighted match. Stir until dissolved. Add coffee, mix, and serve in demitasse cups. Serves 6.

Ready-mix Café Diable may be purchased.

Note: Obviously, the main preparation of this dinner may be done in advance.

Buffet Dinner

Creole Rock Lobster Tails
Poppy-Seed Snacks
Chicken in Foil Brisket of Beef à la Bercy
Asparagus Vinaigrette Green Noodles Amandine
Icebox Parker House Rolls
Orange Mold Glacé
Minted Pears and Spiced Prunes Rum Cream Pie
Coffee

ADVANCE PREPARATION SCHEDULE

Previous Day	Early Morning	Deep Freeze
Lobster tails to fill shells	Rolls	
Prepare chicken for baking	*Stuff lobster tails*	
Cook brisket		
Vinaigrette Sauce		
Orange Mold		
Prunes		
Rum Pie		

9

CREOLE ROCK LOBSTER TAILS

8 frozen rock lobster tails	4 tomatoes, quartered, peeled
6 tablespoons butter	2 10-ounce cans tomato purée
2 medium green peppers, diced	2 cloves garlic, minced
2 onions, sliced	2 tablespoons snipped parsley
1 tablespoon seasoning salt	

Check the weight of each frozen lobster tail. Place, unthawed, in kettle. Add boiling salted water to cover, allowing 1 teaspoon salt per quart of water. Boil, allowing 3 minutes longer than ounce weight of largest tail; for example, 11 minutes for an 8-ounce tail; therefore entire batch cooks for 11 minutes. Drain; with scissors, split, cut through thin undershell of each tail, insert fingers between top shell and meat. Pull out meat. Cut into big pieces. Save shells. Melt butter in a large saucepan or skillet. Sauté green peppers and onions until tender. Add tomatoes, tomato purée, garlic, parsley, and seasoning salt. Cook, uncovered, over low heat for 10 minutes. Stir in lobster meat. Fill shells, serve hot. Serves 8.

POPPY-SEED SNACKS

Use thinly sliced white bread. Butter well. Sprinkle generous amount of poppy seed over butter. Bake in oven at 250°, watching closely, until toast is light brown. Cut in strips.

CHICKEN IN FOIL

6 chicken legs and thighs	1 cup butter-cracker crumbs
6 chicken breasts	½ teaspoon paprika
½ cup butter, melted, or salad oil	1½ teaspoons salt
¼ teaspoon pepper	

Wash chicken pieces. They should be at room temperature. Dip each piece of chicken in the melted butter, then into the crumbs. Season with paprika, salt and pepper. Place on jelly-roll pan. Make a complete, tight cover with foil, sealing in entire contents of pan. Bake in a 350° oven for 30 minutes; remove foil, continue cooking for 25 more minutes. Serves 8.

BRISKET OF BEEF A LA BERCY

2 teaspoons salt
3 tablespoons brown sugar
1 cup chili sauce
1½ cups vinegar

2 teaspoons seasoning salt
5-pound brisket of beef
1 cup chopped celery leaves
2 sliced onions

Mix salt, brown sugar, chili sauce, vinegar, and seasoning salt together. Pour over meat and let stand overnight. Allow one hour per pound for roasting. Place meat in the roaster. Pour marinade over the meat to moisten. Cover with celery leaves and onions. Roast in a 325° oven, basting often with marinade, for 5 hours, or until tender. Cover, if meat becomes too brown. May be prepared in advance. When ready to serve, slice and reheat in strained pan drippings from which fat has been removed. Serves 8.

ASPARAGUS VINAIGRETTE

2 10-ounce packages frozen green asparagus, cooked according to package directions, or 3 pounds fresh asparagus, cooked

Vinaigrette Sauce (Hot)

3 tablespoons pickle relish
2 tablespoons chopped parsley

1 tablespoon chopped pimento
1 cup French dressing

Blend with rotary beater. Heat in double boiler. Serve hot or cold.

Vinaigrette Sauce (Cold)

2 teaspoons salt
6 tablespoons oil
4 tablespoons chopped parsley
2 hard-cooked eggs, riced

6 tablespoons vinegar
2 tablespoons chopped green pepper
2 teaspoons chopped chives
Freshly ground pepper, to taste

Paprika to taste

Mix all above ingredients. Blend with rotary beater.

To cook fresh asparagus: Snap off tough ends of stalk and peel, if desired. Tie stalks together, about ten spears in each bundle. Place upright in bottom of double boiler, cover stems with boiling water, using ½ teaspoon salt per cup of water. Cover with inverted top section of the double boiler and cook about 15 minutes. The tender part of the asparagus will then be steamed and the stalks should be tender. Serves 8.

GREEN NOODLES AMANDINE

1 12-ounce package green spinach noodles	¼ cup melted butter
	⅓ cup slivered almonds
4 quarts boiling, salted water	(blanched)

Boil spinach noodles in salted water for 10 minutes. Drain; melt butter; brown almonds slightly. Pour over noodles and toss together. Serves 8.

ICEBOX PARKER HOUSE ROLLS

1-ounce cake compressed yeast	1½ tablespoons sugar
½ cup warm milk	1 cup boiling water
1 teaspoon flour	1 tablespoon butter
1 teaspoon salt	1 egg, beaten
3 cups all-purpose flour; more, if necessary	

Combine yeast, milk, and flour and let stand for 30 minutes. Meanwhile, mix salt, sugar, water, and butter together. Cool and add to yeast mixture; beat with a rotary beater. Add egg and continue to beat until thoroughly blended. Add flour (3 cups) and beat again with a spoon. If dough is very sticky, add more flour. Place in greased bowl, cover with wax paper and towel and place in refrigerator overnight to rise.

Remove as much dough as is needed, shape into Parker House or any desired shape. Place on baking sheet, cover; set in a warm place free from drafts, and let rise until doubled in bulk, about 1½ hours. Place in a 400° oven for 15 minutes. Remaining dough may be kept several days.

To shape Parker House rolls: Roll dough ¼ inch thick. Cut with 2¾-inch floured biscuit cutter. Make a crease to one side of center. Flatten one side slightly and brush with melted butter. Fold thicker half over thinner half, pressing both together. Place 1 inch apart on greased cooky sheet.

ORANGE MOLD GLACE

2 packages orange-flavored gelatin
3 cups boiling water
2 6-ounce cans frozen orange juice

2 cups Marshmallow Fluff (1 pint jar)
Grapefruit sections
Minted pear halves
Chopped ginger

Dissolve the gelatin in boiling water; add the frozen orange juice, stir until melted. Refrigerate until slightly thickened and add the Marshmallow Fluff, beating with a rotary egg beater until smooth. Pour into a 2-quart mold and chill until firm. Unmold on a bed of salad greens. Surround with Minted Pears and grapefruit sections. Sprinkle with chopped ginger. Serves 8.

MINTED PEARS

1 teaspoon mint flavoring
2 cups pear juice

Dash green food coloring
12 to 14 pear halves (2 No. 2 cans)

Add the mint flavoring to the pear juice; add a dash of green food coloring. Place pears in a flat dish; cover with colored juice. Refrigerate overnight, if possible, as the flavor improves.

SPICED PRUNES

1 pound large prunes
1 cup vinegar
1 cup sugar

1 cup water
1 teaspoon ground cloves
1 teaspoon cinnamon
½ teaspoon salt

Rinse prunes; cover with cold water. Boil 12 minutes; drain. Combine vinegar, sugar, water, spices, and salt. Boil one minute. Add prunes and bring to a boil. Cool; let stand about one week under refrigeration.

RUM CREAM PIE

Crust:

1½ cups chocolate cookie crumbs
⅓ cup soft butter
¼ teaspoon cinnamon

Combine all ingredients and mix well. With the back of a spoon, press mixture on bottom and sides of 9-inch spring form pan. Bake in a 375° oven for 8 minutes.

Filling:

6 egg yolks	½ cup cold water
1 cup sugar	1 pint heavy cream, whipped
1 tablespoon gelatin	⅓ cup dark rum
¼ cup shaved chocolate	

Beat the egg yolk until light; add the sugar, continue beating. Soak the gelatin in the cold water; place over low flame, bring to a boil, and pour it over the sugar-egg mixture, stirring briskly. Fold in the whipped cream; add the rum. Cool until mixture begins to set; pour into crumb shell. Sprinkle with shaved chocolate. Refrigerate until set, or for several hours.

Buffet Dinner

Cocktail Prunes   Liptauer Cheese — Potato Chip Crackers

Chinese Chicken Soup

Dumplings Amandine in Tureen from Tea Cart

Veal Curry Hawaiian   Sole à la Mistral

Fluffy Rice   Potato Casserole

Spinach on Artichoke Bottoms Hollandaise

Salad Havana   Herb Bread

Baked Alaska Aflame   Butterscotch Cookies

Orange Cake

Coffee

ADVANCE PREPARATION SCHEDULE

Previous Day	Early Morning	Deep Freeze
Prunes	*Potato Casserole*	*Ice Cream*
Liptauer	*Artichokes*	*Cookies*
Chicken Soup	*Spinach*	*Orange Cake*
Refrigerate raw	*Herb Bread*	
dumplings		
Veal Curry		
Sole à la Mistral		

COCKTAIL PRUNES

24 cooked or canned prunes, pitted
12 slices bacon, halved
Cocktail onions

3-ounce package cream cheese
thinned with 2 tablespoons
cream
Rolled anchovies
Smoked oysters

Stuff each prune with any one of the suggested fillings — onions,
anchovies, oysters, or cheese. Wrap with a half-slice of bacon and
fasten with a toothpick. When ready to serve, broil for about 5
minutes on each side or until bacon is crisp.

LIPTAUER CHEESE

1 8-ounce package cream cheese
½ cup softened butter
½ cup commercial sour cream
½ teaspoon dry mustard
2 teaspoons capers

2 tablespoons anchovy paste
¼ cup minced green onion
2 teaspoons paprika
1 tablespoon caraway seeds
½ teaspoon salt

Combine all ingredients in blender until smooth. Chill several
hours. Serve with potato chips or crackers. Serves 6 to 8.

CHINESE CHICKEN SOUP

1 5-pound hen
2 quarts water
1½-inch strip ham
2 tablespoons sherry

1 whole onion
3 carrots, sliced
1 tablespoon salt

Put chicken in water with all ingredients except salt and sherry.
Simmer, covered, as slowly as possible for one hour. Then add
salt. Cook another hour or until chicken is tender. Drain soup, and
let stand. Skim fat before reheating. Heat, add sherry and serve
from tureen. (Use chicken next day for Chicken Divan Salad or
Chicken Hash, etc.) Serves 6 to 8.

DUMPLINGS AMANDINE

2 tablespoons chicken fat
1 cup matzo meal
1 egg
1 teaspoon salt
¼ cup diced chicken (optional)

¼ cup finely chopped burnt almonds
1 tablespoon parsley flakes
⅛ teaspoon poultry seasoning
1 cup boiling water

Mix chicken fat with matzo meal. Add egg, salt, diced chicken, almonds, parsley flakes, and poultry seasoning. Add water gradually and blend. Chill in refrigerator for several hours. Roll into balls, using about ½ teaspoon per ball; drop into rapidly boiling uncovered soup. Boil until balls lighten and come to the surface, about 20 minutes.

VEAL CURRY HAWAIIAN

4 tablespoons shortening
2 cloves garlic
3 pounds lean veal, cut into 1½" x 1" pieces
1½ 10-ounce cans condensed cream of mushroom soup, undiluted
1½ soup cans of milk
1½ teaspoons salt

¼ teaspoon pepper
2 to 3 tablespoons curry powder, according to taste
About 10 scallions with green tops, thinly sliced
2½ cups rice
2 cups pineapple chunks, drained
Snipped parsley

In a Dutch oven, heat the shortening. Brown garlic in the shortening and remove. Add veal and brown well. Stir in soup, milk, salt, pepper, curry powder, and scallions. Simmer, covered, about 30 minutes. Refrigerate. Cook rice as package label directs, or cook Fluffy Rice. To serve: Slowly reheat curry, stir in pineapple; sprinkle with parsley, and serve over rice with chutney and other appropriate curry accompaniments (see Index for Curry Accompaniments). Serves 6 to 8.

FLUFFY RICE

1 pound long-grain rice　　3 cups hot water　　1 teaspoon salt

Wash rice thoroughly in cold water. Drain well and combine with the hot water. Add salt. Place in saucepan. Cover tightly and bring to a quick boil. Lower flame and simmer slowly for about 45 minutes, or until rice is dry and the water has been absorbed. Do not remove cover or stir while cooking. When rice is done, shut off heat and allow to stand for 20 minutes.

SOLE A LA MISTRAL

½ cup bread crumbs	6 medium-size fillets of sole
1 medium onion, finely chopped	1 teaspoon salt
4 tomatoes, peeled and chopped	½ teaspoon pepper
1 clove garlic, minced (optional)	1 cup white wine
¼ cup parsley, finely chopped	2 tablespoons butter
1 tablespoon flour	

Cover the bottom of a shallow 9″ x 13″ baking pan with half of the bread crumbs, then with finely chopped onion, chopped tomatoes, garlic, and minced parsley. Spread the sole on top of these. Season to taste and cover with the wine. Bake in a 375° oven for 20 minutes.

To make sauce: Drain liquid into a saucepan. To avoid lumps, first make a paste of the flour with a small amount of the liquid and return to pan. Add butter; cook until thickened (5 minutes). Pour the sauce over the sole, sprinkle with the remaining bread crumbs, and return to oven for 5 more minutes.

POTATO CASSEROLE

1 cup light cream	¼ cup pimento, finely chopped
2 12-ounce packages frozen, shredded potatoes, thawed	1 tablespoon onion flakes (optional)
¼ cup butter	1 teaspoon salt
	½ teaspoon pepper
⅓ cup grated cheese (Parmesan or American)	

Bring the light cream to a boil; add the potatoes. Cook until the cream is absorbed. Mix in the remaining ingredients except the cheese. Transfer to a shallow greased casserole. Cover with grated cheese. Bake in a 350° oven one hour or until brown. May be turned out on serving platter and bordered with the vegetables. Serves 6 to 8.

SPINACH ON ARTICHOKE BOTTOMS HOLLANDAISE

2 10-ounce packages frozen spinach
½ pound fresh mushrooms
6 tablespoons butter
1 tablespoon flour

½ cup milk
½ teaspoon salt
⅛ teaspoon garlic powder
1 No. 2 can artichoke bottoms
(7 to a can)

Cook spinach according to the directions on the package. Reserve 16 mushroom caps; chop remaining caps with stems and sauté in 2 tablespoons butter. Sauté mushroom caps separately in another 2 tablespoons butter.

To make cream sauce: Melt 2 tablespoons butter in saucepan; add flour and cook until bubbly. Add milk, stirring constantly until smooth. Add seasonings; then the chopped mushrooms and spinach. Drain artichoke bottoms and cover with mound of the creamed spinach, then with a generous spoonful of Sour Cream Hollandaise. Top with a whole mushroom. (This dish may be prepared in advance and heated in oven at last minute.) Heat in a 375° oven for 15 minutes.

Variation: Slice 1 pound mushrooms; sauté in 2 tablespoons butter. Make cream sauce as above with butter, flour and milk or light cream and seasonings. Combine with mushrooms and fill artichoke bottoms. Heat in a 375° oven for 15 minutes.

SOUR CREAM HOLLANDAISE

1 cup commercial sour cream 1 cup mayonnaise ¼ cup lemon juice

Combine ingredients, blend thoroughly, and heat slowly.

SALAD HAVANA

Leaf lettuce
3 cucumbers, cut in ½-inch cubes

3 avocados, diced in ½-inch cubes
2 Italian onions, sliced in rings
Vinegar and Oil Dressing (see Index for recipe)

Chill ingredients thoroughly in advance. Line a bowl with lettuce leaves or shredded lettuce. Toss together the cucumber and avocado. Place on lettuce; cover with onion rings. Pour Vinegar and Oil Dressing over all and serve at once. Serves 6 to 8.

HERB BREAD

Slice French bread in ¾-inch-thick slices, to, but not through, bottom crust. Brush with ¼ cup butter, creamed with 4 tablespoons herbs (parsley with chives or thyme, or tarragon with chives). Secure bread in loaf shape. Heat 10 minutes in a 400° oven.

BAKED ALASKA AFLAME

2 pints packaged ice cream	1 teaspoon vanilla
Sponge cake	Brandy
¼ teaspoon salt	2 10-ounce packages frozen berries
4 egg whites	ries
½ cup sugar	

In advance, spread ice cream on sponge cake and place in freezer until ready to serve. To serve, add salt to egg whites and beat until stiff. Add sugar gradually, beating until very stiff. Fold in vanilla. Remove cake from freezer; cover with meringue. Be certain that ice cream is completely sealed by meringue. Place four empty half eggshells in meringue, hollow side up so as to form cups, and space them evenly. Bake 4 or 5 minutes in a preheated 450° oven, or until meringue is slightly brown. Remove and fill egg shells with brandy. Light each with a match and bring it flaming to the table. Serve immediately with thawed frozen fruit of your choice or with crushed strawberries or chocolate syrup. Serves 6 to 8.

BUTTERSCOTCH COOKIES

1 cup butter	2 teaspoons baking powder
2 cups brown sugar	2 cups coarsely chopped pecans
2 eggs, beaten	1 teaspoon vanilla
1½ cups all-purpose flour	⅛ teaspoon salt

Heat butter and sugar until dissolved. Cool. Add eggs, blend, and sift in combined flour and baking powder. Mix well. Add remaining ingredients. Spread on jelly roll pan and bake in a 350° oven about 15 minutes. Cut in squares while hot.

ORANGE CAKE

½ cup butter	½ teaspoon baking soda
1 cup sugar	¼ teaspoon salt
2 eggs, well beaten	1 cup commercial sour cream
2 cups cake flour	Grated rind of orange
1 teaspoon baking powder	½ cup chopped nuts

Cream butter and sugar until light and fluffy, add eggs and beat well. Sift flour, baking powder, baking soda, and salt; add alternately with the sour cream. Fold in orange rind and nuts. Bake in well-greased 8″ x 8″ x 2″ cake pan in a 350° oven for about 40 minutes. Remove from oven and while still hot in pan, pour the topping over the cake. Cool on rack before removing from pan.

Topping: ½ cup confectioners' sugar mixed with the juice of one orange.

Buffet Dinner

Crab Fingers with Mustard Dressing   Caviar Croustades
Quartered Duck à l'Orange   Lamb Curry
Baked Wild Rice
Asparagus Ring centered with Celery Almond
Cranberry Mold   Spiced Crabapples and Peaches
Apricot Refrigerator Cake   Sour Cream Apple Pie
Coffee

ADVANCE PREPARATION SCHEDULE

Previous Day	Early Morning	Deep Freeze
Ready ducks	*Prepare ducks for*	*Lamb Curry*
Cranberry Mold	*baking*	*Rolls*
Apricot Cake	*Prepare rice for*	
Sour Cream Apple	*baking*	
Pie	*Prepare asparagus,*	
	except for egg	
	whites	
	Bake pie	
	Caviar Croustades	

CRAB FINGERS WITH MUSTARD DRESSING

2 pounds crab fingers, fresh or frozen

Mustard Dressing:
⅓ cup commercial sour cream   ⅓ cup salad mustard
⅓ cup currant jelly, melted

Mix all the ingredients and cool. Place in a bowl in the center of a serving platter. Surround the bowl with crab fingers, garnished with endive or parsley. Serves 6 to 8.

CAVIAR CROUSTADES

Cut small rounds (about 1 inch) of bread about ½ inch thick. Scoop out centers to form cups. Dip in melted butter, brown in oven, and fill centers with caviar. Decorate with grated hard-cooked egg.

QUARTERED DUCK A L'ORANGE

2 5- to 7-pound ducks, quartered   1 cup orange juice
2 tablespoons brown sugar   1 tablespoon orange rind
2 tablespoons lemon juice

Season ducks with salt and pepper. Spread with combined mixture of sugar, juices, and rind. Place skin side up in shallow baking pan. Do not cover or add liquid. Do not prick skin. Roast about 4 hours, or until tender, at 325°. Cooking time varies with the age of fowl. If birds are not sufficiently brown, place under the broiler for a few minutes before serving. Serves 6 to 8.

BAKED WILD RICE

1¼ cups wild rice
1½ teaspoons salt
2 cups boiling water or stock
¼ cup butter

1 onion stuck with 4 cloves
⅛ teaspoon ground ginger
1 10-ounce can water chestnuts, sliced thin

Wash rice especially well; place all ingredients in a casserole, burying the onion in the middle of the rice. Cover tightly and bake in a 325° oven for 1¼ hours. When done, stir with a fork and if not fluffy, let stand in oven for 10 minutes with heat turned off. Serve from casserole.

LAMB CURRY

2 tablespoons butter
4 pounds lean lamb, cut in 1-inch squares
2 chopped onions
1 teaspoon salt
½ teaspoon Worcestershire sauce
½ teaspoon prepared mustard

1 bay leaf
2 peppercorns
2 tablespoons catsup
2 teaspoons curry powder
½ teaspoon garlic powder (optional)
2 bouillon cubes
2 cups hot water

Melt the fat or butter in a saucepan. Add lamb and onions and brown. Combine salt, Worcestershire sauce, mustard, bay leaf, peppercorns, catsup, curry and garlic powders. Dissolve bouillon cubes in water and mix with seasoning mixture. Add to lamb, blend well. Bring to a boil; cover and simmer for 2 hours or until tender. If a thicker sauce is desired, make a paste of 1 tablespoon flour and ¼ cup lamb gravy. Return to the curry and cook 5 minutes longer. More curry may be added to taste. Serve with rice and curry accompaniments (see Index for Curry Accompaniments). Freezes well.

ASPARAGUS RING

2 20-ounce cans green asparagus stems and pieces, drained, *or*
3 10-ounce packages frozen asparagus, cooked and chopped
1½ teaspoons salt   ¼ teaspoon paprika
¼ teaspoon pepper   2 eggs, separated
Bread crumbs

Mix asparagus with seasonings and 2 well-beaten egg yolks. Add white sauce (below) to the asparagus mixture. Fold in 2 stiffly beaten egg whites. Sprinkle buttered 6-cup ring mold with bread crumbs. Pour in asparagus and set in pan of warm water. Bake at 350° for 45 minutes. Serves 6 to 8.

Medium White Sauce:

2 tablespoons butter	¼ teaspoon seasoning salt
2 tablespoons flour	2 cups milk
1 teaspoon salt	½ cup cream

Melt butter, add flour. Stir until blended. Add seasoning. Pour in milk and cream gradually, stirring constantly until thickened.

CELERY ALMOND

6 cups sliced celery	2 tablespoons finely chopped green
¼ cup butter	onions
1 teaspoon salt	1 cup slivered almonds
¼ teaspoon pepper	Butter for browning
4 tablespoons dry sherry	

Sauté celery in ¼ cup butter with salt and pepper. Cover and cook until celery is tender, about 10 minutes. Then sprinkle with green onions and cook 2 minutes more. Brown almonds in butter. Stir in wine. Cook 2 minutes; pour over celery and serve. Serves 6 to 8.

CRANBERRY MOLD

2 packages raspberry gelatin	2 cups hot water
2 16-ounce cans whole cranberry sauce	

Dissolve gelatin in hot water. Stir in cranberry sauce. Pour into greased 6-cup mold and refrigerate. Serve surrounded with spiced peaches and crabapples. Serves 6 to 8.

APRICOT REFRIGERATOR CAKE
(Prepare in advance)

1 tablespoon unflavored gelatin	1 cup water
¼ cup cold water	1 teaspoon grated lemon rind
12 ounces dried apricots	2 egg yolks, slightly beaten
1½ cups water	2 egg whites, stiffly beaten
¾ cup sugar	1 10-inch angel food cake
	2 cups heavy cream, whipped

Soften gelatin in ¼ cup cold water; cook apricots (reserving 6) in 1½ cups water about 30 minutes. Force through food mill. Add sugar, remaining water, and lemon rind, and heat to boiling. Add small amount of hot mixture to yolks and return all to pan. Cook 3 minutes, stirring constantly. Add gelatin; stir until dissolved; chill until slightly thickened. Fold in egg whites. Slice cake horizontally into 3 equal layers. Spread apricot mixture between layers and on top. Chill several hours or overnight. Cover with whipped cream; decorate with the halves of apricots which have been reserved.

SOUR CREAM APPLE PIE

Pastry:

1½ cups cake flour	½ cup shortening
¼ teaspoon salt	Ice water

Sift together flour and salt. Cut in shortening with pastry blender. Add sufficient water (3 or 4 tablespoons) to hold together. Roll out for double crust.

Apples for filling:

5 to 7 tart apples	¼ teaspoon nutmeg
¾ cup sugar	2 tablespoons flour
1¼ teaspoons cinnamon	¼ teaspoon salt
	⅔ cup commercial sour cream

Peel and core apples. Slice thin. Add next five ingredients. Fill pastry-lined pan with mixture. Top with sour cream. Put on top crust, press edges together and flute. Prick with fork and bake in a 450° oven for 10 minutes; reduce heat to 350° and bake 40 minutes longer.

Buffet Dinner

Quick Lobster Bisque   Chicken Scampi
Norwegian Bread Snacks   Curried Brown Rice
Buttered Pea Pods   Braised Celery George Rector
Herb Cole Slaw   Apricot Mold — Grapes Garni
Blueberry Meringue
Coffee

ADVANCE PREPARATION SCHEDULE

Previous Day	Early Morning	Deep Freeze
Chicken Scampi (*may be frozen*)	*Blueberry Meringue* *Cole Slaw*	*Chicken*
Apricot Mold	*Norwegian Bread Snacks*	
	Simmer celery hearts	

QUICK LOBSTER BISQUE

1 5-ounce can lobster meat
1 10-ounce can cream of asparagus soup
1 10-ounce can cream of mushroom soup
1 cup light cream
3 tablespoons sherry

Shred lobster. Combine all ingredients except sherry. Heat, but do not boil. Add sherry just before serving.

NORWEGIAN BREAD SNACKS

12 slices Norwegian flat bread   Melted butter
Parmesan cheese grated

Brush the bread with the melted butter. Sprinkle generously with grated Parmesan cheese. Place in a 400° oven for 10 minutes or until brown. Serve hot.

CHICKEN SCAMPI

4 ounces dried mushrooms
1 cup water
1 4- to 5-pound hen, disjointed
3 tablespoons flour
3 teaspoons salt
½ teaspoon pepper
¼ cup shortening

⅓ cup domestic port wine
¼ cup chili sauce
1 bay leaf
½ teaspoon rosemary
¼ pound cooked shrimp, tiny (optional)

Wash mushrooms and soak in water, several hours or overnight. Shake chicken in paper sack containing flour, salt and pepper. Brown chicken in hot fat in a skillet. When golden brown, add port wine, chili sauce, bay leaf, rosemary, dried mushrooms, and liquid in which they were soaked. Cover, and simmer very slowly about 3 hours, or until tender. Just before serving, add the shrimp. The chicken may be cooked in advance, reheated when the shrimp are added.

CURRIED BROWN RICE

1 cup brown rice
1 tablespoon salt
2 quarts boiling water
1 tablespoon minced onion

2 tablespoons butter
¼ teaspoon salt
¼ teaspoon pepper
1 teaspoon curry powder

Drop washed rice gradually into boiling, salted water. Boil rapidly for 25 minutes. Drain. Run cold water over the rice to separate the grains. Drain. Brown onion until golden in the butter. Add the rice, salt, pepper, and the curry powder. Press into 8 individual buttered muffin tins. Place in pan of water. Steam in a 350° oven for 45 minutes. Serve around Chicken Scampi. Serves 6 to 8.

BUTTERED PEA PODS

2 pounds Chinese pea pods, or snow peas
Boiling water to cover

1 teaspoon salt
¼ pound butter (1 stick)

Wash pods. Tie in small bundles. Drop into boiling, salted water. Cook for 10 minutes. Remove; drain. Melt the butter in a skillet.

Add the pea pods. Cook for about 3 minutes, tightly covered.
Serve at once.

BRAISED CELERY GEORGE RECTOR

8 celery hearts	Salt and pepper
4 tablespoons butter	Beef consommé, canned, or stock
2 tablespoons chopped onion	(1 10½-ounce can)
½ teaspoon beef extract	

Trim off the outer stalks and leaves of celery, leaving 4-inch stalks.
Split in half through the hearts. Melt 3 tablespoons of butter and
sauté the onion for 5 minutes. Arrange celery on the onion, season
with salt and pepper, and moisten with 1 cup consommé or enough
to cover bottom of pan. Cover and simmer for 20 minutes or until
celery is tender. Dissolve the beef extract with the liquid in the pan
and add the remaining butter and consommé, if needed. Place the
pan, uncovered, in a 350° oven and bake for 20 minutes, or until
liquid is absorbed. Baste frequently in oven with the pan liquid.
Arrange on platter with Buttered Pea Pods. Serves 6 to 8.

HERB COLE SLAW

1 teaspoon salt	⅓ cup vinegar
¼ teaspoon pepper	1 tablespoon finely chopped pimento
½ teaspoon dry mustard	mento
1 teaspoon celery salt	1 teaspoon grated onion
1 teaspoon caraway seed	1 teaspoon salad herbs
2 tablespoons sugar	3 cups shredded cabbage
3 tablespoons oil	
½ cup green pepper, medium shred	

Mix together the seasonings, oil, and vinegar. Toss together lightly
with the other ingredients. Refrigerate.

APRICOT MOLD

1 pound dried apricots, puréed	1 package orange-flavored gelatin
½ cup sugar	3 cups hot water
1½ cups water	½ pound cream cheese, softened
1 package lemon-flavored gelatin	1 cup crushed pineapple, drained

Cook apricots and sugar in the 1½ cups water until soft; force through a sieve; cool. Dissolve gelatins in hot water; let cool until of jellylike consistency. Mix apricot mixture with gelatin, and pour half into a 6-cup ring mold. Chill until set. Combine cream cheese and pineapple and spread over the gelatin. Pour remaining gelatin mixture on top. Chill until very firm. Serve on bed of greens with clusters of grapes as garnish. Serves 8.

BLUEBERRY MERINGUE

3 egg whites	1 cup heavy cream
⅛ teaspoon salt	1 pint fresh or 1 10-ounce pack-
¾ cup sugar	age frozen blueberries
½ teaspoon vanilla	

Beat whites with salt until they hold a firm peak. Then beat in sugar, a tablespoon at a time, beating thoroughly after each addition. Mix the last ¼ cup of sugar in with a spatula or fork. Add the vanilla. Cut a piece of aluminum foil to fit on your baking sheet. Spoon meringue in a diamond shape, piling it up on the sides to make a shell. Bake one hour in a 250° oven. Remove from foil and place on a platter. Fill with whipped cream and the blueberries.

Thanksgiving Buffet Dinner

Beet Appetizers
Roast Turkey à la Bristol
Giblet Gravy   Holiday Dressing
Fruit Aflame
Jumbo White Asparagus Polonaise
Orange Yams or Apple Yams
Pineapple Spokes — Assorted Fruits
Tossed Green Salad   Royal French Dressing
Pumpkin Chiffon Pie
Coffee   Tea

ADVANCE PREPARATION SCHEDULE

Previous Day	Early Morning	Deep Freeze
Beet Appetizers	*Stuff turkey*	
Pumpkin Pie	*Prepare yams*	
Ready turkey	*Fruit*	
	Chill greens	

BEET APPETIZERS

4 bunches small beets   ¼ teaspoon pepper
2 cups vinegar   3 bay leaves
1 large onion, sliced   2 hard-cooked eggs, finely
2 tablespoons sugar   chopped
1 teaspoon salt   4 ounces anchovies, chopped

Boil the beets until tender; drain, peel and marinate for several
hours in combined vinegar, onion, sugar, salt, pepper, and bay
leaves. Drain. Chop beets very fine and combine with chopped
egg and anchovies. Serve on slices of tomato or cooked celery root
with Thousand Island Dressing and Euphrates Wafers.

To cook celery root: Cut away knobs, scrub, peel and slice. Cook
for 25 minutes in boiling, salted water.

THOUSAND ISLAND DRESSING

1 cup mayonnaise	2 tablespoons chopped stuffed
1 teaspoon onion juice	green olives
2 tablespoons chopped green	½ cup chili sauce
pepper	½ cup commercial sour cream
1 hard-cooked egg, chopped	

2 tablespoons prepared horse-radish

Blend all together, folding in sour cream last.

ROAST TURKEY A LA BRISTOL

1 12-pound turkey, cleaned	1 8-ounce can frozen orange juice
Salt, pepper, paprika	concentrate
¾ cup softened butter	

Allow approximately one pound of turkey per person. Clean and dry turkey. Season with salt, pepper, and paprika inside and out. Stuff with dressing and truss. Rub entire turkey with ¼ cup butter and sprinkle lightly with flour. Place in a 325° preheated oven. Bake for ½ hour, and pour orange juice over all. Baste turkey every 20 minutes. For first basting, use remaining half-cup butter, combined with one-half cup boiling water. Continue to baste every 20 minutes with pan drippings. Turkey should roast approximately 5 hours. So that turkey may be evenly browned, place it first on one side and, when brown, turn to the other side. Finally, place it on its back for remainder of roasting period. Serves 8, generously.

GIBLET GRAVY

4 tablespoons fat   2 tablespoons flour
2 cups stock in which giblets have been cooked

Remove turkey from roaster and pour off liquid. Reserve. Melt 4 tablespoons fat over slow heat in roaster. Add flour; stir until brown and return liquid to flour mixture. Cook until smooth, about 5 minutes. Season with salt and pepper to taste. Add chopped giblets.

HOLIDAY DRESSING

4 tablespoons butter *or* chicken fat
2 good-sized onions, chopped
1 small stalk celery, chopped
1 green pepper, chopped
1 cup matzo meal *or* cracker meal

3 eggs, beaten
1 cup water
1 tablespoon sugar
1 cup almonds (slivered)
4 cups cornflakes

Melt butter or chicken fat. Add onion, celery, and green pepper; sauté in butter or fat to a golden brown. Add all ingredients, except cornflakes, and mix well. Add cornflakes and mix lightly. Pack very loosely as dressing swells a great deal. This amount will stuff a 16-pound bird. The additional dressing may be baked in a separate greased baking dish.

FRUIT AFLAME
(Garnish for turkey)

1 large bunch parsley
8 pineapple slices (1 No. 2½ can, optional)

8 peach halves (1 No. 2½ can)
8 sugar cubes

Lemon extract

Place turkey on a bed of crisp parsley. Drain fruit thoroughly. Place pineapple slices around the turkey, and on each slice place a half peach, hollow side up. Just before serving, dip sugar cubes in lemon extract and place in hollow of each peach. Ignite and bring the turkey to the table in flaming splendor.

JUMBO WHITE ASPARAGUS POLONAISE
2 20-ounce cans white asparagus

Heat gently in liquid from can and drain. Cover with Polonaise Sauce and serve.

POLONAISE SAUCE

½ cup bread crumbs
4 tablespoons butter

Pinch salt, pepper, paprika
1 tablespoon lemon juice

Brown crumbs in butter until golden. Add seasonings and lemon juice. If cheese flavor is desired, substitute ½ cup grated Cheddar or American cheese for lemon juice. Serve over heated jumbo white asparagus. Border with Orange or Apple Yams. Serves 8.

ORANGE YAMS

5 yams, uniform size   2 oranges
¼ pound butter   1 cup brown sugar

Cut yams in half. Peel. Place raw in skillet, flat side down, in melted butter. Place a thick slice of unpeeled orange on each. Pour sugar over all. Cover and cook slowly, basting often. Turn often, replacing orange each time. Cook 45 minutes, or until tender. Serves 8.

APPLE YAMS

8 to 10 large, green, firm apples

Prepare apple shells by scooping out the fruit until wall of apple is ½-inch thick. Stuff generously with marshmallow-potato filling. Place stuffed apples in 350° oven. Bake ½ hour until soft, but not mushy.

Filling:

1 20-ounce can sweet potatoes   ¼ teaspoon cinnamon
¼ cup dark Karo syrup   16 miniature marshmallows
¼ cup butter   1 tablespoon lemon juice
1 teaspoon salt   ¼ cup melted butter

Mash potatoes and combine with remaining ingredients except melted butter. Blend thoroughly; then stuff apples to overflowing. Baste with melted butter. The apples must be tart as contrast to the sweet potatoes. Serves 8.

PINEAPPLE SPOKES

Cut a large, ripe pineapple into six sections lengthwise, retaining the stalk. Remove hard core. With a sharp, curved knife, cut pulp from shell. Cut into bite-sized pieces, but allow the fruit to remain in shell of each section. Arrange pineapple on large, round platter with sections resembling the spokes of a wheel. Place assorted fruits, such as spiced cherries, mangoes, strawberries, and

Minted Pears (see Index) in spaces between sections. Garnish with watercress and sprinkle fruit with pomegranate seeds. Colored toothpicks may be placed in each cube of pineapple for color and for service.

SPICED CHERRIES

1 28-ounce can large Bing cherries, drained
1 cup drained juice
1⅓ cups sugar

⅔ cup vinegar
¼-inch stick cinnamon
1 teaspoon whole cloves

Place drained fruit in a shallow pan. Combine remaining ingredients in a saucepan. Boil 5 minutes. Pour over cherries; cool. Refrigerate at least one hour, but preferably overnight. Serve with or without syrup.

TOSSED GREEN SALAD

Romaine lettuce   Spinach   French endive
Head lettuce   Watercress

Break 3 quarts of greens into bite-size pieces. Toss with Royal French Dressing. Season to taste with salt and pepper. Serves 8.

ROYAL FRENCH DRESSING

½ cup sugar
¼ cup vinegar
1 tablespoon lemon juice
1 small onion, grated

2 tablespoons catsup
½ cup salad oil
1 teaspoon salt
1 teaspoon paprika

Place all ingredients in a bowl and beat two minutes.

PUMPKIN CHIFFON PIE

1 Graham Cracker Crust (see
 Index for recipe)
 or 1 baked Pastry Shell (see
 Index for recipe)
3 eggs, separated
1 cup sugar
1¼ cups canned pumpkin

½ cup milk
½ teaspoon salt
½ teaspoon nutmeg
½ teaspoon ginger
½ teaspoon cinnamon
¼ teaspoon ground cloves
1 envelope unflavored gelatin

¼ cup cold water

Beat egg whites until stiff; gradually beat in ½ cup of the sugar until mixture stands in stiff peaks; refrigerate. Put remaining ½ cup sugar, egg yolks, pumpkin, milk, salt, and spices into top of double boiler and beat with a rotary beater until well blended. Place over boiling water and cook until thickened, stirring constantly. Remove from heat. Soak gelatin in cold water for 5 minutes; stir into hot mixture until dissolved. Cool. When pumpkin mixture begins to thicken, fold in the beaten egg whites. Pour mixture into pie shell and chill until set. Top with 1 cup sweetened whipped cream (1 tablespoon honey for sweetener gives an interesting flavor) and sprinkle with grated orange rind.

For a delicious **Variation**, use ¼ cup sherry and ¼ cup milk instead of ½ cup milk.

Buffet Dinner

Crabmeat and Scallops Breton
Assorted Bread Sticks   Relishes
Beef in Herb Wine Sauce   Chicken Ambassador
Brown Rice
Pineapple-Noodle Ring Mold   Green Beans Sauté
Grapefruit and Avocado Salad — French Dressing
Apricot Pie   Bisque Cream Pie
Coffee

ADVANCE PREPARATION SCHEDULE

Previous Day	Early Morning	Deep Freeze
Prepare scallops, except for eggs	*Partially prepare chicken*	*Bread Sticks*
Apricot Pie	*Partially prepare noodles*	*Rolls*
Bisque Cream Pie		*Bisque Cream Pie*
Beef in Herb Wine Sauce		

CRABMEAT AND SCALLOPS BRETON

2 pounds fresh scallops
6 ounces canned or frozen crab-
  meat, shredded lightly

¼ cup milk
¼ cup flour, mixed with 1 tea-
  spoon salt
2 tablespoons grated cheese

Wash, clean, and dry scallops. Dip in milk and then in flour mixture. Sauté in butter until they are golden brown and tender. Put to one side.

Cream Sauce:

2 tablespoons butter
2 tablespoons flour
2 cups light cream
1 teaspoon curry powder

1 teaspoon salt
¼ teaspoon nutmeg
2 egg yolks
¼ cup sherry

Melt butter; add flour, cook until bubbly and smooth. Stir in light cream slowly; add seasonings. Cook slowly 5 minutes. When ready to serve, heat and pour over beaten yolks. Add scallops, crabmeat, and sherry. Keep hot in chafing dish. Do not boil again. Serves 8.

ASSORTED BREAD STICKS

6 frankfurter rolls
Soft butter or margarine
Minced parsley

Minced chives
Nuts, finely chopped
Poppy or caraway seeds
Grated cheese

Cut the frankfurter rolls in quarters, lengthwise. Spread with soft butter, or margarine, on all sides. Roll in one of the above suggested seasonings. Bake in a 425° oven for 5 to 10 minutes.

BEEF IN HERB WINE SAUCE

3 or 4 medium onions, sliced
2 tablespoons bacon drippings
3 pounds lean beef (sirloin tip),
cut into 1½-inch cubes
1½ tablespoons flour
1 cup beef bouillon
1½ cups dry, red wine

¼ teaspoon marjoram
¼ teaspoon thyme
¼ teaspoon oregano
1 teaspoon salt
½ teaspoon freshly ground pepper
½ pound fresh mushrooms, sliced
lengthwise
¼ cup butter

In a heavy skillet, sauté onions in bacon drippings until transparent, about 5 minutes; remove from pan. Shake meat cubes and flour together in paper bag until meat is well coated. Brown meat in bacon drippings. Add ¾ cup beef bouillon, 1 cup wine, the herbs and seasonings; cover the pan tightly and simmer for 1½ hours, gradually adding the remaining bouillon and wine. Meanwhile, sauté mushrooms in the butter. Finally add mushrooms and onions to the meat and cook about 20 to 30 minutes longer. Serves 6 to 8. Serve with Brown Rice (see Index for recipe).

CHICKEN AMBASSADOR

3 fryers, quartered
2 tablespoons salt
½ teaspoon poultry seasoning
⅓ cup butter, melted

1 can (10½ ounces) consommé
½ cup sherry
½ pound mushrooms
2 10-ounce cans artichoke hearts

Season fryers with salt and poultry seasoning and place in roaster, skin side up. Baste with the combined melted butter and consommé. Bake in a 325° oven for one hour, basting every 20 minutes. Add the sherry and bake for ½ hour longer, using the pan drippings for basting. Meanwhile, steam the mushrooms; add the hearts of artichoke. When ready to serve, combine the drippings in the roasting pan with the mushrooms and artichokes. Arrange chicken on a serving platter and pour the sauce from the pan over the chicken. Serves 8.

PINEAPPLE–NOODLE RING MOLD

1 8-ounce package broad noodles   ½ cup brown sugar, scant
1 16-ounce can crushed pineapple   4 eggs, beaten
½ cup melted butter

Cook noodles for 15 minutes in boiling salted water; drain. After draining the crushed pineapple, combine ¼ cup of it with 2 tablespoons of the brown sugar and set aside. Mix the rest of the pineapple with the juice, brown sugar, beaten eggs, and melted butter. Add the noodles and mix thoroughly. Pour the pineapple and brown sugar mixture which has been set aside into a well-buttered 1½-quart ring mold. Add the noodles and bake in a 350° oven for 30 minutes. Serves 6 to 8.

GREEN BEANS SAUTE

1½ pounds green beans *or*   4 tablespoons butter
2 packages frozen, French-cut   4 slices crisp bacon, crumbled
Salt and pepper to taste

Cook fresh green beans, covered, in a small amount of boiling salted water until tender. Do not overcook. If frozen beans are used, follow directions on the package. Sauté the beans in the butter for 2 to 3 minutes. Sprinkle with the crisp, crumbled bacon. Place in the center of noodle mold. Serves 6 to 8.

GRAPEFRUIT AND AVOCADO SALAD

Limestone lettuce   2 avocados
2 grapefruit   2 persimmons, sliced in sixths

Divide the grapefruit into segments and remove the membrane. Peel the avocados, remove the seeds, and slice lengthwise. Arrange in salad bowl with the limestone lettuce, alternating the avocado slices, persimmon slices, and grapefruit segments. Serve with French Dressing. Serves 8.

FRENCH DRESSING

⅓ cup lemon juice   ½ teaspoon dry mustard
⅔ cup salad oil   ½ teaspoon salt
½ teaspoon paprika   ⅛ teaspoon freshly ground pepper
    2 teaspoons powdered sugar

Blend all ingredients in a bottle or jar. Cover and shake thoroughly. Chill. Pour over the salad just before serving. Serves 8.

APRICOT PIE

1 10-inch baked pie shell   ½ teaspoon vanilla
1 3-ounce package cream cheese 2 cups apricots, puréed (1½
2 tablespoons sugar   pounds uncooked)
2 tablespoons cream   ½ cup currant jelly
               Toasted almonds

See Index for pastry recipe. Cream the cheese with sugar, cream and vanilla; spread on bottom of pie shell. Add the puréed apricots. Melt the currant jelly in the top of a double boiler. Beat well and spread over the fruit. Sprinkle with toasted almonds. Chill for 8 to 10 hours before serving. Prepare in advance.

BISQUE CREAM PIE

Pie Shell:
   1½ cups vanilla wafer crumbs   ⅓ cup melted butter

Roll vanilla wafers to fine even crumbs with a rolling pin. Putting wafers in a plastic bag or between two sheets of wax paper is a convenient way to make the crumbs. As a variation, Cinnamon Crisp Graham Crackers may be used. Mix the crumbs and butter; blend well with fingers, a fork or a pastry blender. Press into a 9-inch pie pan. Bake in a 325° oven for 10 minutes. Cool.

Filling:
½ pound peanut brittle *or* English   2 cups heavy cream, whipped
   toffee

Fold the peanut brittle or English toffee, very finely crushed, into the whipped cream. Pour into the pie shell. Chill very thoroughly and serve. This pie may be frozen. Prepare in advance. Serves 8.

Buffet Dinner

Avocado on the Half Shell
Hot French Dressing
Garlic Olives   Easy Deviled Eggs
Salami and Ham Cornucopias
Vineyard Squab   Standing Rib Roast
Baked Beets   Yorkshire Pudding
Spring Salad Mold
Crêpe Meringue Viennese   Glazed Cheese Pie
Coffee

ADVANCE PREPARATION SCHEDULE

Previous Day	Early Morning	Deep Freeze
Deviled Eggs	*Stuff squabs*	
Spring Salad Mold	*Glaze pie*	
Ready squab	*Prepare crêpe and ar-*	
Cheese Pie	*range in casserole*	
	Make cornucopias	

AVOCADO ON THE HALF SHELL

4 ripe avocados, room temperature   Galax leaves
Hot French Dressing   Ham Cornucopias
Salami Cornucopias   Garlic olives and pimento olives
Deviled eggs

Cut avocados in half, lengthwise. Remove pit, but do not remove peel. Place on a large platter on a bed of galax leaves. Center with a bowl of Hot French Dressing to be served with avocado, and arrange remaining hors d'oeuvres on the leaves, distributing them so as to give color to the platter.

HOT FRENCH DRESSING

⅔ cup salad oil   ⅓ cup Worcestershire sauce
⅓ cup sugar   ⅔ cup vinegar
⅔ cup catsup   ½ teaspoon salt
¼ teaspoon freshly ground pepper

Combine; bring to a boil and serve hot. The dressing should be hot, but the avocado room temperature. Serves 8.

SALAMI CORNUCOPIAS

Slice salami very thin and form cornucopia around a carrot, or stuff with softened cream cheese.

HAM CORNUCOPIAS

Make cornucopias of Westphalian ham around whole, fresh figs. Fasten with toothpicks.

EASY DEVILED EGGS

12 hard-cooked eggs, cut in half   ½ cup pickle relish
lengthwise with French cutter   6 tablespoons mayonnaise
1 teaspoon salt

Remove the egg yolks and mash, or put through sieve. Combine with remaining ingredients. Fill whites. Garnish with paprika and parsley and chill.

VINEYARD SQUAB

8 jumbo squabs   ½ cup red wine (Burgundy)
½ cup melted butter   ¼ cup water
4 cups bread crumbs   Medium-size bunch of green, seed-
2 teaspoons salt   less grapes
½ teaspoon freshly ground pepper   1 tablespoon flour

Wash and dry squabs. Melt ¼ cup butter; add bread crumbs and brown; add seasonings and ¼ cup wine. Stuff each squab, adding about six grapes to each one with the dressing. It is not necessary to close the cavity. Place the birds in a well-buttered baking pan.

Combine remaining ¼ cup butter, ¼ cup water and ¼ cup wine and pour over the birds. Place in a 400° oven for about 30 minutes or until tender, basting every 10 minutes with the drippings. When tender, remove and place squabs on serving platter and keep warm.

Prepare Burgundy Sauce: Add one tablespoon flour to drippings; add remaining grapes and heat. If desired, add additional wine. Serve separately. To add elegance (but added time as well), use peeled and seeded red muscat grapes.

STANDING RIB ROAST

1 3-rib standing roast	1 tablespoon Worcestershire
4 teaspoons salt	sauce
½ teaspoon pepper	1 tablespoon A-1 Sauce
2 large onions, sliced	½ cup chili sauce
	⅛ pound butter

Weigh the roast first. Season well with salt and pepper. Cover with slices of onion which have been secured with toothpicks. Mix Worcestershire sauce, A-1 Sauce, and chili sauce and add to the meat. Dot with butter. Place in a 300° oven. Baste frequently with drippings. *For rare:* Up to the weight of 10 pounds of meat, roast 20 minutes to the pound in a 300° oven. Do not add additional time for a larger roast. The meat should be at room temperature before placing in the oven. Serve with Yorkshire Pudding (see Index for recipe). Serves 6 to 8.

BAKED BEETS

2 28-ounce cans sliced beets,	⅓ cup butter
drained	Few drops onion juice (optional)
⅓ cup sugar	2 tablespoons lemon juice
1 teaspoon salt	½ cup water
¼ teaspoon paprika	

Slice or shred the beets and place in layers in a greased 1½-quart casserole, seasoning each layer with sugar, salt, paprika, butter, onion and lemon juice. Pour water over all. Cover casserole and bake in hot oven (400°) for about 30 minutes, or until tender. Stir occasionally during baking period. Serves 8.

SPRING SALAD MOLD

2 tablespoons unflavored gelatin	1 28-ounce can whole, peeled to-
½ cup cold water	matoes
½ green pepper	½ cup vinegar
5 stalks celery	¼ cup sugar
3 carrots	½ teaspoon salt
4 green onions	Cucumbers, tomatoes, avocado

Soak gelatin in cold water. Chop pepper, celery, and carrots very fine, and slice green onions very, very thin. Quarter tomatoes and place in saucepan and bring to a boil. Add gelatin and dissolve. Let cool and add remaining ingredients. Mix well and pour into a greased 6-cup ring mold. Place your favorite dressing in the center and garnish with sliced cucumbers, tomatoes, and avocado. Serves 8.

CREPE MERINGUE VIENNESE

Casserole ingredients:

Thin pancakes, cut in ½-inch strips	1 cup damson plum or apricot jam
¼ cup butter (approximately)	⅓ cup walnuts, choppea
½ cup powdered sugar	

Thin pancakes for strips:

3 eggs, beaten	⅛ teaspoon salt
1 cup sifted all-purpose flour	3 tablespoons powdered sugar
1 cup milk	2 teaspoons grated lemon rind

Combine above ingredients in order listed. Melt one teaspoon butter in 7-inch skillet. Pour 2 tablespoons batter into pan and tilt pan back and forth so that batter covers bottom completely. When lightly browned, turn and brown lightly on the other side. Use 1 teaspoon butter for each pancake. Stack pancakes on breadboard until all batter is used. Then cut pancakes into ½-inch strips and separate. Place a layer in bottom of well-buttered 2-quart casserole. Spread with jam, sprinkle with nuts, dust lightly with powdered sugar and dot with butter. Repeat layers until all strips are used. When ready to serve, top with meringue; place in a 325° oven for 15 minutes or until meringue is lightly brown Serve slightly warm.

Meringue:

½ cup egg whites, room temperature	6 tablespoons sugar

Beat egg whites until they stand in peaks. Gradually add sugar, continuing to beat very well. Serves 8.

GLAZED CHEESE PIE

1 9-inch unbaked pie shell	2 tablespoons flour
(See Index for recipe)	2 eggs
1 8-ounce package cream cheese	⅓ cup milk
½ cup sugar	1 teaspoon vanilla

Cream the cheese until soft; add sugar gradually. Stir in flour and whole eggs and mix thoroughly. Add milk and vanilla and mix again. Pour into unbaked pie shell. Bake in a moderate oven (350°) for about 40 minutes. Cool and glaze with one of the following glazes:

Pineapple Glaze:
Cook together until bubbly 1 cup pineapple juice, 1 tablespoon cornstarch mixed with 1 tablespoon sugar. Add ½ cup drained, crushed pineapple and 1 teaspoon vanilla. Pour over cooled pie and refrigerate.

Peach Glaze:
Cook together until bubbly ¾ cup peach syrup, 2 tablespoons cornstarch; add 1 teaspoon almond extract. Arrange peach slices in pattern on top of cooled pie and pour cooked glaze over top. Refrigerate.

Blueberry Glaze:
Thaw one package frozen blueberries; drain juice and add mixture of 1 tablespoon cornstarch and 1 tablespoon sugar. Cook until thick and clear; add 1 teaspoon grated lemon rind and the blueberries. Pour over cooled pie and refrigerate.

Cherry Glaze:
Cook together 1 cup cherry juice and 1 tablespoon cornstarch mixed with 1 tablespoon sugar. Stir in 1 teaspoon almond extract and ½ cup cherries. Pour over cooled pie and refrigerate.

Buffet Dinner

Caviar Ring   Crabmeat Imperial
Watercress Sandwiches
Chicken Jubilee
Rice Moderne   White Asparagus Cashew
Cleopatra Salad   Bittersweet Dressing
Crêpes Capri   Pocket Cookies
Coffee

ADVANCE PREPARATION SCHEDULE

Previous Day	Early Morning	Deep Freeze
Caviar Ring	*Chickens, except for*	*Pocket Cookies*
Crabmeat Imperial	*last 15 minutes of*	
Watercress Sandwiches	*preparation*	
	Rice in molds	
	Crêpes Capri	

CAVIAR RING

1 envelope gelatin   1 tablespoon lemon juice
½ cup milk   1 cup heavy cream, whipped
1 cup mayonnaise   1 4-ounce can caviar

Dissolve gelatin in cold milk. Heat in top of double boiler until completely dissolved. Cool. Add mayonnaise, lemon juice, and whipped cream, then the caviar. Place in a 1-quart ring mold. Chill until firm. Unmold on platter of salad greens. Fill center with Crabmeat Imperial. Serves 8.

CRABMEAT IMPERIAL

1 clove garlic   ¼ cup French dressing
2 cups crabmeat   ½ teaspoon curry powder
1 cup finely chopped celery   1 cup mayonnaise
¼ cup finely chopped green pepper Capers
1 teaspoon grated onion   Hard-cooked egg wedges

Rub bowl with cut clove of garlic. Mix crabmeat, celery, green pepper, onion, and French dressing. Marinate until just before serving. Add curry to the mayonnaise and toss with the crabmeat mixture. Garnish salad with capers and egg wedges. Serves 8.

WATERCRESS SANDWICHES — CURRY MAYONNAISE

12 slices thin white bread
¼ cup chopped watercress
1 3-ounce package cream cheese

2 tablespoons mayonnaise
¼ teaspoon salt
¼ teaspoon paprika
¼ teaspoon curry powder

If bread is too thick, flatten with rolling pin. Spread with soft butter. Combine remaining ingredients and mix in blender or with rotary beater. Spread the buttered bread with the paste. Place a small sprig of parsley at one end and roll. Place close together on a flat pan and refrigerate until ready to serve. Serves 8.

CHICKEN JUBILEE

4 fryers, quartered
2 teaspoons salt
½ cup melted butter
¼ teaspoon pepper
1 cup water
½ cup raisins
½ cup brown sugar
1 teaspoon garlic salt (optional)

2 medium onions, sliced (optional)
1 12-ounce bottle chili sauce
1 tablespoon Worcestershire sauce
1 16-ounce can Bing cherries, drained
1 cup sherry

Place chicken in shallow roasting pan, skin side up. Season and dribble with butter. Broil under medium flame until brown. Combine remaining ingredients, except wine and cherries. Mix thoroughly. Pour over the chicken and cover entire pan with aluminum foil. Bake an hour in a 325° oven. Add wine and cherries and remove foil the last 15 minutes of roasting time. To serve, place on a platter and pour sauce over all. Serves 8.

RICE MODERNE

1½ cups cooked white rice, or ½ cup raw rice, cooked
1 20-ounce can cooked, wild rice   ¼ pound butter

Combine cooked white rice and wild rice; add melted butter and seasonings to taste; heat. Serve in a chafing dish or press into individual molds and use as a border for chicken platter. Serves 8.

WHITE ASPARAGUS CASHEW

½ cup slivered cashew nuts   ½ cup butter, melted
2 20-ounce cans of jumbo white asparagus, drained

Brown the cashew nuts in the melted butter. Pour over the asparagus; heat thoroughly. Serves 8.

CLEOPATRA SALAD

1 small head cauliflower, broken
  into buds
2 cups Chinese celery
1 head lettuce
2 heads romaine
¼ cup grated Parmesan cheese
1 2-ounce can anchovies, cut up

Refrigerate cauliflower buds and celery overnight. Drain; dice celery. Tear the lettuce into bite-size pieces. Toss all the ingredients together. Sprinkle with grated Parmesan cheese. Toss with Bittersweet Dressing.

BITTERSWEET DRESSING

1 cup salad oil
¼ cup sugar
1 teaspoon salt
¼ teaspoon pepper
1 teaspoon dry mustard
½ cup catsup
¾ cup vinegar
1 onion, grated

Combine all ingredients in a jar; shake well. Chill. Shake again before serving.

POCKET COOKIES

1 3-ounce package cream cheese
¼ pound butter
1 cup all-purpose flour
2 tablespoons sugar
¼ teaspoon salt
Raspberry preserves

Cut the cheese and butter into the flour. Add the sugar and salt and blend well. Roll into ball and set in the refrigerator overnight. Roll out in ⅛-inch thickness. Cut into 2-inch squares and place one teaspoon preserves in each. Fold into triangles and pinch together. Place on ungreased cooky sheet. Brush with cream if a gloss is desired. Bake in a 425° oven for 10 minutes.

CREPES CAPRI

1 cup all-purpose flour	½ tablespoon grated orange rind
¼ teaspoon salt	2 eggs
2 tablespoons sugar	1 cup milk
	2 tablespoons melted butter

Sift flour, salt and sugar. Add orange rind. Add slightly beaten eggs and milk to butter. Stir into flour mixture and beat until smooth. Grease a 5-inch skillet. When hot, pour in 2 full table-spoons of batter, turning pan so that batter spreads evenly. When brown, turn and brown other side. Stack until ready to serve. These pancakes may be prepared hours in advance.

Butter Cream Filling:

1 cup sugar	½ cup chopped roasted filberts
½ cup butter	(or other nuts)
½ cup rum	

Cream butter and sugar; add other ingredients and mix well. Fill and roll the pancakes and sprinkle with a little sugar. Place in a 375° oven before serving or keep warm and serve in a chafing dish.

Buffet Dinner

Cold Lobster — Mustard Sauce Calcutta

Artichokes à la Grecque   Cheese Strips

Steak Diane   Chicken Louisa

Mushroom Barley Ring   Asparagus Meringue

Jackson Salad

Pan Rolls

Crème Brûlée with Canned Pears   Black Walnut Cake

Coffee

Previous Day	Early Morning	Deep Freeze
Calcutta Sauce	*Chicken Louisa*	*Pan Rolls*
Cook lobster	*Barley Ring*	
Artichokes à la	*Crème Brûlée in cas-*	
Grecque	*serole*	
	Refrigerate salad in-	
	gredients	

COLD LOBSTER CHUNKS WITH MUSTARD SAUCE CALCUTTA

1 pound cooked lobster, cut into chunks

1 cup commercial sour cream
¼ cup chopped chutney
1 tablespoon prepared mustard

Combine the sour cream, chutney, and prepared mustard. Serve in a bowl surrounded by the lobster chunks.

ARTICHOKES A LA GRECQUE

2 10-ounce packages frozen artichokes
2 onions, sliced into rings
1 cup bouillon
½ cup white wine
½ teaspoon salt
⅛ teaspoon freshly ground pepper

1 teaspoon sugar
1 bay leaf
⅛ teaspoon thyme
4 sprigs parsley
Juice of 1 lemon
2 tablespoons olive oil
2 tablespoons tomato paste
Chopped chives

Combine all ingredients except artichokes and chives in a deep saucepan. Cook slowly, uncovered, for about ½ hour or until liquid is thick. Serve artichokes in the sauce and garnish with chives. May be served either hot or cold.

CHEESE STRIPS

Cut crusts from sliced bread. Cut each slice in four squares or four long strips. Dip each side in melted butter. Sprinkle with grated Parmesan cheese, then with poppy seeds. Toast lightly on both sides. Serve hot.

STEAK DIANE

2½ to 3 pounds sirloin steak, boneless and 1-inch thick, cut into
6 portions
Salt and pepper
½ teaspoon dry mustard

6 tablespoons butter
¼ cup minced onion
¼ cup A-1 or Escoffier Sauce
2 tablespoons Worcestershire
sauce
2 tablespoons butter

Trim the fat from the steak, cover with wax paper and pound to ½-inch thickness. Sprinkle with salt, pepper, and mustard, rubbing the seasoning into the steak with the back of a spoon. Melt a tablespoon of butter in a skillet, sear steak for one minute on each side, remove from pan and roll like a pancake for convenience in handling. Melt two tablespoons butter in a chafing dish or skillet; add minced onion, A-1 Sauce, and Worcestershire sauce; place steaks in the sauce. Simmer, turning once until cooked to taste; about two minutes on each side should be sufficient.

CHICKEN LOUISA

2 large frying chickens, disjointed
1 cup bread crumbs, finely
crushed
1 teaspoon salt
¼ teaspoon paprika

¼ cup shortening, preferably
butter
1 cup cream
2 tablespoons sherry (optional)

Wash and dry chickens. Place crumbs and seasonings in a paper sack. Shake the chicken, a few pieces at a time, in the seasoned crumbs, being certain they are well coated. Melt shortening in a skillet and sauté the chicken over very low heat, uncovered, for about 30 to 45 minutes or until tender. If necessary, add additional shortening or consommé to prevent sticking to pan. (This preparation may be done in advance.) To serve, heat chicken, remove to serving platter or casserole; add cream to remaining buttered crumbs in the skillet, blend well and heat thoroughly. Add sherry and pour over chicken.

Variation: Add ¼ cup sliced mushrooms or truffles last 15 minutes of cooking time.

MUSHROOM BARLEY RING

1½ cups dry barley
4½ cups water
¾ teaspoon caraway seeds
¾ teaspoon salt
3 tablespoons butter
½ pound sliced mushrooms

2 tablespoons chopped parsley
1 clove garlic, minced
1 teaspoon salt
⅛ teaspoon pepper
¼ teaspoon marjoram
¼ cup butter
¼ cup water

Place barley, water, caraway seeds, and salt in a saucepan. Bring to a boil, cover and simmer for about one hour or until tender. Melt 3 tablespoons butter in a saucepan and add mushrooms, parsley, garlic, salt, pepper, and marjoram; sauté for 5 minutes. Add ¼ cup butter and water and heat. Drain barley, and combine with mushroom mixture. Pour into a well greased 1½-quart casserole and bake in a 350° oven for 30 minutes. This recipe may be baked in a 6-cup greased ring mold. To prepare, place mold in a pan of water, and bake 45 minutes in a 350° oven. Center mold and/or border with vegetables. Serves 6 to 8.

ASPARAGUS MERINGUE

2 pounds fresh asparagus or 2 packages frozen asparagus

Wash and trim fresh asparagus, remove end of stalk, and lay in a greased 2-quart casserole. (If frozen asparagus is used, separate spears before placing in dish.)

Sauce:

3 tablespoons butter
3 tablespoons flour
1½ cups hot milk
3 egg yolks, well beaten

⅛ teaspoon celery salt
⅛ teaspoon onion salt
½ teaspoon dry mustard
⅛ teaspoon cayenne pepper
2 tablespoons mustard mayonnaise

Melt butter in a saucepan over low heat; blend in flour. Add hot milk slowly, stirring constantly, and cook until sauce is smooth and thickened. Remove from heat; add a little of the hot mixture to the beaten egg yolks, then stir egg yolks into the sauce. Add the celery and onion salts, dry mustard, cayenne pepper, and mustard mayonnaise. Pour this sauce, heated thoroughly, over the asparagus, so that it cooks immediately. Cover with meringue.

Meringue:

3 egg whites, room temperature   Pinch of salt
  3 tablespoons mustard mayonnaise dressing

Add salt to the egg whites and beat until stiff and glossy; fold the dressing into the egg whites. Spoon the meringue over the asparagus and sauce as for a pie. Bake in a 300° oven for 15 to 20 minutes or until thoroughly hot and meringue is slightly browned. Serves 8.

JACKSON SALAD

8 strips of bacon, fried crisp, crumbled
4 hard-cooked eggs, grated
½ cup wine vinegar
2 tablespoons Worcestershire sauce
⅔ cup salad oil
½ cup lemon juice
1½ teaspoons salt
½ teaspoon pepper, freshly ground
½ teaspoon paprika
3 quarts salad greens, washed and chilled

Combine the bacon and the hard-cooked eggs; add seasonings in order as listed. Toss lightly with salad greens. Serves 8.

PAN ROLLS

1 package dry granular yeast
¼ cup warm water
1 cup commercial sour cream
4 teaspoons sugar
⅛ teaspoon soda
1 teaspoon sugar
  3 cups sifted all-purpose flour

Dissolve the yeast in the warm water. Scald cream. Add sugar, soda and salt. Cool to lukewarm. Add yeast solution to cream mixture. Stir well. Add flour gradually and mix thoroughly. When dough is stiff, turn out on lightly floured board and knead quickly for about 3 minutes. Shape into round biscuits and place in two greased 9-inch shallow round pans. Cover and let rise in a warm place until double in bulk. Bake in a 400° oven for about 20 minutes.

CREME BRULEE WITH CANNED PEARS

1 pint whipping cream
8 eggs
½ cup granulated sugar
1 28-ounce can Bartlett pears
  ¾ cup brown sugar

Scald cream in top of double boiler. Beat the eggs and gradually add granulated sugar. Beat together thoroughly; add a pinch of salt. Pour the scalded cream over egg and sugar mixture and return to top of double boiler. Beat with egg beater until it is thick (do not overbeat as it will curdle). After it cools, put in a baking dish, then put pears on top and before serving, sprinkle with brown sugar and run under the flame of the broiler. This will form a thin crust of brown sugar. Serves 8.

QUICK CREME BRULEE WITH CANNED PEARS

1 28-ounce can Bartlett pear halves   1 pint commercial sour cream chilled
½ cup brown sugar, tightly packed

Place pears in shallow 9″ x 13″ baking dish. Spread with sour cream and cover with brown sugar. Broil about 3 inches from heat until sugar caramelizes. Serve hot.

Variations: Fresh, frozen or canned drained fruits may be substituted; for example, peach halves, pineapple chunks, or whole berries in sufficient quantity. Serves 8.

BLACK WALNUT CAKE

13 eggs, separated   3 teaspoons cream of tartar
1 teaspoon lemon flavoring   1 cup sifted cake flour
1½ cups sugar   ½ cup ground black walnuts

Beat egg yolks with flavoring until thick and lemon-colored. Gradually beat in ½ cup of the sugar. Beat egg whites until foamy; add cream of tartar gradually and continue beating until mixture is stiff and glossy. Fold egg yolk mixture into egg whites. Fold sifted cake flour and remaining 1 cup sugar in gradually; fold in nuts gently with as few strokes as possible. Pour into an ungreased 10-inch tube pan. Bake in a moderate oven (350°) for 1 to 1¼ hours, until cake is lightly browned and shrinks from sides of pan. Invert pan on wire rack to cool. When cake is cool, remove from pan. Dust with powdered sugar or use a favorite frosting. Makes 12 to 16 servings.

Buffet Dinner

Cold Trout Hors d'Oeuvre
Shrimp Sauce
Stuffed Cherry Tomatoes   Cucumber Sandwiches
Roast Capon — Corn Bread Dressing   Roast Lamb in Marinade
Vegetable Platter
Celery Heart Salad Platter — Lorenzo Dressing
Coconut Ice Cream Balls
Chocolate Sauce   Toffee Belles
Irish Coffee

ADVANCE PREPARATION SCHEDULE

Previous Day	Early Morning	Deep Freeze
Poach trout	*Sandwiches*	*Toffee Belles*
Shrimp Sauce	*Stuff tomatoes*	*Ice Cream Balls*
Ready capon	*Stuff capon*	
Marinate lamb	*Refrigerate salad in-*	
Bake corn bread	*gredients*	
Chocolate sauce	*Frost Toffee Belles*	

COLD TROUT HORS D'OEUVRE

3½ to 4 pounds of trout, cooked,   Watercress
    skinned   Stuffed Cherry Tomatoes
¼ cup lemon juice   Stuffed eggs
Cucumber slices, fluted   Lemon wedges

Prepare trout in court bouillon (see Index for recipe). Remove
from liquid. Drain and place on platter. Moisten with lemon
juice and refrigerate. Garnish with Stuffed Cherry Tomatoes,
stuffed eggs, fluted cucumber slices, watercress, and lemon wedges.
Serve with Shrimp Sauce. Serves 8.

SHRIMP SAUCE

2 cups commercial sour cream
1 cup commercial salad dressing
2 tablespoons pickle relish
1 pound cooked shrimp, coarsely chopped

2 hard-cooked eggs, coarsely chopped
2 tablespoons lemon juice

Combine all ingredients; mix well. Refrigerate.

STUFFED CHERRY TOMATOES

1 3-ounce package of cream cheese   2 tablespoons cream
24 cherry tomatoes

Soften cream cheese with cream. Scoop a small piece from the bottom of the tomato with a French cutter. Allowing ½ teaspoon per tomato, fill the tomatoes with the cheese mixture. Chill.

CUCUMBER SANDWICHES

Cut thin rounds of bread. Spread one side with mayonnaise. Spread mashed and seasoned cream cheese through a pastry tube, or with the tip of a spoon around the edges. Fill center with chopped cucumber which has been mixed with mayonnaise and finely snipped chives. Serves 8.

ROAST CAPON

1 8-pound capon
Salt, pepper and poultry seasoning
1 10-ounce can chicken consommé

Softened butter
¼ cup butter

Wash and dry bird. Rub inside with salt (allowing ⅛ teaspoon per pound) and pepper. Fill lightly with Corn Bread Stuffing. Truss, season with salt and poultry seasoning, and rub with softened butter. Place in roasting pan in a 325° oven. Baste frequently with ¼ cup butter, heated in the undiluted consommé. Bake, uncovered, for about 2½ hours, or until tender. Bird is done when the flesh on thigh feels very soft. Serves 8.

CORN BREAD DRESSING

2 tablespoons chopped onion
½ cup diced celery
½ cup butter
2 cups toasted, cubed white bread
2 cups unsweetened, coarse corn bread crumbs (may be prepared with a mix)

1 teaspoon seasoning salt
1 teaspoon salt
1 teaspoon poultry seasoning
½ teaspoon pepper
1 egg, slightly beaten
½ cup chopped oysters (optional)

Sauté the onion and celery in the butter; add the bread cubes, crumbs, and seasonings. Now add the egg, mixing lightly with a fork, and, last, the oysters. This is sufficient dressing for one 6- to 8-pound bird.

ROAST LAMB IN MARINADE

2 ounces olive oil
1 ounce lemon juice
1 medium onion, chopped
¼ cup chopped parsley
1 teaspoon salt

½ teaspoon pepper
1 teaspoon marjoram
1 teaspoon thyme
1 teaspoon caraway seed
1 garlic bud

1 6-pound leg of lamb

Combine the olive oil, lemon juice, chopped onion, chopped parsley, and seasonings to make a marinade. Cut slits in the lamb; rub marinade into the meat. Wrap in heavy aluminum foil; marinate for 12 to 24 hours. Open foil and place lamb in roasting pan in a 325° oven for 3½ hours, using marinade and pan drippings for basting. Serves 6 to 8.

VEGETABLE PLATTER

Artichokes with peas:
8 artichoke bottoms (1 20-ounce can)

1 20-ounce can baby French peas
¼ cup melted butter
¼ cup chopped parsley

Heat artichokes in liquid from can and 1 tablespoon butter. Remove and place in shallow pan. Fill artichoke cavity with peas. Pour melted butter over all. Place in a 350° oven for 10 minutes to heat. To serve, sprinkle with parsley.

Corn:

| 8 ears of corn | 1 teaspoon salt |
| 6 tablespoons butter | ½ cup light cream |

Cut corn down on cob to remove kernels, then scrape the pulp from the cob. Place in a skillet with the butter, salt and light cream; cook 5 minutes. Serves 8.

Glazed Carrots:

1 bunch carrots (4 cups cooked) *or*	½ cup brown sugar
2 20-ounce cans baby carrots	¼ cup hot water
	4 tablespoons butter

If carrots are not small, cut them into 1-inch lengths with a French vegetable cutter. Place sugar, water, and butter in a saucepan. Bring to a boil and add the cooked carrots. Simmer slowly, and turn occasionally until carrots are glazed and slightly browned. Place corn in center of platter. Arrange artichoke bottoms and carrots alternately as a border.

CELERY HEART SALAD PLATTER

2 20-ounce cans beets, sliced juliene	Bibb lettuce
1 20-ounce can celery hearts, drained, split lengthwise in 3-inch strips	1 20-ounce can green asparagus
	Hard-cooked egg, grated

Arrange beets and celery in alternating mounds on Bibb lettuce. Separate mounds by placing asparagus stalks between them. Pour Lorenzo Dressing over all and sprinkle with grated egg.

LORENZO DRESSING

| ½ cup chili sauce | 2 tablespoons lemon juice |
| ½ cup chopped watercress | 1 cup French dressing |

Shake together in a covered jar; chill.

COCONUT ICE CREAM BALLS

| 2 quarts vanilla ice cream | 2 cups grated coconut |
| | Kahlua |

Make the ice cream balls in advance using a scoop. Roll in coconut and place in freezer until ready to serve. Balls hold their shape perfectly when wrapped individually in wax paper. To serve, place ice cream in low sherbet glasses. Pour Kahlua over ice cream, or place balls of ice cream in a bowl and serve Kahlua from liqueur bottle. Serves 8.

CHOCOLATE SAUCE

2 squares (2 ounces) unsweetened chocolate
½ cup water

1 teaspoon salt
1½ cups light corn syrup
1 teaspoon vanilla

Cook chocolate and water over low heat until chocolate is melted, stirring constantly. Remove from heat; add salt and slowly mix in corn syrup. Return to heat and simmer for 10 minutes, stirring occasionally. Add vanilla. Makes about 1⅔ cups sauce. Serve hot.

TOFFEE BELLES

⅓ cup melted butter
¾ cup brown sugar
¼ teaspoon salt
2 tablespoons milk
¼ cup chopped nuts

1 teaspoon vanilla
2 cups rolled oats
1 package chocolate bits (6 ounces)

Mix the butter, brown sugar, salt, milk, and vanilla together; stir in the rolled oats. Grease very small muffin tins. Place one table-spoon mixture in each. Bake in a 325° oven for 20 minutes. Cool; frost with melted chocolate bits; sprinkle with the nuts. Makes 16 to 18.

IRISH COFFEE

For each serving: Place 2 cubes sugar in large, stemmed wine glass or coffee cup. Pour 1 ounce Irish whisky over sugar. Fill glass to within one-half inch of top with double strength black coffee. Stir until sugar is dissolved. Place a tablespoon of whipped cream on top. Drink through cream; do not stir.

Buffet Dinner

Apple Curry Soup   Crabmeat Louis — Sauce Louis
Cheese Sticks
Escalopes of Veal   Tomato Sauce Provençale
Broiled Steak with Mustard Crust
Baked Potatoes Drake   Chive Topping   Cauliflower Custard
Fromage à la Crème
Coconut Crisps   Old-Fashioned Cookies
Coffee

ADVANCE PREPARATION SCHEDULE

Previous Day	Early Morning	Deep Freeze
Fromage à la Crème	Soup	*Cheese Sticks*
Sauce Louis	Cauliflower	*Cookies*

APPLE CURRY SOUP

2 10½-ounce cans condensed con- 1 cup light cream
sommé   Salt and pepper
1 apple, grated or chopped fine ½ teaspoon curry powder, or to
1 small onion, chopped   taste

Cook the consommé, apple, and onion together until tender, about
5 or 10 minutes. Put through a strainer. Stir in the cream, and
season to taste. Reheat the soup, but do not boil. Pour into soup
bowls and float a little grated apple on top for interest.

CRABMEAT LOUIS

1 pound crabmeat   1 cup diced celery
1 cup cauliflowerets   Sauce Louis

Marinate all ingredients together in Sauce Louis for several hours.
To serve individually, line a scallop shell with lettuce, place mixture in shells. Chill until serving time.

SAUCE LOUIS

1 cup mayonnaise	1 teaspoon horse-radish
½ cup French dressing	1 teaspoon Worcestershire sauce
¼ cup catsup or chili sauce	½ teaspoon salt

Combine all ingredients. Mix well.

CHEESE STICKS

Bread slices, crusts removed   Softened butter
Sharp Cheddar cheese, grated

Spread bread with butter; sprinkle with sharp grated cheese. Place in refrigerator to harden until ready to serve. Cut each slice into 3 strips. Toast in a 375° oven or under broiler until lightly browned.

BROILED STEAK WITH MUSTARD CRUST

Allow ¾ pound boned beef per person; use strip or sirloin steak. Leave steaks at room temperature for about one hour. Coat steak on one side with prepared mustard about ¼ inch thick. Place in preheated broiler. Broil on one side to personal taste, then coat other side with mustard; broil again. Mustard should form a crust and give the steak a barbecued appearance. Serve at once.

ESCALOPES OF VEAL

6 veal slices (escalopes)	½ teaspoon seasoned salt
⅓ cup butter	2 tablespoons chopped parsley
1 cup soup stock	2 tablespoons chopped onion
¼ teaspoon garlic powder	Salt and pepper

Have veal cut in one-half-inch slices; pound with the edge of a saucer until very thin. Melt butter in a skillet and when very hot sauté escalopes for 3 minutes on each side. Add stock, garlic powder, seasoned salt, parsley, and onion and blend; sprinkle with salt and pepper. Cover and simmer 20 minutes. To serve, arrange escalopes in a circle to border platter and fill center with Tomato Sauce.

TOMATO SAUCE PROVENCALE

8 large tomatoes	1 clove garlic, minced (optional)
1 onion, thinly sliced	1 tablespoon flour
¼ teaspoon thyme	1 tablespoon butter
1 bay leaf	½ teaspoon salt
¼ teaspoon pepper	

Place tomatoes in a heavy skillet and crush. Add onion, thyme, bay leaf, and garlic. Simmer 20 minutes or until tomatoes are tender. Strain through a food mill or ricer. Return to skillet. Blend flour and butter and stir into tomato purée. Season with salt and pepper and simmer 15 minutes.

CAULIFLOWER CUSTARD

1 large head of cauliflower	1 teaspoon salt
2 eggs, beaten	½ teaspoon pepper
1 teaspoon melted butter	1 cup light cream

Trim and wash cauliflower; cook uncovered, in boiling salted water for 15 minutes. Drain and chop fine; combine with remaining ingredients and mix well. Pour into well-buttered 1-quart casserole. Bake in a 325° oven 45 minutes or until custard is set. (Prepare in advance except for baking.)

BAKED POTATOES DRAKE

6 uniform-sized Idaho potatoes	Bowl of crumbled crisp bacon
Salad oil	Bowl of commercial sour cream
Bowls of snipped chives	

Wash and dry potatoes, and rub each with salad oil. Arrange on baking sheet and place in a 450° oven. Bake 45 to 60 minutes or until tender. Remove from oven at once; prick to let out steam and cut a 1½-inch cross in top of each. Holding bottom with a towel (or some protection from heat), press until the fluffy white of the potato bursts through the opening. Top with salt and dust with paprika. Serve with the bowls of bacon, sour cream, and chives to be used as topping.

FROMAGE A LA CREME

1 8-ounce package cream cheese	2 tablespoons lemon juice
2 tablespoons light cream	1 cup heavy cream, whipped
⅛ teaspoon salt	Any fresh or frozen berries

Blend the cream cheese with the light cream until soft. Stir in the salt and lemon juice. Fold cheese into the whipped cream. Put mixture into a quart mold or 6 individual molds, which have been rinsed in very cold water. Chill until set. Unmold and serve with fruit topping, Raspberry Sauce (see Index), or thawed frozen packaged strawberries.

COCONUT CRISPS

¾ cup melted butter	1 cup shredded coconut
2 cups brown sugar	1 cup chopped pecans
2 whole eggs	1½ teaspoons vanilla
1 cup all-purpose flour	⅛ teaspoon salt

Cream butter and sugar; add eggs, then flour, and remaining ingredients. Mix well. Pour into a shallow pan, spread as thin as possible. Bake in a 300° oven for 1 hour. Cut in squares and remove while hot.

OLD-FASHIONED COOKIES

1 cup butter	2 cups all-purpose flour
1 cup confectioners' sugar	1 teaspoon vanilla
1 egg	⅛ teaspoon nutmeg
1 teaspoon baking soda	Sugar
1 teaspoon cream of tartar	Cinnamon

Combine ingredients in order given. Place in refrigerator for one hour. Roll out and cut with cooky cutter; or drop by teaspoon on cooky sheet 2 inches apart and flatten down lightly with bottom of drinking glass covered with damp cloth. Sprinkle with sugar and cinnamon. Bake in a 325° oven for 10 minutes.

Buffet Dinner

Avocado Pineapple Cocktail
Duck or Goose Esterházy
Confetti Rice Mold
Caramelized Tomatoes   Herbed Peas
Fruit Platter   Fruit Mayonnaise
Grand Marnier Soufflé
Coffee

ADVANCE PREPARATION SCHEDULE

Previous Day	Early Morning	Deep Freeze
Ready poultry	*Confetti Rice*	
	Mayonnaise	
	Tomatoes	

AVOCADO PINEAPPLE COCKTAIL

1 No. 2 can pineapple chunks, drained (13½ ounces)
2 avocados, diced same size as pineapple chunks
4 slices bacon, crisply fried and crumbled
Lettuce
2 cups Thousand Island Dressing (see Index for recipe)

Pour pineapple juice over avocado to prevent turning dark and drain. Mix with pineapple chunks. Line sherbet glasses with lettuce leaves, fill with combined avocado and pineapple, cover generously with dressing and sprinkle with crumbled bacon. Serves 8.

DUCK OR GOOSE ESTERHAZY

1 10-lb. goose *or* 2 ducks, 5 to 6 lbs. each
½ teaspoon salt and pepper
1 teaspoon thyme
8 apples
2 oranges
2 cans sauerkraut (28 ounces each)
2 cups raw cranberries
¼ cup sugar
½ cup dark corn syrup
1 cup Madeira *or* sauterne wine

Wash ducks. Rub with salt, pepper, and thyme, inside and out.

Cut apples into quarters and core. Stuff into ducks. Squeeze the juice of an orange into each cavity over the apples; cut orange peel into strips and place with apples. Close duck with skewers. Place on rack in roaster in a 350° oven for 1 hour. Pour off grease and reduce temperature to 325°. Roast another hour. Pour off the grease again. Place sauerkraut and cranberries in bottom of roaster. Sprinkle with sugar. Pour in syrup. Lay the ducks on top, breast side down. Pour wine over all and roast one hour in a 325° oven. Roasting time may vary with age of poultry. Average time is 20 minutes per pound. To serve, place quartered ducks on bed of sauerkraut.

Goose may need an additional hour of cooking time; but the preparation is the same. Serves 8.

Variation: Stuff fowl with your favorite dressing instead of apples.

CONFETTI RICE MOLD

1 cup washed rice	½ cup green onion tops, chopped
1½ cups boiling water	½ cup green onion bottoms,
1 teaspoon salt	chopped very fine
½ cup butter	⅓ cup pimento strips
3 eggs, slightly beaten	1 teaspoon salt
1 20-ounce can bean sprouts, drained	⅛ teaspoon pepper

Place rice in boiling salted water in top of double boiler. Cover and cook about 40 minutes. Melt butter in a large skillet and scramble eggs loosely so that they are moist but set. Add rice and remaining ingredients; mix well and heat. Lower flame, cover and cook very slowly for 10 minutes. If very dry, add 2 more tablespoons butter. This preparation may be made in advance. To serve, reheat rice carefully and pack into a greased 6-cup ring mold which has been heated. Turn out on a platter and border with Caramelized Tomatoes and center with Herbed Peas. Serves 8.

CARAMELIZED TOMATOES

8 uniform, medium-sized toma-   ½ cup brown sugar
   toes   1 teaspoon salt
½ cup butter, melted   ¼ teaspoon pepper
4 slices bread, crusts removed,
   cubed

Remove pulp from tomatoes after cutting off ¼-inch slice from the stem end. Leave enough of the shell so the tomato will not lose its shape. Pour melted butter over the bread cubes; add sugar, seasoning, and 1½ cups of the tomato pulp. Blend well. Fill tomato shells generously. Bake in a 350° oven in a shallow pan for 30 minutes. Serves 8.

HERBED PEAS

3 10-ounce packages frozen peas   3 tablespoons butter
3 tablespoons chopped chives   ½ teaspoon dried sweet basil
   ¼ teaspoon paprika

Cook peas according to the directions on the package. Drain; add remaining ingredients. Thoroughly heat before serving. Serves 8.

FRUIT PLATTER

1 fresh pineapple   2 cups fresh strawberries, washed
8 spiced peaches   but not hulled
2 cups assorted melon balls   ½ cup pomegranate seeds
   Watercress

Remove pineapple top, and cut pineapple into ¼-inch slices. Peel each slice, remove core and cut in half. Border platter with overlapping pineapple slices and center with alternate mounds of melon balls, peaches and strawberries. Sprinkle with pomegranate seeds and garnish with watercress. The pineapple top may be split and used as decoration. Any variety of seasonal fruit is always delicious as well as attractive. Serves 8.

FRUIT MAYONNAISE

2 eggs, slightly beaten	2 tablespoons butter
1 cup pineapple juice	1 teaspoon cornstarch
2 tablespoons lemon juice	1 teaspoon sugar
	1 cup whipping cream

Place all ingredients except cream in the top of a double boiler. Cook over low heat, stirring constantly until thickened. Cool. Before serving, fold in the whipped cream.

GRAND MARNIER SOUFFLE

¼ cup butter	4 egg yolks, well beaten
¼ cup flour	1 teaspoon vanilla
½ teaspoon salt	2 tablespoons Grand Marnier
1 cup scalded milk	½ cup crushed nut brittle
½ cup sugar	(optional)
	4 egg whites, stiffly beaten

Melt butter; add flour, blend, and add salt and milk. Add the sugar to the egg yolks, then gradually to the white sauce, continually beating. Add vanilla, Grand Marnier, and the crushed brittle. Fold in the stiffly beaten whites. Turn into a buttered 1½-quart casserole which has been sprinkled with sugar. Set in a pan of hot water. Bake 1 hour in a 325° oven.

Variations:

Eliminate Grand Marnier and substitute the following:

Chocolate: Add 2 ounces of chocolate, melted, to white sauce.

Mocha: Add 2 teaspoons instant coffee to the white sauce. Good with the chocolate variation also.

Orange: Beat 2 tablespoons thawed frozen or canned orange concentrate into egg yolk mixture and add the grated rind of an orange.

Coconut: Fold in 1 cup grated fresh or chopped canned coconut, just before folding in whites of egg.

SAUCE VANILLE

2 cups light cream or milk
½ vanilla bean or 1 teaspoon vanilla extract
½ cup sugar

4 egg yolks, beaten
½ cup heavy cream, whipped (optional)
¼ cup liqueur or cordial

Combine light cream with vanilla bean in top of double boiler, place directly over heat and bring to a boil. Remove from heat. Add sugar to egg yolks and stir into hot cream. Cook over hot water in double boiler, stirring constantly, until mixture thickens and coats the spoon. If vanilla extract is used instead of vanilla bean, add at this point. Cool. Just before serving, fold in whipped cream and/or liqueur.

Barbecues

*Each recipe
serves six
unless otherwise
indicated*

NO LONGER is the kitchen strictly a woman's domain, for man has invaded it with his knack for the barbecue. The following recipes are a challenge to the man who loves to please his family and friends with his cooking. However, lacking a zealous male host, the hostess will do just as well with these indoor and outdoor menus.

Barbecue foods may also be enjoyed by city dwellers for whom the alfresco type of eating is not available. For them we have included the indoor rotisserie suggestions at the end of the barbecue section.

HELPFUL HINTS FOR BARBECUING
Outdoor barbecues cast a special kind of spell over young and old alike. Fresh air, the sizzle of meat cooking over glowing embers, and the pungent tang of smoke sharpen appetites to razor keenness. Simple or elaborate, each meal becomes an adventure in good eating when served in the open air.

EQUIPMENT

Paper and kindling
Charcoal or dry wood
Poker
Matches
Paper towels and napkins
Bib-type apron
Canvas or asbestos gloves and pot
 holders
Grill
Long-handled fork and spoon

Tongs for turning food
Hinged, log-handled wire broiler
Dutch oven
Platter or pan for cooked meat
Small saucepan for barbecue sauce
Long-handled swab or brush for
 barbecue sauce
Condiment kit of salt, pepper,
 catsup, Worcestershire sauce,
 cream salad mustard

Build your fire early enough so that it will have burned down to coals by the time you are ready to cook the meal.

Build a big enough fire to provide heat for cooking food for all your guests at one time. A shallow bed of coals will do for chops, hamburgers or hot dogs. Roasts and thick meats need a deeper bed.

Charcoal and dry woods that burn with a pleasing aroma make good fuel. Place crumpled newspapers and kindling in the fire pit first, then arrange the fuel on top loosely so that air can circulate freely throughout. Once the coals have burned down to a gray color, lit by a ruddy glow, you will have the steady even heat necessary for barbecuing.

The length of time needed for barbecuing may be shortened by doing some precooking in the oven first. Most of the menus in the barbecue section are written on the assumption that a kitchen is close at hand. However, for those who desire to cook the complete meal out-of-doors, the following recipes may be used in conjunction with the barbecued meats.

BARBECUED SKILLET POTATOES

Peel and thinly slice 4 large potatoes into an iron skillet. Spread butter, salt and pepper between layers and fry on top of barbecue grill, turning as the bottom layer browns.

BARBECUED BAKED POTATOES

Scrub large Idaho potatoes, pierce with fork, wrap in heavy-duty aluminum foil and place in glowing coals of barbecue grill for 45 to 60 minutes. To serve: Fold foil back from top half of potato, slash across and top with a large piece of butter.

ROASTING EARS

Strip outer husks from freshly picked sweet corn, leaving inner husk and silk intact. Wrap in heavy-duty aluminum foil and place in slow-burning coals in barbecue grill for 20 minutes OR: Completely husk corn, rinse in cold water. Spread with butter, sprinkle with salt and pepper. Wrap in foil and roast same as above.

ZIPPER BANANAS (IN THE GRILL)

Strip one section to the bottom of a slightly underripe banana. Spread with 1 tablespoon butter and 1 tablespoon brown sugar and sprinkle with a few drops of lemon juice. Replace folded-back peel. Wrap in heavy-duty foil and place on grate over the coals for 20 minutes. Serve by turning back foil and stripping one section of peel. Scoop out soft pulp with spoon.

Barbecue Dinner

Ham Kabobs   Crabmeat Diable
Roast Beef on a Spit
Marinated Vegetable Platter   Old-Fashioned Baked Beans
Salt Sticks
Rainbow Sundae Buffet   Plum Kuchen
Coconut Squares
Iced Tea   Coffee

ADVANCE PREPARATION SCHEDULE

Previous Day	Early Morning	Deep Freeze
Crabmeat Diable		*Beans*
Baked Beans		*Plum Kuchen*
		Coconut Squares

HAM KABOBS

Alternate cubes of ready-to-eat ham with pineapple cubes on skewers. Marinate in soy sauce for 15 minutes before grilling. Grill until lightly brown.

SOY SAUCE FOR HAM KABOBS

1 teaspoon dark brown sugar
½ cup cold water
1 teaspoon horse-radish

2 teaspoons strong prepared mustard
½ cup imported soy sauce

Mix sugar and water in a pitcher. Then add horse-radish and mustard. Mix well. Add soy sauce.

CRABMEAT DIABLE

2 tablespoons butter
2 tablespoons flour
¾ cup milk
½ teaspoon salt
¼ teaspoon chili powder
⅛ teaspoon Tabasco

½ cup mushrooms, sautéed; or 2-ounce can
1 6-ounce package frozen, canned or fresh crabmeat, coarsely chopped

24 profiterolle shells (see page 187

Melt the butter; add the flour, stirring until smooth. Add other ingredients except crabmeat. Cook 5 minutes. Fold in crabmeat. Cool. May be made in advance and refrigerated. To serve: Fill profiterolle shells, well rounded, and bake for 10 minutes in a 350° oven. The shells may be filled in advance if set in a covered container in refrigerator. They also may be frozen.

ROAST BEEF ON A SPIT

4-pound rib roast, boned and rolled for use on a spit
1 teaspoon rosemary

Salt and pepper
½ cup red wine
¼ cup melted butter

Season roast and center on spit. Allow your fire to burn down until coals are coated with gray ash and no flame is visible. If more coal is needed, place new briquets around outer edges of firebox. Grill 12 to 14 minutes per pound for rare meat. Baste during cooking with mixture of butter and wine.

Variation: Marinate roast in red wine for 3 hours before roasting. Proceed as above with basting.

MARINATED VEGETABLE PLATTER

2 cups peas, cooked	1 cup small, whole canned carrots
2 cups string beans, cooked	24 canned white asparagus spears
1 small cauliflower, cooked	6 broccoli spears, cooked

Drain, then marinate each kind of vegetable separately in Vinaigrette Dressing (see Index). Arrange attractively on large platter.

OLD-FASHIONED BAKED BEANS

1 pound pea beans (navy)	¼ teaspoon pepper
5 cups water	1 tablespoon salt
1 onion	¼ cup brown sugar
½ pound brisket of beef, sliced	½ cup chili sauce
1 teaspoon dry mustard	¼ cup molasses
½ cup strong coffee	

Pick over the beans, wash and cover with 3 cups water. Soak overnight. In the morning, add 2 cups of water or enough to cover and cook until tender. Cooking time is about one hour, but to test them, blow on a bean and if the skin loosens, beans are done. Place the onion in a 2-quart bean pot. Alternate layers of beef and beans, with beans at the bottom. Combine remaining ingredients, pour over the beans and add water to cover. Cover and bake in a 250° oven from 6 to 8 hours. Add boiling water from time to time to keep the beans just covered. Uncover last half-hour of baking.

RAINBOW SUNDAE BUFFET

3 pints of ice cream, assorted   1 cup sliced peaches
   flavors   1 cup crushed pineapple
Banana halves   1 cup chocolate sauce
Fresh strawberries   1 cup marshmallow sauce
½ cup chopped walnut halves   1 cup cherry sauce

Make ice cream balls with a scoop; place in a large bowl. Arrange
the sauces and fruits in separate bowls around the ice cream.

PLUM KUCHEN

½ cup butter   ½ teaspoon baking powder
¼ cup superfine sugar   1 teaspoon vanilla
1 egg   1 28-ounce can drained, halved
1 cup all-purpose flour   plums or 16 fresh prune plums
½ teaspoon salt

Cream the butter and sugar together until light and fluffy; add the
egg; stir in the flour sifted with the salt and baking powder; add
vanilla; mix well. Pat onto the bottom of a 9-inch layer cake tin.
Arrange plum halves over the dough; sprinkle with 3 additional
tablespoons sugar. Bake in a 350° oven for 1¼ hours.

Variation: For glaze, spread with ½ cup beaten apricot jam while
cake is still hot.

COCONUT SQUARES

½ cup butter   ¾ cup coconut
1 cup all-purpose flour   3 tablespoons flour
2 tablespoons brown sugar   ¼ cup brown sugar
1 cup pecans, chopped   1 teaspoon baking powder
                   2 eggs

Blend together the butter, flour and brown sugar. Spread like a
crust on the bottom of an 8-inch-square pan. Bake 20 minutes in
a 350° oven. Meanwhile, grind together the pecans and coconut;
combine this with the flour, brown sugar, baking powder, and
eggs. Spread this over the baked crust and continue baking 25
minutes more. Cut in squares.

Barbecue Dinner

Swiss Fondue
Barbecued Breast of Lamb   Enchiladas Americanos
Cauliflower Supreme
Pickled Beets and Onion Rings
Brownie Alaska Pie   *or*   Chocolate Frosted Brownies
Raspberry Sauce
Coffee

ADVANCE PREPARATION SCHEDULE

Previous Day	Early Morning	Deep Freeze
Brownie Pie	*Parboil cauliflower*	*Enchiladas*
(may be frozen)	*Arrange casserole*	*Brownie Pie*
Pickled Beets and		*with Ice Cream*
Onion Rings		
Raspberry Sauce		

SWISS FONDUE

1 pound Swiss cheese, grated   1 cup dry white wine
2 tablespoons flour   Salt and pepper
Clove of garlic   5 tablespoons kirsch

Grate the cheese and blend into the flour. Rub the top pan of a
chafing dish with a split clove of garlic; add the wine. Place over
boiling water and heat to the boiling point. Add the cheese and
stir constantly with a wooden fork until the cheese has melted.
Season with salt and freshly ground pepper. When the mixture
returns to the boiling point, add the kirsch and serve immediately.
Keep heated in chafing dish. Serve with toast points of French
bread. Dip toast in the fondue. Eat while very hot.

BARBECUED BREAST OF LAMB

3 strips of lamb breast, about 6 pounds
¼ cup water
½ cup chopped onion
2 tablespoons shortening
½ cup lemon juice

½ cup water
1 tablespoon Worcestershire sauce
1 cup chili sauce
1 teaspoon salt
1 teaspoon chili powder
Dash of pepper

Cut lamb into serving pieces and place in covered casserole. Add water and bake for 1½ hours at 350°. Remove meat.

Prepare Basting Sauce: Sauté onion in shortening, mix with lemon juice, water, Worcestershire sauce, chili sauce, and seasonings. Dip each piece of meat in sauce. Place on barbecue grill over low fire for 30 minutes, basting while grilling.

ENCHILADAS AMERICANOS

3 large onions, minced
3 cloves garlic, minced
2 pounds ground beef
4 cups tomato purée
2 cups tomato hot sauce

1 quart cold chili
3 tablespoons chili powder
2 teaspoons pepper
18 tortillas
1 pound Monterey cheese, sliced

Cover the bottom of a large saucepan with olive oil and cook onions and garlic until tender and brown. Add ground beef and cook until meat is crumbly and brown; pour over tomato purée and hot sauce. Let sauce cook down. Mix cold chili and seasonings into smooth paste. Add to the meat mixture; cook until slightly thick.

Cut the tortillas into quarters; line baking dish and add layer of sauce; alternate layers of tortillas and sauce, ending with sauce; cover with cheese. Bake in a 350° oven approximately 30 minutes. We suggest making two casseroles, one to be frozen. Serves 10 to 12.

CAULIFLOWER SUPREME

1 head cauliflower
1 10½-ounce can tomato soup

1 cup commercial sour cream
2 tablespoons butter

Wash cauliflower; drain. Parboil in salted water for about 10 minutes; drain. Place in casserole; cover with soup and then with the cream. Dot with butter; bake in a 350° oven for 30 minutes.

PICKLED BEETS AND ONION RINGS

3 tablespoons sugar
½ teaspoon dry mustard
½ teaspoon ground cloves
½ teaspoon salt

6 tablespoons vinegar
2 cups canned, sliced beets with juice
1 onion, thinly sliced

Mix dry ingredients; add beet juice, vinegar, beets, and onion. Mix. Let stand for three hours. May be kept several days.

BROWNIE ALASKA PIE

1 16-ounce package brownie mix   1 quart vanilla ice cream

Make the brownie mix according to package directions. Pour into two 9-inch pie pans to use as pie shell. (Use one and freeze one.) Fill shell with scoops of ice cream and serve with Raspberry Sauce. If brownie recipe is desired instead of mix, use the one below, omitting frosting.

CHOCOLATE FROSTED BROWNIES

½ cup butter
3 squares chocolate (3 ounces)
2 eggs, well beaten

1 cup sugar
½ cup all-purpose flour
1 teaspoon vanilla

Place butter and chocolate in top of double boiler and heat until melted. Remove and cool. Cream eggs and sugar and add to the cooled chocolate mixture. Add sifted flour and vanilla. Blend well and pour into a greased 8″ x 8″ pan. Bake in a 350° oven for 25 minutes. Frost brownies while hot and cut immediately.

Frosting:

1 square chocolate (1 ounce)
1 tablespoon butter

1 cup confectioners' sugar
½ teaspoon vanilla

1 teaspoon cream

Melt chocolate over hot water. Remove; add butter, sugar and cream. Blend in vanilla and frost. Cut brownies while still warm

RASPBERRY SAUCE

¼ cup sugar   2 teaspoons cornstarch
1 10-ounce package frozen raspberries, thawed

Blend sugar and cornstarch and stir into raspberries. Cook over moderate heat, stirring constantly, until mixture thickens and is clear. Cool before serving.

Barbecue Dinner

Anchovy Cheese Mold   Rye Crackers   Bacon Pizzas
Bologna on a Spit   Hamburgers Gourmet
Midwest Baked Beans   Broccoli Smitane
Onion Salad
Applesauce Pie
Ginger Ale Float   Coffee

ADVANCE PREPARATION SCHEDULE

Previous Day	Early Morning	Deep Freeze
Anchovy Cheese Mold	*Meat for hamburgers*	*Baked Beans*
Onion Salad	*Bacon Pizzas*	
Applesauce Pie	*Sauce for bologna*	

ANCHOVY CHEESE MOLD

6 ounces cream cheese   ½ teaspoon caraway seed
¼ cup butter   2 anchovies, finely chopped
1 teaspoon paprika   1 green onion, finely chopped
¼ teaspoon salt   1 teaspoon capers

Mix the cheese with the butter until smooth. Add the remaining ingredients. Blend well. Form into ball. Chill for several hours. Place on a platter, and surround with assorted small crackers.

BACON PIZZAS

3 English muffins, split and toasted   Salt, pepper, oregano
6 slices Mozzarella or Cheddar   4 slices bacon, crisply fried and
  cheese   crumbled
1 3-ounce can tomato sauce   Grated Parmesan cheese

Place a slice of cheese on each half of muffin. Top with a spoonful of tomato sauce. Sprinkle with the salt, pepper, and oregano and top with bacon bits and grated Parmesan cheese. Place on a cooky sheet, bake 5 to 10 minutes in a 450° oven until cheese is bubbly and slightly browned. Serve at once.

BOLOGNA ON A SPIT

1 whole bologna, about 6 pounds

Sauce:

½ cup chili sauce   ½ teaspoon powdered rosemary
¼ cup red wine   Salt and pepper

For a basting sauce, combine chili sauce, wine, and seasonings. Blend well. Center bologna on a spit; brush frequently with the sauce. Grill for one hour over low, hot coals.

HAMBURGERS GOURMET

6 slices white bread   2 tablespoons chopped onion
1 cup dry, red wine   1 teaspoon salt
1 cup water   ⅛ teaspoon ground pepper
2 pounds chopped beef   Bread crumbs

Trim crust from bread and soak for 10 minutes in mixture of wine and water. Add to chopped meat; mix well and season with onion, salt, and pepper. Shape into patties and dip in bread crumbs. Let set. To serve, sauté quickly in butter. Makes 8 hamburgers.

Note: Reduce quantity of wine if desired.

MIDWEST BAKED BEANS

1 pound navy beans   1 cup brown sugar
½ pound bacon   1 cup catsup
¼ pound butter   1 6-ounce can tomato sauce
     ¼ teaspoon dry mustard

Wash beans. Cover with three cups water and soak overnight.
Add two cups water and boil, covered, about one hour. Place
beans in alternate layers with the bacon in a 2-quart casserole.
Combine remaining ingredients and pour over the beans. Cover
and bake in a 325° oven for 5 hours. Remove the lid the last
hour. If beans become too dry while baking, add additional
tomato sauce. *Note:* This dish freezes well. Serves 6 to 8.

BROCCOLI SMITANE

2 10-ounce packages frozen   ½ cup commercial sour cream
   broccoli   1 teaspoon prepared horse-radish
2 tablespoons butter   ¼ teaspoon salt
2 tablespoons flour   ¼ teaspoon thyme
½ cup water, drained from cooked   ⅛ teaspoon pepper
   broccoli

Prepare broccoli according to package directions. Do not overcook. Melt butter in saucepan over low heat; blend in flour. Add
water gradually, cooking and stirring until thick. Stir in sour cream
and seasonings. Serve sauce over broccoli. Serves 8.

ONION SALAD

Peel and slice 1½ pounds white onions. Separate into rings. Plunge
into boiling water for one minute. Soak in iced water for 15
minutes. Drain and sprinkle with ¼ cup sugar. Cover with the
following dressing:

Dressing:

     ¼ cup Wesson oil   Salt and pepper
     ½ cup vinegar   More sugar, if desired

Can be kept in jar in refrigerator indefinitely.

APPLESAUCE PIE

28 crushed graham crackers 3 cups applesauce, fresh or
¼ pound butter, softened   canned
          ¼ teaspoon cinnamon (optional)
    1 cup heavy cream, whipped

Blend graham crackers and the butter together. Reserve one third of the mixture for topping. Line a 9-inch pie plate with remaining two thirds crumb mixture, pressing firmly against sides of the plate. Pour in the applesauce, combined with cinnamon, and cover with the remaining crumbs. Bake in a 400° oven for 20 minutes. Cool. Serve with whipped cream.

GINGER ALE FLOAT

Place a scoop of orange sherbet in a tall glass, and fill with ginger ale. Garnish with sprigs of mint and orange slices.

Barbecue Dinner

Gazpacho (Spanish Soup)
Relish Tray Savory Bits
Barbecue Pork Loin Roast
Corn and Oyster Bake Marinated Red Cabbage
Broiled Fruit Platter
Lemon Cake
Coffee

ADVANCE PREPARATION SCHEDULE

Previous Day	Early Morning	Deep Freeze
Gazpacho	*Marinated Cabbage*	*Lemon Cake*
Savory Bits	*Corn and Oyster Bake*	
Barbecue Sauces		

GAZPACHO
(Spanish Soup)

¼ cup olive oil
2 tablespoons vinegar
3 cloves garlic, minced
2 large onions

2 thick slices stale brown bread
5 pounds ripe tomatoes
2 cups cold water
1 green pepper

Blend oil, vinegar, garlic, onions, and bread in the blender; then add the remaining ingredients. Blend thoroughly. Chill and serve with a dot of commercial sour cream. This should be made at least four hours in advance to allow flavors to blend. Serve in individual bowls with Poppy-Seed Melba Toast (see Index for recipe).

RELISH TRAY

Raw cauliflower buds, celery hearts, green onions, radish roses, carrot curls. To make carrot curls, cut thin lengthwise slivers of carrot with a vegetable peeler. Roll up tightly and pin together with a toothpick. Drop into ice water and let them remain for about an hour until the curls hold their shape when toothpicks are removed.

SAVORY BITS

1 cup Wheat Chex
1 cup Rice Chex
1 cup Cheerios

⅓ cup melted butter
1½ teaspoons garlic salt
¼ teaspoon salt

Mix all ingredients well. Toast under broiler until brown, stirring frequently; or bits may be heated in a slow oven for 15 minutes, then a hot oven for about 20 minutes longer.

BARBECUED PORK LOIN ROAST

3 cloves garlic
7 whole peppercorns
1 teaspoon salt
1 teaspoon cumin seed

1 tablespoon oregano
1 6-pound rolled, boneless pork
   loin roast

Crush together first 5 ingredients and rub mixture into pork. Place roast on a barbecue skewer, and bake in a moderate oven (350°)

for 1 hour. While roast is baking, start charcoal fire and bring to a white ash. Remove roast from oven and place on revolving spit over the charcoal fire. Cook about 4 hours more, basting frequently with following barbecue sauce for last hour. Serves 12.

QUICK BARBECUE SAUCE

3 cloves garlic, minced	1 cup catsup
1 onion, finely chopped	1 teaspoon chili powder
1 bay leaf	½ cup vinegar
2 tablespoons butter	Salt and pepper

Sauté garlic, onion, and bay leaf in butter until light brown. Add remaining ingredients, and simmer for 30 minutes.

SAVORY BARBECUE SAUCE

2 tablespoons shortening	1½ teaspoons oregano
1 green pepper, chopped	1 teaspoon prepared mustard
1 large onion, chopped	2 tablespoons vinegar
3 cloves garlic, minced	1 tablespoon molasses
2 6-ounce cans tomato paste	1 tablespoon brown sugar
2 cans water	3 dashes Tabasco
1 No. 2 can (2½ cups) tomatoes	½ teaspoon Worcestershire
2 tablespoons chili powder	sauce
⅛ teaspoon cumin seed	1 bay leaf
4 peppercorns	4 whole cloves
Pinch celery seed	Few coriander seeds

Heat shortening in heavy skillet; sauté green pepper, onion, and garlic until golden brown. Add remaining ingredients and simmer one hour. More water may be added if sauce becomes too thick.

CORN AND OYSTER BAKE

1 pint large oysters	1 tablespoon Worcestershire
1 28-ounce can corn, cream style,	sauce
yellow	¼ teaspoon mustard
1 teaspoon salt	½ cup bread crumbs
½ teaspoon pepper	2 tablespoons melted butter

Drain the oysters. Combine with corn and seasonings. Pour into a buttered 1½-quart casserole; top with combined crumbs and butter. Bake in a 350° oven for 45 minutes.

MARINATED RED CABBAGE

1 onion, chopped	2 tablespoons sugar
2 tablespoons chicken fat *or* butter	1 teaspoon salt
	½ teaspoon pepper
2 tablespoons flour	2 medium-sized heads red cabbage, shredded
½ cup vinegar	
3 sour apples, sliced	

Brown onion in fat; blend in flour. Add remaining ingredients and simmer until cabbage is tender, about 25 minutes.

BROILED FRUIT PLATTER

Place your choice of canned, drained pears, peaches, plums, and pineapple in large shallow baking dish. Pour enough of the fruit juices over to cover. Sprinkle with brown sugar, slivered blanched almonds and about ¼ cup of sherry. Place under broiler 4 inches from heat for about 8 minutes until sugar has melted and fruit is lightly browned.

LEMON CAKE

¼ cup butter	1 teaspoon baking soda
1 cup brown sugar	⅓ teaspoon salt
1 egg, beaten	¾ cup sour milk or buttermilk
1½ cups sifted cake flour	¼ cup raisins
Grated rind of 1 lemon	

Cream butter; add sugar gradually and cream well. Beat in egg. Sift flour with baking soda and salt and add alternately with sour milk, beating well after each addition. Beat in raisins and lemon rind. Pour into a greased 8-inch-square pan. Bake in a moderate oven (350°) for about 30 minutes, or until cake bakes away from sides of pan. Remove from oven and, while still hot, pour over the top of the cake the juice of one lemon mixed with ¼ cup brown sugar. Makes 9 2½-inch squares.

Barbecue Dinner

Lobster Parmesan   Seafood on a Skewer
Herbed Lamb Chops   Cold Sliced Turkey
Dill Pickle Relish
Noodle Mold   Spinach Amandine
Salad Imperial   Garden Green Goddess Dressing
Angel Fruit Pie
Mint Tea   Coffee

ADVANCE PREPARATION SCHEDULE

Previous Day	Early Morning	Deep Freeze
Dill Pickle Relish	*Stuff lamb chops*	*Turkey*
Roast Turkey (may be	*Arrange appetizers for*	
frozen)	*skewers*	
Meringue for Angel	*Green Goddess Dress-*	
Fruit Pie	*ing*	
	Complete Angel Pie	

LOBSTER PARMESAN

Place cooked lobster chunks, rolled in grated Parmesan cheese, alternately on skewers with mushroom caps. Broil 3 to 5 minutes, basting with melted butter and sherry.

SEAFOOD ON A SKEWER

Alternate scallops on skewers with stuffed olives and marinated shrimp (see Index for recipe). Broil 5 to 8 minutes, basting with butter, flavored with chopped parsley. These may be done either on a barbecue grill or a rotisserie.

HERBED LAMB CHOPS

Herb Butter:
Whip until creamy ½ cup butter; then mix in one or two **dried** herbs of your choice; minced parsley, mint, crushed rosemary **or** thyme may be used. Add a dash of salt and black pepper **and** seasoning salt, if you desire. Chill.

Lamb Chops:
6 loin lamb chops, 2 inches thick

Using a sharp paring knife, make a deep pocket in the thickest part of the chop. Stuff the pocket with about 1 tablespoon of the herb butter. Close, using round wooden toothpicks. Broil chops over the glowing coals which have burned down to medium heat. When brown on one side, turn and brown on the other side, brushing occasionally with a mixture of equal quantities of oil and lemon juice. Be certain the fat of chops is cooked until crisp. A 2-inch chop will take about 16 minutes to each side to be medium done. Season to taste with salt and pepper before serving.
Variation: Chops may be stuffed with a mushroom cap or **roasted** just with seasoning.

DILL PICKLE RELISH

Grind:
4 dill pickles 6 unpeeled red apples 2 onions

Add:
½ cup vinegar 1 cup sugar

Mix well. Place in jar. Will keep several days in refrigerator.

NOODLE MOLD

2 8-ounce packages broad noodles 4 eggs, beaten
½ cup butter 1 cup sweet cream or milk
1 cup sugar ½ teaspoon salt
1 cup commercial sour cream ½ cup white raisins (optional)

Boil noodles as directed. Drain after washing with cold **water.**
Mash softened butter with sugar, add remaining ingredients, **pour**

into thoroughly buttered 2-quart mold. Place mold in a pan of hot water. Bake in a 375° oven for about 45 minutes or until finger dents the pudding. Turn out onto heated platter and garnish with vegetables. Border the platter with tiny whole butttered beets and center mold with Brussels sprouts. Serves 8.

SPINACH AMANDINE

2 10-ounce packages of chopped,   ½ cup blanched almonds, slivered
    frozen spinach   2 tablespoons butter
1 10½-ounce can mushroom soup

Cook spinach according to the directions on the package. Drain. Sauté almonds in the butter. Add the soup to the spinach. Pour into a buttered 1-quart casserole. Sprinkle almonds on top. Bake in a 350° oven for 30 minutes or until thoroughly heated. Serves 6 to 8.

SALAD IMPERIAL

10 heads limestone lettuce   2 large tomatoes, halved
 8 ounces hearts of palm (1 can)   1 avocado, sliced
4 hard-cooked eggs, sliced

Arrange a bed of the greens in a large salad bowl. Cut hearts of palm in 1-inch lengths, and place on greens in layers with the remaining ingredients, using the contrasting colors of ingredients for garnish. To serve, toss with Green Goddess Salad Dressing. Serve very cold. Serves 8.

GREEN GODDESS DRESSING

1 2-ounce can chopped anchovies   1 cup commercial sour cream
3 tablespoons chopped chives   1 cup mayonnaise
1 tablespoon lemon juice   ½ cup chopped parsley
3 tablespoons tarragon vinegar   Dash freshly ground pepper
½ teaspoon salt

Combine all ingredients in blender and whirl for 20 seconds, or beat thoroughly with rotary beater. Chill.

ANGEL FRUIT PIE

Meringue:

4 egg whites, room temperature   1 cup sugar
¼ teaspoon cream of tartar   1 teaspoon vanilla

Beat the egg whites until frothy, add the cream of tartar. Beat until stiff. Gradually beat in the sugar until glossy. Add the vanilla. Pile into a large Pyrex pie plate which has been well greased. Bake for 1 hour at 300°. Cool.

Custard:

4 egg yolks   2½ tablespoons water
½ cup sugar   1 teaspoon vanilla

Beat the egg yolks until thick and lemon-colored. Add the sugar and water. Cook in a double boiler to a custard consistency. Cool. Add vanilla.

Topping:

1 cup heavy cream, whipped   2 cups fresh fruit — sliced
1 tablespoon confectioners' sugar   peaches, strawberries or rasp-
1 teaspoon vanilla   berries

Add the vanilla and confectioners' sugar to the whipped cream. Spread one half of the whipped cream mixture over the bottom of the pie shell, then the custard. Cover with fruit; then with remaining cream. Chill for several hours before serving. Well-drained frozen fruit may be used.

MINT TEA

3 cups boiling water   Confectioners' sugar
6 teaspoons tea   Ginger ale
1 tablespoon mint jelly   Mint sprigs
Lime juice   Lime slices

Pour the water over the tea. Let steep for 5 minutes. Strain; pour over jelly and stir until dissolved. To frost rims of the glasses, dip into lime juice, then into sugar. GLASSES MUST BE CHILLED. Fill glasses half full of tea. Add crushed ice and ginger ale. Garnish with a sprig of mint and a slice of lime. Serves 8.

Barbecue Dinner

Hawaiian Appetizers   Eggs Anchovy
Chateaubriand à la Pierre
Potatoes Parmesan   Vegetables Mornay
Marinated Tomatoes
Fresh Strawberry Pie
Coffee

ADVANCE PREPARATION SCHEDULE

Previous Day	Early Morning	Deep Freeze
Eggs Anchovy	*Marinate tomatoes*	
Barbecue sauces	*Strawberry Pie*	
Marinate beef	*Arrange appetizers*	
Vegetable casserole	*Potatoes for cooking*	

HAWAIIAN APPETIZERS

Alternate on skewers cubes of cooked chicken, cubes of pineapple, and 1-inch squares of green pepper. Roast 5 minutes, basting with barbecue sauce.

CLEO'S BARBECUE SAUCE

½ cup catsup
2 tablespoons Worcestershire
   sauce
1 tablespoon vinegar
2 tablespoons brown sugar

½ cup water
2 tablespoons butter
2 tablespoons soy sauce
⅛ teaspoon fresh black pepper
1 clove garlic, minced (optional)

Mix and cover. Cook slowly for 30 minutes. (For a more pungent flavor, use Quick Barbecue Sauce. See Index.)

EGGS ANCHOVY

4 hard-cooked eggs
2 tablespoons mayonnaise
2 teaspoons anchovy paste
1 teaspoon chopped parsley
½ teaspoon paprika
8 tiny sprigs parsley

Cut eggs lengthwise with French cutter. Scoop out yolks. Mash together with the mayonnaise, anchovy paste, and chopped parsley. Refill the white with the mixture, dust with paprika, and garnish with sprigs of parsley. Serves 8.

CHATEAUBRIAND A LA PIERRE
(Filet Mignon)

1 whole beef tenderloin (5 to 6 pounds)
1 cup Chablis
¼ pound butter
½ cup cognac
¼ teaspoon thyme
1 bay leaf
1 small onion, thinly sliced
1 pound mushrooms, thinly sliced
1 teaspoon salt
⅛ teaspoon pepper

Marinate the beef overnight in the Chablis. Melt the butter in a saucepan, add cognac and seasonings. Stir well. Add onion slices and cook to half the volume. Add mushrooms and cook approximately 4 minutes. Remove the meat from the marinade; cut a pocket in the tenderloin. Stuff with the onion-mushroom mixture. Skewer together. Secure meat on a spit; tie and roast about 1 hour. Baste with marinade and drippings. It will be rare. Serves 8.

VEGETABLES MORNAY

2 10-ounce packages frozen mixed vegetables
¼ teaspoon thyme
¼ teaspoon nutmeg
2 cups vegetable liquid
Milk
¼ cup butter
¼ cup flour
¼ cup Parmesan cheese (optional)
3 tablespoons sauterne
½ cup soft bread crumbs (day-old)

Cook vegetables according to package directions, adding thyme and nutmeg but cooking one-half the length of time. Drain; reserve liquid. Place vegetables in a greased 1½-quart casserole. Add milk to the vegetable liquid to make 2 cups, if necessary. Melt butter in a saucepan and add flour; stir until smooth. Blend in the vegetable liquid stirring constantly until thick and smooth; add cheese and sauterne. Spread the bread crumbs over the vegetables and pour the sauce over the bread crumbs and vegetables. Bake in a 325° oven for 45 minutes or until brown. Serves 8.

POTATOES PARMESAN

6 tablespoons butter	2 tablespoons chopped parsley
1 teaspoon salt	2 tablespoons grated Parmesan
1½ pounds very small new pota- toes, scrubbed	cheese

Melt butter in skillet over low heat. Add the salt and potatoes. Cover. Cook about 1 hour, turning frequently. Remove the potatoes from the skillet. Place in a serving dish. To the melted butter, add finely chopped parsley and Parmesan cheese. Pour over the potatoes. Serves 8.

MARINATED TOMATOES

8 large tomatoes, peeled and sliced	½ teaspoon salt
	¼ teaspoon dried sweet basil
½ cup thinly sliced scallions	2 cups French dressing
Salad greens	

Place tomato slices in a shallow dish. Sprinkle with scallions, salt and sweet basil. Pour French dressing over all. Marinate for several hours. Lift tomatoes from marinade. Serve on a bed of salad greens on a large platter. Serves 8.

FRESH STRAWBERRY PIE

1 9-inch baked pie shell	1 cup heavy cream
2 tablespoons bread crumbs	1 quart fresh strawberries, sliced
1 6-ounce glass currant jelly	

Prepare pie shell (see Index for recipe). Sprinkle with bread crumbs. Whip the heavy cream. Melt currant jelly over low heat. Spread the cream over the bottom of the pie shell. Add the berries, spreading evenly over the cream. Pour the melted currant jelly over the berries, covering each one. Chill before serving.

Barbecue Dinner

Barbecued Shrimps   Barbecued Lamb Riblets
Jumbo Frankfurters
Cumberland Sauce   Onion Relish
Baked Beans Waikiki
Steamed Corn — Yankee Style
Cabbage Salad with Tomato Mayonnaise
Small Poppy-Seed Rolls (prepared)
Rice Pudding Hofbrau   Molasses Chips
Coffee

ADVANCE PREPARATION SCHEDULE

Previous Day	Early Morning	Deep Freeze
Partially bake beans	*Cabbage Salad*	*Molasses Chips*
Marinate riblets	*Cumberland Sauce*	
Rice Pudding		

BARBECUED SHRIMPS

2 pounds large raw green shrimp   ½ teaspoon salt
½ cup soy sauce   ¼ teaspoon ground pepper
1 garlic clove, mashed   ½ cup parsley, minced
½ cup melted butter

Brush the shrimp with the soy sauce and let stand for 15 minutes. Place in a large sheet of pan-shaped heavy-duty aluminum foil. Add the garlic, salt, pepper, and parsley to the butter. Pour the mixture over the shrimp. Barbecue for 10 minutes over low, hot coals.

BARBECUED LAMB RIBLETS

Pour favorite barbecue sauce or French dressing over lamb riblets. Allow to stand several hours or overnight. Remove riblets from the sauce. Place on rack of barbecue grill 8 inches above the source of heat. Broil about 10 minutes on each side, turning once, brushing occasionally with sauce. Serve piping hot. Best eaten as a finger food.

JUMBO FRANKFURTERS

12 garlic hot dogs

Broil 10 minutes, turning frequently. Serve with Onion Relish and Cumberland Sauce.

CUMBERLAND SAUCE

1 cup currant jelly	1 tablespoon prepared mustard
¼ cup vinegar	2 tablespoons chopped, fresh mint

Blend together all ingredients. Mix well.

ONION RELISH

1 cup onion, finely chopped	1 tablespoon prepared mustard
2 cups India relish	¼ teaspoon salt
1 tablespoon Worcestershire sauce	¼ teaspoon pepper

Combine all ingredients. Mix well.

BAKED BEANS WAIKIKI

2 26-ounce cans baked beans	¼ cup brown sugar
1 teaspoon dry mustard	1 cup canned, shredded pineapple
Canned, sliced pineapple	

Combine all ingredients except the sliced pineapple in a 1-quart casserole. Bake for 1½ hours in a 250° oven. One-half hour before complete baking, add the sliced pineapple on top for garnish and finish baking.

STEAMED CORN — YANKEE STYLE

Husk corn and wash husks. Do not dry. Line heavy kettle with wet husks. Place ears on the husks. Cover tightly. Steam over low fire for 20 minutes.

CABBAGE SALAD — TOMATO MAYONNAISE

1 tomato, coarsely chopped   ½ cup mayonnaise
2 scallions, chopped   2 tablespoons lemon juice or
¼ teaspoon salt   vinegar
        3 cups cabbage, shredded

Combine first five ingredients, then toss with shredded cabbage.

RICE PUDDING HOFBRAU

1 cup medium rice   1½ cups sugar
Water to cover   2 eggs, slightly beaten
1 teaspoon salt   1 teaspoon vanilla
4 cups milk   1 cup whipped cream, if desired

Wash rice. Cover with water and bring to a boil. Add salt. Heat
milk and pour over the boiling rice, very slowly, while stirring.
Cook 20 minutes, stirring frequently. Remove from fire and add
sugar. Cook about 30 minutes or until creamy. Remove from fire
and slowly stir in eggs and vanilla. Pour into 9" x 12" oblong Pyrex
casserole. Chill. Stir the pudding as it is served, and pass whipped
cream, if desired.

MOLASSES CHIPS

¾ cup shortening   1½ teaspoons baking soda
¾ cup sugar   ½ teaspoon ginger
1 egg, unbeaten   ½ teaspoon cinnamon
½ cup molasses   1 6-ounce package (1 cup)
2½ cups sifted all-purpose flour   semisweet chocolate pieces
        ½ cup chopped walnuts

Cream shortening and sugar until fluffy. Beat in egg and molasses.
Mix and sift flour, baking soda, and spices; add. Mix well. Stir
in semisweet chocolate pieces and walnuts. Drop by teaspoonfuls
on ungreased cooky sheets. Bake in moderate oven (375°) for
10 to 12 minutes. Makes about five dozen cookies.

Barbecue Dinner

Hot Cheese Balls   Liver Kabobs
Home-Packaged Halibut   Double-Decker Burgers
Baked Potatoes in Herb Sauce
Cole Slaw Jardinière
Gingerbread Skillet Cake
Coffee

ADVANCE PREPARATION SCHEDULE

Previous Day	Early Morning	Deep Freeze
Cole Slaw	*Ready burgers*	*Hot Cheese Balls*
Skillet Cake	*for cooking*	
Fish in packages		

HOT CHEESE BALLS

¼ cup butter   ½ cup all-purpose flour
1 6-ounce jar sharp cheese   Dash cayenne pepper

Allow butter and cheese to soften. Combine and blend well. Add pepper and flour; make a soft dough. Refrigerate until workable. Make balls the size of a walnut. Bake on cooky sheet in a 350° oven for 10 minutes. Batter will spread and flatten out with baking. May be prepared and frozen unbaked.

LIVER KABOBS

1 pound chicken livers, cut in half   ½ cup salad oil
2 medium onions, cut in ¼-inch   2 tablespoons lemon juice
    slices   1 small clove garlic, mashed
3 oranges, peeled and cut into ½-   1 teaspoon finely chopped onion
    inch slices   ½ teaspoon salt

Thread liver, onion and oranges alternately on metal skewers. Combine oil, lemon juice, garlic, onion, and salt. Pour over appetizers in shallow baking dish. Let stand 30 minutes, basting frequently. Grill 5 inches above heat for 4 to 5 minutes on each side, or until liver is cooked. Serve immediately.

HOME-PACKAGED HALIBUT

6 slices halibut or flounder	½ cup clam juice
¼ cup salad oil	½ cup tomato juice
½ cup chopped onions	Dash Tabasco
½ cup chopped green pepper	1 teaspoon Worcestershire sauce
1 clove garlic, minced	1½ teaspoons salt
1 tablespoon flour	½ teaspoon pepper

Heavy-duty aluminum foil

Heat salad oil in a large skillet; add onions, pepper and garlic and sauté for 5 minutes. Blend in the flour until smooth and add remaining ingredients. Simmer 5 minutes. Place each slice of fish on a large piece of foil and turn up the edges to form a cup. Spoon the sauce, evenly divided, over each portion. Fold two opposite sides loosely over the fish. Bring the other two sides together and fold over as for a seam. Bring down to make a loose package and tuck the ends underneath. Place packages in a pan and bake in a 350° oven for 45 minutes. Bring the wrapped fish out to the barbecue grill and keep hot until ready to serve. Open the packages from the top and eat from the foil.

DOUBLE-DECKER BURGERS

3 pounds ground beef	Dash of pepper
2 eggs	½ teaspoon garlic salt (optional)
½ cup water	½ cup catsup
1 teaspoon seasoning salt	¼ cup bread crumbs
2 teaspoons salt	10 thin slices of onion

10 thin slices of tomato

Mix meat, eggs, water, salt, pepper, garlic salt, catsup, and crumbs. Make 20 thin bun-sized patties. Make a sandwich of the meat with slice of tomato and onion between two meat patties. Press edges tightly to seal. Grill patties 3 to 5 inches from glowing coals about 5 minutes on each side. Serve on hamburger buns. Serves 10.

BAKED POTATOES IN HERB SAUCE

6 Idaho potatoes, washed and dried, uniformly sized

Rub potatoes with butter. Bake in a 450° oven for 45 minutes. These may be wrapped in foil and baked directly on charcoal for 45 minutes. Slash crisscross and serve with sauce.

Sauce:

½ cup butter
3 tablespoons chopped chives

1½ tablespoons chopped parsley
1½ cups commercial sour cream

Melt butter in a small pan. Add chopped chives, parsley, and sour cream; mix well. Allow cream to heat but do not boil.

COLE SLAW JARDINIERE

3 cups shredded cabbage
1 cup mixed slices of radishes, cucumbers, celery

2 tablespoons minced parsley
2 tablespoons grated onion

Toss cabbage and mixed vegetables with dressing.

Dressing:

1 cup mayonnaise
2 tablespoons tarragon vinegar
2 tablespoons prepared mustard

½ cup light cream
1 teaspoon salt
¼ teaspoon pepper

Combine all ingredients; mix well.

GINGERBREAD SKILLET CAKE

1 14-ounce package gingerbread mix
4 squares grated bitter chocolate

¾ cup sugar
½ cup melted butter
2 cups applesauce

Prepare gingerbread according to package instructions. Let stand at room temperature overnight. Crumble with fingers. Add chocolate, sugar, and butter. Pile one-half of the mixture lightly in heavily greased 12-inch skillet. Place applesauce on top. Add remaining half of the crumb mixture. Bake in a 350° oven for 30 minutes. Invert on plate immediately. (Leave skillet on top until cool.) Remove. Decorate with whipped cream. Can be served when cool, but flavor improves when kept for 24 hours under refrigeration.

Barbecue Dinner

Shrimps Gourmet
Boned Leg of Lamb   Noodles and Swiss Cheese
Dilled Green Beans
Baked Apricots Paysanne
Double Chocolate Cake with Chocolate Frosting
Coffee

ADVANCE PREPARATION SCHEDULE

Previous Day	Early Morning	Deep Freeze
Marinate lamb	*Prepare noodles for*	*Chocolate Cake*
Bake apricots	*baking*	
	Brandy Sauce	
	Frost cake	

SHRIMPS GOURMET

2 pounds cooked, cleaned shrimp

Brandy Cocktail Sauce:
4 tablespoons catsup   1 teaspoon salt
4 tablespoons chili sauce   ½ teaspoon pepper
2 teaspoons Worcestershire sauce   2 tablespoons grated onion *or*
4 teaspoons prepared horse-radish   chopped chives
1 cup mayonnaise   ¼ cup brandy

Combine all sauce ingredients except brandy; then add the brandy slowly. Chill. Serve shrimps on bed of lettuce around a bowl of cocktail sauce.

BONED LEG OF LAMB

1 9-pound leg of lamb, boned

Have butcher bone the lamb and shape so that it lies flat.

Marinade:

1 clove garlic, crushed   2 teaspoons barbecue spice
1 cup French dressing   1 teaspoon salt
⅔ cup chopped onions   ¼ teaspoon oregano
       1 bay leaf, crushed

Marinate the lamb overnight in the combined crushed garlic, French dressing, onions and seasonings; drain. When ready to cook, place on wire rack; barbecue 45 minutes to one hour, basting with marinade. To cook in oven: place the lamb, fat side up, in a shallow pan; brush with marinade. Place under flame in broiler 4 inches from heat and broil for 10 minutes until golden brown. Turn, baste, and broil 10 more minutes. Bake, fat side up, for 20 minutes per pound of meat in a 350° oven.

NOODLES AND SWISS CHEESE

1 8-ounce package medium   ¼ cup melted butter
   noodles, cooked, drained, hot   ½ teaspoon salt
½ pound Swiss cheese, grated   ¼ teaspoon pepper
1 tablespoon onion juice   1 pint commercial sour cream
1 teaspoon Worcestershire sauce   ½ cup buttered crumbs

Boil noodles in salted water and add Swiss cheese to the noodles while still hot; add the onion juice, Worcestershire sauce, butter, salt and pepper. Cool. Combine with sour cream; mix lightly, but thoroughly. Place in buttered casserole, top with buttered bread crumbs and bake in a 350° oven for one hour.

DILLED GREEN BEANS

1 cup chopped onions   1 teaspoon salt
4 tablespoons shortening   ⅛ teaspoon pepper
3 pounds whole, fresh beans,   1 tablespoon chopped dill *or*
   cooked, *or* 2 10-ounce packages   ½ teaspoon dill seed
   frozen, thawed and cooked   2 hard-cooked eggs, riced

Sauté onions in shortening until golden; add hot green beans, seasoning, and dill. Toss lightly and top with riced egg.

BAKED APRICOTS PAYSANNE

1 12-ounce package dried apricots,   3 cups water
   or mixed dried fruits   ¼ cup sugar
1 cup seeded raisins   Juice of one lemon
        1 orange, unpeeled and thinly sliced

Wash fruit and raisins. Place in a 1½-quart casserole with the water. Bake in a 325° oven for one hour. Add sugar and lemon juice and stir until sugar is dissolved. Add orange slices. Chill.

DOUBLE CHOCOLATE CAKE

½ cup sifted cake flour   1 teaspoon vanilla
½ teaspoon baking powder   3 squares unsweetened chocolate
¼ teaspoon salt   (3 ounces)
 4 eggs, unbeaten, room tempera- 2 tablespoons sugar
   ture   ¼ teaspoon soda
¾ cup sugar   3 tablespoons cold water

Sift flour once and measure. Combine baking powder, salt and eggs in bowl and beat with rotary beater or electric mixer. Add ¾ cup sugar gradually, beating until mixture becomes thick and lemon-colored. Gradually fold in flour and vanilla. Melt chocolate over very low heat; cool. Stir in 2 tablespoons sugar, soda, and cold water. Quickly fold into batter, stirring until completely blended. Pour into a 10" x 15" x 2" baking pan which has been lined on bottom with wax paper. Bake in a moderate oven (375°) for 15 to 20 minutes. Turn cake out onto a cloth; quickly remove the paper and cut off (using scissors) the crisp edges of the cake. Cool on rack. Cut cake into four equal sections and split each section horizontally, making 8 thin layers. Put layers together with Chocolate Frosting, using about ¼ cup between each layer. Cover top and sides with remaining frosting. Chill before serving. Serves 12.

CHOCOLATE FROSTING

4½ squares unsweetened chocolate   ⅓ cup milk
    (4½ ounces)   2 egg whites, unbeaten
½ cup butter   1 teaspoon vanilla
3 cups sifted confectioners'
   sugar

Melt chocolate and butter together over very low heat. Add sugar, then milk, unbeaten egg whites, and vanilla, stirring until well blended. Place in bowl of ice water and beat with rotary beater until of spreading consistency. Makes about 3 cups frosting.

Barbecue Dinner

Shrimp Rémoulade   Cumin-Seed Wafers
Calf's Liver Roast
Grilled Tomatoes   Chestnuts and Prunes
Rolls (Prepared)
Berry Cobbler   Coffee

ADVANCE PREPARATION SCHEDULE

Previous Day	Early Morning	Deep Freeze
Cook shrimp		*Unbaked Cumin-Seed*
Rémoulade Sauce		*Wafers*
Prunes and chestnuts		

SHRIMP REMOULADE

1 quart water   3 peppercorns
1 tablespoon caraway seeds   2 teaspoons salt
1 slice lemon   1 pound raw shrimp, cleaned

Boil water with seasoning for 5 minutes and add shrimp; boil for 12 minutes. Let shrimp cool in water in which they were cooked;

drain, clean, devein, and refrigerate. Serve with sauce and Cumin-Seed Wafers.

REMOULADE SAUCE

2 tablespoons oil
2 yolks of hard-cooked eggs
1 raw egg
1 teaspoon dry mustard
1 tablespoon parsley
1 tablespoon chives
½ green pepper, chopped
¼ cup capers
¼ onion, chopped
½ cup vinegar
⅛ clove garlic, minced
Powdered sugar to taste
1 teaspoon salt
½ teaspoon freshly ground black pepper

Combine all ingredients, but not in mechanical mixer; stir or shake in covered bottle or jar. Serve with shrimp. This is a thin sauce.

CUMIN-SEED WAFERS

¾ cup softened butter
3 ounces sharp Cheddar cheese
1 cup sifted all-purpose flour
2 teaspoons cumin seed

Combine butter and cheese. Mix well. Gradually add flour and cumin seed. Form into rolls 1½ inches in diameter. Wrap in wax paper or foil and chill. Slice thin and bake on a cooky sheet 6 to 8 minutes in a 400° oven. Dough may be frozen. Makes 6 dozen.

CALF'S LIVER ROAST

1 whole calf's liver

Basting Sauce:
½ cup melted butter
1 clove minced garlic
¼ teaspoon thyme
½ teaspoon salt
Freshly ground pepper

Combine ingredients. Place liver on grill, baste frequently and roast about 1½ hours.

GRILLED TOMATOES

6 medium-sized, firm tomatoes

Cut tomatoes in half, brush the halves with butter, and sprinkle with finely chopped basil and with bread crumbs. Place in a hinged grill and cook over the coals until the tomatoes are lightly browned.

CHESTNUTS AND PRUNES

1 pound chestnuts	1 pound prunes
Canned consommé, or stock	¼ cup sugar
1 tablespoon sugar	1 teaspoon lemon juice
1 tablespoon butter	½ teaspoon cinnamon

Place chestnuts in cold water, bring to a boil and cook 5 minutes. Shell and skin chestnuts. Place in a saucepan and add consommé to cover; add sugar and butter and cook until just tender or about 5 minutes more. Cool, drain and halve.

Place prunes in water to cover in another saucepan. Cook 20 minutes and add sugar, lemon juice, and cinnamon. Add chestnuts and cook 5 minutes more. Serve hot or cold.

BERRY COBBLER

3 cups fresh blackberries *or*	½ teaspoon cinnamon
2 10-ounce packages frozen	½ to 1 cup sugar, as desired
raspberries	1 recipe drop biscuit mix
1 cup cream, whipped	

Mash berries slightly in a Dutch oven or skillet with tight cover. Add sugar and cinnamon. Set aside. Mix a batch of drop biscuits with your favorite mix. Drop by spoonfuls on top of berries, which have been heated. Dot with butter. Put the lid on tightly, and cook as you would dumplings, seeing that the juice does not boil over. It should cook for 15 to 20 minutes on a barbecue grill. Serve warm with whipped cream.

Hawaiian Barbecue Dinner

Sweet Sour Ramaki
Steak Aloha with Seasoned Butter
Apricot Rice Mold   Curried Lima Beans
Fire-and-Ice Tomatoes
Clover-leaf Potato Rolls
Royal Hawaiian Fudge Cake   Island Rum Pineapple
Honolulu Cooler   Coffee

ADVANCE PREPARATION SCHEDULE

Previous Day	Early Morning	Deep Freeze
Fire-and-Ice Tomatoes	*Ramaki*	*Hawaiian Fudge Cake*
Potato Rolls	*Glaze cake*	*Seasoned Butter*
Apricot Rice Mold	*Chill Honolulu Cooler*	
Island Rum Pineapple		

SWEET SOUR RAMAKI

1 6-ounce can water chestnuts   ½ cup vinegar
(about 24 pieces)   ½ cup liquid from chestnuts
12 bacon strips, cut in half

Marinate chestnut pieces for one hour in vinegar and chestnut liquid. Drain. Spread each half-slice of bacon with brown sugar. Roll chestnuts in bacon slices and fasten with toothpicks. Place in a shallow pan and bake for 30 minutes in a 350° oven. Serve hot. Makes 24 ramaki.

STEAK ALOHA

2 2-inch T-bone steaks   1 clove garlic
1 cup soy sauce

Mince garlic; add to soy sauce. Marinate steak for about 15 minutes, turning frequently. Grill 30 to 40 minutes for medium rare, turning once and basting often. Serve in portions, cutting diagonally across the grain of the meat.

Grilling a Thick Steak:

1. Remove steak from refrigerator not more than an hour in advance. Trim, leaving a minimum of fat. Gash edges.
2. Marinate in your favorite dressing for about 15 minutes.
3. Place about five inches from glowing coals.
4. Turn at least once during grilling.
5. To test, cut near bone and note color.
6. It is difficult to specify the exact amount of time needed for barbecuing as there is such a variance in grills and in personal preferences.

SEASONED BUTTER

½ cup butter, softened	1 teaspoon chopped parsley
½ teaspoon seasoned salt	¼ teaspoon basil
½ teaspoon garlic salt	Soy sauce (optional)

Cream butter well with the remaining ingredients. Place on wax paper, and roll into a log ¾ inch in diameter. Wrap securely and place in freezer. To serve, cut in ½-inch slices and place one slice on each portion of beef. Butter melts as it is served and is a fitting crown to a deserving steak.

APRICOT RICE MOLD

1 cup dried apricots	3 cups cooked rice
½ cup chopped onion	1 teaspoon salt
1 cup chopped celery	Dash of pepper
¼ cup butter	2 tablespoons chopped parsley

Soak apricots in water to cover for 30 minutes; drain and put through a food chopper. Sauté onion and celery in butter and add to cooked rice and apricots. Season with salt and pepper. Fold in parsley. Turn into a 6-cup greased mold or casserole. Bake in a moderate oven (375°) for about 40 minutes. Turn out onto serving platter or serve from casserole.

CURRIED LIMA BEANS

2 10-ounce packages frozen baby
lima beans
1 10-ounce can cream of mushroom
soup

1 cup chili sauce
2 tablespoons maple syrup
2 teaspoons curry powder
2 tablespoons brown sugar

Cook beans 10 minutes in one cup water. Place all ingredients including the water in which the beans were cooked into a casserole. Bake, uncovered, in a 350° oven for 30 minutes.

FIRE-AND-ICE TOMATOES

6 large tomatoes, peeled and
quartered
1 large green pepper, sliced in
rings
1 large red onion, sliced in rings
¾ cup vinegar
1½ teaspoons celery salt

1½ teaspoons mustard seed
½ teaspoon salt
4½ teaspoons sugar
⅛ teaspoon cayenne pepper
⅛ teaspoon black pepper
¼ cup water
1 large cucumber

Place tomatoes, green pepper, and onion alternately in a salad bowl. Make a dressing by mixing the vinegar, seasonings, and water together. Boil for one minute. While still hot, pour over the vegetables. Cool and chill. Just before serving, peel and slice the cucumber and add. Without the cucumber, this relish will keep in the refrigerator for several days. Serves 6 generously.

CLOVER-LEAF POTATO ROLLS

1 cake compressed yeast
¼ cup lukewarm water
1 cup scalded milk
2 tablespoons butter
5 to 6 cups all-purpose flour

1 teaspoon salt
3 small potatoes, cooked and
mashed
2 eggs, beaten

Soften yeast in lukewarm water. Pour milk over butter and salt and stir until melted; add mashed potatoes and cool. Stir in eggs and enough flour, gradually, to make dough of kneading consistency. Turn out on floured board and knead until satiny, about 10 minutes. Form dough into ball, place in greased bowl, cover and let rise in warm place until double in bulk, about 2 hours.

Punch down; roll dough into balls the size of large marbles. Place three balls of dough in each greased muffin cup. Cover and let rise again in warm place until double in size. Bake in a hot oven (400°) for 15 to 20 minutes, or until rolls are golden brown.

ROYAL HAWAIIAN FUDGE CAKE

¼ cup butter	1 teaspoon baking powder
1 cup sugar	½ teaspoon salt
2 tablespoons cocoa	1 teaspoon soda
1 egg	½ cup sour milk *or* buttermilk
1½ cups sifted cake flour	¼ cup boiling water
1 teaspoon vanilla	

Cream butter; combine sugar and cocoa, and cream into butter. Beat in egg. Sift flour, baking powder, and salt together. Dissolve soda in sour milk and add to creamed mixture alternately with dry ingredients, beating well after each addition. Stir in vanilla and boiling water. Pour into a well-greased 6″ x 10″ pan. Bake in moderate oven (350°) for about 30 minutes, or until cake bakes away from sides of pan. Cool and glaze.

CHOCOLATE GLAZE

1½ cups water	1 tablespoon cocoa
1 tablespoon butter	1 tablespoon cornstarch
⅔ cup sugar	1 teaspoon vanilla

Heat water and butter in saucepan over low heat. Mix together the sugar, cocoa, and cornstarch and add to the liquid. Cook over low heat, stirring constantly, until sauce is thickened and clear. Remove from heat, stir in vanilla, and pour over top of cooled cake.

ISLAND RUM PINEAPPLE

1 large pineapple   Rum or brandy
Sugar

Cut off the top of the pineapple about 1½ inches from base of stock. Reserve top. Hollow the pineapple, removing fruit and leaving shell. Core fruit and cut into sticks. Roll sticks in sugar and replace in pineapple shell. Pour in sufficient rum to cover.

Replace top of pineapple as a cover and place in refrigerator for several hours or overnight. Serve very cold from shell.

HONOLULU COOLER

½ cup sugar
1 cup water
1 cup strong tea
1 cup unsweetened pineapple juice

¾ cup lemon juice, fresh, frozen, or canned
⅓ cup orange juice
2 cups ginger ale
Orange slices
Mint sprigs

Make a simple syrup by boiling sugar and water 5 minutes; set aside. Combine tea and fruit juices; chill. Just before serving, add ginger ale and syrup to taste. Garnish with orange slices and mint sprigs.

Hasty Barbecue Dinner

Clam Dip with Potato Chippers
Barbecued Ribs (choice of 2 recipes)   Barbecued Cube Steaks
Caraway Potatoes   Lima Beans New Salem
Hush Puppies
Lazy Susan Salad
Entree Sundae   Brownies Alexander
Ginger Ale Iced Tea

ADVANCE PREPARATION SCHEDULE

Previous Day	Early Morning	Deep Freeze
Lima beans	*Crisp vegetables for*	
Brownies Alexander	*Lazy Susan Salad*	
	Clam Dip	
	Basting sauce	
	Chill Ginger Ale Tea	

CLAM DIP

1 8-ounce package cream cheese	1 teaspoon lemon juice
1 teaspoon Worcestershire sauce	1 6-ounce can minced clams
Black pepper, to taste	½ cup commercial sour cream

Blend together all the ingredients. Serve with potato Chippers.

I BARBECUED RIBS

Allow 1 pound ribs per person. Salt ribs lightly and place on a rack in an uncovered roasting pan. Brown under the flame in the broiler. Remove from broiler and baste with ⅓ cup Uncooked Barbecue Sauce, after all excess fat has been poured off from the browned ribs. Place in a 325° oven; baste with the remaining barbecue sauce at frequent intervals until the ribs are fork tender. Roasting of the ribs may be completed on a barbecue grill. Roasting time will be from 1½ to 2 hours.

UNCOOKED BARBECUE BASTING SAUCE

2 cups catsup	½ cup prepared mustard
1 cup vinegar	2 teaspoons chili powder
½ cup molasses	1 teaspoon Worcestershire sauce
2 teaspoons salt	½ teaspoon pepper
4 onions, finely chopped	2 tablespoons butter

Combine all ingredients and mix thoroughly. Do not cook.

II BARBECUED RIBS

3 sides of spare ribs, cut between ribs into serving-size pieces

Place ribs over charcoals; cook slowly 1½ hours. Turn and baste frequently with sauce.

Sauce:

1 cup brown sugar	1 teaspoon dry mustard
1 cup chili sauce	1 tablespoon salt
3 cloves garlic, pressed	1 tablespoon fresh, ground
1 cup tarragon vinegar	pepper
1 bay leaf	½ cup olive oil
1 tablespoon Worcestershire sauce	1 cup tomato paste
2 tablespoons lime or lemon juice	1 cup red port wine

Mix together and boil for 15 minutes. Use as a barbecue sauce on ribs, lamb, beef or fish.

BARBECUED CUBE STEAKS

Cube steaks (allow one per person)   Toasted, buttered sandwich bread
Barbecue sauce (See Index)   Grated cheese

Place steaks on folding wire toasters to keep thin steaks from curling. Broil briefly on both sides, brushing frequently with barbecue sauce. Place steaks between bread slices; sprinkle with grated cheese and serve immediately.

CARAWAY POTATOES

2 cans (4 cups) small potatoes   1 teaspoon salt
2 tablespoons caraway seeds   ½ teaspoon paprika
2 tablespoons onion, grated   ¼ teaspoon pepper
¼ cup butter

Melt butter in a pan. Add the potatoes and the remaining ingredients. Brown lightly. Serves 6 to 8.

LIMA BEANS NEW SALEM

4 cups dried lima beans   ½ cup catsup
¼ pound sliced salt pork   ½ cup molasses
1 tablespoon salt   1 teaspoon dry mustard
1 small onion, minced   ¼ cup butter
½ cup brown sugar

Soak lima beans in warm water for 2 hours, drain off the water and place beans and salt pork in a pan filled with 2 quarts of boiling salted water. Simmer about 2 hours, covered, until the beans are tender, but not mushy. Place the minced onion in bottom of a 3-quart casserole. Pour in the beans and the water in which the beans have been cooked. There will be about one cup of the liquid. Combine the rest of the ingredients and pour over the beans. Lay the strips of salt pork over the top. Dot with butter and bake in a 350° oven for 1 hour, or until a golden brown. Serves 6 to 8.

HUSH PUPPIES

1 cup all-purpose flour
1 tablespoon baking powder
2 cups corn meal
2 eggs, well beaten
1 teaspoon salt

⅛ teaspoon pepper
1 small onion, grated
1 tablespoon chopped parsley
⅔ cup butter
1 cup milk

¼ cup shortening

Add baking powder and corn meal to flour. Mix eggs, salt, pepper, onion, parsley, and butter. Add milk. Blend well. Combine gradually with dry ingredients and mix thoroughly. Melt ¼ cup shortening in griddle. Drop batter in cakes into the hot shortening; fry until golden, or drop into deep fat at 375°.

LAZY SUSAN SALAD

Arrange attractively on a lazy susan, radishes, celery hearts, raw cauliflowerets, carrot curls, olives, and pickles.

ENTREE SUNDAE

4 curved bananas   1 quart, or more, vanilla ice cream
Caramel Sauce (See Index for recipe)

Slice bananas in half lengthwise. Place cut side down on dish. Arrange a scoop of ice cream inside curve of banana. Pour Caramel Sauce over banana.

BROWNIES ALEXANDER

1 16-ounce package brownie mix
¼ cup sugar
2 tablespoons butter
1 tablespoon cornstarch
1 cup dry cottage cheese

1 egg, beaten
2 tablespoons milk
½ teaspoon vanilla
¼ teaspoon salt

Prepare brownie batter according to package directions. Set aside. Cream sugar and butter; blend in the cornstarch. Add remaining ingredients; mix well. Spread half of the chocolate mixture in the bottom of a well-greased rectangular pan, 13″ x 8″ x 2″. Pour cheese mixture over the chocolate layer. Spread remaining chocolate mixture over cheese. The two mixtures will marbleize slightly and this

can be accentuated with a spoon, if desired. Bake in a 350° oven for 40 to 45 minutes. Cool and then cut into squares.

GINGER ALE ICED TEA

Prepare iced tea in usual manner. Fill tall glasses with one half tea and one half ginger ale. Garnish with mint or lemon slices.

Barbecue Dinner

Scallop Kabobs with Dill Sauce   Bacon Curls
Chicken Marinade in Foil
Rice Pilaf   Green Beans in Sour Cream
Watercress and Orange Salad
Lemon Dressing
Bavarian Cream Mold with Raspberries   Walnut Squares
Coffee

ADVANCE PREPARATION SCHEDULE

Previous Day	Early Morning	Deep Freeze
Dill Sauce	*Rice Pilaf*	*Walnut Squares*
Marinate chicken	*Wrap chicken in foil*	
Bavarian Cream Mold	*Prepare green beans for casserole*	
	Crisp salad greens	

SCALLOP KABOBS

18 scallops, halved   ¼ cup butter, melted
3 tablespoons sesame seeds

Skewer scallops; dip in melted butter, then in sesame seeds. Broil, allowing 6 minutes for cooking. Brush liberally with butter during cooking period. Season with salt and pepper. Serves 8.

DILL SAUCE FOR SCALLOPS

⅔ cup mayonnaise
⅔ cup commercial sour cream
2 tablespoons chopped green
　onion

1 tablespoon chopped dill, *or*
　1 tablespoon dry dill weed
2 tablespoons chopped parsley
Salt and pepper

Combine all ingredients, and serve with scallops or other sea-
foods.

BACON CURLS

Raw shrimp, cleaned and deveined
Oysters, halved (if large)
Bacon slices, halved

Seasoning salt
Worcestershire sauce
Lemon juice

Sprinkle oysters and shrimp with seasonings. Wrap each in a
half-slice of bacon. Broil, turning once, for 6 minutes or until
bacon is crisp.

CHICKEN MARINADE IN FOIL

4 pounds chicken thighs, breasts *or*
　drumsticks
1 cup Wine Marinade, or enough
　to cover

½ cup melted butter
¼ teaspoon pepper
½ teaspoon salt

Soak chicken in the wine marinade for several hours. Brush each
piece of chicken with butter. Place two or three pieces of chicken
on a piece of heavy-duty aluminum foil. Sprinkle the chicken
with seasonings and moisten with butter. Bring the edges of the
foil together and seal tightly with a double fold. Place packets
of chicken on grill, or bake in a 350° oven for 40 minutes. If
grilling, turn the packets over once during cooking. Serves 8.

WINE MARINADE FOR CHICKEN

½ cup oil
½ cup white wine
1 onion, grated
1 clove of garlic, mashed
½ teaspoon salt

½ teaspoon celery salt
½ teaspoon pepper
¼ teaspoon thyme
¼ teaspoon marjoram
¼ teaspoon rosemary

Shake ingredients together in a quart bottle or jar.

RICE PILAF

¼ pound butter   1 cup fine noodles, uncooked
1½ cups raw, converted rice   3 cups chicken consommé
        ¼ cup blanched almonds, sautéed in butter

Melt butter and sauté rice and noodles until brown. Add soup and salt, and stir well. Cook in covered iron skillet 40 minutes over very small flame until water is absorbed. Sprinkle almonds over rice and serve hot. Serves 6 to 8.

GREEN BEANS IN SOUR CREAM

2 10-ounce packages of frozen   2 tablespoons butter
   French-cut green beans   1 cup commercial sour cream
½ pound mushrooms, sliced   1 teaspoon salt

Cook the beans according to package directions. Sauté the mushrooms in the butter for 5 minutes. Combine with sour cream and salt. Pour over the beans. Heat, but do not allow to boil. Serves 8.

WATERCRESS AND ORANGE SALAD

1 head lettuce   2 bunches watercress
4 large oranges, peeled, sliced in circles

Line the salad bowl with lettuce. Place a layer of the watercress on the lettuce with the stems toward the center. Cover with the orange slices. Pour Lemon Dressing over and serve immediately.

LEMON DRESSING

4 tablespoons lemon juice   ¼ teaspoon salt
½ teaspoon sugar   Dash of ground pepper
        4 tablespoons olive oil

Dissolve sugar in lemon juice and combine with remaining ingredients.

BAVARIAN CREAM MOLD WITH RASPBERRIES

2 tablespoons unflavored gelatin　　¼ teaspoon salt
¼ cup cold water　　　　　　　　　1½ teaspoons vanilla
2½ cups milk　　　　　　　　　　　8 macaroons, crumbled
¾ cup sugar　　　　　　　　　　　1 cup heavy cream, whipped
Fresh raspberries

Soak the unflavored gelatin in the cold water. Scald the milk and add the sugar and salt. Stir the softened gelatin into this mixture until it is dissolved. Chill. As it begins to thicken, flavor with the vanilla. Beat until fluffy, then fold in the macaroons and cream. Place in a 6-cup ring mold. Chill. Serve with fresh berries or fresh-frozen berries. Serves 8.

WALNUT SQUARES

1 cup butter　　　　　　　　　¾ teaspoon cinnamon
1 cup sugar　　　　　　　　　　1 teaspoon vanilla
2 cups all-purpose flour　　　1 egg white, slightly beaten
1 beaten egg yolk　　　　　　½ cup chopped black walnuts

Cream butter and sugar, add flour; combine thoroughly. Add egg yolk, cinnamon, and vanilla and mix well. Grease a 12" x 8" x 2" baking pan. Pat the dough into the pan evenly and spread egg white over all. Sprinkle with nuts and bake in a 350° oven for 35 minutes or until brown. Cut into squares while warm.

Barbecue Dinner

Crab Louis in Artichokes
Toasted Pecans   Clam Puffs   Roquefort Canapés
Hoosier Chicken   Italian Meat-ball Spaghetti
Green Salad Bowl
Black Raspberry Mousse
Jade Tree Cookies   Jam Cookies
Coffee

ADVANCE PREPARATION SCHEDULE

Previous Day	Early Morning	Deep Freeze
Cook artichokes	*Clam Puffs*	*Jam Cookies*
Prepare Louis Dressing	*Roquefort Canapés*	*Jade Tree Cookies*
Toast pecans	*Crisp greens*	
Meat ball and spaghetti sauce		
Black Raspberry Mousse		

CRAB LOUIS IN ARTICHOKES

8 artichokes, cooked   2 cups shredded lettuce
1 pound crabmeat, coarsely chopped, fresh or frozen

To cook artichokes, see Index for recipe.
Remove chokes and middle leaves from artichokes. Place on shredded lettuce. Fill artichokes with crabmeat, using outer leaves for garnish around serving platter. Serve with Sauce Louis (see Index for recipe).

TOASTED PECANS

¼ cup butter
½ teaspoon hot pepper sauce (Tabasco)

1 teaspoon Worcestershire sauce
1 tablespoon garlic salt
4 cups large pecan halves

Melt butter. Add seasonings and blend well; add pecans. When well coated, spread on a large, flat pan and toast in a 275° oven for 30 minutes. Shake occasionally during toasting. Drain on paper towels. May be made in advance and stored in refrigerator in covered container.

CLAM PUFFS

1 7-ounce can drained minced clams
1 8-ounce package cream cheese
¼ teaspoon salt
2 teaspoons lemon juice, fresh, frozen, or canned
1 tablespoon grated onion
1 tablespoon Worcestershire sauce
1 egg white, stiffly beaten

Chop clams very fine. Beat cheese until smooth. Combine all ingredients. Pile on toasted rounds; bake in a 450° oven for 3 minutes. Makes 36 2-inch puffs.

ROQUEFORT CANAPES

Cream 2 3-ounce packages Roquefort (or blue) cheese. Blend with two stiffly beaten egg whites. Spread on small, round crackers and toast under broiler until cheese is puffed and brown; about 5 minutes. Makes 1 cup spread; about 3 dozen canapés.

HOOSIER CHICKEN

3 spring chickens, fryers, quartered
1 cup olive oil
½ cup sauterne
1 tablespoon minced oregano
1 tablespoon minced rosemary
2 cloves garlic

Marinate chicken one or two hours in sauce made of olive oil, sauterne and herbs. Barbecue over slow fire for about an hour, turning frequently. Sprinkle salt over chicken during last half of cooking time. Just before chicken is finished, burn a big handful of marjoram in the fire. The spicy smoke adds a pungent flavor to the meat. Serves 8.

ITALIAN MEAT-BALL SPAGHETTI

1 clove garlic, minced
¼ cup olive oil
1 large green pepper, chopped
4 large onions, chopped
1 teaspoon salt
¼ teaspoon white pepper
¼ teaspoon black pepper
2 No. 2½ cans whole pack tomatoes (6 cups)
6 6-ounce cans tomato sauce

3 8-ounce cans tomato paste, Italian style
¼ teaspoon thyme
⅛ teaspoon sage
¼ teaspoon poultry seasoning
1 teaspoon sugar
1 teaspoon oregano
1 teaspoon soy sauce
1½ pounds ground round steak

½ pound sautéed mushrooms, thinly sliced

Sauté garlic in olive oil; add green pepper and onions. Sauté well. Add salt, pepper, tomatoes, 4 cans tomato sauce, and 2 cans tomato paste. Cover and cook slowly for 30 minutes, stirring occasionally. Add thyme, sage, poultry seasoning, sugar, oregano, and soy sauce gradually, about a pinch at a time. Add more seasoning, if desired. Cook 2 hours. Add meat to sauce gradually and blend well. Simmer an additional hour. Add 2 remaining cans tomato sauce, 1 can tomato paste, and sautéed mushrooms. Add meat balls. This recipe is as involved as is its background, which is musical; but it is equally enjoyable.

Meat Balls:

1½ pounds ground round steak
1 teaspoon salt
¼ teaspoon pepper

¼ teaspoon monosodium glutamate
¼ teaspoon thyme

Mix ingredients well and form into meat balls the size of a large walnut. Drop into sauce and simmer 45 minutes. Serve over spaghetti (one pound, cooked according to package directions). Drain. Serves 8.

GREEN SALAD BOWL

2 heads lettuce
1 bunch chicory
½ cucumber, sliced

1 green pepper
3 tomatoes
1 can drained anchovies

Tear lettuce; cut chicory in small pieces and combine with cucumber. Place in bowl, toss lightly and arrange sliced green pepper rings and quartered tomatoes over salad. Garnish with strips of anchovies. To serve, pour dressing over greens, toss until thoroughly marinated. Serves 8.

FRENCH DRESSING

1½ cups salad oil	2 teaspoons celery salt
½ cup sugar	1 teaspoon salt
¾ cup vinegar	½ teaspoon paprika
1 cup catsup	1 small onion, grated

Place in covered jar and shake thoroughly.

BLACK RASPBERRY MOUSSE

12 ladyfingers	3 teaspoons lemon juice
2 3-ounce packages black raspberry gelatin	1 pint vanilla ice cream
	1 cup whipping cream
2 cups water	½ cup strawberries

Line a 10-inch pie plate with ladyfingers, split and cut in half, round end up. Line bottom of plate with extra ladyfingers. Pour one cup boiling water over raspberry gelatin. Stir until dissolved. Add 2 cups cold water, lemon juice, and vanilla ice cream. Stir until dissolved. Pour into lined plate and set in refrigerator. To serve, cover with whipped cream and strawberries. Serves 8.

JADE TREE COOKIES

1 egg, beaten	¼ cup all-purpose flour
½ teaspoon vanilla	¼ cup butter
1 cup brown sugar	½ cup chopped nuts
⅛ teaspoon salt	1½ cups Rice Krispies

Combine first six ingredients. Blend well. Mix nuts and Rice Krispies together and add. Drop by teaspoonfuls, two inches apart, on a baking sheet. Spread with a fork. Bake in a 325° oven 10 minutes or until brown. Makes about three dozen.

JAM COOKIES

½ cup butter
¼ cup sifted brown sugar
1 egg, separated

1 cup sifted all-purpose flour
1 cup chopped nuts
Raspberry jam

Cream butter and sugar until light. Mix in egg yolk. Add flour and form small balls of the batter. Dip into egg white, then nuts. Place on cooky sheet; make depression in center of each cooky. Bake at 300° for 8 minutes. Press center again and continue baking an additional 10 minutes. Cool slightly. Remove from sheet and fill centers with jam.

"Do-It-Yourself" Barbecue Dinner

Relish Tray

Ham Deviled Eggs   Chutney Cheese Spread for Celery

Special Hamburgers   Shish Kabobs

Sherried Corn on the Cob

Floating Salad

Ice Cream Cones, Assorted Flavors   Brownstone Front Cake

Marshmallow Frosting

Coffee

ADVANCE PREPARATION SCHEDULE

Previous Day	Early Morning	Deep Freeze
Deviled Eggs	*Arrange ingredients*	*Brownstone Front Cake*
Chutney Cheese Spread	*for Shish Kabobs*	
Marinade for Shish	*Ready meat for ham-*	
Kabobs	*burgers*	
	Floating Salad	
	Frost cake	

RELISH TRAY

Olives   Deviled eggs   Sweet pickle relish   Celery
Chutney Cheese Spread (for stuffed celery)

HAM DEVILED EGGS

6 hard-cooked eggs   4 tablespoons mayonnaise
½ cup chopped ham   1 teaspoon Worcestershire sauce

Shell the eggs, cut them in halves crosswise; flute edges; remove the yolks, crush them with a fork and combine them with the other ingredients. Fill the egg whites with the mixture. Dust with paprika and garnish with a sprig of parsley.

CHUTNEY CHEESE SPREAD

2 tablespoons butter   ½ cup chopped chutney
1 cup Cheddar cheese   ½ teaspoon dry mustard

Cream butter and cheese. Add the chutney and dry mustard. Mix thoroughly. Fill single celery stalks.
Variation: Spread on toasted rounds of white bread. Place in broiler 3 inches from flame until brown. Serves 8.

SHISH KABOBS

This dish is excellent for summer entertaining with a minimum of help. Have each food in a separate bowl, and have the charcoal fire started at least half an hour before your guests arrive. Supply each guest with a 9- or 10-inch wire or steel skewer and let them enjoy some "do-it-yourself" activity.

2 to 2½ pounds lamb (or beef)   Large mushrooms
Green peppers (1-inch squares)   Tiny onions
Small tomatos (cherry, if available)   Bacon squares

Kabobs are nearly always marinated. The meat should be cut in 2-inch squares. Soak the meat in the marinade for several hours, the longer the better. If you are planning the dish for the evening, prepare the marinade in the morning and let the meat soak all day. Show your guests how to arrange the seasoned meat on the skewers, alternating bacon squares, green pepper, tomatoes and onions. Have skewers 3 to 4 inches above the charcoal fire.

Turn frequently so that the meat becomes evenly cooked. Brush occasionally with some of the marinade. Broil for 15 to 20 minutes. Peeled, raw shrimp may be added to the skewers, if desired. Serves 6 to 8.

MARINADE FOR SHISH KABOBS

1½ cups salad oil	1 tablespoon freshly ground pepper
¾ cup soy sauce	
¼ cup Worcestershire sauce	½ cup wine vinegar
2 tablespoons dry mustard	1 clove garlic, crushed (optional)
2½ teaspoons salt	
1½ teaspoons parsley flakes	⅓ cup fresh lemon juice

Blend all ingredients in blender for 30 to 40 seconds. Store, tightly covered, in refrigerator until ready to use. This recipe makes 3½ cups of marinade.

SPECIAL HAMBURGERS

2 pounds ground round steak	2 tablespoons commercial sour cream
Salt and pepper to taste	
2 tablespoons chili sauce	¼ cup finely chopped onions
½ cup finely crushed corn flakes	
1 tablespoon finely chopped parsley	

Mix ingredients thoroughly until well blended. Form into cakes. For rare hamburgers, grill 6 minutes on each side. Serve on hamburger rolls. Serves 6 to 8.

SHERRIED CORN ON THE COB

Fresh corn on cob   1 cup melted butter
2 tablespoons sherry

Remove husks and silk from corn. Drop into enough unsalted boiling water to cover. Boil gently for 8 minutes. Place on platter, cover with napkin to keep hot. Serve at once with the melted butter which has been combined with the sherry. Serve the sherry-butter in sauceboat for convenience.

FLOATING SALAD

In a salad bowl, arrange layers of green pepper rings, unpeeled tomato slices, thinly sliced cucumber, and sliced Bermuda onion rings. Cover with the following refrigerated dressing:

1½ cups water	1½ teaspoons pepper
1½ cups cider vinegar	¼ cup salad oil
1½ teaspoons salt	8 tablespoons sugar

Blend very well. Serves 6 to 8.

ICE CREAM CONES
(Assorted Flavors)

Serve a bowl of assorted ice cream balls, accompanied by a platter of cones and a scoop. Each guest can select his favorite flavor.

BROWNSTONE FRONT CAKE

½ cup butter	2 cups cake flour, sifted
1½ cups sugar	1 teaspoon baking soda
3 eggs	½ teaspoon salt
1 4-ounce bar sweet chocolate	1 cup buttermilk
1 teaspoon vanilla	

Cream butter and sugar until light and fluffy. Beat in 1 egg at a time. Melt chocolate over hot water in a double boiler and add to the mixture. Blend well. Beat in sifted dry ingredients in thirds, alternately with the buttermilk and the vanilla. Pour into 2 well-greased and floured 9-inch pans. Bake in a 350° oven for 30 minutes. Frost with Marshmallow Frosting.

MARSHMALLOW FROSTING

¼ teaspoon salt	¼ cup sugar
2 egg whites	¾ cup light Karo syrup
1¼ teaspoons vanilla	

Add salt to egg whites and beat with electric or rotary beater until frothy. Gradually add sugar, beating until smooth and glossy. Slowly add Karo syrup and continue beating until frosting stands in firm peaks. Fold in vanilla. This recipe makes enough frosting for top and sides of two 9-inch layers.

Flavor variations: Add 2 tablespoons cocoa, or 1 tablespoon grated orange or lemon rind, or sprinkle with 1 cup shredded coconut.

Barbecue Dinner

Relishes
Stuffed Fresh Mushrooms   French-Bread Pizza
Barbecued Beef Tenderloin Flambé
Corn Tamale   Green Salad Epicure
Pan Rolls
Pineapple Frappe
Chocolate Banana Cake with Chocolate Frosting
Coffee

ADVANCE PREPARATION SCHEDULE

Previous Day	Early Morning	Deep Freeze
Prepare Corn Tamale	*Crisp greens for salad*	*Chocolate Banana Cake*
Pan Rolls	*Stuff mushrooms*	
Sauce for pizza	*Chill Pineapple Frappe*	
	Frost cake	
	Bake rolls	

STUFFED FRESH MUSHROOMS

¾ pound mushrooms
1 3-ounce package cream cheese
2 tablespoons lemon juice
2 ounces skinless sardines or anchovies
2 teaspoons chopped chives
½ teaspoon salt
¼ teaspoon ground pepper
1 tablespoon heavy cream (to thin, if necessary)

Remove the stems from the mushrooms. Leave whole and stuff with cream cheese to which the lemon juice, sardines, chives, salt and pepper have been added. Broil under broiler until golden brown. Serve hot.

Note: Omit salt if anchovies are used.

FRENCH-BREAD PIZZA

1 long loaf French bread ½ teaspoon oregano
1 6-ounce can tomato paste Salt, pepper, and garlic salt to taste
¼ cup olive oil 2 2-ounce cans anchovy fillets
½ pound Mozzarella cheese, thinly sliced

Cut loaf of bread in half lengthwise. Make a sauce of tomato paste, olive oil, oregano and seasonings; spread on cut surface of bread. Lay anchovy fillets over tomato sauce and cover with slices of cheese. Place on a baking sheet and heat in a hot oven (450°) for about 10 minutes, or until the cheese starts to melt. Cut diagonal slices and serve hot as an appetizer.

BARBECUED BEEF TENDERLOIN FLAMBE

4- to 6-pound whole beef tenderloin
Salt and pepper ¼ cup cognac

So it will have less fat and grill better, purchase a 4- to 6-pound whole beef tenderloin from a lower grade of beef and have it rolled as for rib roast. Do not add any fat. Roast or cook over a spit. Rub the tenderloin with salt and pepper. Before serving, place on a heatproof platter (or copper or aluminum tray). In a small pan warm ¼ cup cognac slightly. Ignite it with a match, pour it flaming over the beef. When the flame dies down, slice the fillet for serving.

For rare beef: Roast 1½ hours 8 inches from flame or 140° on meat thermometer.

CORN TAMALE

2 1-pound cans tamales 1 4-ounce can mushrooms
1 28-ounce can whole kernel corn ¼ cup bread crumbs
1 8-ounce can tomato sauce 1 tablespoon melted butter
½ cup grated, sharp cheese

Place tamales in 1½-quart greased casserole. Combine corn, tomato sauce, and mushrooms. Pour over tamales. Spread crumbs, butter, and cheese over the top. Bake in a 350° oven for 30 minutes. Serves 8.

GREEN SALAD EPICURE

Mixed salad greens
1 clove garlic
2 coddled eggs
⅔ cup salad oil
⅓ cup vinegar
2 tablespoons prepared mustard mayonnaise

1 teaspoon prepared mustard
1 teaspoon Worcestershire sauce
¼ teaspoon salt
¼ teaspoon pepper, freshly ground
½ teaspoon celery salt
¼ cup Parmesan cheese, freshly grated

Rub salad bowl with garlic. Break coddled eggs over the tossed greens which have been added to the bowl. Combine the other ingredients, and toss lightly with the greens. Lastly, sprinkle with the grated Parmesan cheese.

PAN ROLLS

1 2-ounce cake compressed yeast
1 heaping teaspoon sugar
1 cup milk
½ cup melted butter

½ cup sugar
3 eggs, well beaten
4 cups all-purpose flour
1 teaspoon salt

Combine yeast with sugar and let set. Mix with other ingredients in order given; beat together with a spoon and cover with cloth. Let rise overnight in refrigerator. Roll out on floured board; shape into a 2-inch roll and cut in 1-inch slices. Let rise a second time about 30 minutes in warm place. Bake in a 400° oven about 10 to 15 minutes.

CHOCOLATE BANANA CAKE

2 cups cake flour
1 teaspoon soda
½ cup butter
1½ cups sugar
2 1-ounce squares of chocolate, melted

2 eggs
1 cup commercial sour cream
½ cup nuts chopped
3 bananas, mashed

Sift the flour and the soda together. Cream the butter and add the sugar, then the chocolate and slightly beaten eggs. Add the flour and soda alternately with the sour cream. Add mashed bananas and nuts. Bake in a 350° oven for 30 minutes in two greased and floured 9-inch layer tins. Cool. Frost with Chocolate Frosting.

CHOCOLATE FROSTING

3 tablespoons hot milk   1¾ cups sifted confectioners' sugar
2 tablespoons soft butter   1 teaspoon vanilla
2 ounces melted, unsweetened chocolate

Combine milk and butter. Add sugar and vanilla. Beat until smooth. Add melted chocolate, mix thoroughly. Add more milk if the icing becomes dull before frosting cake.

PINEAPPLE FRAPPE

1 32-ounce can pineapple juice   2 tablespoons lime juice
1 10-ounce package frozen strawberries, thawed

Mix in blender.

Barbecue Dinner

Corn Gumbo   Puffed Crackers
Boneless Strip Sirloin Steaks — Sauce Diable
Creamed Spinach and Chives
Baked Egg Barley
Batter Bread
Hot Fruit Compote   Mocha Spice Cake
Coffee

ADVANCE PREPARATION SCHEDULE

Previous Day	Early Morning	Deep Freeze
Sauce Diable	*Corn Gumbo*	*Mocha Spice Cake*
Egg Barley	*Puffed Crackers*	
	Blend spinach	
	Batter Bread	
	Arrange Fruit Compote	
	Frost cake	

CORN GUMBO

1 tablespoon butter	1 16-ounce can creamed corn, with
1 small onion, diced	liquid
2 10-ounce cans chicken gumbo soup	2 cups milk

Melt butter, brown the onion slightly; add soup, corn, and milk
Heat. Serves 8.

PUFFED CRACKERS

Round soda crackers
Ice water   Paprika
Salt   Butter

Soak the crackers in ice water. Remove from the water gently with
spatula and place on cooky sheet. Sprinkle with salt and paprika;
dot with butter. Bake in a 350° oven for 45 minutes or until the
crackers are puffed and brown, and thoroughly dry.

BONELESS STRIP SIRLOIN STEAKS

8- to 16-ounce strip sirloin steaks (one per person)

Place on glowing ash of barbecue grill and broil until cooked as
desired. (*Note:* A rare steak is spongy to the touch. It becomes more
firm and more crusty with grilling. A well-done steak is quite firm.)
Season to taste. Serve with steak sauce or melted, seasoned butter.

SAUCE DIABLE

¼ pound butter, melted	1 teaspoon salt
1 teaspoon imported prepared mustard	Freshly ground pepper
	Dash Tabasco
1½ teaspoons Escoffier Sauce	

Combine ingredients and heat. Brush over steak as it is taken off
grill. Plain melted butter, seasoned with salt and pepper, may also
be used.

CREAMED SPINACH AND CHIVES

¼ cup water
2 10-ounce packages chopped, frozen spinach

½ teaspoon salt
3 ounces cream cheese with chives
¼ teaspoon garlic powder

Bring water to a boil, add salt and spinach and cook until just defrosted. Drain. Add cream cheese and garlic powder. Cook until cheese melts. Whirl in blender for 1 minute. Heat thoroughly before serving and garnish with grated, hard-cooked eggs and paprika. Serves 8.

BAKED EGG BARLEY

½ pound egg barley
1 egg
1 small onion, grated
½ pound mushrooms, sliced
¼ cup butter

1 cup gravy or consommé
2 tablespoons chicken fat or butter
1 teaspoon salt
¼ teaspoon pepper

Mix egg barley with one egg; let dry for one hour, then toast barley in cast-iron pot until brown. Add enough boiling water to cover barley, cook until water is absorbed; repeat process until barley is tender, about 15 minutes. Sauté the onion and mushrooms in the butter. Combine barley, onion, mushrooms, gravy, chicken fat, and seasonings in a 1½-quart casserole; bake covered in a 350° oven for one-half hour. Serves 8.

BATTER BREAD

1 package dry yeast
1¼ cups warm water
2 tablespoons soft butter

2 teaspoons salt
2 tablespoons sugar (optional)
3 cups sifted all-purpose flour

Sprinkle yeast on warm water and stir until dissolved. Add butter or margarine, salt, sugar, and 1½ cups flour. Beat 2 minutes with electric mixer, using medium speed, or beat 300 vigorous strokes by hand. Scrape sides and bottom of bowl while beating. Add remaining flour and blend in with a spoon. Cover and let rise in a warm place, free from drafts, until doubled in bulk, for about 45 minutes. Punch down the batter by beating it about 25 strokes. Pour into a greased loaf pan, 9" x 5" x 3", and spread evenly. Batter will be sticky. Let rise about 40 minutes or until batter reaches to within 1 inch of top of pan. Bake in a 375° oven 45 to 50 minutes or until brown. To test, tap crust and if there is a hollow sound, the bread is baked. Cool on rack. Makes 1 loaf.

Not only is the bread good but it is fun to bake and smell. Make it in 3" x 6" individual loaves, serve one to each guest, and listen to the happy comments.

HOT FRUIT COMPOTE

12 dried macaroons, crumbled
4 cups canned fruits, drained (peaches, pears, apricots, pineapple or cherries)
½ cup almonds, slivered and toasted
¼ cup brown sugar
½ cup sherry
¼ cup melted butter

Butter a 2½-quart casserole. Cover bottom with macaroon crumbs. Then alternate fruit and macaroons in layers, finishing with macaroons. Sprinkle with almonds, sugar, and sherry. Bake in a 350° oven for 30 minutes. Add melted butter. Serve hot. Serves 8.

MOCHA SPICE CAKE

2 cups sifted cake flour
1 teaspoon baking powder
2 teaspoons instant coffee
1 teaspoon soda
½ teaspoon salt
½ cup breakfast cocoa
1 teaspoon cinnamon
½ cup shortening
1½ cups sugar
2 eggs, unbeaten
1 cup buttermilk
½ cup water
1 teaspoon vanilla

Sift the dry ingredients together three times. Cream the shortening, add sugar gradually, and cream together until light and fluffy. Add eggs one at a time, beating thoroughly after each. Combine buttermilk, water, and vanilla; add to the above mixture alternately with the dry ingredients, beating after each addition until smooth. Turn into two greased 9-inch cake pans. Bake in a 350° oven for 30 minutes or until done. Cool. Frost with 7-minute Mocha Frosting.

MOCHA FROSTING

2 egg whites, unbeaten   ⅓ cup water
1½ cups sugar   2 teaspoons light corn syrup
⅛ teaspoon salt   2 teaspoons instant coffee
1 teaspoon vanilla

Combine egg whites, sugar, salt, water, corn syrup, and coffee in the top of a double boiler. Beat with rotary or electric beater about 1 minute or until completely mixed. Cook over rapidly boiling water, beating constantly for 7 minutes if a rotary beater is used, or until frosting will stand up in peaks. Stir frosting up from the bottom and sides occasionally while heating. If electric beater is used over double boiler, only two minutes of beating time is needed. Remove from heat and add vanilla.

The
Rotisserie

A ROTISSERIE makes indoor barbecuing possible. The preceding barbecue meat recipes may also be prepared on a rotisserie. These are additional suggestions:

BEEF KABOB: For the meal-size kabob, alternate 3-inch portions of 1-inch-thick sirloin steak with whole firm tomatoes, green-pepper halves, and strips of bacon. Broil about 15 minutes for medium rare. Baste with butter and seasoning as you would beef roasts.

DUCKLING: This cooks crisp and juicy with little fat remaining. Stuff with dressing or fill cavity with apple wedges. As the duckling begins to brown, brush with 1 cup orange marmalade thinned with ¼ cup orange or pineapple juice. A 4-pound duckling takes about 1½ hours.

HAM: Select a fully cooked boned ham. Allow one hour for heating an 8-pound ham; during the last 15 minutes, brush on a glaze (combine and cook 1 cup brown sugar, ½ cup canned apricot nectar, ½ cup pineapple juice, and 1 tablespoon dry mustard until thickened).

PORK: Order a boned, rolled, and tied shoulder, leg (fresh ham), or loin roast. A compact, center-cut loin roast can be cooked with the bone. Before roasting, season with salt and herbs. Pork takes 25 to 35 minutes per pound; the shorter time is for larger roasts (over 4 pounds).

Family
Dinners

"WHAT shall I serve tonight?"
This classic dilemma of the housewife, like a durable soap opera, goes on and on. Is there any help for her? Can she get away from the monotony of family meals? But of course! Just read on.

Family Dinner

Jellied Tomato Bouillon with topping of Sour Cream and Caviar
Fish Davo   French-Fried Asparagus
Celery Victor
Cranberry Muffins
Baked Bananas and Blueberries   Mexican Wedding Ring Cookies
Coffee

341

ADVANCE PREPARATION SCHEDULE

Previous Day	Early Morning	Deep Freeze
	Poach fish	*Bouillon*
	Davo sauce	*Mexican Wedding*
	Coat asparagus	*Ring Cookies*
	Victor Dressing	
	Cranberry Muffins	
	Prepare bananas and	
	blueberries for baking	

JELLIED TOMATO BOUILLON

3 13-ounce cans tomato bouillon   ¼ cup commercial sour cream
1 10-ounce can caviar, red or black

Place cans of bouillon in refrigerator to jell. Serve in cups. Top
each with 1 teaspoon sour cream and ½ teaspoon caviar.

FISH DAVO

1 large trout or salmon (about 3   1 onion, chopped
   pounds)   ½ cup chopped celery with leaves
1 cup vinegar, or less, if preferred 1½ teaspoons salt
½ cup water   ⅛ teaspoon pepper

Clean fish; wrap in a clean cloth long enough for ends to extend
over sides of pan. Mix vinegar, water, onion, celery, salt and pepper; pour into saucepan and bring to a boil. Simmer for 15 minutes.
Place fish in hot liquid, reduce heat and simmer gently until tender
(about 12 minutes per pound). Lift out fish by holding ends of
cloth and drain. (Save liquor.) Remove fish from cloth and place
on a serving platter. Serve with a sauce made as follows:

Davo Sauce:

1 cup catsup   2 tablespoons butter
1 cup prepared mustard mayon-   2 tablespoons sweet pickle relish
   naise   ½ small onion, finely chopped
2 eggs, beaten   2 tablespoons chopped parsley
½ teaspoon dry mustard   2 hard-cooked eggs, chopped

Place the catsup, prepared mustard mayonnaise, beaten eggs, dry
mustard, butter, and ¼ cup fish liquor in a saucepan and heat

slowly, stirring constantly, until thickened. Remove from heat and stir in pickle relish, chopped onion and parsley. Serve over fish; sprinkle with chopped, hard-cooked eggs. Serves 6.

FRENCH-FRIED ASPARAGUS

1½ pounds fresh asparagus
Salt and pepper
1 egg, beaten

½ cup fine cracker crumbs
Shortening for deep frying
Paprika

Wash asparagus and drain well. Season with salt and pepper. Dip spears into beaten egg and then into cracker crumbs. Fry in deep fat, a few at a time, until browned. Place on absorbent towels to drain. Sprinkle with paprika. Serve hot. Serves 6.

CELERY VICTOR

2 20-ounce cans celery, drained
½ cup Italian Dressing (see Index) or Caesar Salad Dressing (see Index)
2 tomatoes, sliced

Lettuce cups
2 hard-cooked eggs, sliced
1 2-ounce can anchovy fillets (optional)
Victor Dressing

Marinate canned celery in Italian Dressing for 2 hours. Arrange tomato slices in lettuce cups. Top with marinated celery and garnish with hard-cooked egg slices and anchovy fillet. Pour Victor Dressing over each salad. Serves 6.

VICTOR DRESSING

¼ cup wine vinegar
2 tablespoons drained India relish

1 teaspoon salt
¼ teaspoon freshly ground pepper
½ cup salad oil

Combine ingredients and blend well.

CRANBERRY MUFFINS

2 cups sifted all-purpose flour
3 teaspoons baking powder
4 tablespoons sugar
½ teaspoon salt

1 egg, beaten
¾ cup milk
2 tablespoons melted butter
1 cup raw cranberries, chopped

Sift together flour, baking powder, 2 tablespoons of sugar, and salt into mixing bowl. Combine beaten egg, milk, and melted butter and add all at once to the dry ingredients, mixing until just blended. Mix the chopped cranberries with remaining sugar and fold into the muffin batter. Fill greased muffin pans about ⅔ full. Bake in a moderate oven (375°) for 20 to 25 minutes until muffins are a golden brown. Remove from pans and serve at once. Makes 12 muffins.

BAKED BANANAS AND BLUEBERRIES

6 bananas, peeled and sliced lengthwise
1 cup fresh blueberries

½ cup brown sugar
1 cup orange juice
Butter

Commercial sour cream for topping

Place bananas in buttered baking dish and sprinkle with the blueberries, then the brown sugar. Pour orange juice over all. Dot with butter. Bake in a moderate oven (350°) for 20 minutes. Serve hot, topped with sour cream. Serves 6.

MEXICAN WEDDING RING COOKIES

¼ pound butter
½ cup shortening
½ cup confectioners' sugar
1 tablespoon vanilla

1 teaspoon almond extract
2 cups all-purpose flour
1 teaspoon salt
½ cup ground nut meats

Cream butter and shortening; add sugar gradually, and cream well. Beat in flavorings. Sift flour with salt and add. Blend in nut meats. Shape dough into small balls or crescents. Bake on an ungreased cooky sheet in a slow oven (325°) for about 25 minutes. Cool slightly and roll in confectioners' sugar.

Family Dinner

Chicken Broccoli Soup
Poppy-Seed Melba Toast
Veal Italian with Elbow Macaroni
Fruited Acorn Squash   Celery Slaw
Chocolate Cherry Nut Cake
Coffee

ADVANCE PREPARATION SCHEDULE

Previous Day	Early Morning	Deep Freeze
	Blend soup	*Chocolate Cherry*
	Prepare Poppy-Seed	*Nut Cake*
	Melba Toast	
	Celery Slaw	
	Frost cake	

CHICKEN BROCCOLI SOUP

10-ounce package frozen chopped broccoli
1 cup combined vegetable water and milk
½ teaspoon salt
⅛ teaspoon pepper
¼ teaspoon dry mustard
10½-ounce can cream of chicken soup
1 cup heavy cream

Cook the broccoli according to the package directions. Drain the vegetable water into 1 cup measure; add milk to make 1 cup. Place the broccoli, milk mixture, salt, pepper, and the dry mustard in an electric blender. Cover; blend about 30 seconds. Add the cream of chicken soup; chill thoroughly. When ready to serve, add the chilled cream. Mix well.

To serve hot: Pour blended broccoli mixture into the saucepan; add chicken soup; heat and add cream; heat again to serving temperature but do not boil.

POPPY-SEED MELBA TOAST

Cut unsliced bread slightly thicker than for melba toast. Butter well, sprinkle liberally with poppy seeds, and cut in triangles. Place on a cooky sheet and bake in a 300° oven for about 15 minutes or until golden brown. Watch to be certain it does not brown too quickly.

VEAL ITALIAN WITH ELBOW MACARONI

2 tablespoons butter	¾ teaspoon dried oregano
½ clove garlic, minced	¼ teaspoon pepper
1 small onion, chopped	1 8-ounce package elbow macaroni
2 pounds thin veal steak	roni
2 cups tomato sauce	1½ teaspoons salt
2 cups canned tomatoes	2 tablespoons snipped parsley
1 teaspoon salt	Parmesan cheese

In hot butter in skillet, sauté garlic and onion until lightly browned; remove them and reserve. Cut the veal into 8 pieces and sauté in same skillet until golden brown on both sides. Then add the tomato sauce, tomatoes, salt, oregano, pepper, and the reserved onion mixture. Simmer, uncovered, for 30 minutes or until the meat is fork tender, stirring occasionally. Meanwhile, cook the macaroni until tender in boiling salted water. Drain. To serve: Turn macaroni onto a heated platter; top with meat and sauce, and sprinkle with parsley and Parmesan. Serves 6.

FRUITED ACORN SQUASH

6 acorn squash	4 apples
¼ cup butter	2 oranges
Salt to taste	½ cup toasted slivered almonds
⅓ cup brown sugar	

Cut squash in half lengthwise and remove seeds. Butter insides and sprinkle with salt. Peel, core, and slice apples. Peel and section oranges. Arrange apple and orange slices on the squash, sprinkle with almonds and brown sugar, and dot with butter. Bake in a moderate oven (375°) for about 1 hour, or until squash is tender. Serves 6.

CELERY SLAW

1 teaspoon salt	3 tablespoons wine vinegar
3 teaspoons sugar	½ cup commercial sour cream
⅛ teaspoon pepper	4 cups celery, sliced diagonally,
Dash paprika	¼ inch thick
⅓ cup salad oil	1 1-ounce jar chopped pimento

Combine salt, sugar, pepper, paprika, oil, and vinegar; beat well with a rotary egg beater, then slowly beat in the sour cream. Pour over the celery and marinate in refrigerator about 3 hours. Toss in the pimento. Dust with paprika and add a sprig of parsley for garnish.

CHOCOLATE CHERRY NUT CAKE

½ cup butter	1 ounce unsweetened chocolate,
¾ cup sugar	melted
1 egg yolk, beaten	½ cup chopped walnuts
1½ cups cake flour	1 4-ounce jar chopped mara-
1½ teaspoon baking powder	schino cherries
1 teaspoon baking soda	Juice from maraschino cherries
½ cup commercial sour cream	1 egg white, stiffly beaten with
	¼ cup sugar

Cream the butter with the sugar and blend in egg yolk. Sift dry ingredients together and add alternately with the sour cream. Combine with melted chocolate, nuts, cherries and juice. Fold in beaten egg white and sugar. Pour into an 8″ x 8″ pan which has been greased and lined with wax paper. Bake 35 minutes in preheated 350° oven. Frost with 7-minute white frosting or any chocolate frosting (see Index).

Family Dinner

Oyster Soup Louisiane
Poor Man's Sirloin   Baked Stuffed Eggplant
Marinated Celery Root with Grandmother's Mustard Dressing
Apple Crisp
Coffee

ADVANCE PREPARATION SCHEDULE

Previous Day	Early Morning	Deep Freeze
Marinate celery root	Prepare meat for Poor Man's Sirloin Grandmother's Mustard Dressing Prepare Apple Crisp	

OYSTER SOUP LOUISIANE

1 10½-ounce can condensed tomato soup
3 cups rich milk
1 teaspoon salt
¼ teaspoon pepper
½ teaspoon curry powder *or* dried herb
¼ cup minced celery
1½ teaspoons grated onion
2 10½-ounce cans oyster soup

Combine the condensed tomato soup with the milk, salt, pepper, curry powder, minced celery, and lightly sautéed onion. Heat the soup. Add the oyster soup and continue heating; do not let it boil. (One pint of fresh oysters may be used instead of the canned oyster soup, if preferred.) Serves 6.

POOR MAN'S SIRLOIN

2 pounds round steak, ground
1 cup corn flakes
½ cup light cream
1 teaspoon Worcestershire sauce
1 teaspoon salt
¼ teaspoon pepper
1 small onion, grated

Combine all ingredients. Pat into a greased pie pan. Dot with butter and brown for 5 minutes under the broiler. Turn onto large

plate. Return to pie pan, raw side up. Dot with b
again for 5 minutes under broiler. Serves 6.

BAKED STUFFED EGGP⌐

1 large eggplant 2 tablespoons but⌐
1 cup bread crumbs 1 egg, beaten
1 tablespoon onion, minced 1 teaspoon salt
¼ teaspoon pepper

Parboil the eggplant in boiling water for 10 to 15 minutes. Cut in
half lengthwise with sharp knife. Scoop out the pulp, being careful
not to break the skin and leaving some of the pulp as shell. Chop
the pulp very fine. Sauté the minced onion in butter; add to pulp
the onion, salt, pepper, beaten egg, and ½ cup of the bread crumbs,
mixing thoroughly. Refill the eggplant shell; sprinkle the rest of the
bread crumbs, buttered, over the top. Bake in a 375° oven for 30
minutes. Serves 6.

MARINATED CELERY ROOT

2 pounds celeriac or celery root   French Dressing (see Index)
Boiling salted water, ½ teaspoon salt per cup water

Cut away leaves and root fibers of celery root. Scrub and slice
thin; place in saucepan in boiling salted water. Cook 25 minutes.
While still hot, pour French Dressing over celery root to prevent
discoloring. Marinate several hours or overnight. Drain and serve
with Grandmother's Mustard Dressing.

GRANDMOTHER'S MUSTARD DRESSING

3 tablespoons prepared mustard ½ cup vinegar
3 tablespoons sugar ½ cup commercial sour cream

Combine all ingredients; blend thoroughly.

APPLE CRISP

3 cups canned sliced apples 1 tablespoon lemon juice
2 tablespoons sugar ½ stick (¼ cup) butter
½ teaspoon cinnamon ½ cup brown sugar
½ cup all-purpose flour

Butter a 9-inch square cake pan. Cover the bottom with the apple ces. Sprinkle with the sugar, cinnamon, and lemon juice. Crumble with the hands, fork or pastry blender the butter, brown sugar, and flour. Sprinkle over the apple slices. Bake in a 350° oven for 30 minutes. Serves 6.

Family Dinner – Fish Fry

Mushroom and Barley Soup
Fish Fillets Canadien   Baked Onions
Italian Peppers and Sliced Tomatoes
Sunshine Cake Delmonico
Coffee   Milk

ADVANCE PREPARATION SCHEDULE

Previous Day	Early Morning	Deep Freeze
Mushroom and Barley Soup (make twice amount, freeze half)	*Marinate and coat fish* *Place onions in casserole* *Italian Peppers* *Sunshine Cake Delmonico*	*Soup*

MUSHROOM AND BARLEY SOUP

4 ounces dried mushrooms	1 teaspoon salt
2 large onions	3 pounds short ribs of beef
1 red pepper	1 cup medium barley
3 stalks celery	3 tomatoes, quartered
3 carrots	3 quarts water

1 teaspoon pepper, freshly ground

Wash mushrooms and soak overnight or for several hours. Drain, saving liquid. Put all the vegetables except the tomatoes and mushrooms through the food chopper separately. Wash and salt the meat. Place meat, barley, tomatoes, and onions in the water; cook slowly for 1 hour. Add carrots, mushroom liquid, and mushrooms; cook another hour. Add celery and pepper; simmer ½ hour. Add extra water, if too thick. Salt and pepper soup to taste while cooking. Serves 6.

FISH FILLETS CANADIEN

3 pounds fish fillets (sole, trout,   1½ cups prepared pancake mix
  bass or flounder)   1½ tablespoons salt
1½ cups white wine   ¼ teaspoon pepper
              ½ cup butter

Marinate the fish in the wine for one hour; drain. Season and coat well with the prepared pancake mix. This may be done by shaking a few pieces at a time in a bag. Melt the butter in a skillet, and when the fish is well coated, place it in the hot butter. Cook slowly until golden brown. Serve with Mustard Sauce (see Index). Serves 6.

BAKED ONIONS

2 cans small onions   1 cup water
1 tablespoon beef concentrate   4 tablespoons butter
          Pimento strips

Place onions in a well-buttered, shallow baking dish. Pour over them the beef concentrate which has been dissolved in the water. Dot with butter; top with pimento strips. Bake in a 350° oven for 45 minutes, basting frequently. Serves 6.

ITALIAN PEPPERS

2 pounds green peppers   ½ teaspoon oregano
½ cup oil   ⅛ teaspoon crushed Italian pep-
1 clove minced garlic   per
2 teaspoons salt   Sliced tomatoes
     Salad greens, washed and chilled

Place green peppers on a cake rack. Roast for 15 minutes in a 450° oven. Remove skin and seeds; cut into long strips. Combine oil, garlic, salt, oregano, and Italian pepper. Pour mixture over green peppers and marinate at least two hours. Serve on salad greens and garnish with sliced tomatoes. Serves 6.

SUNSHINE CAKE DELMONICO

8 egg yolks, well beaten
1 cup sugar
¼ cup orange juice, scant
2 tablespoons grated orange rind

1 cup sifted cake flour
½ teaspoon baking powder
8 egg whites, stiffly beaten
¾ teaspoon cream of tartar

Add the sugar to the well-beaten egg yolks; beat again; add orange juice and grated orange rind, continuing to beat. Sift flour and baking powder and fold into yolk mixture. Beat egg whites until foamy, add cream of tartar and beat until stiff. Fold carefully into the batter and pour into ungreased angel food pan. Bake in a 325° oven for 30 minutes; raise heat to 350° and bake another half-hour until done. To test, lightly touch center of cake with finger; cake should spring back and leave no imprint. Invert to cool.

WHIPPED CREAM FROSTING

2 cups heavy cream, not whipped
1 cup confectioners' sugar

5 tablespoons breakfast cocoa
1 teaspoon vanilla

Combine all ingredients in a bowl. Refrigerate for at least 2 hours. Remove and whip until stiff. Cut the cake into 3 equal layers. Place cream filling between layers; combine and frost the sides and the top. Chill until ready to serve.

Family Dinner

Tomato Vegetable Soup with Thin Crackers
Belgian Brisket of Beef
Noodle Broccoli Casserole
Hearts of Lettuce with Roquefort Dressing
Blueberry Betty
Coffee

ADVANCE PREPARATION SCHEDULE

Previous Day	Early Morning	Deep Freeze
Vegetable Soup	*Roquefort Dressing*	
Brisket of Beef	*Crisp greens*	
	Prepare Blueberry Betty	
	Prepare Noodle Broccoli Casserole	

TOMATO VEGETABLE SOUP

5 cups water	1½ cups sliced onion
1 beef soup bone with meat, *or*	1½ cups diced carrots
1 veal knuckle bone	2 potatoes, diced (optional)
¼ cup parsley, chopped	3 cups tomatoes, solid pack
1½ cups celery, cut into pieces	2 teaspoons salt
½ teaspoon pepper	

Simmer the soup bone in the water for about 2 hours, covered, over a low flame. Add the parsley, celery, onion, carrots, potatoes, tomatoes, and seasonings. Simmer another hour, or until the vegetables are cooked. Adjust the seasonings. Serves 6.

BELGIAN BRISKET OF BEEF

5 pounds brisket of beef	2 onions, sliced
2 teaspoons salt	4 whole celery stalks
¼ teaspoon pepper	1 cup chili sauce
1 can beer	

Place the beef in the roaster, fat side up. Season. Place onions,

celery stalks, and chili sauce over the beef. Add ¼ cup of water in
the bottom of the pan. Allow one hour per pound for roasting in
a 325° oven. Roast uncovered, basting often with drippings, until
meat becomes well browned, then cover. After beef has baked
for 3½ hours, pour the beer over it, re-cover and cook 1½ hours
longer or until tender. Remove meat and cool. Strain gravy into
a bowl and let it set until fat rises. Skim off as much as possible.
(The preparation to this point may be made a day in advance.)
Slice meat and reheat it in skimmed gravy. Add ½ cup water, if
necessary. Serves 6 to 8.

NOODLE BROCCOLI CASSEROLE

4 cups cooked noodles (1 8-ounce
package, uncooked)

2 10-ounce packages of broccoli,
cooked

½ cup sharp Cheddar cheese,
grated

1 cup medium white sauce

Cook the noodles in 2½ quarts water with one tablespoon of salt
for about 10 minutes. Place alternate layers of noodles, broccoli,
and grated cheese in a 1½-quart casserole dish. Pour the white
sauce over the layers. Bake in a 350° oven for 30 minutes. Serves
6 to 8.

White Sauce:

2 tablespoons butter
1 tablespoon flour
¼ cup broccoli water

¾ cup cream
½ teaspoon salt
1 teaspoon Worcestershire sauce

Melt butter, add flour, and cook until golden. Add liquids slowly,
stirring constantly. Add salt and Worcestershire sauce and blend
well.

HEARTS OF LETTUCE — ROQUEFORT DRESSING I

½ teaspoon dry mustard
½ teaspoon salt
¼ cup wine vinegar
1 cup salad oil
2 tablespoons cream

1 tablespoon Worcestershire
sauce
½ cup crumbled Roquefort *or*
blue cheese
Croutons

Lettuce hearts

Combine all but croutons and lettuce and blend well. Break enough

lettuce into chunks to make about 6 cups. Spri[n]
and pour dressing over each serving.

Croutons:
Cut 3 slices of bread in ½-inch cubes. Melt 2 t[]
in saucepan and toss bread cubes in butter until
Cool before using.

ROQUEFORT DRESSING L[]

½ teaspoon dry mustard	6 tablespoons olive oil
½ teaspoon salt	2 tablespoons cream
2 tablespoons wine vinegar	4 drops Tabasco

½ cup freshly ground blue or Roquefort cheese

Combine and blend well.

BLUEBERRY BETTY

1 quart fresh blueberries, *or*	1 cup all-purpose flour
2 10-ounce packages frozen	1 cup sugar
berries, thawed	½ cup butter
1 tablespoon lemon juice	1 quart of ice cream, *or*
¼ teaspoon cinnamon	1 cup whipped cream

Place washed fresh berries in a 1½-quart casserole. Add the lemon
juice; sprinkle with cinnamon. Sift the flour and the sugar together;
chop in the butter until crumbly. Spread over the berries. Bake
in a 375° oven for 45 minutes. Serve with ice cream or whipped
cream. Serves 6.

Family Dinner

Quick Petite Marmite
Baked Whitefish with Minced Clam Stuffing
Cole Slaw   String Beans Martinique
Velvet Baked Custard — Butterscotch Sauce
Nut Ball Cookies
Coffee

Previous Day	Early Morning	Deep Freeze
	Soup	*Nut Ball Cookies*
	Prepare fish for baking	
	Make custard	
	Make sauce	

QUICK PETITE MARMITE

1 package dehydrated onion soup
1 cup leftover meat or chicken, or ½ pound ground beef
3 cups boiling water

1 10½-ounce can condensed chicken gumbo soup
3 slices toast, cut in triangles
¼ cup grated cheese

Place onion soup and cooked meat in 2 cups of boiling water and cook for ten minutes. Add gumbo and remaining water; let simmer for 5 minutes. Pour into heated soup bowls. Sprinkle toast triangles with grated cheese and place on top of soup. If fresh ground meat is used instead of leftover meat or chicken, sauté for 5 minutes in 1 tablespoon of butter before adding to the soup. Serves 6.

BAKED WHITEFISH WITH MINCED CLAM STUFFING

3-pound whitefish
¼ cup lemon juice
Salt and pepper to taste
3 cups toasted bread cubes
1 can (7-ounce) minced clams

Pinch of tarragon
¼ cup melted butter
2 tomatoes, sliced
1 medium onion, sliced
½ cup butter

Wash fish and pat dry with paper towel. Sprinkle fish, inside and out, with lemon juice, salt and pepper. Combine the bread cubes, minced clams, tarragon, and the ¼ cup of melted butter. Lay fish in a buttered baking dish and with a spoon stuff the bread mixture inside the fish. Arrange the rest of the stuffing around the fish. Place tomato slices topped with onion slices on the stuffing. Dot fish, stuffing, and onion slices with ½ cup butter. Bake in a moderate oven (350°) for 30 to 40 minutes, or until fish flakes easily when tested with a fork. Serves 6.

lettuce into chunks to make about 6 cups. Sprinkle with croutons and pour dressing over each serving.

Croutons:
Cut 3 slices of bread in ½-inch cubes. Melt 2 tablespoons butter in saucepan and toss bread cubes in butter until nicely browned. Cool before using.

ROQUEFORT DRESSING II

½ teaspoon dry mustard
½ teaspoon salt
2 tablespoons wine vinegar
½ cup freshly ground blue or Roquefort cheese
6 tablespoons olive oil
2 tablespoons cream
4 drops Tabasco

Combine and blend well.

BLUEBERRY BETTY

1 quart fresh blueberries, *or*
2 10-ounce packages frozen berries, thawed
1 tablespoon lemon juice
¼ teaspoon cinnamon
1 cup all-purpose flour
1 cup sugar
½ cup butter
1 quart of ice cream, *or*
1 cup whipped cream

Place washed fresh berries in a 1½-quart casserole. Add the lemon juice; sprinkle with cinnamon. Sift the flour and the sugar together; chop in the butter until crumbly. Spread over the berries. Bake in a 375° oven for 45 minutes. Serve with ice cream or whipped cream. Serves 6.

Family Dinner

Quick Petite Marmite
Baked Whitefish with Minced Clam Stuffing
Cole Slaw   String Beans Martinique
Velvet Baked Custard — Butterscotch Sauce
Nut Ball Cookies
Coffee

ADVANCE PREPARATION SCHEDULE

Previous Day   Early Morning   **Deep Freeze**

Soup   *Nut Ball Cookies*
Prepare fish for baking
Make custard
Make sauce

QUICK PETITE MARMITE

1 package dehydrated onion soup
1 cup leftover meat or chicken,
  or ½ pound ground beef
3 cups boiling water

1 10½-ounce can condensed
  chicken gumbo soup
3 slices toast, cut in triangles
¼ cup grated cheese

Place onion soup and cooked meat in 2 cups of boiling water and cook for ten minutes. Add gumbo and remaining water; let simmer for 5 minutes. Pour into heated soup bowls. Sprinkle toast triangles with grated cheese and place on top of soup. If fresh ground meat is used instead of leftover meat or chicken, sauté for 5 minutes in 1 tablespoon of butter before adding to the soup. Serves 6.

BAKED WHITEFISH WITH MINCED CLAM STUFFING

3-pound whitefish
¼ cup lemon juice
Salt and pepper to taste
3 cups toasted bread cubes
1 can (7-ounce) minced clams

Pinch of tarragon
¼ cup melted butter
2 tomatoes, sliced
1 medium onion, sliced
½ cup butter

Wash fish and pat dry with paper towel. Sprinkle fish, inside and out, with lemon juice, salt and pepper. Combine the bread cubes, minced clams, tarragon, and the ¼ cup of melted butter. Lay fish in a buttered baking dish and with a spoon stuff the bread mixture inside the fish. Arrange the rest of the stuffing around the fish. Place tomato slices topped with onion slices on the stuffing. Dot fish, stuffing, and onion slices with ½ cup butter. Bake in a moderate oven (350°) for 30 to 40 minutes, or until fish flakes easily when tested with a fork. Serves 6.

COLE SLAW

6 cups finely shredded cabbage
1½ cups finely diced celery
2 teaspoons caraway seeds
2 teaspoons salad herbs
¾ teaspoon paprika
¾ cup water
¼ cup salad oil
Sugar to taste
¾ cup vinegar

Combine all ingredients except cabbage and celery. Blend thoroughly and then pour over vegetables. Toss lightly. Serves 6.

GREEN BEANS MARTINIQUE

1½ pounds French-cut green beans, or
2 10-ounce packages frozen green beans
1 10½-ounce can condensed cream of mushroom soup
1 3½-ounce can French-fried onions

Cook beans until tender; drain. Stir in the condensed mushroom soup. Pour into a greased casserole and bake in a 350° oven for 15 to 20 minutes. Heat the French-fried onions in the oven in a separate pan while the beans are heating thoroughly. When ready to serve, sprinkle the hot onions over the beans. Serves 6.

VELVET BAKED CUSTARD

1½ cups evaporated milk
½ cup water
⅓ cup sugar
¼ teaspoon salt
3 eggs, beaten
1 teaspoon vanilla
¼ teaspoon cinnamon or nutmeg

Combine milk, water, sugar, and salt. Heat to scalding, but do not boil. Pour over the beaten eggs; mix thoroughly. Add vanilla. Pour into custard cups; dust with the cinnamon (or nutmeg). Set in a pan of boiling water, making certain that the water comes to the level of the custard in the cups. Bake in a 325° oven for 30 to 35 minutes. Serve with Butterscotch Sauce. Serves 6.

BUTTERSCOTCH SAUCE

1 3¼-ounce package instant butterscotch pudding mix
1 cup milk
½ cup heavy cream, whipped

Combine milk and pudding mix. Add cream just as pudding

begins to set. If too thick to serve, stir in additional milk as needed.

NUT BALL COOKIES

¼ pound butter	1 tablespoon lemon juice
¼ cup sugar	1 teaspoon vanilla
1 egg yolk	1 cup sifted cake flour
1 tablespoon grated orange rind	1 egg white, slightly beaten
1 teaspoon grated lemon rind	¾ cup finely chopped nuts

Cream butter; add sugar gradually, and cream until the mixture is light and fluffy. Add egg yolk and orange and lemon rinds, lemon juice, and vanilla; mix thoroughly. Blend in flour; chill thoroughly. Form into ½-inch balls and roll first in the slightly beaten egg white, then in the chopped nuts. Place on a greased cooky sheet and bake in a 375° oven for 15 minutes, or until lightly browned.

Family Dinner

Pot Roast California Style

Potato Pancakes　　Tomato Pudding

Spinach Salad — Garlic Cheese Dressing

Banana Pie

Coffee　　Tea

ADVANCE PREPARATION SCHEDULE

Previous Day	Early Morning	Deep Freeze
	Pot Roast	
	Potato Pancake batter	
	Banana Pie	

POT ROAST CALIFORNIA STYLE

5 pounds boned rump pot roast   1 cup commercial sour cream
2 teaspoons salt   1 tablespoon flour
½ teaspoon pepper   ¾ cup red wine
2 tablespoons melted shortening 1 onion, chopped
                  6 carrots

Sprinkle beef with salt and pepper. Melt shortening in Dutch oven. Brown meat on all sides. Combine the sour cream and flour; pour over the beef. Add the wine and onion. Cook covered over low flame until tender, about 3 hours. Add carrots; continue cooking 30 minutes longer or until the meat and carrots are both tender. Arrange meat on serving platter; surround with cooked vegetables. Serves 8.

POTATO PANCAKES

2 cups raw grated potatoes   ⅛ teaspoon baking powder
  (about 4 large)   1 teaspoon salt
2 eggs, separated   1 tablespoon flour
              ¼ cup shortening

Peel potatoes and soak in cold water for several hours. Grate and then drain well, so that all starch is removed. Beat egg yolks, stir into potatoes. Mix baking powder, salt, and flour together and stir into potato-egg mixture. Beat egg whites until stiff and fold into potatoes. Heat shortening in heavy skillet until very hot. Drop potato mixture by spoonfuls in the hot shortening and fry until golden brown. Turn and brown on other side. Serves 6.

TOMATO PUDDING

1 No. 2½ can tomatoes, sieved   1 cup brown sugar
  (3½ cups)   8 slices bread, cubed, stale or
½ teaspoon salt   toasted
⅛ teaspoon pepper   ⅓ cup melted butter

Bring sieved tomatoes, salt, pepper and sugar to a boil. Place bread cubes in a buttered 1½-quart casserole; pour melted butter over the cubes and toss lightly with a fork. Pour hot tomato mixture over the buttered bread cubes and bake uncovered in a moderate oven (350°) for about 45 minutes.

SPINACH SALAD

6 cups washed, well-dried spin-   4 hard-cooked eggs, sliced
    ach, torn into small pieces   1 teaspoon salt
1 medium Bermuda onion, sliced   ¼ teaspoon pepper
½ cup diced celery

Garlic Cheese Dressing:
    1 cup commercial sour cream   1 pkg. garlic-cheese salad dressing
    3 tablespoons lemon juice   mix

In a large bowl, combine the spinach, onion, celery, eggs, salt and pepper; refrigerate. Combine dressing ingredients and refrigerate. When ready to serve, pour dressing over spinach and toss well. Serves 6.

BANANA PIE

1 3¼-ounce package instant ba-   1 cup milk
    nana pudding mix   1 pint vanilla ice cream
                  Fresh bananas

Line a 9-inch pie pan with Graham Cracker Crust, reserving ¼ cup of the mixture for topping. Chill. Beat the milk into the pudding mix; then beat in softened ice cream. Slice one or more bananas and arrange on bottom of shell. Pour in the pudding. Chill until firm. To serve, place overlapping banana slices around the edge of the pie and sprinkle with remaining crumb mixture.

GRAHAM CRACKER CRUST

1¼ cups fine graham cracker   ½ cup sugar
    crumbs   ⅓ cup melted butter

Crush graham crackers. Add sugar and melted butter. Mix well. Reserve ¼ cup of mixture for topping. Press remainder on bottom and sides of 9-inch pie plate. Chill until set.

fruit is in the syrup, and heat thoroughly. F
a low, flat container and cover with remainin
stand 24 hours. Use as needed. Serves 6.

FRENCH APPLE SLICES

ll-purpose flour   2 egg yolks
ng   7 tablespoons cold water
                     1 tablespoon lemon juice

10 or 12 apples   ¼ teaspoon salt
¼ cup sugar   1 tablespoon flour
½ teaspoon cinnamon

nfectioners' sugar   1 tablespoon water
lla

and salt together. Cut in the shortening with a
until the mixture resembles corn meal. Add the
r, and lemon juice; stir until a soft ball is formed.
s. Slice thin. Add sugar, salt, flour, and cinnamon.
that all the slices are coated. Roll one-half of the
ured board. Place in the bottom of a shallow 7" x 12"
Fill with the apples. Roll the top crust. Cut several
or steam to escape. Place on top of the apples. Seal
crust. Bake in a 350° oven for 50 minutes. Remove
ool. Combine the confectioners' sugar, vanilla, and
ng a sugar glaze. Glaze top crust. Cut into squares.

Family Dinner

Cheese Crisps

Egg Timbale in Aspic with Green Mayonnaise

Liver Imperial

Potato Puffs   Peas Paprika

Pickled Fruit

French Apple Slices

Coffee

ADVANCE PREPARATION SCHEDULE

Previous Day	Early Morning	Deep Freeze
Egg Timbale	*Prepare potato balls*	*Cheese Crisps*
Aspic	*French Apple Slices*	
Green Mayonnaise		
Pickled Fruit		

CHEESE CRISPS

½ cup enriched corn meal   ⅓ cup shortening
1 cup sifted all-purpose flour   ½ cup grated cheese
1 teaspoon salt   ¼ cup milk

Sift together corn meal, flour, and salt; cut in the shortening until
the mixture resembles coarse crumbs. Mix in the grated cheese.
Add milk, stirring lightly, only until ingredients are dampened.
Knead gently a few seconds on a lightly floured board. Roll out
to ⅛-inch thickness. Cut into strips, triangles, diamonds, or other
fancy shapes. Sprinkle with paprika, if desired. Place on a baking
sheet. Bake in a moderate oven (350°) for 12 to 15 minutes, or until
lightly browned. Serve hot or cold. Makes 36 Crisps.

EGG TIMBALE

4 hard-cooked eggs, sieved   ¼ teaspoon onion juice
2 tablespoons melted butter   ½ teaspoon salt
1 teaspoon Worcestershire sauce   ¼ teaspoon pepper

Combine all ingredients; shape into ½-inch balls. Place in aspic
as it begins to thicken. Serves 6.

ASPIC

1 10-ounce can tomato soup (un-diluted)	¼ teaspoon pepper
2 cups prepared canned tomato juice cocktail	1 teaspoon sugar
	1 tablespoon chili sauce
¼ cup sliced onion	½ teaspoon Worcestershire sauce
½ teaspoon salt	Dash of Tabasco
	2 tablespoons unflavored gelatin

¾ cup cold water

Heat together to boiling point the soup, tomato juice cocktail, onion, salt, pepper, sugar and sauces. Soak the gelatin in the water; when softened, stir into the hot mixture. Strain. Pour into a 6-cup mold and when slightly congealed, place egg balls, evenly spaced, in the aspic. Chill until firm. Unmold on a bed of romaine lettuce. Serve with Green Mayonnaise. Serves 6.

GREEN MAYONNAISE

2 bunches parsley, finely chopped	1 pint mayonnaise
	Juice of one lemon

½ cup anchovies, finely chopped

Mix all the ingredients together. If too thick, add small amount of lemon juice until the desired consistency is obtained. May be made in meat grinder or blender. Keep under refrigeration.

LIVER IMPERIAL

2½ to 3 pounds whole calf's liver, unsliced	2 tablespoons lemon juice
	1 teaspoon salt
¼ cup brandy	¼ teaspoon pepper
¼ cup parsley	½ cup butter, melted
½ cup salad oil	½ cup consommé
2 bay leaves	2 medium onions, sliced

¼ cup butter

Marinate the liver for ½ hour in the combined brandy, parsley, oil, bay leaves, lemon juice, salt and pepper. Place liver in roasting pan, season with salt and pepper, and spread with melted butter. Bake in a 375° oven for 15 minutes. Reduce heat to 300°. Baste with marinade, to which the consommé has been added. Cover and bake for one hour. Sauté onions in butter until golden brown and serve around liver. Serves 6.

Quick Family Dinner

Clam Chicken Broth
Monday's Chicken *or* Tuesday's Veal
Buttermilk Biscuits (Prepared)
Herb Slaw Jardinière
Butter Coffee Cake
Coffee

ADVANCE PREPARATION SCHEDULE

Previous Day	Early Morning	Deep Freeze
	Prepare soup	*Butter Coffee Cake.*
	Prepare entree	
	Prepare cole slaw	

CLAM CHICKEN BROTH

2 7½-ounce cans minced clams
  with juice
2 10-ounce cans chicken broth

2 10-ounce cans chicken and rice
  soup
Chopped parsley

Combine the clams and soups; mix in blender for 1 minute. Heat through. Top with chopped parsley. Serves 8.

MONDAY'S CHICKEN

2 10-ounce packages frozen broccoli
1 10½-ounce can condensed mushroom soup
⅓ cup heavy cream
⅛ teaspoon coarsely ground black pepper

¼ teaspoon rosemary
1 teaspoon Worcestershire sauce
2 tablespoons dry sherry
6 to 8 slices leftover or canned chicken or turkey
4 slices processed American cheese

½ cup buttered soft bread crumbs

Cook broccoli until fork tender and drain. Meanwhile, combine the soup, cream, pepper, rosemary and the Worcestershire sauce.

Heat, stirring until smooth; add the sherry. Arrange the broccoli in a shallow, greased casserole; cover with sliced chicken. Arrange the cheese slices on the chicken. Pour sauce over all; top with buttered crumbs and place in a 425° oven until crumbs are golden brown, about 10 minutes. Serves 6.

TUESDAY'S VEAL

2 cups leftover veal, cut in cubes
2 cups gravy
1 cup commercial sour cream
2 tomatoes cut in eighths

1 green pepper, chopped
1 No. 2 can whole kernel corn, drained (2 cups)
1 1-ounce jar pimento, sliced

Salt to taste

Mix all ingredients together, pour into a 1½-quart casserole, and bake 30 minutes in a 375° oven. Serves 6.

HERB SLAW JARDINIERE

4 cups finely shredded cabbage
6 green onions, chopped
2 carrots, grated
2 cups chopped celery
½ cup wine vinegar
½ cup salad oil
¼ cup sugar

1 cup water
2 teaspoons salt
¼ teaspoon each, basil, dill seed and tarragon (optional)
½ teaspoon each, salad herbs, celery seed
1 cup sliced cucumber

2 tomatoes, cut in wedges

Toss cabbage, onions, carrots, and celery together. Refrigerate. Mix vinegar, oil, sugar, water, and seasonings together. When ready to serve, pour over the mixed vegetables. Turn into salad bowl, toss and garnish with tomatoes and cucumbers. Serves 8.

BUTTER COFFEE CAKE

¾ cup butter
2 cups sugar, sifted
4 egg yolks
Grated rind of one orange
Grated rind of one lemon

½ teaspoon salt
3 cups cake flour
2¾ teaspoons baking powder
1 cup milk
4 egg whites, stiffly beaten

Cream butter and sugar; add egg yolks, one at a time, beating well after each addition. Add rind of orange, rind of lemon, and salt. Sift flour and baking powder together and beat in thoroughly. Blend in the milk and fold in egg whites carefully. Place in a buttered 11" x 7" greased pan and bake in a 325° oven for one hour. Dust with powdered sugar.

Family Dinner

Oxtail Soup

Veal Roast Godfrey

Eggplant Parmesan   Poppy-Seed Noodles

Sautéed Fruit

Mocha Float   Freezer Cookies

Coffee

ADVANCE PREPARATION SCHEDULE

Previous Day	Early Morning	Deep Freeze
Oxtail Soup (make twice quantity, freeze half)	*Prepare veal* *Prepare eggplant for cooking*	*Freezer Cookies* *Ice Cream*

OXTAIL SOUP

1 pound lean beef	3 celery stalks, with leaves
1 small oxtail, cut in ½-inch pieces	3 quarts beef stock
Seasoned flour	Salt and pepper to taste
1 tablespoon shortening	1 8-ounce can tomato sauce
1 onion	1 tablespoon lemon juice
3 carrots	1 teaspoon Worcestershire sauce

Wash beef and oxtail pieces thoroughly and roll in seasoned flour. Melt shortening in a large kettle and brown the oxtail and beef. Add vegetables and stock; cover tightly, and simmer gently for 3 hours or until the meat is thoroughly tender. Remove vegetables;

adjust seasonings and add tomato sauce. To serve, add lemon juice and Worcestershire sauce. Serves 6 to 8.

VEAL ROAST GODFREY

3 tablespoons butter
6 pounds boned veal rump roast
1 pint commercial sour cream
1 package onion soup mix
2 teaspoons dill seed
1 teaspoon salt
¼ teaspoon pepper

Melt butter in Dutch oven and brown veal well on all sides. Combine sour cream and onion soup mix; spread over top and sides of roast. Add dill seed, salt, and pepper. Simmer, covered, 2½ to 3 hours (or until meat is fork tender). Remove veal to heated platter. Serve gravy separately. Serves 6 to 8.

POPPY–SEED NOODLES, DUTCH STYLE

3 tablespoons butter
3 tablespoons poppy seeds
½ cup slivered almonds, blanched
and toasted
1 tablespoon lemon juice
1 8-ounce package broad
noodles (cooked)
Dash cayenne pepper

Melt the butter. Add the poppy seeds, almonds, and lemon juice. Pour this mixture over the hot noodles and toss lightly with fork. Serve hot. Serves 6.

EGGPLANT PARMESAN

1 large eggplant
2 eggs, beaten
1 cup dry bread crumbs
¾ cup olive or salad oil
1½ cups tomato sauce
½ cup grated Parmesan cheese
2 teaspoons dried oregano
½ pound sliced Mozzarella
cheese

Pare eggplant; cut into slices. Dip each slice first in egg, then into crumbs. Sauté in oil until brown on both sides. Place eggplant in a 2-quart casserole. Sprinkle with Parmesan and oregano. Cover well with tomato sauce. Repeat until all eggplant is used, topping last layer with Mozzarella. Bake in a 350° oven for 30 minutes. Serves 6 to 8.

SAUTEED FRUIT

Use one kind or any combination of the following fruits:

Canned pears, drained   Bananas
Canned pineapple, drained   Flour
Canned apricots, drained   Cinnamon
Canned peaches, drained   Butter
Mint

Flour each piece of well-drained fruit lightly; sprinkle with cinnamon. Sauté in butter. Sauté quickly to keep crust from forming. Garnish with sprigs of mint and use as meat accompaniment.

MOCHA FLOAT

1 quart chocolate ice cream   ½ cup heavy cream, whipped
6 cups double-strength hot coffee Cinnamon

Place a scoop of ice cream in a 10-ounce glass. Fill with coffee, top with spoonful of whipped cream, and dust with cinnamon.

FREEZER COOKIES

1 pound butter or margarine   3 eggs, well beaten
1 cup sugar   5 cups all-purpose flour
1 cup brown sugar   2 teaspoons soda
1 tablespoon cinnamon   ¼ pound nuts

Cream butter and sugar well and combine with remaining ingredients. Form into six loglike rolls 1½ inches in diameter. Place in freezer until firm. Remove one roll at a time, as needed. Cut in thin slices and bake in a 350° oven for about 10 minutes, or until slightly brown.

Deep-Dish
Dinners

THE HOUSEWIFE'S DREAM: A minimum of pots and pans, but a maximum of good eating in one dish.

Deep-Dish Dinner

French Onion Soup

Stuffed Sandwiches   Tossed Salad — Lime French Dressing

Orange Marble Cake

Coffee   Café au Lait

ADVANCE PREPARATION SCHEDULE

Previous Day	Early Morning	Deep Freeze
Onion Soup	Frost cake	Cake
Sandwiches	Assemble salad	Onion Soup

370

FRENCH ONION SOUP

4 large onions, sliced
4 tablespoons butter
3 cups condensed consommé
1 cup tomato juice
1 chicken bouillon cube

¼ teaspoon basil
¼ teaspoon tarragon
Salt and pepper to taste
Parmesan cheese, grated
French bread

Sauté sliced onions in butter until transparent, but not browned for about 5 minutes. Add remaining ingredients and simmer 10 minutes. Slice bread ¾ inch thick and butter on both sides. Toast one side, turn and sprinkle with grated Parmesan cheese. Toast. To serve, float a slice on each bowl of soup.

STUFFED SANDWICHES

6 chopped hard-cooked eggs
1 12-ounce can corned beef,
  chopped, or
1½ cups cooked leftover beef or
  poultry, chopped

¼ cup sweet pickle relish
2 teaspoons prepared mustard
½ cup mayonnaise
Salt and pepper to taste
Soft butter

12 frankfurter rolls

Combine all ingredients except rolls and butter, and blend well. Slice off the top of each roll and hollow out slightly; brush inside with butter. Fill with egg mixture and replace tops. Wrap in foil or waxed paper and refrigerate. Serve hot or cold. To heat, place wrapped in a 350° oven for 20 minutes.

TOSSED SALAD

2 quarts salad greens
1 cup shredded raw carrots
1 cup sliced radishes

½ cup sliced cucumber
1 green pepper, sliced in rings
½ cup Lime French Dressing

Toss salad ingredients with Lime French Dressing, using just enough to coat greens.

LIME FRENCH DRESSING

1 cup salad oil	1 teaspoon celery salt
½ cup lime juice	½ teaspoon onion salt
½ teaspoon dry mustard	½ teaspoon finely ground black
1 teaspoon salt	pepper
½ teaspoon oregano	

Combine in covered jar; shake thoroughly. Shake each time before using.

ORANGE MARBLE CAKE

½ cup butter	2½ teaspoons baking powder
1 teaspoon salt	2 cups sifted cake flour
½ teaspoon vanilla	⅔ cup milk
1¼ cups sugar	1 ounce unsweetened chocolate
2 eggs	2 tablespoons water
2 tablespoons grated orange rind	

Cream butter, salt, vanilla, and sugar together. Mix until light and fluffy. Add eggs separately, beating well after each addition. Sift dry ingredients together. Add alternately with the milk. Divide the batter into two parts. To one part, add the orange rind. To the other part, add the chocolate which has been melted in the hot water. Grease a 9-inch square pan. Pour in the white, orange-flavored batter. Then pour over it the chocolate batter. Cut through the batter with a knife, several times, for marbled effect. Bake in a 350° oven for 30 minutes.

ORANGE FROSTING

1 egg yolk	3 tablespoons orange juice
3 tablespoons softened butter	1 teaspoon grated orange rind
2 cups sifted confectioners' sugar	Dash of salt

Beat egg yolk. Combine all ingredients and blend very well. This recipe is especially good when made with a blender.

Variation: Lemon-Orange Icing:

2 tablespoons lemon juice	1 cup confectioners' sugar
1 tablespoon grated lemon rind	

Add to above recipe.

CAFE AU LAIT
Freshly brewed coffee   Hot milk or light cream

Brew coffee and heat same amount of milk. Pour both into coffee cup simultaneously.

Deep-Dish Dinner

Hot Spiced Consommé
Egg Timbale on Celery Root   Relishes
Lamb Stew Marocain
Rhubarb and Applesauce   Buttermilk Biscuits
Chocolate Chip Cake — Caramel Frosting
Beverage

ADVANCE PREPARATION SCHEDULE

Previous Day	Early Morning	Deep Freeze
Egg Timbale	*Lamb Stew (may*	*Chocolate Chip Cake*
Thousand Island	*be frozen)*	*Lamb Stew*
Dressing	*Chill compote*	
	Frost cake	

HOT SPICED CONSOMME

Combine three 10½-ounce cans condensed consommé, 4 tablespoons chili sauce, 1 tablespoon Worcestershire sauce, and a dash of Tabasco. Heat and strain. Serves 6.

EGG TIMBALE ON CELERY ROOT

8 hard-boiled eggs   ½ teaspoon pepper
1 teaspoon salt   ¼ cup butter
1 tablespoon finely chopped parsley

Chop eggs finely; season with salt and pepper; add softened butter and parsley. Butter ring or timbale forms. Place in refrigerator until set. Serve with Thousand Island Dressing. Serve on celery root or slice of tomato. Serves 6.

LAMB STEW MAROCAIN

4 tablespoons shortening	6 large mushrooms, sliced
Salt and pepper to taste	3 medium carrots, quartered
3 pounds lamb, cut in 1-inch chunks	5 small onions
2 tablespoons flour	5 medium potatoes, quartered
2 cups water	1 teaspoon sugar
1 clove garlic, minced	1 cup cooked peas
2 tablespoons tomato paste	3 tablespoons sherry

Heat 2 tablespoons shortening in skillet. Season meat with salt and pepper, sprinkle with flour, and brown. Add water, garlic, and tomato paste; bring to a boil, stirring constantly. Pour into a 3-quart casserole; cover and bake in a moderate oven for about 30 minutes. Heat remaining 2 tablespoons shortening in skillet. Add mushrooms, carrots, onions, and potatoes. Sprinkle sugar over vegetables and cook only long enough to glaze them. Pour vegetables into casserole with meat; cover and bake in a 350° oven for 1 hour. Just before serving, stir in peas and sherry; sprinkle with chopped parsley if desired. Serve at once. Serves 6.

RHUBARB AND APPLESAUCE

Cook one package of frozen rhubarb according to package directions; cool. Stir in 1 No. 303 can (2 cups) applesauce. Chill.

BUTTERMILK BISCUITS

2 cups sifted all-purpose flour	4 tablespoons shortening
½ teaspoon salt	⅓ teaspoon soda
2 teaspoons baking powder	2 tablespoons water
1 cup buttermilk (scant)	

Sift flour, salt, and baking powder into a bowl. Cut in shortening with a pastry blender until the mixture is the consistency of coarse corn meal. Dissolve the soda in water and add to the buttermilk.

Add the liquid slowly until all dough is dampened and will hold in a ball. Turn out on lightly floured board, knead gently once or twice and roll out to about ½-inch thickness. Cut into rounds with biscuit cutter and brush tops with melted butter. Bake in a very hot oven (475°) for 10 to 12 minutes. Makes 18 small biscuits.

CHOCOLATE CHIP CAKE

½ cup butter	1 teaspoon vanilla
1 cup sugar	2 cups cake flour
2 whole eggs, beaten	1 teaspoon baking powder
1 cup commercial sour cream	1 teaspoon baking soda

1 cup chocolate bits

In electric mixer, cream the butter and sugar. Add the eggs and beat until fluffy. Add vanilla to the sour cream. Sift the flour, baking soda, and baking powder together. Add the sour cream and the dry ingredients alternately to the butter and sugar until combined. Dust the chocolate bits with 1 tablespoon flour and fold into the batter. Pour into 8-inch-square pan which has been well greased and floured. Bake in a 350° oven 35 to 40 minutes.

CARAMEL FROSTING

1½ cups brown sugar	2 tablespoons butter
¾ cup cream	½ teaspoon vanilla

Cook sugar with cream to soft ball stage (238°). Add butter and vanilla; remove from heat and beat until of consistency for spreading.

Deep-Dish Dinner

Beef Stew with Red Wine   Spaetzle Polonaise
Tossed Salad Romaine — French Dressing
Coronado Baked Apples   Meringue Cookies
Coffee

ADVANCE PREPARATION SCHEDULE

Previous Day	Early Morning	Deep Freeze
	Beef Stew	
	Meringue Cookies	

BEEF STEW WITH RED WINE

3½ pounds beef for stew
12 small, white onions
12 small carrots, cut in 2-inch lengths
⅛ pound salt pork, or other shortening
2 tablespoons flour

2 tablespoons tomato paste
1 cup bouillon, canned *or* cubes
1 cup red wine
1 teaspoon salt
1 bay leaf
½ teaspoon pepper
6 to 8 peppercorns

¼ teaspoon basil (optional)

Brown meat, onions, and carrots in the fat in an iron skillet; transfer to a 3-quart casserole. Drain surplus fat from the skillet. Sprinkle flour in the skillet, add the tomato paste, bouillon, and wine, gradually, stirring until thickened. If more liquid is required add more bouillon and wine, alternately. Add the seasonings and simmer a few minutes. Pour the liquid over the contents of the casserole. Place casserole in a 250° oven for 2 hours. (The stew can be cooked on top of the stove over a low flame until the meat is tender.) This dish may be prepared, or partly cooked, early in the day and heated or finished just before serving. Heat gently if cooked in advance. Do not boil; simmer. Serves 6.

SPAETZLE POLONAISE
(Dumplings)

1½ cups all-purpose flour   ½ teaspoon baking powder
1 teaspoon salt   ½ cup water
1 egg, well beaten

Mix dry ingredients; stir in the water and the egg. Beat until a smooth batter is formed. Drop by teaspoonfuls into boiling salted water. (A moistened teaspoon will prevent sticking.) Cook for 15 minutes. Test one by pulling it apart to make sure the dough is cooked through. Drain; serve hot, garnished with a Polonaise sauce made by combining ¼ cup of cracker crumbs with 2 tablespoons of melted butter.

TOSSED SALAD ROMAINE

Romaine lettuce   Julienne beets
3 ounces blue cheese, crumbled

Place the lettuce and the julienne beets in a salad bowl. Serve with French Dressing. Sprinkle with blue cheese.

FRENCH DRESSING

½ cup sugar
1 tablespoon dry mustard
⅔ cup undiluted tomato soup
2 teaspoons paprika
½ teaspoon garlic powder

1 cup white vinegar
1 cup salad oil
2½ teaspoons Worcestershire sauce
3 teaspoons salt

Combine all ingredients in a small bowl. Beat with a wire whisk or a fork until they are smooth. If an electric mixer or blender is used, combine all the ingredients in the small bowl and beat at top speed for 4 minutes.

CORONADO BAKED APPLES

½ cup brown sugar   2 tablespoons butter
½ cup water   1 orange, sliced
6 tart apples, pared and cored

Combine sugar, water, and butter in a saucepan; add orange slices and bring to the boiling point. Place cored and peeled apples in a shallow pan. Pour the sauce over the apples; bake uncovered in a 350° oven for 1 hour, or until done. Baste occasionally with the syrup in the pan. Serves 6.

MERINGUE COOKIES

¼ pound butter	1 egg white
½ cup sugar	¼ cup finely chopped nuts
1 egg yolk, slightly beaten	2 tablespoons sugar
1 cup cake flour	¼ teaspoon cinnamon

Cream the butter and sugar until light and smooth. Stir in the egg yolk; mix thoroughly. Sift flour twice; measure. Add to the batter and mix well. Grease and flour a 9″ x 12″ cake pan. Spread dough very thin, using a wet knife if necessary. Beat egg white until stiff. Spread over the dough; top with mixture of the finely chopped nuts, sugar, and cinnamon. Bake in a 400° oven until golden brown in color. Cut immediately into diamond shapes. They must be cut very quickly because this cookie cools and becomes crisp rapidly.

Deep-Dish Dinner

Chicken and Vegetable Soufflé
Wax Bean Salad Bowl
Cherry-Cranberry Compote
Oven-Iced Cupcakes
Coffee

ADVANCE PREPARATION SCHEDULE

Previous Day	Early Morning	Deep Freeze
	Wax Bean Salad Bowl	
	Bake cupcakes	
	Refrigerate compote	

CHICKEN AND VEGETABLE SOUFFLE

8 slices bread
¼ cup grated onion
½ cup finely chopped green pepper
½ cup finely chopped celery
2 cups cooked poultry or meat, diced
1 10-ounce can cream of mushroom soup

1½ cups milk
3 eggs, beaten
½ cup mayonnaise
½ cup sharp processed cheese, sliced
¾ teaspoon salt
⅛ teaspoon pepper

Trim crusts from slices of bread. Place four slices in bottom of an 8" x 8" x 2" baking dish. Combine onion, pepper, and celery with the meat or chicken and spread over the bread. Cover with remaining four slices of bread. Mix soup, milk, eggs, mayonnaise and cheese together; add seasoning. Blend well and pour over the mixture in pan. Bake 45 minutes in a 375° oven. (Leftover dry meat or chicken may be used.) Serves 6.

WAX BEAN SALAD BOWL

2 10-ounce packages frozen French-style wax beans
1 tablespoon minced onion
1 teaspoon salt
2 tablespoons salad oil or olive oil

1 tablespoon sugar
¼ cup wine vinegar
¼ cup cold water
⅛ teaspoon pepper
Red onion slices

To be prepared in advance: Cook the beans according to the directions on the package, until just tender. Do not overcook. Drain and cool. Combine the remaining ingredients, reserving onion slices for garnish, and toss lightly with beans. Chill several hours. To serve, arrange on lettuce-lined bowl. Top with slices of red onions. Serves 6.

CHERRY-CRANBERRY COMPOTE

2 16-ounce cans whole cranberry sauce

1 28-ounce can pitted Bing cherries
1 tablespoon grated orange peel

Heat ingredients together until the sauce melts. Chill. Serves 6.

OVEN-ICED CUPCAKES

⅓ cup shortening	1⅔ cups cake flour
1 cup sugar	2 teaspoons baking powder
1 egg	½ teaspoon salt
1 egg yolk	½ cup milk
1 teaspoon vanilla	

Topping:

1 egg white	2 tablespoons cocoa
½ cup brown sugar	¼ cup chopped nuts

Cream the shortening and the sugar until light and fluffy. Add egg and the egg yolk and beat thoroughly. Sift flour, baking powder, and salt and add alternately with the milk. Beat until smooth after each addition. Add vanilla. Fill greased cupcake pans about half full. Beat egg white until stiff. Mix cocoa and brown sugar; gradually beat into egg white. Pile lightly on cupcakes. Sprinkle with nuts. Bake in a moderate oven (350°) for 30 minutes.

Deep-Dish Dinner

Marzetti
Three-Bean Salad
Caraway French Bread
Chocolate Marshmallow Soufflé — Foamy Vanilla Sauce
Coffee

ADVANCE PREPARATION SCHEDULE

Previous Day	Early Morning	Deep Freeze
	Prepare Marzetti	
	Three-Bean Salad	
	Vanilla Sauce	

MARZETTI

2 pounds ground chuck and veal
2 tablespoons shortening
1 large onion, chopped
⅔ cup chopped green pepper
2 8-ounce cans sliced mushrooms, drained
1½ teaspoons salt
½ teaspoon pepper

1 teaspoon oregano
2 10-ounce cans condensed tomato soup
1 6-ounce can tomato paste
⅔ cup water
2 tablespoons Worcestershire sauce
8 ounces broad noodles

½ pound shredded sharp cheese

Brown meat in shortening in a heavy skillet. Add onion, green pepper, mushrooms, and seasonings; cook until tender, about 5 minutes. Combine with tomato soup, tomato paste, water, and Worcestershire sauce. Cook noodles in boiling water until almost tender; drain and rinse. In a large, greased baking dish, spread half of noodles, cover with half of meat and sauce mixture, and sprinkle with half of cheese; repeat, using remaining ingredients. Bake in a moderate oven (375°) for about 45 minutes or until heated. Serves 8.

THREE-BEAN SALAD

1 16-ounce can French-cut green beans
1 16-ounce can yellow wax beans
1 16-ounce can red kidney beans
½ cup minced green pepper

½ cup minced onion
½ cup salad oil
½ cup cider vinegar
¾ cup granulated sugar
1 teaspoon salt

½ teaspoon pepper

Drain beans; place in glass bowl. Add green pepper and onion. Mix oil and vinegar with sugar, salt, pepper. Pour over bean mixture. Toss. Refrigerate, covered, until served. Makes 10 servings.

CARAWAY FRENCH BREAD

⅓ cup soft butter   1 teaspoon caraway seeds
2 small loaves prepared French bread

Cream the butter with the caraway seeds. Cut loaves of bread into 2-inch slices, cutting close to bottom, but not through loaf. Spread each slice with butter and place in hot oven according to package directions. Serves 6.

CHOCOLATE MARSHMALLOW SOUFFLE

3 tablespoons butter or margarine
3 tablespoons all-purpose flour
¼ teaspoon salt
1 cup milk
¼ cup sugar

3 1-ounce squares unsweetened chocolate, grated
32 marshmallows
3 egg yolks, beaten
1 teaspoon vanilla

3 egg whites, stiffly beaten

Melt butter or margarine in a saucepan; blend in flour and salt. Add milk and cook over low heat, stirring constantly, until thickened and smooth. Add sugar, chocolate, and marshmallows; stir until chocolate and marshmallows are melted. Remove from heat. Slowly add egg yolks and vanilla to chocolate-marshmallow mixture and mix well; cool. Fold egg whites into cooled chocolate mixture. Turn into a 1½-quart casserole and place in pan of hot water. Bake in moderate oven (350°) for 1 hour or until set. Serve warm or chilled, with cream or custard sauce.

FOAMY VANILLA SAUCE

1 3¼-ounce package instant vanilla pudding mix
1 cup milk

½ teaspoon vanilla
1 cup cream, whipped
Dash salt

Make instant pudding according to package directions, using only one cup of milk. Add vanilla and salt to beaten cream and fold into the custard just as it begins to thicken.

Deep-Dish Dinner

Bouillabaisse   French Onion Bread
Tossed Green Salad — Gladys's Dressing
Baked Apricot Whip
Coffee

ADVANCE PREPARATION SCHEDULE

Previous Day	Early Morning	Deep Freeze
	Bouillabaisse	
	Spread French bread	
	Crisp greens	
	Prepare Gladys's	
	Dressing	
	Cook apricots	

BOUILLABAISSE

3 cups fish broth *or* 2 10-ounce cans consommé, plus ½ cup water
1 package frozen shrimp (10 ounces), shelled, deveined
½ cup salad oil
1 cup thinly sliced onion
1 clove garlic, minced
2½ cups tomatoes
¼ cup fresh lemon juice
3 strips lemon peel
2 bay leaves
¼ teaspoon pepper, coarsely ground
8 whole cloves
1½ teaspoons salt
2 pounds fish fillet, fresh or frozen
12 oysters
1 can (6 ounces) lobster
½ cup sherry
1 lemon, thinly sliced

To make the fish broth: Combine water in which the shrimp was cooked, the liquid from the oysters, and enough cold water to make 3 cups.

To make Bouillabaisse: Cook the shrimp according to the directions on the package. Heat oil in a large saucepan; sauté the onion and garlic until tender. Add the tomatoes, lemon juice and peel, the seasonings and the fish broth. Simmer for 30 minutes. Cut the fish fillets into 2-inch pieces and add to the soup mixture; simmer 8 minutes longer. Drop in the oysters and simmer until the edges curl, about 3 minutes. Then add the lobster, shrimp, and sherry. Heat gently. Garnish with thinly sliced lemon. Serves 6 to 8.

FRENCH ONION BREAD

1 large loaf French bread	½ cup Parmesan cheese, grated
½ cup grated onion	1 cup mayonnaise

Combine the onion, cheese, and mayonnaise. Slice bread 1½ inches thick; spread with the onion mixture. Heat under the broiler for a few minutes. Serve hot.

TOSSED GREEN SALAD

A tossed salad of mixed greens such as head lettuce, leaf lettuce, romaine, endive, escarole, and watercress with Gladys's dressing.

GLADYS'S DRESSING

¾ cup salad oil	½ teaspoon dry mustard
¾ cup wine vinegar	1 teaspoon paprika
½ cup maple syrup	1 clove garlic
1 sliced onion	

Shake all the ingredients in a covered bottle. Chill. Remove the onion and the garlic before pouring over the mixed greens. Toss gently.

BAKED APRICOT WHIP

3 egg whites	1 tablespoon lemon juice
6 tablespoons sugar	1½ cups cooked puréed apricots

Beat egg whites until stiff. Beat sugar in slowly; combine juice and apricots. Fold gently into whites. Place in 1-quart casserole. Set in pan of water. Bake 45 minutes in a 300° oven. Serves 6.

Deep-Dish Dinner

Fish Chowder
Combination Salad — Spiced Dressing
Bread Pudding
Coffee   Milk

ADVANCE PREPARATION SCHEDULE

Previous Day	Early Morning	Deep Freeze
	Fish Chowder	
	Spiced Dressing	
	Crisp greens	
	Prepare Bread Pudding	
	except for egg whites	

FISH CHOWDER

5 tablespoons butter or bacon drippings
2 large onions, sliced
5 medium potatoes, pared and diced
3 teaspoons salt
2½ cups boiling water

1-pound can whole kernel corn
½ teaspoon Tabasco
1½ pounds fresh or frozen fish fillets, thawed
2 cups milk and 1 cup evaporated milk
Paprika or finely chopped parsley

Melt butter in a deep kettle; add onions and cook until tender, but not brown. Add potatoes, salt, water, drained corn liquid, and Tabasco. Cut fish fillets into 2-inch pieces and add. Cover; simmer 25 minutes or until fish is tender. Add milk and corn; heat to serving temperature. When serving, sprinkle with paprika or parsley. Prepare in advance so flavors blend. Serves 6.

Variation: Add 1 10-ounce can clam chowder and 1 can water just before reheating to serve.

COMBINATION SALAD

Tear a head of crisp lettuce into bite-sized chunks. Top with sliced tomatoes and cucumbers. Toss lightly with dressing.

SPICED DRESSING

1 tablespoon chopped parsley
½ teaspoon chopped chives
¼ teaspoon dry mustard
1 teaspoon salt
½ cup salad oil

⅛ teaspoon pepper
2 tablespoons wine vinegar
1 teaspoon prepared horse-radish
1 shallot or green onion, finely chopped

Combine ingredients and beat well. Chill.

BREAD PUDDING

2 cups dried bread crumbs
1 quart milk
2 egg yolks, beaten
½ cup brown sugar
½ cup granulated sugar
2 tablespoons butter

1 teaspoon grated lemon rind
1 teaspoon grated orange rind
½ teaspoon vanilla
½ cup raisins
1 large cooking apple, cut into thin, fine slices

2 egg whites, stiffly beaten

Dry bread and roll into crumbs. Heat milk and pour over bread crumbs. Combine egg yolks, brown and white sugar, butter, lemon and orange rind, vanilla, raisins, and apple. Add to bread mixture. Fold in stiffly beaten egg whites. Pour into a well-buttered 1½-quart casserole, and bake in a pan of water in a 350° oven for 1 hour or more until set. Serves 6.

Deep-Dish Dinner

Old-Fashioned Vegetable Soup
Lettuce Salad
Thousand Island Dressing
Burgundy Bread
Cherry Pie
Coffee   Milk

ADVANCE PREPARATION SCHEDULE

Previous Day	Early Morning	Deep Freeze
	Vegetable Soup	
	Crisp lettuce	
	Thousand Island	
	Dressing	
	Prepare bread	
	Prepare Cherry Pie for	
	baking	

OLD-FASHIONED VEGETABLE SOUP

2 pounds soup bone sawed open
   to expose marrow
1½ pounds lean beef, cut in ½-
   inch cubes
3 teaspoons salt
1 bay leaf
½ teaspoon sugar
2 to 3 quarts cold water, approximately

1 cup chopped onion
1 cup sliced celery
1 cup sliced carrots
1 cup canned tomatoes
4 small potatoes, pared and quartered
½ cup peas
½ cup cut-up green beans
½ cup rice

Place soup bone, meat, salt, bay leaf, and sugar in a deep kettle.
Cover with cold water and heat slowly until water boils. Skim.
Add onion and celery. Cover kettle and reduce heat so the soup
will simmer. Do not boil. Keep the soup at simmer temperature
for about 3 hours. Remove and discard bones. Add carrots, toma-

toes, potatoes, peas, beans, and rice. Cover and simmer about ½
hour. Adjust salt and pepper to suit taste. Ladle out meat, vegetable and broth into soup plates. Serves 6.

LETTUCE SALAD
1 large head lettuce, divided into 6 portions.

THOUSAND ISLAND DRESSING

1 cup mayonnaise
1 teaspoon Worcestershire sauce
1 teaspoon onion juice
¼ cup sweet pickle relish
½ cup chili sauce

2 tablespoons finely chopped
green pepper
1 hard-cooked egg, finely
chopped
1½ cups commercial sour cream

Combine all the ingredients, folding in the sour cream last.

BURGUNDY BREAD

4 tablespoons Burgundy (or other
dry red wine)
½ cup butter, softened

1 large loaf French bread
⅛ teaspoon salt
Dash cayenne

Mix wine, butter, and seasonings. Slice bread into 1½-inch slices,
cutting to, but not through, bottom crust. Spread each slice lightly
with wine butter. Press bread together and then spread butter
over the top. Heat ten minutes in a 400° oven.

CHERRY PIE
Pastry for 2-crust 9-inch pie. (See Index.)

Filling:

¾ to 1 cup sugar
4 tablespoons flour
¼ teaspoon almond extract
1⅓ tablespoons butter

2½ cups cherries and juice or 1
No. 2 can
Dash red food coloring

Mix sugar, flour, and almond extract in saucepan; stir in cherries,
juice, and coloring. Cook over moderate heat, stirring constantly
until mixture boils and thickens. Pour into pastry-lined pan, dot
with butter. Quickly cover with top crust and slash. Bake 30 to
40 minutes until nicely browned and juice bubbles through slits in
crust. Serve warm, not hot. Serves 6.

Deep-Dish Dinner

Poulet au Pot (Chicken in the Pot)
Matzo Dumplings
Wilted Lettuce
Ozark Pudding
Coffee   Milk

ADVANCE PREPARATION SCHEDULE

Previous Day	Early Morning	Deep Freeze
Cook chicken in pot *Refrigerate dumplings*		

POULET AU POT
(Chicken in the Pot)

2 fryers, about 2½ to 3 pounds
  each, plus 2 breasts
8 cups water
1 very small bay leaf
2 tablespoons minced onion
2 tablespoons salt

¼ teaspoon white pepper
½ teaspoon celery salt
1 bunch of carrots, cut in halves
1 4-ounce package noodles, ¼
  inch wide, boiled in salt water
  10 minutes

1 12-ounce package frozen peas

Wash and dry chickens and cut each into 5 pieces. Place in 5-quart saucepan with the breasts. Add water, bay leaf, minced onion, and seasonings. Cover saucepan and bring to quick boil. Reduce flame and simmer for 30 minutes, gently. Then add scrubbed and halved carrots. Cover saucepan and simmer gently 15 minutes. Add cooked noodles and frozen peas. Cover and simmer gently 15 minutes, or until tender. Do not overcook. Serve from tureen with Matzo Dumplings. Serves 6. *Note:* If a stronger soup is desired, add 4 or more bouillon cubes to taste.

MATZO DUMPLINGS

2 eggs, well beaten   ½ teaspoon baking powder
2 tablespoons cold water   ½ teaspoon salt
½ cup matzo meal   1 tablespoon chopped parsley
                Pinch of nutmeg

Blend all ingredients well. Form into balls size of marbles. Refrigerate several hours. Thirty minutes before serving, drop into 5 cups boiling water to which 3 bouillon cubes have been added. Drain and place in soup.

WILTED LETTUCE

1 or 2 heads lettuce, torn in bite-   ½ cup vinegar
    sized pieces   ¼ cup water
1 onion, thinly sliced   2 tablespoons sugar
4 slices bacon   ½ teaspoon salt
                ⅛ teaspoon pepper

Place lettuce and onion rings in a salad bowl. Dice bacon, fry until brown. Add vinegar, water, sugar, and seasonings and bring to a boil. Pour hot mixture over lettuce and onion. Serve immediately. Serves 6.

OZARK PUDDING

1 egg   ⅛ teaspoon salt
¾ cup sugar   1½ cups chopped nuts
2 tablespoons flour   ½ cup chopped raw apple
1¼ teaspoons baking powder 1 teaspoon vanilla

Beat egg until yolk and white are partially mixed, or for 1 minute at low speed in electric mixer. Add sugar gradually; beat mixture until it is very smooth. Sift flour, baking powder, and salt together; fold into first mixture. Add nuts, apple, and vanilla; blend well. Pour into well-greased 9-inch pie pan. Bake in a moderate oven (350°) 35 minutes. Serve with whipped cream or ice cream. The pudding will rise during the first part of the baking. Do not be alarmed when it settles. Serves 6.

Deep-Dish Dinner

Swiss Steak Indienne
Noodle Shells Italian
Apricot Applesauce
Valencia Angel Food Cake
Coffee   Milk

ADVANCE PREPARATION SCHEDULE

Previous Day	Early Morning	Deep Freeze
	Swiss Steak	
	Refrigerate applesauce	
	Bake Angel Food Cake	

SWISS STEAK INDIENNE

3 pounds round steak	2 large onions, thinly sliced
2 tablespoons flour	2 stalks celery, diced
1½ teaspoons salt	1 clove garlic, minced
⅛ teaspoon pepper	2 tablespoons bottled thick meat
2 tablespoons fat	sauce
2 8-ounce cans tomato sauce	¼ cup light or dark raisins
3 fresh tomatoes, cut into pieces	1 20-ounce can small potatoes
¾ cup water	1 No. 2 can carrots

Trim excess fat from meat; combine flour, salt and pepper. Lay meat on board, sprinkle with half of mixture. With rim of saucer, pound in mixture. Turn meat and repeat the pounding process, first covering meat with remaining half of flour, salt and pepper mixture. Brown meat in hot fat in skillet, browning well on both sides. Remove meat from pan. Place on paper towel to drain off fat. Remove all fat from pan, then return meat. Add rest of ingredients, except potatoes and carrots; stir well. Simmer, covered, about 2 to 2½ hours. Just before serving, add potatoes and carrots; reheat. Serves 6.

NOODLE SHELLS ITALIAN

1 8-ounce package noodle shells	1 clove garlic, minced
¼ cup butter	1 cup cooked peas (optional)

Cook shells in boiling, salted water as directed until tender. Melt butter in saucepan, add garlic, sauté one minute. Toss with noodles (and peas, if desired). Serves 6.

APRICOT APPLESAUCE

2 20-ounce cans applesauce *or*	2 cups apricot purée
2 20-ounce cans appleberry sauce	1 teaspoon Curaçao (optional)

Combine ingredients and mix well. Chill before serving. Serves 6.

For apricot purée: Wash 1 pound dried apricots, cover with water and cook 45 minutes. Force through food mill; add sugar to taste.

VALENCIA ANGEL FOOD CAKE

1⅓ cups egg whites (10 to 12 eggs)	2 tablespoons grated orange rind
1⅓ teaspoons cream of tartar	1½ cups sugar
¼ teaspoon salt	2 tablespoons orange juice
	1 cup sifted cake flour

Beat egg whites, cream of tartar, and salt until egg whites are stiff, glossy and finely grained. Add orange rind and 1 cup sugar gradually, folding in well. Fold in orange juice. Sift the flour with the remaining ½ cup sugar several times and fold into the mixture. Bake in ungreased 10-inch tube pan at 325° for 1 hour, or at 375° for about 40 minutes. Cake is baked when it springs back to the touch. Invert pan and let cake cool. Frost with Orange Frosting.

Variation: Tangerine rind in both cake and frosting gives unusual flavor.

ORANGE FROSTING

⅓ cup butter	3 tablespoons orange juice
1½ cups confectioners' sugar, sifted	1 tablespoon grated orange rind

Cream butter, add sugar gradually; blend well. Add orange juice and rind and beat until smooth.

Beverages and Drinks

The following section offers a variety of thirst-quenching drinks, as well as suggestions for something more potent to serve when the occasion demands. Included are a few of the old stand-bys, along with some tantalizing new taste treats.

Alcoholic Drinks

VINEYARD PUNCH

1 cup water
3 sticks cinnamon
2 6-ounce cans undiluted grape juice (frozen)
2 6-ounce cans undiluted grapefruit juice (frozen)
½ cup lemon juice
2 cups port wine
2 quarts ginger ale

Simmer water and spice for 5 minutes; cool and strain. Combine the spiced water with the fruit juice and wine. Chill for several hours. When ready to serve, pour into a punch bowl and add the iced ginger ale. Serves 8.

DUBONNET ON THE ROCKS

Place 2 cubes of ice in an old-fashioned glass; pour in 1 jigger of Dubonnet and add a strip of lemon peel. One portion.

GINGER BLOSSOM COCKTAIL

1 quart orange sherbet   2 jiggers brandy, more if desired
1 pint ginger ale

Place in blender (or use rotary beater). Mix well; garnish with a sprig of mint. Serves 12.

HOT BRANDY TODDY

Place 1 cube of sugar in a 5-ounce glass. Add slice of lemon and 1 jigger of brandy. Fill with boiling hot water. Dust with nutmeg.

For **German Grock:** Add 2 cloves and stick of cinnamon to above.

One portion.

STINGER

½ glass shaved ice   1 jigger brandy
½ jigger white crème de menthe

Shake well. Strain into cocktail glass. One portion.

SCORPION

For 1 portion, place ½ scoop shaved ice in a blender. Add:

2 ounces orange juice   1 ounce brandy
2 ounces light rum   ½ ounce orange brandy

Give it a whirl for 30 seconds, add cracked ice, pour into a brandy snifter and just relax.

FROZEN DAIQUIRI

6-ounce can frozen concentrate   2 cans light Cuban rum
for limeade   3 cans water

Mix and freeze. When you wish to serve daiquiris, spoon some of the mixture into your blender, give a quick whirl, and pour it, partially frosted, into champagne or daiquiri glasses. Use a sprig of mint for garnish. Ten portions.

ORANGE GROVE

Golden Jamaica rum
Freshly squeezed orange juice
Orange slices
Ice cubes
Quinine water

Pour equal parts rum and freshly squeezed orange juice into a tall glass. Add ice cubes; fill with quinine water; stir. Then garnish with a slice of orange and/or mint. One portion.

ZOMBI

For each serving, place in blender:

½ ounce dark Jamaica rum
½ ounce vodka
1 tablespoon lime juice
Cracked ice
1½ ounces pineapple juice
(canned or frozen)
½ teaspoon sugar

Whirl for 10 seconds.

BORSCHT CIRCUIT

2 ounces vodka
¼ teaspoon Worcestershire sauce
¼ teaspoon dill
Beet borscht, strained

Serve in mugs. Put 2 ice cubes in each serving. Add vodka, Worcestershire sauce; stir. Add sufficient borscht to fill mug. Sprinkle with dill weed. One portion.

BLOODY MARY

¾ cup tomato juice
1 teaspoon Worcestershire sauce
Dash of Tabasco (optional)
1 tablespoon lemon or lime juice
1 jigger vodka

Mix together first 3 ingredients. Pour vodka over ice in a tall (10-ounce) glass. Add tomato juice mixture and dash of Tabasco, if desired. Stir. One portion.

BULL WHIP

In double old-fashioned glass, put 2 cubes ice, 1½ ounces vodka
dash celery salt, pepper, salt, dash of Worcestershire sauce, an
1 tablespoon lemon juice. Fill with beef bouillon. May be serve
hot. One portion.

FROZEN WHISKEY SOUR

1 6-ounce can frozen lemonade
   concentrate
3 6-ounce cans water

1 tablespoon frozen orange
   concentrate (optional)

2 6-ounce cans bourbon (measured into can)

Mix and freeze. When ready to serve, spoon some of the mixture
into blender or beater, give it a quick whirl and serve with a
maraschino cherry and a slice of orange. Serves 8.

"CIN AND GIN"

For each serving, place 2 cubes of ice, 1 dash orange bitters, ½
jigger of Italian vermouth, and 1 jigger of gin, into mixing glass.
Stir, then strain into chilled cocktail glasses. Serve with a twist of
lemon.

RASPBERRY LEMONADE

2 6-ounce cans lemon concentrate
6 cans water (6 ounces each)

1 10-ounce package frozen raspberries

1 jigger gin per serving (optional)

Combine and blend well. Pour over ice cubes in 10-ounce glasses.
Serves 10 (6 ounces in each glass, plus gin).

ORANGE BLOSSOM COCKTAIL

For each serving, pour into a mixer 3 tablespoons of orange juice
with 1 jigger of gin. Shake. Serve in chilled glass.

GINGER PEACH COOLER

1 10-ounce package frozen sliced peaches, thawed
¾ cup sugar
¼ teaspoon nutmeg
¼ teaspoon ginger
2 tablespoons lemon juice
4 jiggers gin
4 small bottles ginger ale
Orange slices

Dice peaches. Add sugar, nutmeg, ginger, and lemon juice. Mash lightly and mix well. When ready to serve, spoon mixture equally into 4 tall glasses. Add ginger ale. Stir well. Serve iced. Garnish with orange slices.

DUBONNET COCKTAIL

Place 2 cubes of ice in a mixing glass. Add ⅔ jigger Dubonnet and ⅔ jigger gin. Stir. Strain into cocktail glasses and garnish with maraschino cherry. Two portions.

PINK CARNATION

1 6-ounce can pink lemonade concentrate
1½ cans cold water
1½ cans vodka (measured into 6-ounce can)
Shaved ice

Blend ingredients together in electric blender. Serve in frosty, cold cocktail glasses. The rim of the glass may be dipped in lemon juice and then in powdered sugar. About six portions.

TWISTER

1 wedge of lemon
Twist of lemon peel
2 ounces of vodka
Ginger ale or 7-up

Fill highball glass half full of ice cubes, add lemon peel, and vodka; fill glass with ginger ale or 7-up. Separate lemon peel from pulp halfway through length of wedge. Place on rim of glass. One portion.

Nonalcoholic Drinks

ROSEMARY FIZZ

2 tablespoons crushed rosemary leaves	½ cup water
3 tablespoons sugar	2 cups apricot nectar
¼ teaspoon salt	1 quart ginger ale
	1 cup lime juice

Simmer rosemary leaves, sugar, and salt in the water for 2 minutes. Cool and strain. Combine the apricot nectar with the ginger ale and lime juice. Add the rosemary syrup. Serve in tall, chilled glasses over chipped ice and garnish with twists of lime rind.

RASPBERRY SODA

1 10-ounce package frozen raspberries, thawed
1 quart ginger ale

Place ice cubes in 10-ounce glass. For each serving, add ¼ cup raspberries and fill glass with ginger ale.

PINEAPPLE NECTAR

3 cups pineapple juice   3 cups apricot nectar
Ice cubes

Combine juices; serve in tall chilled glasses over ice cubes.

PINK PUNCH

4 cups cranberry juice	1 cup lemon juice
2 cups unsweetened pineapple juice	7 cups chilled pale-dry ginger ale
	Lemon slices
Sprigs of mint	

Combine juices and chill. Just before serving, pour into punch bowl; add ice cubes or block of ice. Add ginger ale, slowly. Garnish with lemon slices and sprigs of mint.

MINTED GRAPE FIZZ

1 cup ice-cold water
2 cups chilled grape juice
2½ cups chilled orange juice
2 tablespoons lemon juice

3 tablespoons sugar
2 teaspoons peppermint extract
1 pint lemon sherbet
6 mint sprigs

Mix first six ingredients together; pour into tall, chilled glasses; top with a spoonful of lemon sherbet and a sprig of mint. Serves 6.

HERBED TOMATO COOLER

3½ cups tomato juice
2 tablespoons crushed basil leaves

1 tablespoon lemon juice
½ cup commercial sour cream

Simmer ½ cup tomato juice with the basil leaves for 3 minutes. Chill and strain. Add remaining tomato juice and lemon juice. Mix with the sour cream and beat thoroughly. Chill. Serves 6.

CURRIED TOMATO JUICE

Mix thoroughly the juice of two lemons with 2 teaspoons curry powder. Stir into one quart chilled tomato juice. Serves 6.

MULLED CIDER

1 teaspoon whole allspice
2 2-inch sticks cinnamon
12 whole cloves

2 quarts apple cider
⅔ cup brown sugar, packed
Ground nutmeg

Tie allspice, cinnamon, and cloves together in cheesecloth. Combine cider and brown sugar in saucepan. Heat and add spice bag; simmer 10 minutes. Remove bag. Serve piping hot in mugs and add dash of nutmeg. Serves 8.

Hints to
Help-Less Housewives

1. Wash strawberries before hulling.
2. Drop peeled avocado or banana in lemon juice to prevent its turning dark.
3. When peeling citrus fruits or pineapple, do so over a bowl so as to catch the juices.
4. To ripen avocado or pineapple, place in a brown paper bag; seal and let stand in a warm, not hot, spot.
5. To store a ripe pineapple in a refrigerator, wrap well to prevent other foods from absorbing odor.
6. Be certain nut meats are fresh before using as they will spoil the flavor of baked products if at all rancid. Taste before using.
7. Dehydrated onion soup is excellent seasoning for stews, ground beef, etc.
8. Use undiluted consommé to baste poultry.
9. The volume of beaten egg whites is increased when eggs are at room temperature.
10. When preparing meringue for desserts, add two tablespoons flavored gelatin to a four-egg recipe for color and flavor.

11. Do not beat quick breads after adding dry ingredients, just stir.
12. Heavy cream doubles and often triples in volume when whipped.
13. One cup of raw rice becomes three when cooked.
14. Fresh tomatoes keep longer when placed with stem end down.
15. A boned or rolled roast requires ten more minutes cooking time per pound than one cooked with bones.
16. Meats cooked in liquid should be simmered slowly. Fast cooking causes meat to become stringy.
17. When roasting meat, do not prick with a fork; if necessary to turn it, use tongs.
18. To avoid worry when roasting, use a meat thermometer.
19. Liver loses its flavor if stored longer than 24 hours.
20. Do not separate slices before placing bacon in pan as they slide apart when warm.
21. To remove kernels from a cob of corn, place ear in the funnel of an angel food pan and shave down on the cob; kernels will fall in pan.
22. Cook cheese at a low temperature as it becomes stringy when subjected to high heat.
23. Do not freeze cheese. It becomes mealy.
24. To prevent steaks and chops from curling, slash through outside fat at one-inch intervals.
25. For quick snacks, freeze small amounts of leftovers.
26. When cooking for the family, prepare double portions and freeze half.
27. Cooked foods of any kind have a limited life in freezer; check before using.
28. Store sugar peppermint patties uncovered to prevent drying.
29. To make chocolate curls, use a vegetable peeler on a bar of the bittersweet kind.

Just Helpers

30. When boiling cabbage, add a piece of rye bread to the water to eliminate odor.
31. Raw potato in the refrigerator absorbs odors.

32. To deodorize jars and bottles, pour in a solution of dry mustard in water.

33. To remove fish odors on hands, wash first with salt, then with cold water.

34. Store flour sifters in a brown bag or hang them in a shopping bag to prevent flour dust sifting over other utensils.

35. Sharpen your scissors by cutting sandpaper.

36. Beat egg whites before beating yolks. No wash, no waste.

37. Chill beaters and bowl in refrigerator before whipping cream.

38. To prevent brown sugar from lumping, place a piece of rye bread in the covered container with it, or store brown sugar in the refrigerator. To restore lumpy dried brown sugar, place in sugar box a piece of crumpled, thoroughly dampened paper toweling. Close box securely and leave 24 hours.

39. Add salt to water when cooking eggs to prevent shell from cracking.

40. Prick the skin of a raw apple to prevent splitting when baking.

41. To clarify soup, remove scum from the first boiling.

42. When rolling dough, place a wet cloth under board to prevent slipping.

43. When making tart shells, prick the dough with a fork before baking to prevent puffing.

44. To cut fresh bread easily, warm the knife.

45. To remove cranberry sauce from can with ease, open one end and puncture the other.

46. If soup is too well salted add a half of a peeled raw potato. If still too salty, add the other half.

47. If potatoes are too salty, add sugar while cooking.

48. When sour milk is indicated, add one tablespoon vinegar to one cup of milk.

49. Before measuring molasses, grease the cup and it will not stick.

50. To insure safe removal of a frozen salad, grease the mold instead of moistening it.

51. A round measuring spoon makes nicely shaped drop cookies. Fill it heaping full.

52. Ingredients to be cooked should be room temperature unless otherwise specified.

53. For especially good flavor, cook noodles, rice, barley, etc., in bouillon.
54. To freshen cookies, place a piece of rye bread with them in a covered container for 24 hours.
55. For crisp fried potatoes, peel and slice, and soak them in cold water in refrigerator overnight.
56. When cooking a starch such as rice or noodles, grease the kettle before boiling water to keep a ring from forming.
57. To freshen marshmallows, place in covered container with a slice of fresh apple.
58. Though cheese may mold in the refrigerator, it does not spoil. Cut off the mold and use the balance.
59. Leftover egg whites stored in a tightly covered jar will hold for ten days in the refrigerator.
60. Grind meat once for patties, but two or three times when making small meat balls or meat loaf.
61. Use cold water when washing dishes soiled with egg.
62. To remove fish odor from dishes, wash with cold water and soap and rinse with hot water.
63. Olives which have been opened should be stored in an uncovered container in refrigerator.
64. When pounding raw meat, moisten it to prevent sticking to hammer.
65. For crisp bacon, pour off fat continually while frying.
66. For a subtle flavor, use green olives in cooking. Bring them to a quick boil, then blanch immediately in cold water.

RECIPES THAT CAN BE USED FOR LEFTOVERS

TABLE OF WEIGHTS AND MEASURES

3 teaspoons	=	1 tablespoon
2 tablespoons	=	1 liquid ounce
4 tablespoons	=	¼ cup
1 pint	=	2 cups
1 quart	=	4 cups
1 fluid ounce	=	2 tablespoons
8 fluid ounces	=	1 cup
16 fluid ounces	=	1 pint or 2 cups
1 pound butter	=	2 cups (4 sticks)
½ pound butter	=	1 cup (2 sticks)
¼ pound butter	=	½ cup (1 stick)

APPROXIMATE CAN SIZES

Regulation can of soup	=	10½ ounces
#1 meats and fish	=	16 ounces
#1 flat	=	13 ounces
#1 half-flat	=	7 ounces
#2	=	20 ounces or 2½ cups
#2½	=	28 ounces or 3½ cups
#303	=	16 ounces or 2 cups
#10	=	96 ounces or 12 cups

APPROXIMATE SUBSTITUTIONS
OF ONE INGREDIENT FOR ANOTHER

1 tablespoon flour	½ tablespoon cornstarch or ¾ tablespoon tapioca
1 cup cake flour	⅞ cup all-purpose flour
1 cup corn syrup	1 cup sugar plus 1 cup liquid
1 cup honey	1 cup sugar plus 1 cup liquid
1 ounce chocolate	3 tablespoons cocoa plus 1 tablespoon fat
1 cup butter	1 cup oleomargarine
1 cup coffee cream	3 tablespoons butter plus ⅞ cup milk
1 cup heavy cream	⅓ cup butter plus ¾ cup milk

Index

Note: Unless otherwise indicated in the text,
the recipes in this book will make six servings

406

Unless otherwise indicated in the text,

the recipes in this book will make six servings

Unless otherwise indicated in the text,

the recipes in this book will make six servings

Unless otherwise indicated in the text,

the recipes in this book will make six servings

Unless otherwise indicated in the text.

the recipes in this book will make six servings

Green beans (*continued*)
  vinaigrette, 57
Green goddess dressing, 294
Green mayonnaise, 362
Green noodles amandine, 221
Guacamole salad, 127

Half-and-half bars, 79
Halibut, home-packaged, 303
Ham
  baked, with orange glaze, 158
  cornucopias, 249
  deviled eggs, 328
  kabobs, 279
  rotisserie, 399
  upside-down cake, 25
Hamburgers
  double-decker, 303
  gourmet, 286
  special, 329
Hard sauce, brandy, 113
Harvey roast, 172
Hash au gratin, baked, 17
Hasty barbecue dinner, 315–19
Hawaiian appetizers, 296
Hearts of lettuce — Roquefort dressing,
  354
Hearts of palm salad bowl, 212
Herb
  bread, 228
  -buttered French bread, 112
  cole slaw, 236
  dressing, 62
  lamb chops, 293
  peas, 273
  shrimp, 154
  slaw jardiniere, 366
  tomato cooler, 399
Holiday dressing, 240
Hollandaise sauce, 44
Home-brandied fruits, 164
Home-packaged halibut, 303
Honolulu cooler, 315
Hoosier chicken, 324
Hoppel poppel, 14
Horse-radish ring, 164
Hostesses, memo to, 2
Hot brandy toddy, 394
Hot buttered syrup, 23
Hot fudge sauce, 97
Housewives, hints to, 400–403
Hungarian goulash Szekely, 134
Hush puppies, 318

Ice cream, *see* Desserts
Icebox Parker House rolls, 221
Iced cherry soup, 33

Iced pineapple cubes, 124
Icing, *see* Frostings
Irish coffee, 266
Island rum pineapple, 314
Italian buffet, 141–45
  hot, 145–48
Italian fettucini, 135
Italian meat-ball spaghetti, 325
Italian peppers, 351

Jackson salad, 260
Jade tree cookies, 326
Jambalaya, 115
Jams, jellies, marmalades, preserves,
    etc.
  apricot conserve, 31
  apricot marmalade, 70
  peach jam, 16
  peach marmalade, 66
  pickled fruit, 130, 363
  pineapple, 50
  pinecot preserves, 73
  plum jam, 54
  plum marmalade, 20
  preserved kumquats, 124
  strawberry preserves, 8
  watermelon rind, 36
Jelly, *see* Jams
Jiffy coffee cake, 35
Jubilee Bavarian cream, 109
Jubilee sauce, 110
Jumbo frankfurters, 300
Jumbo white asparagus Polonaise, 240

Kabob
  beef, rotisserie, 339
  liver, 302
  scallop, 319
  shish, 328
    marinade for, 329
Key lime pie, 83
Kolacky, 59
Kuchen
  bundt, 27
  peach, 12
  plum, 281
Kumquat(s)
  preserved, 124
  ring, 151

Lace cookies, 193
Lamb
  barbecued breast, 283
  barbecued riblets, 299
  chops, herbed, 293
  curry, 231
  leg, boned, 305

Unless otherwise indicated in the text,

the recipes in this book will make six servings

Unless otherwise indicated in the text,

the recipes in this book will make six servings

Unless otherwise indicated in the text,

the recipes in this book will make six servings

Unless otherwise indicated in the text,

the recipes in this book will make six servings

Soups
  hot (*continued*)
    tomato-vegetable, 353
    vegetable, old-fashioned, 387
Sour cream
  apple pie, 233
  coffee cake Grandmère, 20
  cole slaw, 115
  dip, 5
  dressing, 116
  hollandaise, 227
  noodles, 25
Southern carrots, 93
Soy sauce for ham kabobs, 279
Spaetzle, 77
  polonaise, 377
Spaghetti, *see also* Noodles
  Italian meat-ball, 325
  with meat sauce, 146
Spareribs, sweet and sour, 122
Spiced cherries, 242
Spiced chicken, 190
Spiced dressing, 386
Spiced French dressing, 187
Spiced prunes, 222
Spiced rice crisps, 5
Spinach
  amandine, 294
  casserole, 156
  creamed, with chives, 336
  on artichoke bottoms hollandaise, 227
  salad, 360
  vinaigrette, 77
Spring salad mold, 251
Squab
  Savannah, 162
  Vineyard, 249
Squash
  acorn
    chutney, 159
    fruited, 346
  ring, 201
  zucchini
    Cantonese, 123
    sautéed, 86
Steak
  aloha, 311
  baked, 155
  barbecued cube, 317
  broiled, with mustard crust, 268
  Diane, 258
  ground round (poor man's sirloin), 348
  sirloin strip, boneless, 355
Stew
  beef, with red wine, 376
  lamb, Marocain, 374

Stinger, 394
Strawberry
  Charlotte Russe, 131
  pancakes, 32
  pie
    fresh, 298
    glacé, 175
  preserves, 8
String bean(s)
  casserole, 163
  Martinique, 357
Strip sirloin steaks, boneless, 335
Strudel, apricot, 160
Stuffing for poultry
  chestnut, 177
  corn bread, 264
  for breasts, 11
  holiday dressing, 240
  mushroom, 162
  wild rice, 200
Substitutions (table), 405
Sunshine cake Delmonico, 352
Supper buffets, 75–116
  football, 114–16
  New Orleans, 110–13
  short-notice, 95–97
Supreme sauce, 29
Swedish heirloom cookies, 79
Swedish trout, 132
Sweet and sour
  ribs, 122
  meat balls, 92
  Ramaki, 311
  sauce, 92
Sweetbreads
  glazed, 88
  Marechal, 48
  ragout fin, 103
  velouté, 89
Swiss cheese scrambled eggs, 7
Swiss fondue, 282
Swiss steak Indienne, 391
Syrup, *see* Sauces, sweet

Tables
  can sizes, 404
  substitutions, 405
  weights and measures, 404
Tahiti fruit cup, 38
Tarragon mayonnaise, 72
Tart shells, 28
Tarts, blueberry, au Cointreau, 27
Tea
  ginger ale iced, 319
  mint, 295
Tenderloin sandwiches, 81
  sliced, 88
Thanksgiving buffet dinner, 238–43

Unless otherwise indicated in the text,

the recipes in this book will make six servings